PROFESSIONALS IN SEARCH OF WORK

Coping with the Stress
of Job Loss and Underemployment

PROFESSIONALS IN SEARCH OF WORK

Coping with the Stress of Job Loss and Underemployment

H. G. KAUFMAN, Director
Research Program in Science, Technology and Human Resources
Polytechnic Institute of New York, Brooklyn, New York

Foreword by
Jerome M. Rosow, Former Assistant Secretary of Labor

1807 1982

A Wiley-Interscience Publication

JOHN WILEY & SONS

New York · Chichester · Brisbane · Toronto · Singapore

Library of Congress Cataloging in Publication Data:

Kaufman, Harold G.
 Professionals in search of work.

 "A Wiley-Interscience publication."
 Includes index.
 1. Professional employees--Psychology. 2. Un-
employment--Psychological aspects. 3. Under-
employment--Psychological aspects. I. Title.

HD8038.A1K38   650.1'4'019 82-2061
ISBN 0-471-46069-9   AACR2

Printed in the United States of America

10 9 8 7 6 5 4 3 2 1

Foreword

Unemployment at current levels is reaching epidemic proportions. Economists use such esoteric terms as "frictional" and "short-term" and "recession-related" to depersonalize the meaning and to divorce economic action from social and political action. Now that the Organization for Economic Cooperation and Development is predicting 28 million people unemployed by 1983 in the western industrialized countries, we see the global proportions of this dilemma.

Here in the affluent United States with a 3 trillion dollar economy, the presence of over 10 million unemployed and over 5 million employed part-time (who want to work full time) and millions of others too discouraged to look for work, we are approaching crisis level. The full employment goal has suffered a severe setback and is rapidly slipping away from our eager grasp. During the last twenty years, we have seen unemployment rise from 3 percent (full level) to 9 percent (a serious problem) and we have elevated our definition of "full employment" to 5 or 6 percent or even higher levels.

Against this economic background, Prof. H. G. Kaufman's comprehensive evaluation of unemployment and underemployment among professionals is a major contribution to knowledge. This scholarly work deserves the attention of professionals in search of work in terms of immediacy of need and usefulness in providing personal insight and an intelligent set of options for action. This book addresses the psychological effects of unemployment and underemployment coupled with a critical analysis of individual differences to avoid generalizations and pinpoint meaning.

The schematic separation of unemployment into four stages is especially valuable to professionals themselves as well as the concerned institutions: universities, employers, social agencies, government, and society. Prof. Kaufman focuses especially well on "Stage II—concerted effort," which occurs within the second to third month of unemployment and may last up to three months. This is the period of opportunity and high motivation and he links it up with detailed analyses of finding work, job search methods, improving employability, and adjustment strategies. Then moving from individual strategies he defines extensive and practical tested options for response by our institutions to reduce the adverse effects of professional unemployment and underemployment. Finally, he concludes with a comprehensive model for future policy action, which is aimed directly at the needs of professionals.

Unemployment no longer wears only a blue collar. It is a national problem affecting the complete spectrum of the labor force—young, middle-age and older, men and women, and every occupation including our most respected professions. Professionals by virtue of their education represent the nation's most valuable resource. These individuals have made a great investment in themselves through formal education, extended work experience, career knowledge, and skill development. The majority of professionals out of work have *lost their jobs*. Despite popular opinion, they have great difficulties in relocating in the career of their choice. These difficulties are increasing.

The supply–demand balance for professionals has shifted radically since 1970. College education has expanded as a function of an open society with great opportunities for economic and social progress. Education has been the passport. The energy price shocks of 1973 and 1980 have hurt productivity, created inflation, and slowed economic growth. Further, the failure to plan for the demographic shifts has created a massive oversupply of teachers and further feeds the growing imbalance. Despite these facts, we continue to assume that a free market economy can achieve equilibrium by some self-regulating miracle. So the weak national labor market exchange system has been cut, the duration of unemployment insurance payments shortened, the information services and job retraining programs eliminated, and the valuable lessons of our history ignored.

The nation cannot afford to waste its own talent and human genius. The professionals themselves, as thinking, intelligent people, feel deep resentments to both unemployment and the growing underemployment. Prof. Kaufman alerts us to the propensity for political activism. The thwarted desire for job involvement could find its outlet in political action to change the system itself.

This is the right time to face up to unemployment among professionals. It is time to realize one obvious fact: as America has opened the gates to higher education, it has created a new society of professionals who number close to one-fifth of the labor force. They are at the upper and middle rungs of the ladder of success and power. When they fall off or are pushed down by forces beyond their control, how do they cope? What is the message to future generations seeking to invest in education and careers? What are the implications for our economy and our society? This book addresses these critical questions and provides workable solutions for the individual and society.

JEROME M. ROSOW

Scarsdale, New York
March 1982

Preface

The origins and development of this book are best understood in a historical context. My research on unemployment has its roots in the recession of 1970–1971. I began the book during the recession of the mid-1970s and continued to work on it through a third recession at the beginning of a new decade. As the book goes to press, the United States (and most other industrialized nations) is in the midst of yet another recession and experiencing the highest levels of unemployment since the Great Depression. Indications are that the situation will get worse. Even if improvement should occur, high levels of joblessness and underemployment are likely to continue into the foreseeable future, affecting the health and well-being of all segments of society.

My involvement with the problems of unemployed professionals began in 1971, when many of my students (primarily engineers pursuing part-time masters degrees in management) began coming to me with anguished stories of job loss and an inability to find work. Having grown up in the post-Depression generation, I had experienced a job market in which the highly educated (especially engineers) were in such demand that employers vied with one another to lure new college graduates as well as experienced professionals. Therefore, widespread job loss among my students came as a shock to me as well as to them. My concern with their problems led to the research reported in this book. In addition, since this book deals with career problems encountered by professionals, it is a logical extension of my two previous books, *Obsolescence and Professional Career Development* and *Career Management: A Guide to Combating Obsolescence*.

As the problem of unemployment began to affect various types of professionals, I became more aware of the widespread traumatic effects of joblessness among the highly educated. It also became clear to me that there was a need for integrating research on the psychological impact of unemployment on professionals into a cohesive framework. While an increasing number of studies focusing on jobless professionals has been carried out by psychologists and other social scientists, they are difficult to locate because they tend to be widely scattered in diverse and often obscure sources. Most books on unemployment have been produced by economists, and the few that have examined the psychological impact of job loss have typically concentrated on blue-collar workers. In addition, it became clear to me that underemployment among the highly educated is an even greater problem than unemployment. Nevertheless, few researchers have attempted to address the impact of underemployment on the individual and society.

Given these gaps in knowledge and a lack of integration of that which does exist, I set out to fill the need for a book that views unemployed and underemployed professionals primarily from a psychological perspective, but is also multidisciplinary in its approach. Therefore, a unique aspect of this book is that it deals with the complex, multifaceted problems of joblessness and underemployment among professionals by integrating unpublished research with existing literature from a variety of disciplines.

Many of the research results reported in this book appear in print here for the first time and are based on several studies carried out by myself as well as others. A major source of the data for this book was an investigation I began in 1972 which was supported, in part, by PHS Research Grant No. MH 21965-01, from the National Institute of Mental Health. The cross-cultural results reported from Israel were obtained primarily from studies carried out by Gili Shield and Yehudit Varsher under the direction of Rivka Bar-Yosef. I analyzed some of the data they collected while I was a Lady Davis Postdoctoral Fellow at the Hebrew University in Jerusalem during 1976–1977. The unemployment–reemployment results from the National Sample of Scientists and Engineers came from a study that I began in 1977 and was supported, in part, by National Science Foundation Grant No. SRS 77-20737. Any opinions, findings, conclusions or recommendations expressed here are mine and do not necessarily reflect the views of the National Institute of Mental Health, the Lady Davis Foundation, or the National Science Foundation.

The preparation of this book has taken me on a long, tortuous path. While the aforementioned awards were helpful in initiating some major facets of the research for this book, a great deal of additional work was conducted without funding. Moreover, for several years I found myself in the ironic situation of carrying out objective research on unemployed professionals while I was experiencing enduring anxiety about my reappointment and tenure in an extremely tight academic job market. Hence I had great empathy with those about whom I was writing.

The completion of this book is due in no small measure to numerous people who gave me their support and who assisted in untold ways in its development. Unfortunately, space does not permit citing all who contributed one way or another to this book. However, I feel obliged to mention the contributions of several individuals.

While thanks are due my many colleagues who read early drafts of selected chapters and provided positive and constructive feedback, I would especially like to single out Richard Kopelman. He not only provided some useful insights on the chapters dealing with the psychological impact of unemployment, but he also kept me informed of relevant references that came to his attention and helped stimulate my work on the book by his continuing enthusiasm for it.

Colleagues who shared research results or case study material with me are too numerous to mention but their names are cited thoughout the book, as is the information they provided. Much of the published material I discuss was tracked down with the dedicated assistance of the reference librarians at the Polytechnic Institute of New York. The unpublished research data that I report were analyzed largely with the very capable programming assistance of Stuart Klein and Mark Levine. These data could not have been collected without the many graduate management students at the Polytechnic who assisted in various ways. The contributions of all are deeply appreciated.

Several individuals read the complete manuscript and provided editorial suggestions. Grateful acknowledgment for that gargantuan task goes to Karen Craig, Ann Meadows, Steve Ross, and Anita Tierney. Over several years, many contributed to the crucial but onerous task of typing and retyping the various drafts from my often illegible handwriting. Special appreciation goes to Honorata Czarny, who not only typed most of the final drafts but also helped in the early organization of the references, and Martha Willett, who came through in critical periods when I had last-minute revisions and needed editorial assistance.

Others who helped in various aspects of the manuscript preparation include Hilda Barreto, Paulette Barrick, and the staff of the Word Processing Center as well as the Graphic Arts Department at the Polytechnic Institute of New York. Ann Kennehan and Zvi Ostrin assisted in the difficult task of indexing the book and Raymond Chan, John Kas, Violet Low, and Soo Ching Yan provided computer and word processing help in preparing the index. My sincere thanks to all of them.

Finally, I wish to express my gratitude to those unemployed and underemployed professionals who were willing to take the time to share their emotions, opinions, and experiences with me. Their problems, failures, and successes truly provided the inspiration for this book. My hope is that by making the individual and societal implications of their experiences known, this book will contribute to efforts that ameliorate the detrimental consequences of job loss and underemployment.

H. G. KAUFMAN

New York, New York
March 1982

The Plan of the Book

The job market and unemployment have typically been studied from the perspective of economists. Although some labor economists have investigated issues such as job search, only in rare instances have they focused on the impact of unemployment or underemployment on the well-being of the individual. Such concern has generally been left to other social scientists. However, surprisingly few psychologists have attempted to study the effects of job loss or underemployment and even fewer have investigated these problems among professionals. One purpose of this book then is to remedy this deficiency by taking a psychological perspective on professionals in search of work.

Although the book's overall orientation is psychological in nature, the problems of unemployment and underemployment are so complex that a multidisciplinary approach cannot be avoided. Therefore, information has been integrated from a diversity of relevant fields, which, in addition to psychology, include health, labor economics, sociology, social work, career counseling, management, education, and public policy. Indeed, practitioners as well as researchers in these fields will find an abundance of information throughout the book relevant to their respective disciplines. The multidisciplinary approach is clear from the contents of each chapter.

Chapter 1 sets the stage for the book by scrutinizing the decline in the professional job market so as to understand better the causes of the problem, who has been affected, and the prospects for the future. The second chapter evaluates job loss as a major life stress and closely examines the psychological impact of unemployment, particularly as regards professionals. How individual differences are related to unemployment stress among professionals is the focus of Chapter 3. An examination of the impact of job loss on professionals continues in Chapter 4 with an exploration of the stages of unemployment through which many jobless professionals pass and how these stages fit with various theories of stress.

In Chapter 5, attention is directed to individual barriers and facilitators that affect professionals in their search for work, including those involving discrimination. The various ways in which professionals search for and find employment are examined extensively in Chapter 6, along with an attempt to analyze individual differences associated with the use of particular search strategies. This is followed in Chapter 7, by an evaluation of individual change strategies for enhancing job opportunities as well as attaining adjustment. These strategies include relocation, continuing education, retraining, and counseling. The all-important problem of professionals who take jobs that leave them underemployed is explored in Chapters 5 through 7.

In Chapter 8, societal responses to the changing professional job market are discussed, with particular emphasis on the role played by government, employers, professional societies, and educational institutions. Finally, Chapter 9 provides an overview beginning with a model that uses a systems approach to summarize individual adjustment to job loss. This is followed by an examination of the mental health professional's role in dealing with the psychological problems associated with unemployment and underemployment. The last section presents a proposed employment system designed to enhance cooperation among societal institutions for the purpose of providing more effective assistance and support to professionals in search of work.

Contents

CHAPTER EIGHT   SOCIETAL RESPONSES: OPTIONS
FOR INSTITUTIONAL CHANGE   231

PROFESSIONALS IN SEARCH OF WORK

Coping with the Stress
of Job Loss and Underemployment

CHAPTER ONE

The Changing Job Market for Professionals

A professional[1] occupation was once an almost assured path to a secure and rewarding career. For many who have such aspirations, this is no longer true. Professional workers were in great demand for over a generation following World
War II. During this period, those entering professional careers were relatively immune to the disruption and long-term joblessness faced by their predecessors in
the Great Depression.

By 1970, however, a sudden deterioration in the job market for the college educated made it increasingly difficult to pursue a professional career. With this ab-
rupt change, record numbers of professionals found themselves joining the ranks
of the unemployed. Moreover, many were forced into accepting jobs that were
well below their knowledge and skill capabilities, leaving them underemployed.
In this chapter we examine briefly the decline in the professional job market in
order to understand better how the problem evolved, who has been affected, and
what the future career prospects are for educated workers.

EMERGENCE OF THE PROBLEM

In the 1970s unemployment again emerged as the most important problem facing
Americans (Gallup Opinion Index, 1977; Opinion Research Corporation, 1975).
Not since the Great Depression was joblessness so prevalent, and although minority youth with limited education and skills were hardest hit, no segment of the
population was left untouched. Between 1969 and 1971, a record number of professional workers became unemployed, rising 125 percent compared to the 80
percent increase in the total number of unemployed persons (Crowley, 1972).
This record was again to be broken during the recession of the mid-1970s. At that
time more than three-fifths of the Fortune 500 largest industrial companies made
significant cutbacks in personnel (Hershfield, 1975). Among these companies,
the incidence of permanent separations was greater for higher-level employees

than for blue-collar workers, who were much more likely to experience only temporary layoffs.[2] Unlike blue-collar workers, professionals were generally not protected by unions, making them highly vulnerable to permanent job loss. There is clear evidence that in the early 1970s professionals felt as threatened by unemployment as did the working population as a whole (Strumpel, 1976). Indeed, by 1976 professionals were more likely than other workers to be looking for a position because their job was ending (Rosenfeld, 1977).

A college education, which typically provided entry into a professional occupation, apparently offered little protection against job loss. In fact, between 1969 and 1977 the percentage of workers who had jobs that provided regular steady work decreased only among college graduates; job security increased for those with less than a college education (Quinn and Staines, 1978). A survey of households during the recession of 1975 revealed that 15 percent of those with a college education had lost their job during the previous six months (Opinion Research Corporation, 1975). This was only slightly lower than the 19 percent experiencing job loss among those who did not complete high school. Furthermore, during the same period about one-tenth of those in both groups experienced a reduction of work hours, thereby becoming underemployed. It would thus appear that perhaps one-fourth of all college-educated workers lost their jobs or became underemployed just during the first half of 1975.

Employment problems during the 1970s were obviously a result of the economic slowdown and recurring recessions, but the economy had experienced such downturns before, most notably in the late 1950s and early 1960s, and professional workers then were not hurt as badly (Ginzberg, 1972). The difference was that, during the 1970s, we entered what has been called "a new economic era" (Katona and Strumpel, 1978). During this period a variety of complex and, at times, interrelated events came together that served to stabilize or reduce the demand for many types of professionals while the supply of college-educated workers continued to grow to record numbers. Among the events that appear to have contributed to diminished demand were changes in national priorities, foreign competition, and the financial crisis of the cities. The rapid expansion in supply was stimulated by such factors as the great increase in college-educated workers, the changing role of women, and the so-called "brain drain" to the United States. Both supply and demand were probably affected by changes in population growth, the war in Vietnam, and the energy crisis. It is obvious that these are only some of the many factors that could have contributed to the emergence of joblessness among professionals during the 1970s, but a brief examination of these factors will demonstrate their impact on supply and demand.

Rise of a College-Educated Labor Force

One of the most dramatic changes in the American labor force has been the rapid increase in the number of college-educated workers, the major source of supply for professional occupations. In 1940, at the end of the Great Depression, only 5.7 percent of the labor force had completed four or more years of college, but by the recession of 1975 this percentage had almost tripled, to 16.4 percent (U.S. Department of Labor, 1976). In absolute numbers this increase was even more dramatic, growing almost fivefold, from less than 2.9 million college graduates in the 1940 labor force to almost 14 million in 1975. A comparable number had completed some higher education, and thus by the mid-1970s about one-third of all American workers had attended college.

During the 1950s and 1960s, the increased supply of college-educated workers could barely keep pace with the demand for such workers to fill the expanding number of professional positions. This demand was spurred on by the increasing allocation of resources to education as well as to research and development, which, when combined, accounted for approximately 10 percent of the GNP during the late 1960s, about double that of the early 1950s. The result was a 3.7 million increase between 1960 and 1970 in the number of professional workers, which was over twice the growth rate for total employment (Crowley, 1972). By 1970, however, it was clear that highly educated workers, by becoming such a large segment of the labor supply, had also become more vulnerable to the vicissitudes of the economy affecting the demand for professionals.

Changes in Population Growth

Changes in the age distribution and growth rate of the population have had a pervasive impact on both the supply and demand of professionals. Not only do such demographic changes determine the size of the labor force but they also are the major determinants of labor demand in the educational sector, which employs more professionals than any other industry—about 4 million teachers and administrators. Primarily in response to the post–World War II "baby boom" that extended through the 1950s, the great demand for teachers and other educational professionals continued to increase during the 1960s and burgeoning numbers of college graduates were easily absorbed in elementary and high schools as well as in higher education. In fact, one-fourth of the increase in professional employment during the decade of the 1960s was accounted for by teachers, primarily at the elementary and secondary school levels (Crowley, 1972). By the 1970s, however, the diminished rate of population growth following the postwar baby boom began to be reflected in declining student enrollments, first in elementary and then in high school. In response to this reversal in growth, the demand for teachers tapered off. According to data from the U.S. Bureau of Labor Statistics, the total number of employed elementary school teachers actually began to decline in the early 1970s. Simultaneously, schools of education, with burgeoning enrollments of postwar babies who had reached adulthood, were churning out an increasing number of teachers. By 1972, a record 338,000 persons completing teacher training were clamoring for only 197,000 new teaching positions (Carnegie Commission on Higher Education, 1973). Although the number of new graduates eligible to teach declined to 261,000 by 1975, almost half of all the new teachers who applied to teach still were not able to find full-time teaching positions (National Center for Educational Statistics, 1978). Even teachers who were working experienced a loss of job security. Surveys indicate that among professionals employed in education only about 6 percent characterized their job as not providing steady work in 1969, but by 1977 almost 18 percent reported such insecurity (Quinn and Staines, 1978). Although changes in population growth have had their most extreme impact on the teaching profession, the great increase in the number of young, highly educated workers entering the labor force during the 1970s contributed to a general job market turnaround, with the supply suddenly exceeding the demand in many professions.

Changing Role of Women

College enrollments in the late 1960s were fed not only by the large number of postwar babies entering postsecondary studies but also by the high rate of women continuing on to higher education, many of whom were preparing to become elementary school teachers, a ''traditionally female'' profession. The rate of women entering college continued to increase and in 1977 the U.S. Bureau of the Census found that the number of female undergraduates exceeded that of males. In the early 1970s the changing role of women in society had begun to affect dramatically the choice and nature of female careers. Stimulated by changing role perceptions vis-à-vis career and family as well as by job market factors such as affirmative action programs and limited opportunities in teaching, women began moving into ''traditionally male'' professional schools for training in fields such as engineering, law, and medicine (Parrish, 1974). Furthermore, by deferring (or even abandoning) marriage and childbearing, women were more readily able to establish themselves in professional careers. In fact, among college-educated women, nine-tenths of those who remained single were in the labor force compared to fewer than six-tenths of those who were married (Taeuber and Sweet, 1976).

To summarize, the changing role of women during the 1970s was not only manifested by a greater participation in the labor force associated with their rising levels of education but also by their entry into previously male-dominated professions. The rapid increase in the number of educated women was occurring at a time when the demand for professionals was diminishing, particularly in teaching, an occupation which had traditionally absorbed large numbers of women college graduates. These circumstances served to increase further the supply of college-educated workers competing for professional positions.

Changes in National Priorities

Major shifts in national priorities that began in the late 1960s had their repercussions in the recessions and unemployment during the 1970s. Nowhere was this change more evident than in Federal research and development (R&D) and defense expenditures. R&D, in particular, grew rapidly during the 1950s and, spurred on by the space race, increased from $5 billion in 1954 to $19 billion by 1964, when it accounted for 3 percent of the gross national product (GNP). A parallel increase in employment of engineers and scientists, second in magnitude only to the growth in teachers, could be attributed largely to the increase in R&D and defense spending. During the 1950s the number of engineers and scientists doubled, rising from about 600,000 to nearly 1.2 million. An almost equivalent increase in the number of technical professionals occurred during the 1960s, so that by 1970 the total exceeded 1.7 million (National Science Foundation, 1975a). Over half the growth in engineering employment occurred in aerospace and defense work, and by 1970 these industries accounted for about one-fifth of the 1.1 million engineers (Crowley, 1972). Almost one-half of the increase in the number of scientists occurred in colleges and universities, primarily in response to increased federal R&D funding, which also helped support burgeoning numbers of graduate students.

By the late 1960s the proportion of the GNP spent on R&D began a sharp decline, largely as a result of reductions in federal funding in aerospace and defense programs. With such a significant segment of technical professionals employed in these programs, they became highly vulnerable to termination. In 1970, growth in total employment of engineers and scientists ceased and among those working in R&D an immediate decline began (Crowley, 1972). In private industry, by far the largest employer of engineers and scientists (over 1 million), there was a 5 percent drop in the employment of such professionals between 1970 and 1975 (National Science Foundation, 1977). During this period the number of industrial R&D scientists and engineers declined by 11.6 percent (National Science Foundation, 1978).

Contraction in government research funds to colleges and universities combined with a diminished growth in enrollments, led to reduced demand for faculty (Crowley, 1972). In fact, data from the U.S. Bureau of Labor Statistics indicate that the number of faculty members actually began to decline in 1976. Other data indicate that between 1976 and 1978 there were declines ranging between 9 and 14 percent in the total number of physical, earth, and social scientists (National Science Foundation, 1980). The reduced demand for faculty in most fields has contributed greatly to the much publicized ''Ph.D. glut,'' since doctoral recipients had typically been employed by academic institutions (Cartter, 1974, 1976).

Unlike demographic changes, which have a long-lasting impact on the labor force, the effects of changes in national priorities tend to be of relatively shorter duration. Hence the surplus of engineers and scientists during the early 1970s was eased considerably by the late 1970s and shortages again began to appear, particularly in fields requiring highly trained professionals to meet new national priorities in areas such as energy (National Science Foundation, 1977). The job market for college and university faculty, however, did not revive in most fields (engineering and computer science are among the exceptions).

The academic job market is determined by demographic and other factors in addition to national priorities. Although the effects of changes in national priorities may be of shorter duration than demographic changes, it is clear that the fluctuating and unpredictable nature of government allocation of resources can be highly disruptive to the careers of the increasing number of college-educated workers whose jobs are dependent on federal funding.

The Vietnam War

Changes in national priorities also affected the Vietnam war, which had a pervasive impact on the labor force. The personnel requirements of the Vietnam war served to hold unemployment down until 1969—not only directly, by removing large numbers of men and some women from the labor force, but also because of the many men who had enrolled in college to obtain a student draft deferment (King, 1976). In fact, for one-fifth of college students, avoiding the draft was one of the most important reasons for entering college (Johnston and Bachman, 1972). Higher education did help men avoid the draft since those who had entered college by 18 years of age were much less likely to serve in the military (Kohen and Shields, 1977). Furthermore, many college men prepared to enter fields that offered the potential of an occupational deferment—the most popular choice being teaching at the elementary and secondary school levels (Grasso and Myers, 1977). For those college graduates who could not obtain an occupational deferment, the presence of the draft served as an inducement to enlist (Helmer, 1974). These ''reluctant volunteers,'' by deferring their entry into the labor force, helped further to keep the unemployment rate down among professionals.

It has been found that even with the temporary departure of draft-deferred students as well as the reluctant volunteers from the labor force during the Vietnam war, only workers who were college educated experienced rates of unemployment higher than those that would have occurred without the war (King, 1976). With the winding down of the war, record numbers of college graduates began entering a labor market where the shortage of teachers, engineers, and other professionals had suddenly become a surplus. In fact, at least one-fourth of the increase in unemployment between 1969 and 1971 could be attributed to the winding down of the war, and the college educated did not escape the higher rates of joblessness (King, 1976).

In sum, the war served not only to increase the numbers of college graduates but also encouraged many men to enter draft-deferred occupations such as teaching, in which large surpluses began to appear even before the war ended. The United States withdrawal from Vietnam brought with it a sharp decline in the demand for military personnel. Therefore, in the midst of a recession in the early 1970s, male college graduates, who no longer needed to postpone entry into the labor force because of military service, were joining large numbers of college-educated Vietnam veterans to further swell the ranks of those seeking professional jobs. It should be noted, however, that with the end of the Vietnam war and the elimination of the draft, there was a decline in male college enrollments attributed to the drop in the approximately 400,000 "reluctant students" who were motivated to enter college each year because of the threat of the draft (King, 1976). Athough this may have served to hold down the increase in the number of male college graduates, the immediate effect was to exacerbate an already poor job market for college teachers as a result of the diminished growth in student enrollments.

The Energy Crisis

The Arab oil embargo directed against the United States and other industrialized countries served to awaken the world to the energy crisis. Recovery from the 1970–1971 recession came to a grinding halt in the final months of 1973 when the Arabs unleashed their "oil weapon" (Early, 1974; Flaim, 1974). In fact, the unemployment rate had dropped to a low of 4.6 percent in the fall of 1973, but it rapidly increased following the Arab oil embargo and continued to rise to the highest levels experienced since the Great Depression. The immediate impact of the oil shortage was felt largely by blue-collar workers, particularly in manufacturing (Flaim, 1974). However, the potential longer-range effects of the energy crisis began to become apparent as the Arab oil producers transformed their boycott into higher oil prices via the international cartel, the Organization of Petroleum Exporting Countries (OPEC). As OPEC proceeded to quadruple the price of oil, a worldwide economic slump was precipitated involving balance-of-payment deficits for oil-importing countries, accompanied by high levels of inflation as well as widespread unemployment.

Although the Arab oil embargo may have had only a limited immediate effect on the unemployment of professionals, the subsequent sudden increase of petroleum prices was one of the factors that contributed to the 1974–1975 recession, which saw record numbers of professionals encounter joblessness. The great amount of R&D funding directed toward energy problems (National Science Foundation, 1977) created a demand for professionals, particularly engineers and scientists who specialized in energy-related fields. It remains to be demonstrated whether the increase in professional workers as a direct result of the energy crisis offset the reduction in the demand for professionals because of the consequent economic slowdown. Nevertheless, it is clear that as the cost of oil spiraled upward because of unpredictable cutbacks in production (such as those created by the Iranian revolution) or OPEC price increases, it exacerbated worldwide economic instability and increased employment insecurity for all workers.

Foreign Competition

Although the war in Vietnam and the emergence of OPEC were among the more visible international events affecting the labor market, there were clearly other, less noticeable changes occurring abroad that had a pervasive effect on the economy. Of particular concern was the loss of jobs because of the inability of American industry to compete with less expensive foreign imports. This applied not only to small manufacturers of clothing and shoes but also to giants in the steel industry and to high technology electronics firms. In fact, by the early 1970s two-thirds of American executives reported that increasing foreign competition was an important factor contributing to unemployment (Goble, 1973). On this issue, at least, organized labor was in agreement with management. In recognition of this problem, the United States became the only country in the world that provided economic assistance to workers who had been adversely affected by the influx of imports (Henle, 1977). However, only workers of manufacturing firms were eligible for such trade adjustment assistance. Those supplying services associated with a product were not eligible. Nor were workers who had been employed in firms that moved their operations overseas to reduce production costs. Because of these and other limitations, it is difficult to determine from adjustment assistance data to what extent professional workers have been affected by foreign competition. However, one need only examine the experience of individual firms that carried out mass terminations as a result of foreign competition to realize that professionals have also been affected. For example, because of foreign imports, Bethlehem Steel, the nation's second-largest steel producer, terminated about 10 percent of its salaried employees at all levels, which was comparable to the rate for all its workers (Clarity, 1977). Following the pattern among television and stereo equipment manufacturers, Zenith Radio Corporation, a giant in the industry, responded to foreign competition by terminating one-fourth of its work force, including many salaried employees, and shifting its operations overseas (Kleinfield, 1977). Imports of small foreign cars were considerably enhanced by the energy crisis, which resulted in consumer demand for smaller fuel-efficient vehicles. American auto manufacturers were not producing such vehicles on a large scale and sales began to slump. By the 1980 model year General Motors, Chrysler, and Ford cut costs by terminating 42,600 salaried employees, which was about twice the number of Big Three factory workers who lost their jobs permanently during the same period (Stuart, 1980). It would appear that in industries forced to curtail operations because of foreign competition, professionals were at least as affected as other workers in having their jobs eliminated.

Financial Crises of the Cities

For college graduates desiring job security, professional-level civil service jobs in municipalities have offered a traditional haven, even during times of recession. However, by the mid-1970s security began crumbling in the face of the financial crises confronting many of America's cities (Stanley, 1976). As is the practice in the private sector, attempts at reducing city budget deficits included mass layoffs of municipal employees. The most extreme case was that of New York City, both in terms of the magnitude of the crisis and in the number of workers affected. By 1976, New York City lost about one-fifth of the almost 300,000 jobs that existed at the end of 1974 (Ferretti, 1976). In fact, over one-half of the 111,800 jobs lost in New York City during fiscal year 1975–1976 were in local government (Burks, 1976). Poor job prospects for teachers and other educational professionals were further exacerbated since more than one-third of the Civil Service jobs lost in New York City came from the instructional staff of the city-run school systems, including those in higher education. If these are added to the jobs lost among health specialists, social workers, and other highly educated personnel who help to provide a myriad of municipal services, it appears that professionals were affected by New York City's budget crisis much more than other workers.

Despite the economic recovery following the recession of the mid-1970s, an increasing number of cities of all sizes were having budget problems, resulting in reductions in their work forces (Joint Economic Committee, 1980). It would appear that the contraction of job opportunities in local governments that occurred at a time when record numbers of college graduates were seeking work served to further worsen an already bad job market for professional positions, particularly in education.

The Brain Drain

The international migration of professionals has, in recent years, typically involved a "brain drain" from less developed countries to those that are more highly developed (Adams, 1968; Niland, 1970). Discussion of the problem has focused on the loss to countries experiencing the drain. During the 1960s the demand for educated personnel in the United States and other developed countries easily absorbed professionals emigrating from developing countries. Engineers and scientists alone accounted for 56,300 immigrants to the United States between 1966 and 1970 (National Science Foundation, 1973). In fact, many of these professionals came from other developed countries, particularly Great Britain, in search of greater opportunities in the United States. However, in the 1970s, the brain drain from less developed countries to the United States increased to record numbers, despite unemployment among American professionals. For example, India's annual brain drain to the United States had grown from only about 190 in 1965 to over 7000 by 1972, according to one estimate (*The New York Times*, 1974). These included highly trained professionals such as doctors, engineers, scientists, and teachers.

In addition to immigrants entering the United States officially as professionals, untold numbers of illegal aliens were also competing for work. In fact, almost one-half of the illegal aliens from Europe, Africa, and Asia who were apprehended had a college education and one-third were found to be working as professionals or managers (North and Houstoon, 1976). Moreover, many of the official immigrants first came to the United States as students and then remained to work after they completed their studies (National Science Foundation, 1973). This process has gained momentum with the stimulus of oil wealth from some developing countries that began sending increasing numbers of students to the United States in the 1970s (*The New York Times,* 1977b). Indeed, by 1979, 33.8 percent of the record 264,000 foreign students in the United States came from OPEC countries (Institute of International Education, 1980). In some fields, the influx of large numbers of immigrants had been seen as further exacerbating an already difficult job market for professionals (Feerst, 1977).

The factors thus far discussed should suffice to indicate why there was a job market turnaround for professionals in the 1970s. It would appear that the problem of unemployment among professionals emerged as a result of the confluence of far-reaching demographic and value changes, together with a complex series of local, national, and international events that served to stifle the growth of what had been a robust job market for those with a college education.

A WORLDWIDE PROBLEM

The surplus of highly educated workers is not unique to the United States. In fact, by the 1970s it had become a worldwide problem. At first, unemployment among the educated had attained serious proportions only in some of the less developed countries, particularly in Asia, and this served to stimulate the brain drain from these areas (Perez de Tagle, 1973). For example, in India over one-fourth of the country's total engineers were reported to be unemployed in 1968 (Richman and Copen, 1972). High unemployment among Indian professionals grew to such an extent that even doctors were affected (*The New York Times,* 1974).

By the mid-1970s a worldwide job crisis faced college-educated persons that extended to the highly industrialized nations (Scully, 1976). In western European countries such as France, it was estimated that half the university graduates were unable to find jobs. Even in the Soviet Union, with its educational system geared toward the country's needs, an oversupply of trained professionals has been reported (Austin, 1980b). Some of the same factors that contributed to unemployment of professionals in the United States were also evident in other developed countries. In western Europe there was an enormous expansion in the numbers of college and university students during the 1960s that continued into the 1970s. For example, in 1973–1974 there were 800,000 university students in Italy, over two and a half times the 313,000 enrolled in 1962–1963 (Scully, 1976). Declining birthrates reduced the demand for teachers just as many new teachers were entering the job market (Laderriere, 1976). This surplus was reported to be most acute in already financially hard-pressed countries such as Italy and Britain (Shuster, 1976). In fact, the few countries in which the demand for professionals tended to exceed the supply were the newly rich oil-producing nations. With these exceptions aside, for most countries of the world, the problem of not having enough professional-level jobs for the rapidly increasing number of highly educated workers seeking such positions has become the norm. In some countries the problem has reached crisis proportions. Although this book focuses on professionals in the United States, the changing job market is worldwide and therefore cross-cultural data from other countries are evaluated in subsequent chapters.

WHO ARE THE UNEMPLOYED PROFESSIONALS?

Now that we have some understanding of how the problem of joblessness emerged among highly educated workers, it would be useful to determine who the unemployed professionals are. A somewhat limited picture can be obtained from data supplied by the U.S. Bureau of Labor Statistics.

The unemployed are classified by the U.S. Department of Labor as either job losers, leavers, or entrants. During the 1970s the largest single group among unemployed professionals were job losers, those who experienced involuntary termination of their employment. By 1975 a majority (51 percent) of professionals who were out of work had lost their jobs. One-third were job entrants, including new graduates as well as those who had worked previously and were reentering the work force. Job leavers, those who quit or left voluntarily, accounted for only 16 percent. Thus it is clear that professionals during the 1970s were most likely to become unemployed as a result of job loss and in this respect had become similar to the rest of the work force.

According to U.S. Bureau of Labor Statistics data, 56 percent of unemployed professionals were male in 1970, but by 1973 a reversal occurred and 54 percent were female. Subsequently, women continued to be a slight majority among unemployed professionals despite the fact that they were still a minority in the professional work force (42 percent in 1976). Contributing to the predominance of women among unemployed professionals was the poor job market for elementary and secondary school teachers. Since 1972, about one-fifth of unemployed professionals were teachers and these were primarily women. In fact, about one-third of the jobless women professionals were teachers. For male professionals, among those unemployed during the early 1970s over one-fifth were engineers, but subsequently this was reduced by almost half because of an improved job market. However, since engineering is the largest male profession, engineers tend to be more predominant among highly educated jobless men.

Much has been made of youth unemployment, and rightly so, because young job seekers comprise the single largest group among the unemployed. For example, in 1976 the U.S. Bureau of Labor Statistics found that 46 percent of the jobless were persons under 25 years of age. However, among professionals unemployed in 1976, only 27 percent were under age 25. The dominant age group was between ages 25 and 34, accounting for 38 percent of unemployed professionals, a considerable increase from 29 percent in 1970. This is understandable insofar as professionals typically defer their entry into the labor force until they complete their higher education. In addition, by 1976 most of the postwar babies had already passed age 25. Nevertheless, since two-thirds of unemployed professionals were under age 35, it is primarily those at the early stages of their career who were affected by joblessness. The most notable exception to this trend appears in engineering, where most of the unemployed were in mid or late career (Kaufman, 1980; National Science Foundation, 1975b).

Thus far, we have avoided using unemployment rates primarily because they do not tell us which types of professionals are predominant among the jobless. However, unemployment rates indicate which groups are relatively more prone to joblessness and have more difficulty finding work. For example, among technical professionals, high unemployment rates were generally experienced by younger workers (Kaufman, 1980; National Science Foundation, 1971). However, older professionals with low seniority had the highest likelihood of losing their jobs (Kaufman, 1980). In fact, at any given level of seniority, the older professionals were more prone to job loss. Evidence also indicates that other factors, such as an individual's performance, may be more important than age in personnel cutbacks among technical professionals (Thompson, 1973).

Among elementary and high school teachers, as well as other civil service professionals, terminations are decided on the basis of seniority, and thus it is the younger workers who are least secure (Guyot, 1976). Even among recent college graduates, it is the youngest who experience the highest unemployment rates (Perrella, 1973). It would therefore appear that not only do those who are at an early stage of their career predominate among the unemployed professionals, but they are also more likely than those who are older to be out of work.

Graduates in some fields are more prone to unemployment. These have consistently been found to include humanities and social science graduates (Eckland and Wisenbaker, 1979; Perrella, 1973). Among such graduates with Ph.D.s who are typically employed as college teachers, philosophy and modern language majors have the highest unemployment rates (National Research Council, 1978).

In engineering and science, where unemployment rates are typically cyclic, certain fields were more susceptible to job loss than others. For example, technical professionals most likely terminated during the recession of 1969–1971 included aeronautical, industrial, and electrical engineers as well as computer programmers (Kaufman, 1980). However, those scientists and engineers who were underemployed as subprofessionals or in occupations outside science or engineering were clearly most prone to termination. Professionals without a bachelor's degree have also been found to be highly susceptible to job loss (Kaufman, 1980; National Science Foundation, 1971).

This brief examination is designed to provide a somewhat clearer picture of the professionals who were unemployed during the 1970s.[3] They were most likely to have experienced job loss, were predominantly under age 35, and somewhat more likely to be female. Furthermore, if female, they had a higher probability of being teachers than any other type of professional; if male, they were more apt to be in engineering than in another occupation; and if in engineering, they were more likely to be older. It is obvious that the characteristics of the professionals who were unemployed parallel, to some degree, the makeup of the population of working professionals. It is also clear that some professionals were more prone to termination, including those who were either younger, had low seniority, did not have a college degree, or had been underemployed.

UNDEREMPLOYMENT

The discrepancy between the supply and demand for professional-level workers has not only resulted in joblessness but has also created the even more widespread problem of underemployment—having to take a job that does not require a high degree of utilization of the individual's ability, knowledge, or skills. Underemployment among the highly educated has long been rampant in some developing countries. For example, a study of the fertilizer industry in India during the mid-1960s revealed that 63 percent of those with general science degrees were employed in subprofessional positions, as were 87 percent of the arts and commerce graduates (Merrett, 1971). Being able to find only part-time work is another form of underemployment that has been widespread in developing countries. For example, in Uruguay, during the mid-1960s, 15 percent of all professionals worked less than a 30-hour week, even though they wanted to work longer (Beller, 1970). Despite their centrally controlled economics, underemployment may also be a serious problem in some Communist countries (Mesa-Lago, 1968, 1971; Yanov, 1977).

Although problems of underemployment among professionals have also existed in the United States (Berg, 1970; Bisconti and Solmon, 1976; Kaufman, 1974c; Ritti, 1970) and other industrialized countries, such as England (Stanic and Pym, 1968), it was not until the great imbalance in the supply and demand for college-educated workers during the 1970s that such problems began to increase dramatically. Data indicate that a clear-cut increase in underemployment among college graduates in the United States occurred between 1969 and 1971 (Grasso and Myers, 1977). During the 1960s, only one-tenth of new college graduates accepted a subprofessional position (U.S. Department of Labor, 1978). Among new college graduates in 1970–1971, over one-third took subprofessional jobs (Perrella, 1973). Furthermore, the jobs of over half of these graduates were not directly related to their field of study, primarily because those were the only jobs they could find. Three-fourths of the social science graduates and two-thirds of the humanities majors were employed in such jobs. By 1975 almost one-fourth of all workers who had completed college were in positions that were subprofessional (U.S. Department of Labor, 1976). Thus underemployment has become pervasive not only among recent college graduates but also in the educated work force as a whole.

Researchers have noted that when highly educated workers take subprofessional positions, they deprive job opportunities to less qualified workers (Berg, 1970; O'Toole, 1975). Therefore, not only has the shortage of professional-level jobs created underemployment among the growing number of highly educated workers, it has also served to exacerbate the problem of unemployment among workers who would normally occupy subprofessional positions.

OUTLOOK FOR THE FUTURE

There does not seem to be much doubt that the demand for new professionals in the 1980s will be well below the available supply of college graduates; the only disagreement pertains to the size of the surplus. The various estimates of this surplus range from the 2.7 million projected by the Bureau of Labor Statistics up to a possible 8 million calculated by the U.S. Office of Education (Best and Stern, 1977; Hecker, 1978).

A major contributing factor to this surplus is the continuing increase in the percentage of college-educated workers in the labor force, which by the 1980s will be fed annually by more than 1 million new baccalaureate recipients and over half a million master's, doctoral, and professional-degree graduates (Frankel, 1978). The projections for the 1980s includes a labor force in which about one-fourth of all workers have a college degree and over one-tenth have completed advanced study beyond the baccalaureate degree (Golladay, 1976). If we include those who have completed less than four years of higher education, such as the burgeoning numbers of community college graduates, 40 percent of the labor force will have received some college education by the closing years of the 1980s. However, although the proportion of workers with higher education will continue to increase during the 1980s, the percentage of professional and technical workers in the labor force will tend to stabilize at between 15 and 17 percent (Best and Stern, 1977; Golladay, 1976).

As a result of an inadequate demand for professionals, about one-fifth of the openings for college graduates are expected to come from increasing educational prerequisites in jobs that formerly had not required a college degree (Carey, 1976). Such ''educational upgrading'' in managerial, administrative, and even sales jobs may be quite legitimate, owing to the increasingly complex knowledge and skills required for many such positions. In fact, a college education and a professional specialization has long been the path to high levels of management (Gould, 1966). This process of the "professionalization" of management has continued with the entry of college graduates into managerial positions occurring at an increasingly rapid rate (Folger, 1972). Indeed, by 1977 over half of all managers had acquired some college education (Michelotti, 1977). Thus most salaried managers may be considered to be professionals.

Because of a lack of professional-level jobs, however, it is clear that many highly educated workers will be forced to find subprofessional employment in sales, clerical, or even blue-collar jobs in which they will be underemployed. Such underemployment is expected to be the major problem encountered by highly educated workers, with unemployment being less widespread (Carey, 1976; Folger, 1972; Vetter, 1977). That is not to say that unemployment of professional-level workers will cease to be a problem in the future, but rather that underemployment will continue to increase. Indeed, an evaluation by management analyst Peter Drucker (1980) concludes that "to create and find productive jobs for knowledge workers will be the first employment priority for this country" (p. 32).

Even the more optimistic forecasts that point to an improved job market for new college graduates in the 1980s, take a much less sanguine view of the prospects for experienced college-educated workers as well as for many graduate degree recipients (Freeman, 1976). There is no question that the Ph.D. glut will continue well into the future, although there are variations by field (National Science Foundation, 1975b; U.S. Department of Labor, 1975b; Vetter, 1977). Doctorates in the humanities and social sciences will be hardest hit, as academic opportunities decline in response to a shrinking student population. Projections indicate that there will continue to be a great excess in the supply of teachers at all levels into the 1980s for most specialties (Golladay, 1976; Frankel, 1978).

Perhaps indicative of the deteriorating market for professionals is the projected shortage of jobs for lawyers (Ginther, 1975; Goldstein, 1977, 1978). The cause again is the rapid increase in the supply of lawyers. Just between 1970 and 1976, the number of law degrees earned increased 116 percent, to over 32,000 (National Center for Educational Statistics, 1978). In California, which is the state with the most lawyers, 40 percent of those admitted to practice in 1978 were having significant difficulty finding law jobs (Goldstein, 1979).

Moreover, some are beginning to predict future surpluses in "recession-proof" professions such as accounting as a result of soaring increases in enrollments (Fiske, 1977). Even medicine may no longer be immune to the job market difficulties experienced by other professions, since according to projections, growth in medical school graduates plus the influx of foreign-trained physicians will lead to surplus of doctors in the United States (Office of Technology Assessment, 1980). The number of medical degrees earned in the United States between

1970 and 1980 doubled, to over 16,000. Surpluses of as many as 185,000 doctors have been projected by 1990 (Office of Technology Assessment, 1980).

It is clear that a rapid growth in supply has occurred in all professions, with the result that supply may exceed demand in most fields. With the raising (and possible elimination) of the mandatory retirement age combined with continuing inflation, professionals are likely to remain longer in the labor force, thereby further exacerbating the supply-and-demand problem among educated workers.

All predictions of future occupational requirements are risky owing to the unpredictable nature of the factors that affect the job market. In fact, when forecasts for specific professions have been made, the projections differ widely depending on the assumptions regarding national priorities (Bezdek, 1973). Furthermore, these forecasts are made assuming that there will be no wars or major recessions. Despite a caveat regarding occupational projections, all indications are that many professionals are likely to experience even greater difficulties in finding appropriate work in the future. Given continuing worldwide economic problems and persistent high rates of joblessness, there is no reason to believe that the job insecurity and unemployment experienced by professionals in the 1970s will not be repeated in the decades to come.

NOTES

1. The term "professional" has been defined in many ways. For the purposes of this book professionals include those in occupations requiring a base of knowledge and skills acquired through higher education and subsequent experience. These occupations typically include those classified as professional by the U.S. Department of Labor in the *Dictionary of Occupational Titles*. In addition, since salaried managers are often required to have higher education, they are considered as professionals for our purposes. Also included within the broad focus of this book are college graduates whose education has prepared them for professional-level positions but who are either unemployed or underemployed in jobs that considerably underutilize their knowledge and skills.

2. Since job loss is more likely to be permanent for professionals than for other workers, it is generally referred to in this book as termination rather than layoff, which may be temporary because of recalls.

3. For a more detailed study of those more likely to get terminated among engineers and scientists during the recession of the early 1970s, see Kaufman (1980).

CHAPTER TWO

Psychological Effects
of Unemployment

The effects of economic change on human well-being were studied by social scientists at least as far back as the late nineteenth century (e.g., Durkheim, 1897). However, it was not until the Great Depression of the 1930s that psychologists began to be seriously concerned with the problem of unemployment and its impact on people. At least some of that concern seems to have been generated by motives of self-interest since psychologists, particularly the academically oriented, were themselves threatened by the specter of joblessness. Largely in response to that threat, they organized themselves into activist groups such as the Psychologists League and the Society for the Psychological Study of Social Issues (Finison, 1976, 1978). These groups fought for programs such as federal support for unemployed psychologists through the Works Progress Administration, and they strived to shift the emphasis of psychology from academia toward social action.

Psychologists' concern about unemployment during the Great Depression was also demonstrated by some research efforts directed toward understanding and dealing with the mental health consequences of joblessness. A review of the research literature carried out in 1938 revealed that by the waning years of the Depression, a small body of knowledge had accumulated concerning the psychological effects of unemployment (Eisenberg and Lazarsfeld, 1938). Since that time, additional studies have been carried out by psychologists and other social scientists, but the knowledge gained from the more recent research is frequently difficult to locate because, even when published, much of it is widely scattered and often in obscure sources.

In this chapter we review the current state of knowledge regarding the impact of unemployment, particularly on professionals, and attempt to integrate that knowledge to attain a more accurate and comprehensive understanding of the psychological consequences of joblessness. Unemployment will first be examined broadly as a stressful life event and as a factor in societal health. The widespread impact of unemployment on the individual will then be demonstrated by showing how even those who do not lose their jobs can be adversely affected. An analysis of the differences in the work motivation between professionals and other workers and their differential reactions to being out of work serves to introduce an extensive examination of unemployment stress among jobless professionals.[1]

UNEMPLOYMENT AS A LIFE STRESS

Unemployment is often exprienced as a highly stressful life change. Studies have consistently found that job loss ranks between seventh and ninth in the degree of stress it creates relative to as many as 61 life changes (Holmes and Rahe, 1967; Masuda and Holmes, 1967; Paykel, 1971). In terms of life stress, job loss is comparable to other traumatic losses; it can create almost as much stess as the death of a loved one and has been found to be more stressful than divorce or the death of a close friend. Psychoanalytically oriented evaluations have described the psychic consequences of job loss as similar to "the loss of love the child suffers from a rejecting parent, especially a child who has not done anything to deserve it" (Ginsburg, 1942, p. 442). Since job loss is such a highly stressful life change, it would be expected to precipitate psychological disturbances as well as the physical illness that typically accompanies such events (Langner and Michael, 1963; Rahe, McKean, and Arthur, 1967; Vinokur and Selzer, 1975). This, indeed, appears to be true, as we shall see by examining the available research dealing with epidemiological as well as individual data.

UNEMPLOYMENT AND SOCIETAL HEALTH

A growing body of epidemiological evidence, especially the work of M. Harvey Brenner, indicates that an increase in joblessness can have a widespread impact on mental and physical health and that sustained unemployment may continue to take its toll years after the increase actually occurred. Brenner has demonstrated that admissions to mental hospitals go up during recession periods and diminish when the economy is strong (Brenner, 1967, 1976). His research revealed that for every sustained 1 percent increase in unemployment, subsequent admissions to state mental hospitals rose by 3.4 percent. For example, the 1.4 percent rise in unemployment that occurred just in the year 1970 was associated with an additional 5520 admissions in 1975. This does not include admissions associated with increases in the unemployment rate that occurred after 1970, so it is clearly an underestimate of the total number of people who entered mental hospitals in 1975 which can be attributed to the rise in joblessness between 1970 and 1975.

There is consistent evidence that suicides increase during periods of economic decline (Brenner, 1976; Dublin, 1963; Henry and Short, 1954; Pierce, 1968), notwithstanding arguments by the economist John Kenneth Galbraith (1961) that suicide is not related to unemployment. Galbraith's conclusions may be due to his restricting the range of data to a relatively short period consisting of the years immediately before and during the Great Depression. Using a much longer period, it has been shown that for every sustained 1 percent increase in unemployment, there is a subsequent 4.1 percent increase in suicides, which means that in 1975, 1540 additional suicide deaths were related to the rise in unemployment during 1970 (Brenner, 1976).

Social pathologies, including extremely aggressive behavior, have also been found to be strongly related to unemployment. For example, it was revealed that a 5.7 percent increase in homicides occurs with every 1 percent rise in unemployment (Brenner, 1976). The increase of joblessness in 1970 was associated with an additional 1740 murders in 1975. Alcoholism also has been found to increase during periods of economic decline, as indicated by a rise in alcohol consumption, number of arrests for driving while intoxicated, and increased admissions to mental hospitals for alcoholic disorders (Brenner, 1975). Even mortality from cirrhosis of the liver, which is related to alcohol abuse, was found to go up 1.9 percent for every sustained 1 percent increase in unemployment, and the 1970 rise in joblessness was related to 870 additional such deaths in 1975 (Brenner, 1976).

Increases in mortality from various physical illnesses have also been attributed to the stress created by unemployment. It has been shown that as the unemployment rate increases, so does the death rate due to heart disease; economic upturns are associated with decreased mortality resulting from heart disease (Brenner, 1971). For every sustained 1 percent increase in unemployment there is a 1.9 percent rise in mortality from stroke, heart, and kidney disease, and in 1975, 26,440 additional such deaths were related to the rise in unemployment just during 1970 (Brenner, 1976). Reactions to stress, as well as inadequate diet and poor medical care as a consequence of unemployment, may also affect maternal health, since joblessness has been tied to increases in fetal and infant mortality (Brenner, 1973a).

Even if we consider the costs of unemployment only in economic terms, the estimates are staggering. The 1.4 percent increase in the unemployment rate in 1970 alone may have cost the nation at least $21 billion between 1970 and 1975 in terms of jobless and welfare payments, prison and mental hospital outlays, and lost income due to illness and mortality (Brenner, 1977). This, of course, does not include the economic impact of the increases in unemployment subsequent to 1970.

The unemployment rate has been found to be the best economic predictor of community mental health; in contrast, inflation appears to be totally unrelated (Catalano and Dooley, 1977). Clearly, the epidemiological evidence has established a consistent association between unemployment and psychological disturbance as well as mortality resulting from stress. If these are, in fact, causal relationships, by the 1980s we can look forward to rates of mental hospital admissions and mortality three times greater than those reported for 1975 as being attributable the high unemployment rates of the 1970s (Brenner, 1976).

UNEMPLOYMENT STRESS AMONG THE EMPLOYED

One possible implication of the epidemiological evidence is that anxiety about job loss during periods of high unemployment can affect even those who are still working. Public opinion polls have indicated that anxiety is quite high during periods of economic decline. A survey carried out by Yankelovich in 1974 (Lynn, 1974), when unemployment began a steep increase, found that almost half the residents of New York State were very worried about losing their jobs because of the recession. Nationwide polls indicated that by May 1975, 54 percent of Americans were concerned about losing their jobs, with one-third expressing great worry (Social Science Data Center, 1978).

Anxiety over possible termination may affect mental health even when the unemployment rate is low. For example, among industrial workers studied in 1953–1954, a period of relatively low unemployment, those concerned about possible job loss exhibited poorer mental health than did workers who felt more secure in their jobs (Kornhauser, 1965). If it is assumed that anxiety about job loss, in fact, results in poorer mental health, the relationship between the two is probably exacerbated in times of very high unemployment, when finding another job is much more difficult.

Employed professionals appear to be greatly affected by the anxiety of anticipated job loss. A study of engineers during 1932 revealed that the lowest morale among those who were still working was exhibited by the individuals who expected to be terminated (Hall, 1934), and this seems to be corroborated by more recent research (Kopelman, 1979). Of greater significance was that the Depression-era engineers anticipating job loss were even lower in morale than many of their colleagues who had already been terminated (Hall, 1934).

It has been demonstrated that professionals who survived the mass terminations of their coworkers in the early 1970s experienced high anxiety, were resentful of their employers, and exhibited low interest in their work (Blonder, 1976). Such individuals would probably feel compelled to leave their employer at the first opportunity for a more secure job elsewhere. Indeed, one study revealed that when health care professionals (including doctors and nurses) found themselves in an insecure work environment, they were more likely than nonprofessionals to quit their jobs voluntarily, even after terminations were completed (Greenhalgh and Jick, 1979). Although quit rates drop when terminations occur in a recession period (Valdes, 1971), some professionals may seek a job or career change to cope with the stress generated by insecurity.

There is some very persuasive evidence that the career motivation of individuals who retain their jobs is affected by the stress of adverse economic conditions. In one longitudinal study, technical professionals in three companies were first investigated in 1967 and then followed up in 1969 when their organizations were hit by reduced government spending or market setbacks (Hall and Mansfield, 1971). The study found that as the economic climate deteriorated, the professionals perceived that their jobs offered significantly less security as well as growth, with satisfaction of both these needs plummeting accordingly. Similarly, a study carried out during the 1970 recession found that security needs increased greatly among engineers and scientists (Bucher and Reece, 1972). Other evidence indicates that the lasting effects of job insecurity during that recession involved some drastic changes in career goals among professionals who had retained their jobs (Dewhirst and Holland, 1975). Even after the recession of 1970–1971 had ended, anxiety over job security remained and, in fact, was found to be the most important factor affecting dissatisfaction with career choice among professionals (Greenwald, 1978).

Not only can the career orientation of those who retain their jobs be affected by economic recession, but their personal life and normal activities may also be altered. For example, a study by psychologists of male professionals whose work was involved with investments revealed that almost nine-tenths reported sexual difficulties, especially impotence, following the stock market decline (Dorfman, 1975). Anxiety over job loss may also affect physical health. Unpublished studies carried out at various NASA sites, where most employees were engineers and scientists, revealed that reductions in force (RIF) not only had an immediate impact on illness but also apparently affected the health of those who were not terminated (Mockbee, 1978). For example, Figure 2.1 illustrates that employee illness visits involving a blood pressure review at the NASA Lewis Research Center increased

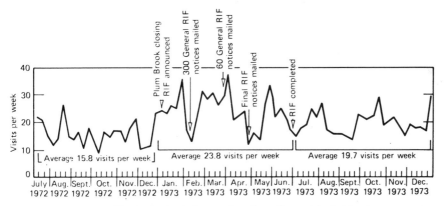

Figure 2.1.   Relationship of reduction in force and employee illness visits for blood pressure review at NASA Lewis Research Center during 1972–1973.

sharply immediately following RIF notifications, despite the fact that the RIF occurred primarily at one location (Plum Brook). Such blood pressure checks were encouraged among NASA employees whose pressure was elevated or who had been diagnosed as hypertensive. The blood pressure visit rate was consistently observed to be sensitive to periods of organizational stress. Before the RIF was announced, such visits averaged 15.8 per week but increased sharply to an average of 23.8 per week after the announcement. However, after the RIF was completed, the visits dropped to 19.7 per week, considerably above the rate prior to the RIF. Thus it appears that organizational stress persists among RIF survivors well after terminations are completed.

It can be concluded that one does not have to undergo job loss to experience stress due to unemployment. The anxieties generated by recessions and joblessness appear to have an ecological impact that can affect those who retain their jobs. Indeed, the anxieties and stress felt by many who remain working may be even greater than that experienced by their colleagues who have been terminated. There is longitudinal evidence that more stress can be generated by the anticipation of job loss than by the actual termination itself (Cobb and Kasl, 1977). For those who are terminated, the stress created by the uncertainty of whether or not they will lose their job has been eliminated, whereas stress persists for those still working but anxious about their job security. Moreover, anxiety over job loss appears to result in a loss of productivity and increased resistance to change (Greenhalgh, 1978). Thus terminations can be disruptive and potentially damaging to the health and well-being not only of the survivors but also of their organizations.

DIFFERENCES BETWEEN PROFESSIONALS AND OTHER WORKERS

Most studies investigating the psychological effects of job loss on the individual have focused on workers other than professionals. Since there are some salient differences between professionals and those in other occupations with respect to the role of work in their lives, it is important to examine those differences, particularly as they affect the impact of job loss.

In one of the first nationwide studies of mental health among American workers, it was revealed that professionals gain much more intrinsic or "ego" satisfaction from their work than do other occupational groups (Gurin, Veroff, and Feld, 1960). The differences were quite dramatic, with 80 percent of professionals and 68 percent of managers deriving ego satisfaction from their work as compared to only 39 percent of clerical workers and 29 percent among the unskilled. Comparable differences between occupations were also reported when work was investigated as a "central life interest" (Orzack, 1959). Professionals and managers not only view work as more central than do other workers, but it is even more important than leisure, which is the opposite view found for nonprofessionals (Staines and O'Connor, 1979). Moreover, the intrinsic nature of the work is crucial to professionals but not to other workers (Friedlander, 1966; White, 1977).

Thus it would appear that professionals are much more likely than those in other occupations to obtain their identity or self-concept from their work. In fact, there is evidence that for the professional, work is a greater potential source of both frustration and satisfaction than it is for other workers (Danielson, 1960; Seybolt, 1976). Furthermore, when individuals perceive work as important to their identity, their satisfaction with life is to a large degree determined by their satisfaction with work (Brayfield, Wells, and Strate, 1957). Indeed, it has been demonstrated that for college-educated workers, job satisfaction is more strongly related to life satisfaction and quality of life than it is for those without a college education (Bamundo, 1977; London, Crandal, and Seals, 1977). There does not seem to be any doubt that, at least among professional workers, there is a "spillover" effect in which satisfaction with one's work results in a more satisfying life (Orpen, 1978).

Since the identity and life satisfaction of the highly educated are so strongly intertwined with their work, it is reasonable to expect that professionals would experience more severe psychological problems resulting from joblessness than would those in other occupations. The evidence available from the few studies that compare unemployed professionals with other workers tends to support this. However, there are some inconsistent results, such as a study of the unemployed carried out during the Great Depression (Watson, 1942) in which life satisfaction was found to be lowest for factory workers and highest among media professionals (e.g., editors, writers, radio announcers, advertising agents). Lawyers, teachers, social workers, and librarians were also high in life satisfaction, whereas physical and life scientists, medical professionals, clerical personnel, and semiskilled workers tended to be low. Some categories of sales personnel were high in life satisfaction, whereas others were quite low. A factor possibly contributing to the inconsistent results may be that professionals are more likely to be higher in life satisfaction prior to job loss than are nonprofessionals. It is the change following job loss that is important. Perhaps the level of life satisfaction dropped more among the professionals, but this could only be ascertained by a longitudinal study that compared life satisfaction before and after job loss among the same individuals.

Other Depression-era research, however, does indicate that those in higher-level occupations were much more affected by job loss. For example, one major study found that the unemployed who had been in higher-level occupations were "more likely to go through more critical disorganization than semiskilled and unskilled workers before readjusting their relations and activities on the basis of lowered standards" (Bakke, 1947, p. 232). Not only were unemployed men who had been in higher-level occupations more affected psychologically by job loss during the Depression, but their wives and children were also more severely affected than those of other workers (Elder, 1974).

Studies carried out since the Depression tend to be consistent in their implication that job loss has a greater psychological impact on professionals than on other workers. Perhaps the only exception is a longitudinal study that found blue-collar workers affected more by unemployment than white-collar workers, but the latter were much more likely to have voluntarily quit than the former (Cohn, 1977). Since the effects of involuntary job loss were not determined, the results are equivocal. (For a further analysis of these results, see the discussion later in the section on self-esteem.) Other studies have more clear-cut results. One such study involved a small group experiment that investigated the effects of unemployment as a function of social status and duration of unemployment (Goodchilds and Smith, 1963). The study found that among high-status unemployed men, those who were out of work longer tended to be more defensive, as well as less self-confident and lower in ego strength, than were the short-term unemployed. Among low-status men, on the other hand, there was no such decline in these traits with length of time out of work; to the contrary, those unemployed the longest appeared to be better adjusted. Other research has revealed that unemployment is much more strongly associated with low self-esteem and stress among whites than blacks (Yancey, Rigsby, and McCarthy, 1972). In fact, studies of stressful life events have revealed that job loss for middle-class whites ranked eighth as a life stress, whereas for poverty-level blacks it ranked fourteenth (Komaroff, Masuda, and Holmes, 1968). These results may be taken as a further indication that unemployment has a greater psychological impact on those of higher socioeconomic status.

A few studies provide more direct evidence for the greater impact of joblessness on professionals relative to other workers. A study during the 1970–1971 recession of the long-term unemployed found that "professionals felt the most dissatisfaction about the way in which they spent their time while their non-professional counterparts were not as dissatisfied" (Briar, 1976). During the recession in 1975, mental health workers reported an upsurge of middle-class clients seeking psychotherapy, whereas few reported an increase among the lower class (Dooley and Catalano, 1977).

In a survey during 1976 carried out in New York City (where unemployment remained high), the negative impact of the economy was most widespread among professionals; blue-collar workers were least affected (Shama, 1979). Interestingly, in a follow-up survey in 1978, when unemployment rates had declined but inflation was rampant, the negative impact of the economy on professionals was less widespread than in 1976 but the opposite occurred among blue-collar workers. This suggests not only that professionals are more negatively affected by recession than are other workers but also that the effect of recession on professionals is worse than that of inflation.

There is also striking epidemiological evidence that the psychological impact of long-term unemployment may be greater on professionals than on other workers, although the opposite may be true in the short run (Dooley and Catalano,

1979). Epidemiological studies of long-term effects reveal that the rate of admissions to mental hospitals of those groups highest in socioeconomic status, as well as those with a college education, is most sensitive to economic change (Brenner, 1967, 1973b). The mental hospital admission rates of those with the highest level of socioeconomic as well as educational attainment go up more during recessions than do the admission rates of those with the lowest attainment. Similar relationships have been revealed for suicides (Henry and Short, 1954; Powell, 1958), although such findings have by no means been universal (see Rushing, 1968). Although the impact of unemployment on job satisfaction remains to be studied, data indicate that between 1969 and 1977 job insecurity increased only among college graduates; in this same period they also experienced the greatest decline in job satisfaction (Quinn and Staines, 1978).

Several explanations have been suggested for the differential sensitivity to recessions among different socioeconomic groups. Brenner, who as we have seen is responsible for much of the epidemiological research on the impact of unemployment, suggests "that relatively high status persons suffer more during an economic downturn than those of relatively low economic status because they have more to lose. . . . Then secondly, it is possible that higher status groups generally have a greater *concern* with socioeconomic status and, therefore, experience greater psychological loss during the downturn" (Brenner, 1967, p. 186). In addition to greater economic loss and concern with socioeconomic status, we have noted that work is generally much more central to the identity of professionals than it is to those in other occupations. Consequently, job loss is probably a greater blow to the ego and self-esteem of professionals than of other workers, and the former would be expected to experience more severe psychological stress. One researcher, who found such differential effects among the unemployed, noted that "professionals, who had previously thrown themselves into a working career . . . were now victims of their own zealousness for work" (Briar, 1976). Others have gone even further by explaining that, whereas unemployment was a "loss of ego-rewarding occupational interactions for the higher status individual, a young unskilled laborer might well have welcomed the furlough from his dull, ego-deflating job" (Goodchilds and Smith, 1963, p. 293). Although the evidence is not completely consistent, the weight of support favors the conclusion that the psychological effects of unemployment are likely to be more extreme for professionals than for other workers.

PREVALENCE OF PSYCHOLOGICAL EFFECTS AMONG JOBLESS PROFESSIONALS

The research examined thus far clearly implies that joblessness can have a severe impact on the psychological well-being of many professionals. The question of how many are affected and in what ways has been the subject of some conjecture.

Therefore, it would be useful to examine the available evidence in some depth to determine more precisely the prevalence of psychological reactions to unemployment among professionals who experience joblessness.

The subjective experience of unemployment was assessed in an investigation we carried out among unemployed, most of whom were terminated from technical jobs during the 1970–1971 recession.[2] The subjective reaction of professionals to being unemployed was assessed by their responses to a question[3] that was originally used to determine how severely blue-collar workers were affected by termination (Kasl, 1971; Cobb and Kasl, 1977). This self-assessment approach revealed that the effects of unemployment were extremely severe for 6 percent of the professionals, who reported that it had changed their whole lives. An additional 33 percent described it as very disturbing and 31 percent somewhat disturbing.

The subjective experience of being unemployed was also measured by how long the professionals believed it would take their lives to return to normal.[4] This question was found to be very sensitive in detecting psychophysiological stress effects of job loss among blue-collar workers (Kasl, 1971). In response to this question, 16 percent of professionals thought it would take over a year for their lives to return to normal and 11 percent felt that they would never be normal again. Almost half (47 percent) predicted that it would take between several months and half a year for there to be a return to normalcy. The longer the professionals felt it would take their lives to return to normal, the more severe they rated their unemployment experience ($r = .68, p < .001$). Thus it would appear that both self-assessment questions measure the subjective experience of unemployment stress.

Although our results indicate that the stress of being out of work is high for perhaps 3 or 4 out of 10 unemployed professionals, a comparable number do not appear to be affected much by joblessness. It was found that 14 percent felt only a little upset by being unemployed and 16 percent reported that they were hardly affected at all. Furthermore, 27 percent reported that their lives had already returned or were about to return to normal despite the fact that they were not working. Some of the factors affecting the differential reaction to unemployment are explored in Chapter 3. What is clear, however, is that professionals do exhibit a wide range of individual reactions to being unemployed.

How does the mental health of jobless professionals compare to that of those who are still working? In an attempt to answer this question, the unemployed professionals in our study were compared with a comparable matched group of employed professionals.[5] The unemployed group was found to be significantly poorer on an index of overall adjustment than those who were still working.[6] Another study, which measured the level of emotional stress experienced by a diverse group of professionals, found that the unemployed exhibited significantly higher stress than those who held jobs (Estes, 1973). The stress index used in that study has been found to reflect the degree of psychological impairment among psychiatric patients.[7] In comparison with the employed group, the psychological impairment exhibited by those who were unemployed was quite high, with 7 percent of the jobless professionals being in the most serious impairment category and an additional 29 percent being at the moderate level, compared to only 1 percent and 15 percent, respectively, among the employed group. Minimal impairment was indicated by only 36 percent of the unemployed and 29 percent were in the mild category. For the employed, 60 percent had minimal and 25 percent mild impairment. The distribution of psychological impairment among jobless professionals is remarkably similar to the one we found for the self-assessed severity of unemployment. It would thus appear that 3 or 4 out of 10 professionals who become unemployed experience psychological impairment extreme enough to require mental health assistance. This may be as much as three times the rate of impairment among professionals in the overall population (see Srole, Langner, Michael, Opler, and Rennie, 1962).

Thus far we have seen that for many professionals, high levels of psychological stress accompany their unemployment. It would be even more useful if we could identify the stress-related psychological changes they are likely to experience as a direct result of being out of work. Unfortunately, our knowledge of such changes comes almost exclusively from studies comparing unemployed with employed professionals, which cannot demonstrate cause-and-effect relationships. Keeping this limitation in mind, we attempt to identify the most important psychological characteristics that have been found to differentiate consistently between unemployed and employed professionals.

Self-Esteem

The drastic reduction in status and prestige following job loss and the failure to find work would be expected to affect the individuals's self-esteem. Diminished self-esteem accompanying job loss has been consistently found among blue-collar workers (e.g., Sheppard, 1965; Wilcock and Frank, 1963), even in studies that were longitudinal in nature (Cohn, 1977; Cobb and Kasl, 1977; Kasl and Cobb, 1970). Thus there is little doubt that job loss does result in lower self-esteem.

Because of professionals' greater identification with their work, their self-esteem should be affected at least as much as that of blue-collar workers. Perhaps the only research that has attempted to compare the impact of unemployment on evaluations of self between blue and white-collar workers has yielded results that were far from clear, despite the fact that it was a longitudinal study (Cohn, 1977). Although both groups experienced a similar decrement in self-confidence as a result of unemployment, a decline in satisfaction with self was evident only among blue-collar workers. There were several explanations given as to why white-collar workers failed to show a similar decline in their satisfaction with self. Perhaps the most important was the fact that 38 percent of white-collar workers were unemployed because they quit their last job, which was twice the rate among blue-collar workers. Indeed, white-collar workers who became unemployed were very likely to have low satisfaction with self while they were still working, possibly indicating problems with their job. Thus it would appear that for many of the higher-status workers, dissatisfaction with themselves may have been more a cause of unemployment than an effect. It is noteworthy that becoming unemployed as a result of the job ending reduced satisfaction with self more than having quit, but this was not determined separately for blue- and white-collar workers. Therefore, from the results presented, it could not be ascertained whether job loss had a greater impact on self-evaluations of higher-status workers. Regardless of what types of workers are more affected by unemployment, there is consistent evidence that professionals who are unemployed are lower in self-esteem than their colleagues who are working, and job loss would appear to be the primary cause (Kaufman, 1973; Estes, 1973).

A loss of self-esteem is likely to be quite disruptive to the professional career, given the centrality of the self-concept to overall career development (Super, 1963, 1970) and the crucial role played by self-esteem in occupational choice decisions (Korman, 1966, 1967; Oppenheimer, 1966). The evidence indicates that those who have low self-esteem tend to choose occupations less congruent with their self-perceived characteristics and abilities. Therefore, a loss of self-esteem may lead to inappropriate job search behavior and poor reemployment decisions. Furthermore, the diminished self-esteem that follows termination has been tied directly to unemployment stress, as indicated by increased blood pressure levels as well as greater self-assessed severity of job loss (Kasl and Cobb, 1970).

The evidence suggests that those suffering from loss of self-esteem as a result of unemployment are prime candidates for psychological assistance. In fact, reviews of studies concerned with self-esteem "reveal that persons who seek psychological help frequently acknowledge that they suffer from feelings of inadequacy and unworthiness" (Coopersmith, 1967, p. 3). Research has also revealed that "changes in self-evaluation resulting from failure are likely to be accompanied by an increase in spontaneous thinking about death" (Diggory, 1966, p. 259). It is noteworthy that the latter research found that suicide proneness was associated with poor self-evaluations only for those whose concern about the future was focused on finding work. In fact, low self-esteem was one of the dominant characteristics of men who committed suicide primarily because of job loss or other failures associated with the work role (Breed, 1972). It was noted that such individuals become susceptible to committing suicide since "failure in cherished roles become crucial to one's self-esteem" (Breed, 1972, p. 16). The psychoanalytical literature suggests that suicide occurs when "the loss of self-esteem is so complete that any hope of regaining it is abandoned. . . [and] to have a desire to live evidently means to feel a certain self-esteem" (Fenichel, 1945, p. 400).

The relationship between suicide and unemployment is evaluated more extensively in subsequent sections of this chapter.

There does not appear to be any doubt that loss of self-esteem because of joblessness is likely to accompany a deterioration not only of the occupational identity of professionals but also of their overall health. The crucial role played by self-esteem for individual well-being will become clearer as we proceed to examine other psychological effects of unemployment on professionals.

Anxiety

The loss of self-esteem is apparently related to the person's sensitivity to anxiety-provoking situations such as that created by unemployment stress. Studies have indicated the following characteristics of individuals who are low in self-esteem:

> These people see themselves as . . . lacking the inner resources to tolerate or reduce anxiety readily aroused by everyday events and stress . . . Clinical studies repeatedly demonstrate that failure and other conditions that threaten to expose personal inadequacies are probably the major cause of anxiety. Anxiety and self-esteem are closely related; if it is threat that releases anxiety. . . .it is the person's esteem that is being threatened (Coopersmith, 1967, pp. 3–4).

It seems obvious that unemployed professionals would be highly prone to anxiety. Indeed, one study did find that jobless professionals exhibited significantly greater anxiety than those who were still working (Estes, 1973). In that study about three-tenths of the unemployed admitted being worried about the future. This was more than twice the rate of the employed who expressed such anxiety. In our research, we also found that somewhat more of the unemployed (59 percent) worried about things that might happen to them than did those who were still working (48 percent). However, this difference was not significant. It is quite likely that the high anxiety levels found among both groups in our study could be attributed to the fact that most of the respondents were technical professionals, many of whom were facing an uncertain future during the recession of 1970–1971, regardless of their employment status. As we have already noted, anxiety increases during periods of high unemployment, even among those who are working.

It can be concluded that not only does the experience of joblessness make the unemployed professional more anxiety prone, but the threat of job loss also creates high levels of anxiety among those who remain working. However, as far back as the Great Depression it was noted that although many may suffer from great anxiety because of unemployment, they are not necessarily neurotic (Eisenberg and Lazarsfeld, 1938). Therefore, at least some of the anxiety generated by unemployment can be considered a normal reaction to the very real uncertainties and threats resulting from job insecurity.

Anomie

Unemployment may also lead to anomie, a concept first formulated by sociologist Emile Durkheim (1897) and used to explain reactions to sudden societal changes, such as an economic depression. One researcher studying the effects of job loss described anomie as "a condition of normlessness, in which the individual no longer feels himself a part of or restrained by the prevailing norm, which in turn can result in apathy and depression" (Sheppard, 1965, pp. 170–171).

Anomie has been found to be prevalent among unemployed blue-collar workers (Aiken, Ferman, and Sheppard, 1968; Sheppard, 1965). Although there is some longitudinal evidence that anomie increases significantly following job loss (Kweller, Zalkind, and Dispenzieri, 1972), research results are not entirely consistent, at least with respect to blue-collar workers (see Cobb and Kasl, 1977).

Studies of unemployed professionals have revealed that they suffer from significantly higher levels of anomie than do those who are still working. For example, in a study of technical professionals, 55 percent of those who had been terminated were high on normlessness compared to 33 percent of those still employed (Little, 1973). In our study, 45 percent of the unemployed compared to 19 percent of those working reported feeling that they "just were not a part of things." This discrepancy between the two groups was the greatest difference found for any of the dimensions of adjustment in our study. Furthermore, the degree of anomie experienced by the unemployed professionals was related to their self-assessed severity of joblessness ($r = .27$, $p < .05$) as well as how long they felt it would take their lives to return to normal ($r = .34$, $p < .01$). Other research has found that the financial impact of unemployment was significantly related to increased normlessness among professionals (Little, 1973).

From its very conceptualization, anomie has been directly connected to suicide (Durkheim, 1897). Research into anomie has demonstrated that people most prone to suicide during periods of high unemployment were those who worked in a professional–managerial occupation, as well as retired males, who appeared suicide prone at all times (Powell, 1958). The latter research found that suicide for males is connected primarily to loss of occupational status, explaining that it "is an ultimate expression of accumulated self-contempt . . . and both guilt and self-contempt are rooted in anomie which results in the inability to act, i.e. impotence" (Powell, 1958, p. 136). There is evidence that suicidal individuals suffer not only from low self-esteem but also from impotence, or what could more accurately be described as helplessness (Neuringer, 1974), a problem discussed at greater length later in this chapter.

As already noted, the loss of status that occurs among unemployed professionals is related to a loss of self-esteem that may have consequences in terms of psychopathology. Job loss can create a condition of severe anomie for professionals and in such a state, loss of self-esteem, helplessness, and other manifestations of psychological deterioration can ultimately lead to suicide. Since suicide has also been found to be related to depression and self-blame, it may be instructive to examine how such reactions are affected by unemployment stress.

Self-Blame and Depression

A loss of self-esteem among the unemployed also appears to be associated with self-blame and depression. Studies reveal that individuals who fail to achieve their aspirations evaluate themselves as inferior and "are likely to report feelings of guilt, shame, or depression" (Coopersmith, 1967, p. 3). In psychoanalytic terms, guilt and shame are considered to be expressions of self-blame that typically motivate a quest for self-punishment (Fenichel, 1945).

Unemployed professionals appear to be more likely to manifest self-blame than do those who are still working. In one study, about two-fifths of unemployed professionals attributed blame for job loss to the person who was out of work—almost double the rate among those still employed (Estes, 1973). However, in a review of research on attribution theory, it has been suggested that when facing personal crises "people make attributions to protect their self-esteem and sense of personal worth. One would expect that, if anything, people faced with such outcomes would go to great lengths to avoid personal blame and feelings of guilt" (Wortman, 1976, p. 45). Indeed, it has been found that most unemployed professionals do not blame themselves for being out of work but rather attribute blame to external causes (Estes, 1973; Little, 1973). We have more to say about this later in our discussion of helplessness.

One way of avoiding blame for job loss is to take on the "sick role," which was described as follows:

> The sick role frees one from usual demands of work and other social role obligations without the stigma that it is one's own fault. Thus, it becomes a valuable role for many people. To the extent that a person can be unemployed without the stigma that it is his own fault (for example, if general economic conditions are poor and unemployment is widespread), then the unemployed role may contain certain benefits such as relaxation, sympathy from "understanding" friends and relatives, more freedom with one's time, etc. In sum, under certain conditions unemployment like the sick role may be a welcome haven from everyday obligations with the added bonus that, when unemployed, one does not even have to stay in bed (Little, 1973, p. 148).

Actual sick-role behavior among the unemployed has been observed by Sidney Cobb, a physician who was part of a research team that carried out a major longitudinal study of mass terminations and their effects on the health of blue-collar workers. According to Cobb, because "the unemployed role is one that is looked on with disfavor in our society, it is not surprising that some people prefer to move into the sick role and accept the identity 'sick' in preference to the identity 'unemployed.' These persons must be among the more flexible and presumably will have had recent experience with the sick role" (Slote, 1969, pp. xvii–xviii). There is evidence that those who behave as if they are ill are not only more likely to be under more stress but also to have had a strong tendency to adopt the sick role in the past (Mechanic and Volkart, 1961). It would appear that, at least for some individuals, taking on a sick role following job loss may serve as a defense in the avoidance of self-blame.

Although there is some indication that individuals who attribute blame to themselves for failure are more likely to experience depression (Abramson, Seligman, and Teasdale, 1978), research with unemployed professionals indicates that feelings of depression are relatively independent of self-blame (Little, 1973). Furthermore, depression appears to be more widespread than self-blame among unemployed professionals. High or moderate levels of depression have been found for three-fourths of jobless professionals, compared to two-fifths of their employed colleagues (Little, 1973). It is possible that the relatively high levels of depression found even among the employed (although significantly lower than among the unemployed) may be a result of the likelihood that as survivors, they experience a loss because of coworkers being terminated and realize that their own positions are not secure. As we have seen earlier in this chapter, professionals who remain working can be greatly affected by the stress generated when mass terminations occur among their colleagues.

When professionals are out of work or even anticipating job loss they may be more susceptible to self-blame and depression than other workers because of their much greater sensitivity to status inconsistency, as the following explanation would imply:

> A person whose achieved ranks are inferior to his ascribed rank is likely to view his situation as one of personal failure. Unlike the low status inconsistent, he cannot justify his lack of success in terms of ascribed handicaps. His difficulties therefore tend to stimulate feelings of personal deficiency and self-blame, thus increasing the likelihood of intrapunitive response such as symptomization (Jackson, 1962, pp. 476–477).

Being identified as an unemployed professional clearly denotes status inconsistency, since having become unemployed is an inferior rank to one's professional status. It has been found that status inconsistency as well as symptoms manifested as psychosomatic disorders are strongly related to depression among unemployed professionals but only weakly to self-blame (Little, 1973). Furthermore, evidence indicates that "intrapunitive responses" such as suicide are related to both depression and self-blame, but here again depression appears more predominant (Barraclough, Nelson, and Sainsbury, 1967). The relationship between depression, mental illness, and suicide has been examined in an extensive review of research and it was concluded: "Depression preceding suicide is probably universal and may be a feature of all types of mental disease associated with suicide and in fact, of all types of suicide" (Silverman, 1968, p. 62). Depression is explored further in our discussion of helplessness later in this chapter.

Research indicates that following job loss among blue-collar workers, there is an increase in depression as well as intrapunitive responses such as hypertension, peptic ulcers, arthritis, alcoholism, and loss of hair, as well as an abnormally high incidence of suicides and sudden death from heart attacks among men without previously known coronary disease (Cobb and Kasl, 1971, 1977). Although such direct evidence is lacking for professionals, the research already cited clearly indicates that the stigma and shame of unemployment is likely to be quite devastating to their self-esteem. Hence out-of-work professionals should be even more prone to experiencing the intrapunitive responses that have been found to result from joblessness among other workers.

Relative to depression, the impact of self-blame on the health of unemployed professionals would appear to be much more benign. This may be due to the fact that for some individuals or under certain circumstances attribution of blame to oneself may be quite adaptive (Bulman and Wortman, 1977; Wortman, 1976). However, self-blame when manifested as shame may be maladaptive since it has been identified as central to the "basic suicide syndrome" formulated by Warren Breed (1972). This syndrome is highly relevant to the unemployed, since it is based on the finding that the primary precipitating factor among male suicides was job loss or other loss of status related to their work.

Breed's (1972) basic suicide syndrome, derived from a study of white males, consists of the following five components:

1. *Failure* is the basic concept of the suicide syndrome. Many of those studied had committed suicide after being fired or otherwise experiencing failure at work. At the time of death only half were fully employed.

2. *Commitment* to a goal or role that becomes "part of the person's self or identity" (p. 7). People experience failure when they believe they have not attained a goal or fulfilled a role to which they were strongly committed.

3. *Rigidity* is an inability to change roles or goals. Those who committed suicide did not have "the flexibility to try new paths . . . and they settled deep into resignation over their own failure . . . . For this kind of person, rigidity may be an unconscious attempt at security maintenance when faced with the threats of identity diffusion" (p. 7).

4. *Shame* is a way in which people who commit suicide respond to failure in fulfilling a role or reaching a goal that is an integral part of their identity.

"Such a failure and the anticipation of negative reactions from other people constitute not only a source of anxiety but a disastrous blow to the self-esteem. The self-image presented to others is felt to be shattered; the 'depression' often found among suiciders can easily follow" (pp. 7–8).

5. *Social isolation* is a defense used by those who experience failure to avoid negative evaluations from others that threaten to be painful to their self-image. "Once a committed person feels shame over failure and cannot create a new life because of his rigidity he feels worthless, and moreover, feels that other people also see him as worthless" (p. 8).

The individual who experiences this syndrome no longer has the ego-defense mechanisms "used by the ordinary person *to escape the effects of heavy blows to self-esteem*" (Breed, 1972, p. 16). Defenses such as rigidity and withdrawal would certainly be dysfunctional in dealing with a problem such as being out of work. In fact, in our study we found that as overall adjustment deteriorated among the unemployed professionals, the type of occupational role they desired became more rigid[8] ($r = .41, p < .01$). Because of the strong commitment of professionals to their work, they are prime candidates for experiencing the basic suicide syndrome following job loss, since "without commitment, there would be no sense of failure, no self-blame and avoidance of social contacts" (Breed, 1972, p. 6).

Social Relations and Support

The social isolation identified as part of the basic suicide syndrome was reported as far back as the Great Depression to be a characteristic of those suffering job loss (Bakke, 1940; Elder, 1974; Jahoda, Lazarsfeld, and Zeisel, 1971). The widespread feelings of shame and stigma from unemployment apparently do lead professionals and other workers to isolate themselves socially to protect their self-image (Briar, 1976). However, professionals appear much more likely than others to seek such protection by avoiding social contacts (Elder, 1974). In fact, a longitudinal study has shown that only among white-collar workers is satisfaction with self related to evaluations of self by others, with the importance of those evaluations declining as a result of unemployment (Cohn, 1977). The following explanation for these findings was offered:

Higher status individuals appear to base their own evaluations of self more on others' evaluations than do lower status individuals. With a public failure such as unemployment, white collar workers discount the importance of others' evaluations and by doing so reduce the impact of employment status change on own evaluation of self. Because blue collar workers are not so dependent on others' evaluations as a source of own evaluation, this ability to discount the importance of others' evaluation does not reduce the impact of employment status change on self evaluations. As to why there is a basic difference between blue and white collar workers in the importance of others' evaluations on own evaluation we can only speculate. If past achievements make an individual more sensitive to others' evaluations (the converse of "ego defense"), then the greater reliance on others' evaluations among white collar workers is expected (Cohn, 1977, pp. 127, 129).

Since evaluations of others are important to the self-image of the professional, that image can be protected by avoiding others through social isolation or by diminishing the importance of their evaluations. It appears that either or both of these defenses are used by unemployed professionals.

During the recession of 1970–71, it was revealed that the major change in activities following job loss was an increase in the amount of time the individual spent alone (Briar, 1976). During that recession, unemployed professionals were found to be considerably less sociable than their colleagues who did not lose their jobs (Estes, 1973). For example, despite their need to find work, 61 percent of the jobless professionals reported that they rarely sought help from others compared to only 46 percent of the employed who reported this. Social isolation may even extend to sexual relations since over one-fourth of unemployed professionals reported that they did not have a regular sex partner, about twice the rate among those who were still working (Estes, 1973). However, contrary to popular myth, fears of marital breakups were equally prevalent among out-of-work and employed professionals (7 percent). The impact of unemployment on marital relationships is evaluated when the role of the spouse is discussed in Chapter 3.

Social support has been found to be important in cushioning the effects of job loss (Cobb and Kasl, 1977; Gore, 1973, 1978). It would appear that social support would suffer as a result of a withdrawal from social contacts and thus be detrimental to the well-being of the jobless individual. However, there is evidence that, although there is a withdrawal from old friends because of the shame and stigma of unemployment, more time is spent with new friends who are also out of work (Briar, 1976). It is their common problem of joblessness that brings the unemployed together for mutual understanding and support. In our study, we found that 53 percent of the unemployed believed that "others really cared about them" compared to 62 percent who believed this among those still working, but the difference was not significant. It may be that the increased social isolation of the unemployed was partly compensated by the social support received from new friends among the jobless. In fact, there is longitudinal evidence that although loss events reduce the size of one's social network, sufficient social support may be obtained from remaining or new relationships (Coyne and Lazarus, 1979).

Anger and Aggression

Social support apparently can help diminish the anger of jobless professionals. For example, in our study those who received high levels of social support felt less resentment about what happened to them ($r = -.37, p < .01$). This is important since the unemployed may be highly prone to hostile feelings. As far back as the Great Depression, resentment and hostility against employers was found to be much more extreme among terminated professionals than among their employed colleagues (Hall, 1934). In our study we found that resentment was exhibited by one-third of the unemployed, almost three times the rate for those still working. Such resentment was associated with the severity of the professionals' unemployment experience ($r = .51, p < .001$) as well as the length of time they felt it would take for their lives to return to normal ($r = .25, p < .05$). Thus feelings of resentment appear to be related to elevated levels of unemployment stress.

Despite the greater resentment expressed by professionals who were out of work, we failed to find significant differences in irritability or outward aggression between the unemployed and employed groups. Although another study revealed that jobless professionals had stronger feelings of overall hostility toward others than did their employed colleagues (Estes, 1973), it also found that extreme anger was expressed by about three-fifths of both unemployed and working professionals, who said that "they boil inside because of others." In our study, too, we found aggression directed toward others among almost half of the employed as well as the jobless. Apparently, feelings of extreme anger toward others are quite prevalent among professionals, regardless of their employment status, at least during a recession period. It may be that in times of high unemployment, anxiety and frustration become so widespread that even persons who still have work not only become extremely angry toward those perceived to be responsible for job insecurity but may also displace this anger toward others or themselves. The evidence presented thus far lends some credibility to the existence of great anger generated by job loss even among those who continue working. This would certainly help to account for the increases in aggressive behavior observed during economic recessions directed either against others or oneself.

There is some indication that feelings of hostility following job loss are directly related to intrapunitive responses. For example, among unemployed technical professionals, irritation and hostility were strongly related to psychosomatic symptoms as well as depression (Little, 1973). It was also found that the degree to which they perceived deterioration in their career was a major factor related to feelings of irritation and hostility. In our study, those unemployed who expected to experience difficulty in taking on new assignments in their career because they had become obsolescent were also more resentful ($r = .26, p < .05$). Such results would seem to fit into a model of societal aggression suggested by Korman (1974), in which an environment that creates low self-esteem results in increased aggression toward others as well as oneself, and ultimately leads to low achievement and dissatisfaction. The latter consequences are examined in the sections that follow.

Motivation to Work and to Achieve

The loss of self-esteem and the deteriorated psychological state of many unemployed professionals would be expected to have some effect on their motivation to work and drive to achieve. Some studies have found "work inhibition" or a "withdrawal syndrome" among the chronically unemployed (Lawlis, 1971; Tiffany, Cowan, and Tiffany, 1970). There is also limited evidence that unemployment does affect work motivation among professionals. For example, a study of Depression-era engineers found that three-tenths of those who had lost their jobs believed that it did not pay to work too hard because employers would only take advantage of them (Hall, 1934). This was three times the rate who felt this way among their employed colleagues.

We found some evidence in our study that a motivation loss may be associated with unemployment. For example, in an attempt to determine motivation in terms of a need hierarchy such as that suggested by Abraham Maslow (1943), it was revealed that unemployed professionals were significantly weaker than their employed colleagues only in their needs for self-esteem and self-actualization.[9] The unemployed also felt it was less necessary to be working to fulfill these higher-order growth needs than did those who were still employed, although the difference was significant only for self-esteem needs. Apparently, not only can growth needs be diminished among unemployed professionals but the "instrumentality" of working to attain those needs may be reduced for them as well. Instrumentality is the individual's perception that a particular behavior will lead to some outcome and is central to the expectancy theory of work motivation (see Lawler, 1973).

Further analyses indicated that those jobless professionals for whom becoming employed had low instrumentality for attaining self-esteem also tended to have a weaker identification or involvement with their work.[10] However, this relationship was very strong only for those who already were low in self-esteem[11] ($r = .60$, $p < .001$). No such relationship was evident for those with high self-esteem. It would appear that for unemployed professionals who have acquired a negative self-concept, the degree to which their self-esteem will be enhanced through reemployment may be determined by how much that self-concept involves their work. On the other hand, it may be that for those who maintain high self-esteem, the need to return to work to protect their self-concept was not affected by their ego involvement with work. Since unemployment very likely resulted in a loss of self-esteem for many (Kaufman, 1973), these results are in accord with those who have argued that the protection of one's self-concept is likely to occur under conditions of situationally devalued self-esteem (Dipboye, 1977; Wiener, 1973). In sum, it would appear that (1) there is a reduced need among unemployed professionals to return to work in order to maintain self-esteem and (2) the strength of this need may be affected by how much their self-concept is tied to their work, particularly for those whose self-esteem has been diminished.

To investigate the relationship between achievement motivation and unemployment among professionals, we analyzed data from a nationwide survey of young professionals (mostly in their late 20s) carried out during the 1971 recession by the American Council on Education (El-Khawas and Bisconti, 1974). We selected from this sample all college graduates and compared those who were employed full time with the unemployed who were looking for a job on self-ratings of various personal traits.[12] The traits in which the graduates most frequently rated themselves above average were academic ability and drive to achieve. There was little difference in rating of academic ability as a function of employment status. Among males, 67 percent of the unemployed versus 62 percent of those who were working rated themselves above average in academic ability. Sixty-six percent of the females responded this way, regardless of employment status. However, great discrepancies were apparent in ratings of drive to achieve. Among males only 45 percent of the unemployed felt that they were above average in achievement drive compared to 64 percent of those working. Among females the percentages were 46 percent and 57 percent for unemployed and employed, respectively.

Although there is a possibility that professionals who are initially lower in achievement motivation are those who become unemployed, it seems more likely that being terminated or not being able to find a job appropriate to their qualifications would lead to a diminished drive to achieve.[13] If the latter is true, the achievement motivation of professionals can decline because of the unemployment experience, even when their perceived ability is not diminished. Ability is a much more stable trait than motivation (Kaufman, 1974c), and thus would be less likely to be seen as diminished in the face of failure associated with being out of work. This is supported by the view that people attribute outcomes involving loss or failure to characteristics that are modifiable rather than those that are fixed and unchangeable (Wortman, 1976).

A loss in achievement motivation among unemployed professionals may reflect an attempt to lower their level of aspiration to be more congruent with a diminished self-esteem. Such an explanation is in accord with current thinking concerning the need for individuals to bring their cognitions about themselves in balance and thereby reduce cognitive inconsistencies (see Korman, 1974). As was already indicated, such an attempt at attaining congruency between one's self-concept and the reality of joblessness can be quite disruptive to the professional's career, particularly in making appropriate reemployment decisions. In fact, unemployed professionals have been found to experience significantly more difficulty in making decisions than those who did not experience job loss (Estes, 1973). In our study, the decision-making ability[14] of the jobless professionals was found to be related to their overall adjustment ($r = .26, p < .05$). Thus not only does the unemployment experience appear to affect the achievement drive of professionals, but it may impair their ability to make appropriate decisions affecting their career.

In our study of jobless professionals, we found that those whose values were more achievement-oriented had greater needs for self-esteem ($r = .32, P < .05$) and self-actualization ($r = .48, p < .01$).[15] However, achievement values also appeared to be affected by the unemployment experience to varying degrees depending on the individual's actual self-esteem. For example, for those who were low in self-esteem, lower achievement values were associated with how long they felt it would take them to return to normal ($r = .50, p < .01$), how severely unemployment affected them ($r = .37, p < .05$), and their rigidity with regard to the job they were willing to take ($r = .65, p < .001$). No such relationships were found for professionals who had high self-esteem. It may very well be that those whose self-esteem has been diminished because of being out of work also have difficulty maintaining their achievement values when subjected to high unemployment stress. Again this is in accord with Korman's (1974) model that low achievement is one of the consequences of an environment that creates low self-esteem.

Maintaining high achievement motivation as well as a strong motivation to work may help guard against the social stigma of unemployment. Indeed, those unemployed who had a higher motivation to achieve or to work were found to be more likely to discount the importance of others' evaluations of themselves (Cohn, 1977). It was noted that "they are more likely to take an ego-defensive position with regards to others' evaluations" (Cohn, 1977, p. 168). Such an ego defense may, however, be useful in protecting against the basic suicide syndrome, which depends on evaluations of others.

Thus far, the overall implication of the findings is that the motivation to work in order to satisfy higher-order growth needs is considerably reduced as a result of joblessness. Furthermore, unemployed professionals who are low in self-esteem may reduce their motivation to attain reemployment to the extent that their work is not, or ceases to be, part of their self-concept. Those who are low in self-esteem also appear most vulnerable to losing their orientation toward achievement as a result of unemployment stress. It is interesting to note that in our study the need to work to attain security among the unemployed was comparable to that of those who were still working. Since it is the higher-order needs rather than those related to security that motivate professionals to work (Gurin et al., 1960; Herzberg, Mausner, and Snyderman, 1959; Kaufman, 1974c), they may in fact become work inhibited because of reductions in their growth needs resulting from unemployment stress.

Professional Obsolescence

The motivation to work among professionals also appears to be related to their obsolescence, defined as the degree to which they lack the up-to-date knowledge or skills necessary to maintain effective performance in their current or future work roles (Kaufman, 1974c). In our study, professional obsolescence[16] was found to be associated with unemployment. For example, we found that the unemployed rated themselves significantly less up to date in their profession than did those who were working continuously. Twenty-two percent of the unemployed clearly viewed themselves as professionally out of date compared to only 9 percent of those who were continuously employed. Not only was obsolescence among jobless professionals related to poor overall adjustment ($r = -.42$, $p < .001$), but it was also the most obsolescent professionals who exhibited the weakest needs for self-esteem ($r = -.34, p < .01$) as well as self-actualization ($r = -.29, p < .05$). This may indicate that work inhibition had already set in for those who were obsolescent. However, only among professionals who had high self-esteem was obsolescence related to occupational rigidity as indicated by an unwillingness to take risks with respect to job choice ($r = .48, p < .01$). This tends to be in accord with the research finding that occupational choice is consistent with the persons' perceptions of their own capabilities primarily for individuals possessing high self-esteem (Korman, 1967a). One implication of our findings is that even if unemployed professionals maintain their self-esteem, it does not necessarily protect them from occupational rigidity if they become obsolescent.

Although professionals who were initially more obsolescent may be more prone to termination (Kaufman, 1974c), it is also likely that those who are not utilizing their professional knowledge and skills because they are out of work may lose their competence as well as confidence in being able to effectively carry out assignments in their field. This latter explanation receives support from another study in which 36 percent of unemployed technical professionals reported a high degree of career deterioration after being terminated (Little, 1973). In addition, those who experienced career deterioration not only tended to exhibit greater irritation and hostility, as was already noted, but they were also more likely to suffer from self-blame and depression. It would appear that unemployment, by inhibiting professional development, can create the motivational conditions that lead toward obsolescence, career deterioration, and ultimately, work inhibition.

Life Satisfaction

Since the role of their work is central to the lives of almost all professionals, unemployment is likely to result in an overall deterioration of their satisfaction with life. All evidence appears to support this. In fact, one study found the greatest difference between out-of-work and employed professionals was in their life satisfaction (Estes, 1973). To illustrate this difference, 44 percent of the unemployed reported that they were usually not in good spirits, three times the rate reported among those who were working.

In our study we also found a significant difference in life satisfaction between the unemployed professionals and their employed colleagues. Only 56 percent of the jobless felt they were generally satisfied with life compared to 76 percent of those still working. Furthermore, those unemployed professionals who expressed a greater dissatisfaction with life were much more likely to be severely affected by being out of work than were the unemployed who were satisfied ($r = .46$, $p < .001$). Dissatisfaction with life was also among the strongest factors related to poor overall adjustment ($r = .68, p < .001$).

The evidence is rather clear that unemployment stress contributes to a general deterioration in the lives of many professionals. However, such deterioration may be affected by the individual's self-esteem. For example, only among those professionals high in self-esteem was a dissatisfaction with life strongly related to how long they felt it would take their lives to return to normal ($r = .60$, $p < .001$). This would appear to indicate that the life satisfaction of professionals is most affected by unemployment stress when they possess high self-esteem. Although such a finding seems to be contradictory to the results we found with motivation, it nevertheless is in accord with studies of satisfaction which indicate that those who are high in self-esteem have a greater need for cognitive consistency (see Korman, 1967b), and hence their life satisfaction would be strongly related to the degree of unemployment stress they perceive. It should also be noted that only among those unemployed who were high in self-esteem was life satisfaction strongly related to their belief that others cared about them ($r = .58, p < .001$). Apparently, receiving social support is most effective in promoting the life satisfaction of the unemployed when they have maintained a positive self-concept.

The evidence indicates that over two-fifths of professionals who are unemployed experience general dissatisfaction with life. This is close to the estimate we made earlier in this chapter regarding the number of professionals who would experience psychological impairment extreme enough to require mental health assistance as a result of being out of work. Since life satisfaction appears strongly related to unemployment stress, the degree of satisfaction with life could therefore serve as another global indicator of the psychological impact of joblessness among professionals.

Locus of Control

Of relevance to adjustment among the unemployed is their locus of control, a concept originally formulated and measured by Rotter (1966). According to this concept, people who feel they have little influence over what happens to them and attribute outcomes to outside forces such as fate or luck have an external locus of control, whereas those who believe that outcomes can be determined by their own behavior are internally controlled. Research has consistently demonstrated that work-inhibited or chronically unemployed people differ significantly from those who are working in their belief that they are controlled by the external environment (Searls, Braucht, and Miskimins, 1974; Tiffany et al., 1970).

Locus of control appears to affect individual responses to stress. A longitudinal study has found that entrepreneurs who feel controlled by the external environment perceived greater stress following extensive business losses than did those with an internal locus of control (Anderson, 1977). However, the coping behavior of externals involved fewer attempts at dealing directly with the objective problem and a greater dependence on defensive responses such as emotional or anxiety reactions. It was concluded that "the task-oriented coping behaviors of internals are apparently associated with a more successful solution of the problems created by the stressful event" (Anderson, 1977, p. 450). In addition, it was indicated that locus of control not only affects success in dealing with a stressful situation but that success influences future locus of control. That is, internals not only are more successful in dealing with stress, but success leads to an even greater internal orientation. It seems clear that locus of control and how one copes with stress are intimately connected. However, having an external orientation does not make one more prone to unemployment (Andrisani and Nestel, 1976).

Other research has revealed that locus of control can be divided into two independent dimensions (Gurin, Gurin, Rao, and Beattie, 1969). One dimension refers to people in general and is called control ideology. It measures the individual's "ideology or general beliefs about the role of internal and external forces in determining success and failure in the culture at large" (Gurin et al., 1969, p. 35). The other dimension is personal control, which measures the degree to which the individual "believes that he can control what happens in his own life" (Gurin et al., 1969, p. 35).

Longitudinal studies of a national sample of workers have provided "some evidence that locus of control is both an antecedent and a consequence of work experience, although the evidence for the former is stronger than that for the latter. . .[and] that personal control is more strongly related than control ideology to work experience" (Andrisani and Abeles, 1976b, p. 28). This longitudinal research also indicated that a voluntary change of employer strongly increased the personal control of the individual, whereas involuntary change had a slight tendency to diminish a belief in such control. Another analysis of this sample, however, revealed that personal control was significantly reduced following job loss (Parnes and King, 1977).

Studies of professionals indicate that unemployment may affect their control ideology to a greater degree than their personal control. As far back as the Great Depression, it was found that unemployed professionals had a significantly stronger belief in an external control ideology than did those who were employed. For example, in a study of jobless engineers during the Depression, half believed that success was more dependent on luck than on real ability compared to only three-tenths of their employed colleagues who felt this way (Hall, 1934). A more recent study of unemployed professionals found that more than one-fourth believed that "progress depended on luck and pull," twice the rate among those who did not lose their jobs (Estes, 1973).

We investigated personal control and found that the out-of-work professionals were more externally controlled than the employed group, but the difference was not significant.[17] Similar results were found in another study (Little, 1973), but significant differences were found for control ideology, with over one-third of the unemployed strongly believing that external forces are the controlling factors in the society, more than twice the rate among the employed. A possible explanation for control ideology being more affected than personal control among unemployed professionals is that an ego-defense mechanism may be operating in the face of failure. It was noted "that higher acceptance of a doctrine of luck or unfair pull serves as a defense against attack upon the employed man's self-esteem" (Little, 1973, p. 80). This is in accord with our earlier discussion on attributions of blame.

When an individual's self-esteem is already low, protection against the consequences of not being in control may be considerably diminished. For example, in our study it was only among professionals who were low in self-esteem that those who believed that they were not in control exhibited lower achievement values ($r = .48, p < .01$). It is likely that professionals whose self-esteem has been diminished as a result of unemployment have difficulty maintaining their achievement values if they do not believe that they have any control over what happens to them. Again this supports the theory of Korman (1974) that an environment that results in low self-esteem and takes control away from the individual creates the conditions that lead to a low achievement orientation.

A belief that one lacks control may have detrimental effects on an individual's mental health. For example, we found that regardless of self-esteem, as the belief in personal control diminished among unemployed professionals, the more likely they were to experience anomie ($r = .39, p < .01$), depression or hopelessness ($r = .29, p < .05$), and rigidity in the type of work role they were willing to accept ($r = .45, p < .001$). Since these are all characteristics associated with suicide, the feeling of failure experienced with job loss among professionals, when combined with a belief that they are not in control, may create conditions that can precipitate suicidal behavior.

Helplessness

Believing that external forces exert control over outcomes that cannot be influenced by the individual implies a helplessness in which the person can do little if anything to change the situation. Such feelings of helplessness create the psychological conditions, such as depression, that can lead to suicide. For example, Martin Seligman (1975) has evolved a theory based on experimental and clinical evidence that cognitions of helplessness in the face of loss, failure, or threat are the basic cause of depression: "The depressed patient believes or has learned that he cannot control those elements of his life that relieve suffering, bring gratification, or provide nurture—in short, he believes that he is helpless" (p. 93). It is further suggested that self-esteem and feelings of competence are directly related to such control. According to Seligman (1975), "what produces self-esteem and a sense of competence, and protects against depression, is not only the absolute quality of experience, but the perception that one's own actions controlled the experience. To the degree that uncontrollable events occur . . . depression will be predisposed and ego-strength undermined" (p. 99). In a subsequent reformulation of learned helplessness in terms of attribution theory (Abramson, et al., 1978), it was suggested that although helplessness results in depression, a loss of self-esteem is greater for individuals who attribute their helplessness to themselves than for those who blame external forces. Such differences were illustrated by the following relevant example:

> Suppose two individuals are depressed because they expect that regardless of how hard they try they will remain unemployed. The depression of the person who believes that his own incompetence is causing his failure to find work will feel low self-regard and worthlessness. The person who believes that nationwide economic crisis is causing his failure to find work will not think less of himself. Both depressions, however, will show passivity, negative cognitive set, and sadness, the other three depressive deficits, since both individuals expect that the probability of the desired outcome is very low and that it is not contingent on any responses in their repertoire (Abramson et al., 1978, p. 166).

The dependency of self-esteem on labor market forces was corroborated by a longitudinal study which found that jobless workers' evaluations of themselves were diminished only under conditions of low unemployment (Cohn, 1977). When the unemployment rate was high, self-evaluations were positive. These results supported the "hypothesis that the unemployed individual will use environmental information in an evaluation of whether his current status reflects personal failure" (Cohn, 1977, p. 155). However, job loss can still have an effect on self-evaluations, even if it is caused by factors external to the individual. This is indicated by the observation

> that when an external attribution of cause for unemployment is available, such as a high local area unemployment rate, the unemployed are not as dissatisfied with themselves as when no external cause for unemployment is available. Yet those individuals who become unemployed because of their job ending, an obvious source for external attribution, do appear to experience low self confidence and dissatisfaction with self (Cohn, 1977, pp. 159–160).

It seems that just the experience of job loss may be sufficient to result in feelings of personal failure and loss of self worth. However, such feelings are likely to be exacerbated if the individual attributes blame for job loss to oneself.

Premature Death

The state of helplessness brought on by a loss of control may even contribute to premature death. Seligman presents a variety of anecdotal and experimental findings that "seem to show death from helplessness. In the course of such deaths an individual losses control over matters important to him. Behaviorally he reacts with depression, passivity, and submission. Subjectively, he feels helpless and hopeless. Consequently, unexpected death ensues" (1975, pp. 187–188).

Evidence relating job loss to death is generally indirect in nature. For example, sudden death has been found to be most frequently precipitated by a loss situation which for men (but not women) includes a loss of status or self-esteem (Engel, 1971). A reduction in self-esteem is a usual consequence of job loss. Of relevance here is that self-esteem associated with work has been found to be related to elevated heart disease risk only for older men in higher-level white-collar occupations (House, 1972). Hence the older male professional may be more susceptible than others to premature death as a result of job loss. Although there is some evidence that job loss can precede death from congestive heart failure, such death is apparently more likely when high stress is coupled with a lack of social support (Chambers and Reiser, 1953). We have already noted that support from others is important in reducing stress, but social support may be crucial in avoiding stress-related death (Lynch, 1977).

There is other evidence, based on longitudinal research, that the most important factor in predicting longevity for older men (but not women) is their satisfaction with work (Palmore, 1969). Indeed, work satisfaction was even a better predictor of longevity than life expectancy based on actuarial predictions. This may help explain why life expectancy is generally lower for men than for women. It was suggested that for men, "the maintenance of a satisfactory and useful work role is more important for longevity than is their chronological age" (Palmore, 1969, p. 106). Therefore, when a useful and satisfying work role is disrupted by joblessness, the likelihood of death would be increased. Longitudinal studies have, in fact, found that sudden death from myocardial infarction was three times the expected rate among men who lost their jobs (Cobb and Kasl, 1977). The epidemiological evidence reported earlier in this chapter indicating that mortality from a variety of causes is linked to unemployment certainly lends credence to the notion that death does occur as a result of the helplessness and hopelessness associated with the loss of control experienced following job loss.

Since stress-related death, as well as suicide, may be viewed as aggression against oneself, the model suggested by Korman (1974) would again be applicable. According to Korman, an environment that takes control away from the individual creates the conditions that lead to aggression against oneself as well as toward others. It would appear that feelings of futility about being able to control the outcomes in one's environment in the face of failure associated with job loss can result in a psychological deterioration that threatens the very life of the individual.

SYNDROMES OF UNEMPLOYMENT STRESS

The experience of unemployment can clearly have a variety of effects on the individual. It also appears that some of these effects may occur together, possibly as symptoms that comprise a syndrome. In fact, counselors have reported as widespread among terminated workers an "unemployment syndrome" that is characterized by a lack of confidence and low self-esteem (United Way of King County, 1974). To further explore the nature of such a syndrome, we utilized the multivariate statistical technique of factor analysis[18] and found that the effects associated with unemployment were divided into three largely independent factors. The factors could be termed syndromes since each factor comprises responses or symptoms that occur together. Accordingly, there may be three relatively independent syndromes of unemployment (see Table 2.1).

The first factor we called the "general unemployment stress syndrome" since it accounted for over half the variance (52 percent) and its most important constituent was a lack of general life satisfaction. In addition, the self-assessed severity of the unemployment experience and the time estimated for a return to normalcy were highly loaded on this factor. Those professionals who exhibit the general unemployment stress syndrome are also more resentful about what happened, experience greater anomie, have lower self-esteem, receive more limited social support, and feel that they have become more obsolescent in their field than others. Professionals who manifest this syndrome appear to be in a considerably weakened state in terms of their perceptions of themselves, their relations with the outside world, and their professional capabilities. Hence they appear quite vulnerable to further psychological deterioration.

The second factor (accounting for 26 percent of the variance) tended to include more specific symptoms than the general syndrome and involved some of the more extreme reactions to joblessness that are likely to be associated with psychopathology. Therefore, we labeled it the "psychopathological unemployment stress syndrome." Those who manifest this syndrome feel extremely burdened by responsibility and have a strong need to return to work for security reasons. Furthermore, they not only exhibit high levels of irritation and outward aggressive behavior but also suffer from depression or hopelessness and have acquired an occupational role rigidity. These professionals also experience greater anxiety and believe that they lack personal control, implying feelings of helplessness. Those who exhibit the symptoms of this syndrome are likely to have reached an advanced state of psychological deterioration as a result of unemployment.

TABLE 2.1.   Syndromes of Unemployment Stress

	Factor Loading
General Unemployment Stress Syndrome	
Life satisfaction[a]	−.85
Resentment[a]	.67
Time for life to return to normal	.62
Severity of unemployment	.61
Self-esteem[a]	−59
Anomie[a]	.54
Social support[a]	−.37
Obsolescence	.35
Psychopathological Unemployment Stress Syndrome	
Irritation[a]	.81
Burdened by responsibility[a]	.62
Occupational role rigidity	.50
Depression[a]	.49
Aggression[a]	.43
Need to work for security	.42
Personal control	−.37
Anxiety[a]	.32
Work Inhibition Syndrome	
Need to work for self-esteem	−.73
Need to work for self-actualization	−.53
Work involvement	−.42
Achievement values	−.36

[a]Based on items from the index of overall adjustment (see note 6).

The third factor (accounting for 22 percent of the variance) was highly specific to work motivation. Hence we have labeled it the "work inhibition syndrome." Unemployed professionals who manifest this syndrome are not motivated to work to attain either self-esteem or personal growth and development. They also have a weak involvement with work and lack achievement values. The professionals who exhibit this syndrome are well on their way to becoming work-inhibited and are not likely to make much of an effort to attain reemployment.

It would appear from the factor analysis that unemployment does create a type of stress among professionals which is more general in nature and may even be considered as a "normal" reaction to being out of work. However, joblessness can also elicit specific reactions, largely independent of the general stress, that are related to symptoms of psychopathology or work inhibition. This may imply that an individual can be experiencing any one of these unemployment syndromes without necessarily exhibiting either of the other two. We explore these factors further in the coming chapters. However, since the syndromes are global indices, our focus will remain on the specific attributes that comprise these factors. This will permit a more precise interpretation of how professionals respond to unemployment.

EFFECTS ON THE FAMILY

Beyond its effect on the jobless individual, the stress of unemployment may have an "ecological" impact on the whole family. In fact, one longitudinal study demonstrated that the wives of terminated blue-collar workers also experienced psychophysiological stress, indicated by their developing hypertension and peptic ulcers (Cobb and Kasl, 1971, 1977). It may be that the increase in stress among the wives of the unemployed contributes to the higher rates of infant mortality associated with joblessness.

Studies of families during the Depression indicated that wives of middle-class men (primarily professionals) who had lost their jobs had significantly greater feelings of dissatisfaction, inadequacy, insecurity, and fatigue than those whose husbands had not experienced job loss (Elder, 1974). However, such differences were not observed among wives of working-class men. In fact, it appeared that regardless of their husbands' employment status, the working-class women tended to be in a better emotional state then the wives of middle-class men who were unemployed. This implies that not only are professionals more vulnerable to unemployment stress than are other workers but that their wives are similarly affected. More recent research indicates that wives of professionals who lost their jobs became as emotionally involved as their husbands in efforts to cope with the unemployment experience (Powell and Driscoll, 1973). Such emotional involvement in their husbands' plight may explain why the wives of unemployed professionals also suffer from depression and a loss of self-esteem (Segrè, 1978).

One of the greatest impacts of job loss on the family is that of role changes for husband and wife. An extensive analysis of role reversal and its associated problems appears in the discussion in Chapter 3 of the wife's role. The impact on women who experience job loss is also discussed in that chapter.

Research indicates "that occupational change on the part of the father initiates a period of stress within the family with detrimental consequences for the child's behavior" (Kantor, 1965, p. 117). One consequence of unemployment was found to be a loss of the father's authority, especially among teenage children (Komarovsky, 1971). Older children tended to view their fathers as failures and were highly frustrated by the effects the loss of their fathers' income had on their own needs and interests. Younger children were less affected than teenagers and may have enjoyed their fathers' presence at home. In fact, there tended to be an increase in the father's authority among children under age 12 when he lost his job. Nevertheless, even for younger children, the change in the role model provided by the father may affect their own personality and behavior, resulting in poorer mental health (Eisenberg and Lazarsfeld, 1938). There is some rather clear-cut evidence that the father's unemployment experience (but not the mother's) can drastically affect their children's self-esteem. Only 7 percent of children whose fathers were at least occasionally out of work had high self-esteem compared to 44 percent among those with fathers who were rarely out of work (Coopersmith, 1967).

There is some longitudinal evidence that children of middle-class families (headed primarily by professionals) are affected differently from those of the working class when the father is unemployed. For example, among middle-class children, those whose father was unemployed perceived him as being lower in status compared to the perceptions of those whose father was not out of work (Elder, 1974). No such difference in perceived status was found among working-class children. The perceived loss of the father's authority and an increase in the mother's power was especially pronounced in middle-class homes. Furthermore, the prevalence of emotional stress among children was found to increase markedly with economic and status loss, which was greatest in middle-class families. Among middle-class families, boys manifested their emotionality primarily in anger, whereas girls more frequently exhibited anxiety reactions. Furthermore, boys reacted to the loss of status in their family by striving toward status, but this did not carry over to achievement motivation or occupational orientation, at least initially. Follow-up evaluations of these boys as adults indicated that the economic and status loss they experienced as children helped them attain a greater maturity, commitment, and achievement with respect to their careers. Furthermore, both sons and daughters of middle-class families that were most economically deprived manifested significantly better mental health as adults than did the offspring of middle-class families that did not experience economic deprivation. No such differences were found among the children of the working class. Thus it would appear that while children from middle-class homes may be more affected by their father being out of work, the experience may help them be more adaptive in dealing with the crises of later life. This adaptability has been explained as follows:

It seems that a childhood which shelters the young from the hardships of life consequently fails to develop or test adaptive capacities which are called upon in life crises. To engage and manage real-life (though not excessive) problems in childhood and adolescence is to participate in a sort of apprenticeship for adult life. Preparedness has been identified repeatedly as a key factor in the adaptive potential and psychological health of persons in novel situations (Elder, 1974, pp. 249–250).

Despite results such as these, most unemployed professionals reported that high tension levels in their family resulting from job loss had a negative effect on their children (Leventman, 1974). It would appear that unemployment cannot only create emotional stress for the individual who is out of work but can have a far-reaching impact on other family members which may affect the next generation, for better or worse. Clearly, the effect of unemployment on child development is an area in need of increased attention.

Children may not only experience psychological stress as a result of unemployment, but they can suffer physical harm at the hands of their parents. Stress created by life crises has been found to be an important factor predisposing parents to child abuse (Justice and Justice, 1976). The stress created by unemployment appears to create the highest risk environment leading to child abuse, as the following research indicates:

> The environmental condition that is cited most often as placing a family at risk in terms of child abuse is unemployment. The stress created by idleness and the lack of a certain source of income predisposes a family to abuse. Our groups of abusing parents contain mothers as well as fathers who have inflicted violence on a child during periods of unemployment. An especially explosive situation is created when the daily child-care duties are turned over to a father who is accustomed to being the breadwinner in the family. Mothers who are in the habit of working and keeping busy outside the house also suffer from frustration and feelings of failure when they are unemployed (Justice and Justice, 1976, p. 255).

Although child abuse is commonly associated with families from lower socioeconomic levels, there is consistent evidence that it is not limited to any specific class (Justice and Justice, 1976). In fact, in the study cited above, 20 percent of the men and women who had abused their children were college educated. However, whether unemployment was also the highest-risk environment leading to child abuse among the most highly educated was not indicated. Unemployed professionals have been reported to displace their own anger and hostility by using their children as scapegoats (Leventman, 1974).

Parents who commit child abuse tend to turn to their children for support when the stress created by life crises is exacerbated by conflicts with their spouses; this is accompanied by feelings of being burdened with responsibilities, isolation from others, and loss of control (Justice and Justice, 1976). These are precisely the symptoms that are associated with the stress of unemployment. If the child does not respond to such "last-ditch" efforts by the parent to find support, the frustration generated is likely to be unleashed in the form of overt aggression directed against the child. Indeed, there are even indications that at least some violence directed against wives can be attributed to the loss of status and frustration experienced by husbands who have lost their jobs or who have become underemployed (O'Brien, 1971; Steinmetz, 1977). Given the evidence we have, it would appear that dealing effectively with joblessness could go far in helping ameliorate the problem of family violence, especially child abuse.

CROSS-CULTURAL COMPARISONS

Until now we have focused primarily on the psychological effects of unemployment among professionals in the United States. However, the question that arises is whether the results thus far reported are replicated in other countries. The very limited evidence that is available indicates that replication does occur.

Although few cross-cultural studies of life stress have been carried out, there is a clear indication that stress created by job loss in western Europe and Japan ranks at about the same level (eighth or ninth) relative to other stressful life events as it does in the United States (Masuda and Holmes, 1967; Harmon, Masuda, and Holmes, 1970). These are all work-oriented societies and it is not known whether job loss creates high levels of stress in countries where the work ethic is less important.

Epidemiological research has demonstrated a consistent relationship between unemployment and mortality rates in industrialized countries such as Sweden, England, and Wales (Brenner, 1976). The effect of joblessness on life expectancy in Germany was noted by Curt Donig, a psychiatrist who studied over 3000 men and women in his Berlin clinic and concluded ''that unemployment and its attendant anxieties can reduce a person's life expectancy by as much as five years, especially if they have been job-seeking for more than a year'' (*Parade Magazine,* 1975, p. 6).

There is also some cross-cultural evidence that professionals are more affected by unemployment than other workers. For example, research in England indicated that the impact of the Great Depression was much more traumatic among the middle class than for manual workers and their families (Runciman, 1966). A cross-national study that included citizens of 20 diverse countries linked the unemployment rate to the work adjustment of those who were still working (Hinrichs and Ferrario, 1974; Hinrichs, 1976). The study found that professionals employed by a multinational corporation in countries with high levels of joblessness derived less satisfaction from their jobs than those in countries with low unemployment rates. The professionals were apparently most affected, since they exhibited the strongest negative correlation between satisfaction and unemployment rate of any occupational group ($r = -.54, p < .01$). Lower job satisfaction may be due to a greater anxiety over security accompanying the anticipation of job loss in countries where unemployment levels are high. In fact, security anxiety was found to be strongly related to unemployment levels in these countries only among assembly line workers ($r = -.61, p < .01$) and professionals ($r = -.51, p < .01$). Anxiety concerning security among other white-collar workers and technicians was not significantly related to the unemployment rate. It appears that professionals across cultures are more sensitive than most workers in feeling dissatisfaction and anxiety when confronted by the threat of unemployment.

Very few studies have actually attempted to determine the psychological effects of joblessness on professionals in other countries. Research on unemployment and health in Canada during the Great Depression indicated that anxiety states and feelings of inadequacy were widespread and most prevalent among those who had been in higher-level occupations (Marsh, 1938). However, more recent research carried out in England did not find that those in higher-level occupations were psychologically more affected by unemployment than were lower-level workers (Hepworth, 1980). Nevertheless, the unemployed in every occupational level exhibited greater psychological problems than those who were working. A study of managers unemployed in England during the late 1970s revealed that they were significantly higher than the norm on stress indicative of "non-psychotic psychiatric illness" (Fineman, 1979). However, another study in England failed to find a significant difference in self-esteem between unemployed and employed managers (Hartley, 1980).

What impact does unemployment have on professionals in less developed countries? The psychological effects of unemployment on professionals has been explored in India. As we have seen in Chapter 1, India has a severe chronic unemployment problem among its professionals. Studies carried out with Indian professionals have found significantly higher levels of anxiety among those who were unemployed as compared to those who were working (Santhanam, 1973).

Although the evidence is admittedly limited, most of the cross-cultural research that deals with the psychological effects of unemployment on professionals supports the results found in the United States. This may indicate that for professionals, work is central to their identity regardless of nationality. Although cultural differences may create some differential reactions to unemployment, professionals throughout the world are likely to be prone to psychological deterioration as a result of joblessness in developed, as well as in developing, countries.

EVIDENCE FOR CAUSALITY

The question of causality must be considered in arriving at any conclusions. Did joblessness create stress or did stress-inducing factors involving the job, family, or the psychological state of the individual result in unemployment? The evidence clearly points to unemployment as the cause and not the effect of stress. Longitudinal studies of blue-collar workers have demonstrated that job change, in general, has a significant effect on self-esteem (Lefkowitz, 1967) and that job loss results in increased psychological and physiological stress (Kasl and Cobb, 1970;

Cobb and Kasl, 1977). In another more limited longitudinal study, emotional stress among a small group of professionals was found to increase significantly following job loss (Estes, 1973). Perhaps the clearest evidence of causality comes from a longitudinal study which revealed that job loss results in reduced self-confidence and self-satisfaction after having controlled for these characteristics prior to unemployment (Cohn, 1977).

Indirect evidence that joblessness causes stress and not vice versa was obtained by comparing the responses of unemployed with those of employed professionals on a standard life-stress scale (Estes, 1973). As expected, the unemployed scored significantly higher in overall life stress. However, the only significant difference in the life-stress items occurred among those events relevant to the unemployment experience either directly or as a result of a "domino" effect in a related sequence of life changes. For example, those who were unemployed more frequently indicated having been fired at work and experiencing changes in their financial state, line of work, working conditions, residence, and recreation, as well as having their wives begin to work. Furthermore, there was no significant difference in the incidence of prior psychiatric therapy between professionals who lost their jobs and those who did not, with the latter actually having a slightly higher frequency of such assistance. On the basis of the available evidence there is little doubt that the unemployment experience is responsible for causing stress and precipitating the psychological and physical deterioration accompanying such stress.

SUMMARY AND CONCLUSIONS

In this chapter we have seen that the degree of stress created by job loss is comparable to that of other losses in life, such as divorce and the death of a spouse or a close friend. The epidemiological evidence also indicates that joblessness has a widespread impact on mental and physical health. The rise in unemployment has been associated with subsequent increases in mental hospitalization, suicides, murders, and alcoholism. Infant mortality and deaths from stroke, heart, and kidney diseases have also risen following periods of high unemployment. Stress created during recession periods appears quite pervasive, affecting not only the unemployed, but also those who are still working.

There does not seem to be any doubt that work is much more central to the identity of professionals than of other workers. Therefore, since work becomes a greater potential source of both frustration and satisfaction for professionals, they would be more likely to experience severe stress as a result of unemployment than would other workers. Furthermore, jobless professionals have consistently been found to exhibit significantly more stress than their colleagues who remain employed, with perhaps as many as two-fifths experiencing psychological impairment extreme enough to require mental health assistance. Those professionals who are affected by unemployment stress are likely to manifest at least some of the following psychological changes and symptoms:

1. Low self-esteem.
2. High anxiety.
3. Anomie.
4. Self-blame.
5. Depression.
6. Social isolation.
7. Anger and resentment.
8. Aggression toward others.
9. Psychosomatic disorders.
10. Occupational rigidity.
11. Professional obsolescence.
12. Low motivation to work.
13. Low achievement motivation.
14. External locus of control.
15. Helplessness.
16. Premature death from suicide or illness.

A factor analysis revealed that the unemployed professional may undergo stress which is either general in nature or more specific, involving symptoms of psychopathology or work inhibition. It is likely that those who exhibit the more extreme psychopathological characteristics would be more prone to experience intrapunative symptoms manifested by psychosomatic disorders and even premature death from either stress-induced illness or suicide. In fact, failure in the work role for males precipitates the basic suicide syndrome. Applied to job loss, this syndrome involves failure in a work role to which one is strongly committed, followed by occupational rigidity or inability to change roles, feelings of shame, and finally, social isolation as a defense to protect oneself against such feelings. Although job loss and other types of failure in the work role are apparently the most important cause of male suicides, clearly most unemployed professionals do not resort to this self-destructive path in dealing with their failure. Responses such as withdrawal and work inhibition are much more likely to occur, but as defense mechanisms these become highly dysfunctional in dealing with the problem of finding a job.

There is some evidence that unemployment can have an "ecological" effect on the whole family. Wives of unemployed men have been found to experience psychophysiological stress accompanying that of their husbands. Older children particularly may also suffer psychological effects, such as a loss of self-esteem as a result of their father being out of work. Furthermore, the stress created by unemployment has been identified as the highest risk factor predisposing parents to child abuse.

The drastic psychological changes that some professionals experience as a result of job loss may be explained as resulting from the need to bring their cognitions about themselves into balance and thereby reduce cognitive inconsistencies. Accordingly, a reduction in the motivation to work would reflect an attempt to lower one's level of aspiration to be more congruent with a diminished self-esteem. Nevertheless, despite their devalued self-esteem, professionals for whom work remains an important part of their identity appear to maintain a high motivation to return to work for restoration of their self-esteem.

The reactions of many professionals to unemployment can also be understood in terms of a societal model in which an environment that devalues self-esteem and diminishes the individual's control can result in low levels of achievement and satisfaction, in addition to aggression toward oneself and others. Widespread unemployment creates just such an environment and it is the resulting loss of self-esteem and the emergence of helplessness that appears to be central to the psychological consequences of joblessness among professionals. This helps explain why unemployment has been found to be the best economic predictor of mental health, whereas inflation appears totally unrelated.

NOTES

1. Definitions of the term "stress" vary considerably. Stress has been used to indicate an environmental stimulus or condition that is disruptive as well as the responses to that disruption. Furthermore, stress has been identified as either physiological or psychological and occasionally even as sociological (e.g., organizational stress, societal stress). We have taken the person–environment interaction approach of Lazarus (1971) in which stress refers to "*any demands which tax the system,* whatever it is, a physiological system, a social system or a psychological system, *and the response of the system*" (Lazarus, 1971, p. 54). Therefore, unemployment stress here refers to the environmental condition of joblessness and the individual's psychological or physiological responses to that condition. Accordingly, although unemployment stress applies primarily to those who are out of work, it can also affect those who are still working or family members of the unemployed. This is discussed later in this chapter as well as in Chapter 3.

2. The study we report in this book was supported, in part, by a grant from the National Institute for Mental Health. The results are presented here for the first time. It involved jobless professionals who answered an extensive questionnaire administered during the fall of 1971 while they were still unemployed. This

sample was selected from a larger pool of unemployed professionals as part of the NIMH study. The sample pool was obtained primarily with the assistance of part-time graduate management students at the Polytechnic Institute of Brooklyn (now New York), who identified unemployed friends and colleagues. Out of 54 selected to participate in the study, 51 returned their questionnaires (see note 5 and Chapter 5 for further deails of the sample selection). Reflecting the way the pool was constructed, the unemployed sample was essentially male (94 percent), mostly with degrees in engineering (84 percent). The average age of the sample was 29 and 82 percent held a bachelor's degree, 14 percent a master's degree, and 4 percent a Ph.D. degree. They had been out of work an average of 25.4 weeks at the time of the study. The majority were involuntarily terminated because their jobs were abolished due to personnel cutbacks (67 percent). The rest either entered the job market directly from school (15 percent) or voluntarily quit for various reasons (17 percent).

3.   The question used to determine self-assessed severity of unemployment was the following:

How did this unemployment affect you?

1. Hardly at all	2. A little upsetting	3. Somewhat disturbing	4. Very dis- turbing	5. Changed my whole life

4.   The subjective experience of unemployment was determined by responses to the following question:

How long do you think it will take for your life to return to *normal?*

1. Its now normal	2. Less than a month	3. Several months	4. Half a year	5. Over a year	6. Never

5.   The matching group of 54 continuously employed professionals was obtained in the same manner as the sample of unemployed (see note 2) and all responded to the questionnaire. Individuals in each sample had been matched person-by-person on the basis of age, occupation, education, and other salient demographic characteristics. Statistical analyses showed that the two groups did not differ significantly on the characteristics used for matching.

6.   The index of overall adjustment was constructed with items judged to have face validity from the scales used in a longitudinal study of blue-collar workers undergoing job loss (Cobb and Kasl, 1977; Hunt, Schupp, and Cobb, 1966). The 10 items used for the index of overall adjustment as well as the scales from which they came (indicated in parentheses) were the following:

	Strongly Agree	Tend to Agree	Uncertain	Tend to Disagree	Strongly Disagree
These days I get the feeling that I'm just not a part of things. (anomie)	1	2	3	4	5
I often feel that my life is very useful. (self-esteem)	1	2	3	4	5
I worry about things that might happen to me. (anxiety)	1	2	3	4	5
As bad as things are, they never seem hopeless. (depression)	1	2	3	4	5
Even important things seem to irritate me. (irritation)	1	2	3	4	5
I sometimes feel like arguing with my family or friends. (aggression)	1	2	3	4	5
I believe that others really care about what happens to me. (social support)	1	2	3	4	5
When I look back on what has happened to me, I feel resentful. (resentment)	1	2	3	4	5
I feel burdened with responsibility. (burden)	1	2	3	4	5
Considering everything, I feel generally satisfied with my life. (life satisfaction)	1	2	3	4	5

7.   Estes (1973) measured psychological impairment by means of scores on the Index of Emotional Stress (IES), a modified version of the Index of Emotional Health developed by Kornhauser (1965). In a validation study, the IES compared favorably with independent clinical judgments made by practicing mental health professionals (Estes, 1973). In addition, the IES was reported to be particularly sensitive to detecting differential levels of psychoneurotic and psychological stress. When the scores on the IES were classified according to the level of psychological impairment used by mental health clinicians in assessing disability, the distribution closely approximated that characteristic of psychiatric patients.

8.   Rigidity with respect to the desired occupational role was measured by the Job Preference Inventory (JPI) developed by Williams (1965). While intended as an index of risk-taking propensity with respect to job choice, the validity evidence indicates that the JPI may also be used as a measure of flexibility vis-à-vis occupational role, since the higher one scores on the JPI "the more one is inclined to seek and accept jobs that are different from those that have been experienced before" (Williams, 1965, p. 305). Conversely, low scores would be indicative of rigid attitudes towards the type of job one would seek and accept.

9.   The scales used to measure the strength of needs were as follows:

Individuals differ with respect to the strength of various needs. Please indicate how strongly you need the following: (Circle one in each line across)

	Indifferent	Somewhat Strong			Moderately Strong		Quite Strong		Extremely Strong
To feel secure	1	2	3	4	5	6	7	8	9
To develop friendships	1	2	3	4	5	6	7	8	9
To have self-esteem	1	2	3	4	5	6	7	8	9
To grow and develop	1	2	3	4	5	6	7	8	9

The scales used to measure the instrumentality of being employed in the attainment of these needs were as follows:

How necessary is your being employed for your: (Circle one in each line across)

	Not at all Necessary		Slightly Necessary		Moderately Necessary		Quite Necessary		Extremely Necessary
Feeling secure	1	2	3	4	5	6	7	8	9
Developing friendships	1	2	3	4	5	6	7	8	9
Having self-esteem	1	2	3	4	5	6	7	8	9
Growth and development	1	2	3	4	5	6	7	8	9

10.   The work involvement measure was an adaptation of a subset of six items from the widely used job involvement scale of Lodahl and Kejner (1965). This scale was designed to provide a measure of "the degree to which a person is identified psychologically with his work, or the importance of work in his total self-image" (Lodahl and Kejner, 1965, p. 24), and was found to be related to reemployment success among laid off blue-collar workers. For a more recent evaluation of this measure, see Rabinowitz and Hall (1977). The six items used in this study were based on those found by a factor analysis to load most highly on involvement among engineers (Lodahl and Kejner, 1965), and they are as follows:

	Strongly Agree	Tend to Agree	Uncertain	Tend to Disagree	Strongly Disagree
1. The major satisfaction in my life comes from my work.	1	2	3	4	5
2. The most important things that happen to me involve my work.	1	2	3	4	5
3. I have other activities more important than my work.	1	2	3	4	5
4. I live, eat, and breathe my work.	1	2	3	4	5
5. To me, my work is only a small part of who I am.	1	2	3	4	5

	Strongly Agree	Tend to Agree	Uncertain	Tend to Disagree	Strongly Disagree
6. I am very much involved personally in my work.	1	2	3	4	5

11.   Self-esteem was measured by the self-assurance scale from the Self-Description Inventory of Ghiselli (1971). The self-assurance scale has been popularized by Korman (1970) as a measure of "chronic" self-esteem and has been widely used by others (e.g., Greenhaus and Badin, 1974; Wiener, 1973). Chronic self-esteem has been conceived by Korman as "a relatively persistent personality trait that occurs relatively consistently across various situations" (1970, p. 32). However, this notion has been criticized since evidence indicates that self-esteem does "vary in response to changes in the situation rather than endure across situations" (Dipboye, 1977). Indeed, our research strongly suggests that self-esteem, as measured by the self-assurance scale, may be diminished under the stress of unemployment (Kaufman, 1973). Although that evidence is not conclusive, it does bring into question whether the self-assurance scale actually measures chronic self-esteem, and if it does, whether chronic self-esteem remains a persistent personality trait when subjected to situations of extreme devaluation of one's self-image.

12.   The item used from the American Council on Education survey was the following: "Rate yourself on each of the following traits as you really think you are when compared with the average person of your own age. We want the most accurate estimate of how you see yourself" (Bisconti and Astin, 1973, p. 97). Respondents rated themselves as either above average, average, or below average on a series of 12 traits.

13.   There is considerable evidence from the research literature indicating that achievement motivation becomes consistent with one's expectancies based on previous experience of failure or success (Korman, 1974; Vroom, 1964).

14.   Decision-making ability was measured by the scale of the same name from the Self-Description Inventory developed by Ghiselli (1971).

15.   Achievement values was measured by a scale developed by Rosen (1956). This measure was found to be related to reemployment success among laid-off blue-collar workers (Sheppard and Belitsky, 1966).

16.   Professional obsolescence was operationalized on the basis of the definition developed by Kaufman (1974c) and was measured by the following item: How up-to-date do you think you are with respect to knowledge and skills relevant to your professional discipline (e.g., electrical engineering, physics, mathematics, management, accounting)?

1	2	3	4	5	6	7	8	9
Considerably less than		Slightly less than		About as much as		Slightly more than		Considerably more than

is required to effectively carry out new assignments in my professional discipline.

is required to effectively carry out new assignments in my professional discipline.
Internal-External (I-E) scale of Rotter (1966), which were identified by Gurin et al. (1969) as loading highly on this factor. The scale used was the following:

1.

_____ (1)   I have often found that what is going to happen will happen.
_____ (2)   Trusting to fate has never turned out as well for me as making a decision to take a definite course of action.

2.

_____ (1)   When I make plans, I am almost certain that I can make them work.
_____ (2)   It is not always wise to plan too far ahead because many things turn out to be a matter of good or bad fortune anyhow.

3.

_____ (1)   In my case getting what I want has little or nothing to do with luck.
_____ (2)   Many times we might just as well decide what to do by flipping a coin.

4.

_____ (1)   Many times I feel that I have little influence over things that happen to me.
_____ (2)   It is impossible for me to believe that chance or luck plays an important role in my life.

5.

_____ (1)   What happens to me is my own doing.
_____ (2)   Sometimes I feel that I don't have enough control over the direction my life is taking.

18.   The factor analysis used the varimax orthogonal rotation available in the Statistical Package for the Social Sciences (SPSS).

CHAPTER THREE

Individual Differences and Unemployment Stress

All evidence indicates that some professionals experience severe stress as a result of joblessness, whereas others are minimally affected. Thus certain individuals appear to be more susceptible to experiencing unemployment stress than others. To shed more light on why such differential susceptibility might occur, this chapter focuses on identifying those individual differences found to be associated with high levels of unemployment stress among professionals.

AGE AND EXPERIENCE

Although it is the very youngest professionals who are most prone to being unemployed (see Chapter 1), there is consistent evidence that professionals in their 30s experience the greatest stress following job loss. This was first discovered in a study carried out during the Great Depression which compared various characteristics between matched groups of unemployed and employed engineering professionals (Hall, 1934). The unemployed engineers were significantly poorer on measures of occupational morale as well as attitudes toward employers than were those still working. These differences were significant at all age levels. Morale was a composite measure of several psychological characteristics, including locus of control, self-esteem, and achievement motivation. Thus, regardless of age, professionals who experienced job loss compared to those who did not were more likely to believe that they were controlled by external events, and to lack self-confidence as well as the drive to succeed. However, this apparent deterioration among the unemployed Depression-era engineers was greatest for those between 31 and 40 years of age. Among those over 40, unemployment had less of an impact with increasing age. Engineers under 30 were least affected by job loss.

The Depression-era results were largely substantiated by a more recent study which found that, among a diverse group of unemployed professionals, those between age 31 and 40 suffered the most emotional stress (Estes, 1973). It was also revealed that the greatest significant difference in stress between the jobless and employed professionals occurred among those in their 30s. But contrary to the findings of the Depression-era study, the unemployed under 30 years old exhibited the second highest level of stress. Furthermore, for those over age 50, the differences in stress between the unemployed and employed groups ceased to be significant. In fact, the least stress among the unemployed occurred among those between age 51 and 60. Since age was highly correlated with work experience ($r = .84$), it was not unexpected that the highest levels of stress were found for professionals approaching midcareer with 11 to 15 years of experience. After reaching this peak, stress diminished among the groups with the most experience. As was found for older professionals, those who had lost their jobs after more than 16 years' experience were not under significantly more stress than those with comparable years of service who were still working.

Other types of studies also indicate a greater sensitivity to unemployment stress for those in their 30s who are entering midcareer. For example, epidemiological evidence shows that the relationship between the economy and mental hospitalization of males begins to peak for those in their 30s and then drops off among those in their 50s (Brenner, 1973b). During the recession of the mid-1970s, a survey of agencies providing family financial counseling reported that for "all economic groups, people in the range of 30 to 40 years of age . . . are the ones who are expressing resentment and frustration" (Roberts, 1975, p. 183).

Turning now to the self-assessed effects of the unemployment experience among the professionals we studied, stress was again significantly different among age groups. As reported in other studies, stress was found to be most extreme for those in their 30s, with 64 percent indicating that unemployment was either very disturbing or had changed their lives. Corroborating the results found for Depression-era engineers, our study revealed that those under age 30 had experienced the least stress. Only one-fourth of those 21 to 25 years of age reported a severe reaction to unemployment, with 32 percent hardly affected at all. Similar to the results of other studies, professionals over 40 reported less stress than did those in their 30s. Nevertheless, half of those over 40 experienced severe effects due to unemployment. This relatively high stress among the older professionals was reflected in a positive correlation between age and the degree to which the individual was affected by unemployment ($r = .26$, $p < .05$)[1].

An examination of specific dimensions of adjustment also indicates that problems tended to be greatest for the unemployed in their 30s; they felt most burdened with responsibility and exhibited high levels of depression, irritation, and anomie. Perhaps most revealing was that only 36 percent of the unemployed in their 30s reported that they were satisfied with their lives, compared to about twice that rate among the rest of the jobless, as well as those who were working, regardles of age.

The type of stress experienced by the various age groups may be affected by their self-esteem. For example, among professionals who were low in self-esteem, the psychopathological unemployment stress syndrome was least noticeable for the youngest group but increased precipitously to extremely high levels for those in their 30s and then dropped just as sharply for those over 40.[2] In contrast, professionals who were high in self-exteem exhibited low psychopathological stress regardless of age. Although the self-exteem of those experiencing low unemployment stress may not be affected, it is also likely that those who are able to maintain high self-esteem in the face of joblessness can keep their stress levels down. However, among the unemployed professionals whose self-esteem is low, it is those in their 30s who are clearly most vulnerable to experiencing the more extreme symptoms of unemployment stress.

The correlation between age and experience was extremely high in our study ($r = .92$) and therefore the relationships between years of work experience and stress parallels that found for age. As the number of years of experience increased, there was a correspondingly steady increase in disturbance resulting from unemployment, reaching a peak among professionals who had worked 6 to 14 years, followed by a slight drop among those with 15 or more years of experience. Every one of the professionals who reported being hardly affected by unemployment had been working only five years or less. However, when experience at their most recent job was examined, unemployment was highly disturbing to about one-half the professionals who had been with their last employer for at least two years. Only about one-fifth were so affected among those whose length of service was one year or less. Apparently two years is sufficient time for many professionals to become so involved in a job that losing it is highly disturbing.

The consistent findings from all studies leave no doubt that job loss creates the greatest stress among professionals who are in their 30s and entering midcareer. [/] One can speculate why this particular age group should be so highly susceptible to unemployment stress. It is during their 30s when male professionals typically "settle down" in their chosen fields and strive to attain career success in order to "become one's own man," according to the life-cycle research of Dr. Daniel Levinson (1978). Levinson found that some men do not reach their goals and experience failure and decline during this period, resulting in a deterioration in mental and physical health during the transition to midlife.

There is other evidence that as professionals enter the threshold of midcareer they are most prone to feelings of frustration and personal failure (Jacques, 1965; Kaufman, 1974c; Levinson, 1970). The midcareer crisis typically begins when professionals are in their 30s and those with low self-esteem may be more susceptible because of their weaker defenses. Some professionals entering midcareer may feel that what they have been doing is no longer fulfilling or important and that the level of success they expected has not been, and will not be, attained. With little to look forward to in the future, careers, as well as marriages begin to disintegrate and high rates of alcoholism, depression, serious accidents, and suicides occur. The high death rate among those between ages 35 and 40 may be attributed to the psychophysiological reactions accompanying the emotional stress and severe depression that follow the perception of being on an irreversibly downward path.

If employed professionals in their 30s are prone to a midcareer crisis, the experience of losing one's job in this age group is likely to be perceived as the most extreme form of personal frustration and failure, and would be accompanied by even more severe consequences. In fact, it has been found that professionals' perception that their career goals were being blocked or could not be attained following job loss were the most significant factors related to severe stress responses such as depression and psychosomatic symptoms (Little, 1973). Failure associated with career has already been identified as the most important cause of suicides among men of working age. Since there are personal factors which may predispose professionals in their 30s to such extreme psychological reactions to job loss, these factors are examined more closely in the sections that follow.

SEX, MARITAL STATUS, AND DEPENDENTS

A group of interrelated personal factors that appear to influence the stress experienced by unemployed professionals are sex, marital status and number of dependents. Each of these factors are explored separately.

Sex

It has been found that among unemployed professionals, there was a tendency for males to exhibit higher levels of stress than females, although this difference was not statistically significant (Estes, 1973). Among male professionals, the unemployed were significantly higher in stress than those who had continuous employment. The difference in stress between the unemployed and employed females, however, was not significant. One can easily jump to the conclusion that loss of work to male professionals is more of a psychological crisis than it is to their women colleagues and then attempt to explain it in terms of ego satisfaction and self-esteem derived by males from work. There is limited support for the latter explanation, such as the fact that men were less willing than women to turn to nonprofessional jobs as salespersons, bartenders, or typists (Estes, 1973). However, the conclusion that there is truly a sex difference in unemployment stress among professionals appears to be somewhat simplistic.

Marital Status

Marital status seems to be more important than sex in determining the levels of unemployment stress among professionals. Although unemployed professionals who were single had higher levels of emotional stress than those who were married or formerly married (Estes, 1973), the relationship is more complicated than it first appears. Single women exhibited negligibly higher stress than single men, but among those who were not single, a clear-cut difference appears, with married, divorced, or separated men experiencing significantly higher emotional stress than women in these categories. On the basis of such results it can be concluded that the stress experienced by unemployed professionals is greater among males than females, but only among those who are not single. Single professionals also experience high unemployment stress, with negligible differences related to sex.

Several explanations have been offered for these results. As far back as the Great Depression, one researcher observed "the tottering morale of the unemployed living in families. Still worse often is the condition of the unemployed living alone. Misery loves company even though it be miserable company" (Williams, 1933, p. 96). This explanation is the essence of a more recent formulation that single people, unlike those who are married, do not have an opportunity to share their stressful experience with supportive spouses (Estes, 1973) and therefore may lack a good deal of the social support that can help them adjust more easily to the crisis of job loss. Indeed, in our study of unemployed professionals we found that one-third of single men reported a lack of social support compared to only one-eighth of those who were married. There is even evidence from a longitudinal study of unemployed blue-collar workers that social support has an important moderating effect on stress (Gore, 1973). The lack of such support apparently resulted in depression, self-blame, higher cholesterol levels, and physical illness after job loss.

Dependents

Another explanation of the differences found for marital status and sex is that the highest emotional stress is exhibited by those professionals who must take on financial responsibilities for themselves or others. These include those who are single of either sex. They also include married males who are responsible for their families as well as men who are divorced or separated and who often provide financial support to former wives and dependent children. Although unemployed professionals who are married exhibit, on the whole, lower stress than do those who are single, there is evidence that unemployed male professionals who have dependent school-age children manifest stress far exceeding that of those who are single (Estes and Wilensky, 1978).

The relationship between number of dependents and self-assessment of the unemployment experience was further examined in our study and it was found that, among professionals with three or more dependents, over half (54 percent) reported experiencing severe effects as a result of unemployment. In contrast, only one-fourth of those with one dependent (themselves) were severely affected by their unemployment experience, despite the fact that 43 percent of this group reported that they did not receive social support compared to not one person who indicated such a lack among those with three or more dependents. It appears that even when social support is present, professionals who have primary economic responsibility for others are most likely to be subjected to the highest stress as a result of being unemployed. One can speculate that professionals who are single parents (of either sex), with custody of and primary financial responsibility for their children, are potentially most vulnerable to experiencing high unemployment stress. Since financial responsibility appears to play an important role in the stress response of professionals to unemployment, a more extensive examination of this factor is appropriate.

FINANCIAL STATUS

Although the relationship between financial impact of joblessness on the level of stress experienced by professionals has been brought into question (Little, 1973), the weight of evidence still indicates that those with the most financial resources are best able to withstand the stress of unemployment. In a study of jobless engineers during the Great Depression, it was found that men who were in no immediate need of financial help maintained a positive mental state; those who were in desperate financial straits manifested the most extreme psychological deterioration (Hall, 1934). A more recent study also revealed that professionals who received the highest incomes (over $600 per month) from all sources while unemployed had the lowest stress levels; those with the lowest income (under $100 per month) exhibited the highest emotional stress (Estes, 1973). Furthermore, individuals who had been earning the highest salaries ($20,000 and over) exhibited the lowest level of emotional stress after losing their jobs. They apparently had greater financial resources to fall back on than those with more limited incomes. But regardless of their previous salary brackets, the unemployed professionals still exhibited much higher stress than those who were employed. These findings indicate that adequate financial resources can reduce stress during unemployment but only to a degree.

Nevertheless, financial security appears to be one determinant of the stress professionals experience following the loss of their jobs, particularly for those in their 30s or those with dependent children. The greatest psychological deterioration among unemployed engineers during the Great Depression was exhibited by those between ages 31 and 40 whose economic situation was desperate (Hall, 1934). This finding was borne out in a more recent study showing that the most extreme emotional stress was experienced by unemployed professionals in their 30s who had dependent children and who were financially insecure (Estes and Wilensky, 1978). These results were attributed to the so-called "life-cycle squeeze" which occurs when income fails to match family consumption requirements among those in their 30s.

The need to work in order to have economic security appears to be an important factor affecting unemployment stress. In our study we found that among professionals for whom being employed was very necessary for feeling secure, two-thirds reported that the unemployment experience was severe, three times the severity rate for those who did not have such strong security needs. The need to be working in order to feel secure, as well as to have self-esteem, was found to be higher as the number of dependents increased but peaked among those professionals in their 30s, which is in accord with the life-cycle squeeze theory.

There is some indication that perceived economic deprivation is lower among those with greater social support (Gore, 1973). But the converse may be true as well—namely, that social support is maintained because the economic problems are not so great as to create interpersonal conflicts, particularly within the family. This issue is elaborated on later in the section on the wife's role.

It can be concluded that financial resources can help relieve stress to some degree following job loss. Stress resulting from unemployment is likely to be greatest among married males in their 30s not only because of the crises precipitated by feelings of midcareer frustration and failure, but also because of their greater financial responsibility for dependent children. The financial burdens of this group are likely to be exacerbated by their greater debts involving home mortgage, health and life insurance, and other payments that have to be continued while their relatively modest savings are rapidly expended. Job loss strikes just when these professionals are on the verge of attaining their career goals as well as financial security for their family. Being in such a vulnerable psychological and economic situation makes professionals in their 30s highly prone to severe unemployment stress.

ROLE OF THE WIFE

In the light of the need for financial security, it is not surprising that one study found that 42 percent of the unemployed professionals reported that their wives began to work following their job loss (Estes, 1973). Other research found similar results (Leventman, 1974). In total about three-fourths of unemployed male professionals reported that their wives were working (Leventman, 1974; Little, 1973). Even among married women who were college graduates, reentry into the work force at middle age was much more likely if their husbands had experienced long-term joblessness (Segrè, 1978). Thus in families where there are severe financial problems as a result of the husband's unemployment, the wife will frequently attempt to ease the economic hardship by going to work. This does not appear to diminish the need for the husband to find work. In fact, in our study we found that the opposite may be true. Among families where the wife was working, 62 percent of the unemployed husbands reported that it was very necessary for them to return to work in order to attain security compared to only 27 percent of those unemployed married men whose wives were not working. Although it is possible that the former were in a more desperate financial situation, there are role-related reasons for their pressing need to return to work, as we shall see shortly.

It appears that the income provided by the wife may or may not diminish the stress experienced by the unemployed husband. Although one study of unemployed professional males noted "that the reduced financial strain which is associated with the loss of the breadwinner role ameliorates some of the stress that might be associated with it" (Little, 1973, p. 142), we found that significantly more jobless men whose wives were working reported severe disruption of their lives (69 percent) than did those whose wives were not working (27 percent). Among the unemployed men whose wives were working, two-fifths felt that they had become a burden. In contrast, none of the unemployed whose wives were not working felt this way.

Although much of unemployment stress can be attributed to financial insecurity, there is evidence that when the wife goes out to work as the breadwinner and the husband stays home to take care of the house and children, the sudden reversal of role and status can result in severe emotional disruption in the family. In fact, longitudinal evidence has demonstrated that when married men become unemployed, a decrease in their contribution to family income, as well as the increase in the amount of time they spend doing housework, has a significant effect on their self-esteem (Cohn, 1977). A review of studies on family reactions to unemployment indicates that "when some members of the family usurped the role of the husband as chief wage earner, interpersonal relationships became strained. Apparently, actual reduction in dollars earned was less devastating than change in roles" (Cavan, 1959, p. 140). This was particularly true for the upper middle-class unemployed. Similar results were reported in a survey of family financial counseling agencies during the recession of the mid-1970s: namely, "that when the wife returns to work because of financial necessity alone, this seemingly practical solution may result in even more disruptive problems within the family" (Roberts, 1975, p. 184). Here, too, the problems were attributed to the acceptance of traditional roles "with the husband as the wage earner and the woman in the role of wife and mother. . . . Within the last two years, a shift has been noted in these predetermined positions, because of financial necessity, not emotional fulfillment. The case material shows that the result is often not only resentment by the wife, but also great guilt on the part of the husband" (Roberts, 1975, p. 184). Such role reversals were studied among the unemployed in the Seattle area, where large numbers of aerospace professionals were out of work, and the following conclusion was reached:

> Sex role stereotypes built on images of the male as provider and head of the household undermine the self-image of the jobless husband. Even when it is financially

necessary for the wife to go to work, sex role stereotyping serves to exacerbate the guilt feelings of the unemployed husband and is a constant reminder of his failure (Briar, 1976, p. 52).

The disruption of family life and the diminished status of the husband as a consequence of unemployment has been well documented in a study of skilled workers who were terminated during the Great Depression (Komarovsky, 1971). In that study, 22 percent of the families exhibited clear symptoms of marital breakdowns, but the evidence indicates that preexisting problems in the marriage were exacerbated by the role changes in the family and the husband's loss of status. Such loss of status occurred only in those households where the husband's base of authority was instrumental, that is, where he had provided only material rewards.

Studies of unemployed male professionals during the recession of the early 1970s indicates that several factors can affect the marriage relationship when job loss occurs. For example, one study, which reported that marriages were dissolving for 12 percent of the professionals, with increased family tension for most of the others, found that tension to be related to financial stress and the wife taking on the breadwinner role (Leventman, 1974). These factors were illustrated in the comments of an engineer who had been out of work for 13 months:

> The kids don't even ask for money anymore. My wife is taking over the role as breadwinner. I hear them whispering, "Don't tell Daddy." I feel like I'm out of the family unit. I guess they are all having a hard time with me. I feel like a piece of shit and take it out on my wife. Who else? I fly off the handle. My wife can't take it. My kids can't take it. It hurts so deeply when you can't take care of your family (Leventman, 1974, p. 385).

Comparable research also carried out during the recession of the early 1970s found that 13 percent of the unemployed male professionals who were married reported a deterioration in their marriage (Jacobson, undated). Here, again, it appeared that marital discord may have been aggravated by job loss but that the root of the problems existed prior to unemployment. Although in most cases the conflicts centered on money and budgetary matters, this discord exacerbated more basic problems associated with role reversal. For example, one unemployed engineer whose wife was working and supporting them reported that she was highly critical of his lack of aggressiveness in finding a job. This attitude manifested itself in other ways, such as deterioration in their sex life which, according to the husband, occurred "because it's difficult for his wife to be a woman when she's acting like a man" (Jacobson, undated, p. 8).

Another case of role reversal was reported by a jobless construction engineer we interviewed whose credentials included a professional engineering license and two master's degrees. But he noted that "all those degrees don't help much for changing diapers." His wife went out to work immediately after he lost his job and he remained home to take care of their baby and the house. The role reversal was rather clear cut, as he noted after a month of being out of work: "I am mastering the housework, washing dishes, cleaning, changing and feeding the baby. My wife takes her work with a lot of determination, although she complains about not seeing the baby enough." After three months of unsuccessful job hunting he developed an ulcer. Although he tried to rationally accept the role reversal, it apparently continued to take a toll on his well being. He describes his situation after five months of joblessness:

> I am a professional babysitter by now. I take it logically, like an educated man should, but I feel that I am losing confidence. I am not feeling well. The doctor says those are anxiety attacks. He suggests analysis—I can't afford it. I think I will go out and buy myself a new dress.

The cynical joke about buying a new dress was clearly indicative of his resentment about the reversal of roles. In this case, at least, the role reversal did create a strain in the marital relationship and was accompanied by a deterioration in the man's physical and mental health. However, such cases appear to be the exception rather than the rule since not only has unemployment *not* been found to result in the deterioration of family relations for most professionals, but it actually has helped improve them for some. In fact, the study reported above found that 15 percent of the unemployed male professionals felt that their marriages were better after they had lost their jobs, which is slightly more than those reporting a deterioration (Jacobson, undated).

Despite some equivocal evidence (Leventman, 1974), it would appear that, in general, wives of professionals *are* supportive of their unemployed husbands. In a follow-up study we carried out with male professionals one year after their company terminated them, 30 out of 31 who were married reported that their wives were always or usually completely understanding, supportive, and cooperative while they were unemployed. Similarly, executives who had lost their jobs generally had high praise for the attitude of their wives, who provided very much needed sympathy and understanding (Diamond, 1974). There is evidence that job loss can result in an improvement in the marital relationship, as was indicated in research among the unemployed in Seattle, many of whom were aerospace professionals:

> Some find that there is a great deal of support and sharing generated by the husband's joblessness. In some instances, this sharing may be partly related to the fact that the worker pitched in with the chores, becoming a "help to his wife." One worker who felt very dissatisfied with the way he was spending his time when not working, claims that there has been a "change for the better" since he's been home. For his "wife is behind him," and he "gets much encouragement." They divide the chores, and there are more conversations than before (Briar, 1976, p. 51).

A case study of a stockbroker who had been out of work over a year further illustrates how family relationships can actually improve as a result of unemployment:

This year, my relationships with my wife, the kids, have been terrific. It isn't that we didn't get along, because we did, but I never had time to sit down with Carole and talk about how she really felt about life, me—whatever. When the kids come home from school, they can tell me what happened at length rather than feeling that they have to condense it into 30 seconds for a tired daddy after his day's work (Wilkes, 1975, p. 85).

Having the time to spend with his family could have resulted in conflicts, particularly those related to loss of status, but since the marriage was one based on mutual respect and equality, such conflict was minimal. As his wife explained:

Sure it's tense at times, all this togetherness. But early on we decided we would still lead independent lives. If John wants to sleep in, there's no reason why he shouldn't. If I want to spend a whole day away from the house, he doesn't have to be along. And John pitches in on housekeeping; our marriage is more equalized now (Wilkes, 1975, p. 85).

With this strong foundation to their marriage, his wife was able to provide the necessary support for him to continue looking for a job which he really wanted and not one which would merely provide an income to pay the bills. As his wife recalls:

I didn't want John to have to take something just to relieve pressure, so I didn't want to increase that pressure. We were doing OK; it was great to have him home. So I just vowed to myself that the unemployment money would pay the bills, the food stamps would take care of food, and the frills would have to go (Wilkes, 1975, p. 79).

Although there generally are positive as well as negative aspects to the unemployment experience, in this case the positive appeared to outweigh the negative, as the terminated stockbroker explains:

It's one of the best things that's ever happened to me. I broke away from a business that would have killed me. I have a whole new perspective on life. Now love making isn't reserved for two tired people late at night. It's love in the afternoon (Wilkes, 1975, p. 85).

The case just cited may not be typical, but it is similar to others that have been reported (Briar, 1976) and illustrates how the unemployment experience can actually reinforce family ties. However, such a strengthening of family bonds can occur only if the relationship was a good one to begin with. It is clear that when a marriage is not based on rigidly defined roles, a wife can much more readily provide the support needed to relieve the stress her husband experiences as a result of his job loss.

Although there is evidence that even employed professional men tend to feel that their family life was negatively affected by their wives working, (Sears, 1977), rigidly defined roles may be breaking down. As one researcher explains the difference in a husband's reaction to his wife working today as compared to what it would have been in the Great Depression: "Cultural differences in expectations with respect to the woman's role as a provider in the family may have greatly diminished loss of the breadwinner role as a stressor for the contemporary middle-class unemployed professional" (Little, 1973, p. 143). In fact, epidemiological research has found that marital breakups were related to unemployment rates during the 1950s but not during the 1960s (Miao, 1974).

With the increasing popularity of the dual-career marriage in which both husband and wife pursue their respective professions, job loss may become a less stressful experience for some married men since the breadwinner's job would be shared. As the wife of an unemployed publishing executive in his 50s asked: "Why should he work, when we don't really need the money?" (Crittenden, 1977). Her husband decided to stay at home and write rather than deal with the possible humiliation associated with job hunting at middle age. This solution would not be appropriate for many of the younger professionals who are still in the process of developing their careers. Nor would it be appropriate if there was marital discord prior to job loss, since even in the dual-career family, existing problems are likely to be aggravated by the husband's loss of status. In any case, it is the way the husband integrates work and family that appears to be crucial to the success of his wife in combining a career with her family role (Bailyn, 1970).

Although it is clear that the role of the wife is important in helping her husband cope with unemployment, relatively little is known about the effects of the wife's support on her own well-being. One of the few studies that collected data on this question focused on middle-aged, college-educated wives of professionals (Segrè, 1978). The study revealed that while marital happiness may be decreased for these women because of their husbands' unemployment, the psychological state of those who remain housewives may deteriorate to a greater degree than those who reenter the work force. Housewives whose husbands experienced long-term joblessness were significantly lower in self-esteem and far more depressed than were housewives whose husbands did not undergo such job instability. However, no such differences were found as a function of husbands' job status among wives who returned to work full time. While the wife who reenters the work force after her husband loses his job may not be terribly happy, she nevertheless appears to be able to maintain her mental health more than the wife who remains at home. Career reentry for women may provide them with a new fulfilling role in life. However, whereas the psychological effects of such a return to work can be positive for the wife, they may be negative for her husband with regard to role reversal, as was already noted.

In contrast to the potentially severe effects of unemployment on married male professionals, there appear to be hardly any such effects among professional women who are married when they experience job loss. In fact, their stress levels were lower than those of employed women (Estes, 1973). Such low stress levels may result from the women returning to their traditional role in the family while their husbands are providing them with financial security.

One longitudinal study indicated that "having the alternative role of mother does remove the negative effect of unemployment on satisfaction with self" (Cohn, 1977, p. 123). Thus, by having an alternative role, women can more easily accept being out of work, and some may even prefer it. Indeed, another longitudinal study even found that two-fifths of unemployed women who found jobs subsequently desired to return to their jobless state (Fidell, 1970). Since these women were not professionals, their negative reaction to working is probably more extreme than it would be among those who are highly career-oriented. Nevertheless, the evidence indicates that women professionals do experience great stress as a result of the role conflict between career and family (Hall and Gordon, 1973). Unemployment for some married professional women may actually serve to reduce the stress resulting from this role conflict, at least until they feel a need to reenter their career. For those wives who are strongly career-oriented, however, periods out of work can be very stressful (Faver, 1980).

EDUCATION, OCCUPATION, AND CAREER

Factors involving education, occupation, and career have been found to be associated with stress among unemployed professionals. Although these factors are closely related to one another, each nevertheless deserves individual examination.

Education

It has been found that for every educational level at or above the baccalaureate, the unemployed are significantly higher in stress than are those who had continuous employment (Estes, 1973). Maximum stress was exhibited by unemployed professionals who hold a doctorate. The results of our study also indicated that the level of education attained by professionals was significantly related to the stress created by joblessness. We found that two-thirds of professionals who completed at least a master's degree reported high stress resulting from unemployment which was more than twice the rate (28 percent) among those without any graduate work. Further evidence that stress among the unemployed professionals is related to education was provided by the significant negative correlation between educational level and overall adjustment ($r = -.27$, $p < .05$).

One possible reason that Ph.D.s experience the highest unemployment stress is the fact that they typically work as college teachers and often are denied tenure when they are in their 30s. Losing their faculty position at an age when they are highly prone to stress helps explain in part why Ph.D.s are psychologically most affected by job loss. Although there is almost no research on the impact of tenure denial on faculty members, there does not seem to be any doubt that it can be a shattering experience of professional and personal failure. Perhaps typical of many who are denied tenure is the following case study reported by Daniel Levinson in his research on adult development:

> Norman Kromer, a biologist who was let go at 39, had strong feelings of failure about himself as a scientist and a person. He felt that he had not been able to speak with his own voice, and therefore could not gain recognition as an eminent biologist. In planning his next move, he could not begin by asking, "Where can I get a job?" He had to start with more fundamental questions: "Have I anything important to contribute as a scientist? Shall I maintain my primary commitment to theory and research, despite my limited success? Or shall I settle for a position involving mainly teaching and administration, though I (and my discipline) value these less? Or perhaps I should get out of the university altogether and pursue other interests that I have neglected for years (Levinson, 1978, pp. 155–156).

Regardless of the possible impact of the age at which Ph.D.s are likely to lose their position, the higher stress levels exhibited among the unemployed who have the most education may be a result of two interrelated factors. First, they have invested more time, money, and effort for educational and professional development than have those who completed only a baccalaureate. Consequently, job loss may be perceived not only as a poor return for their considerable investment but also as a highly unjust outcome given the professional rewards expected to follow advanced graduate study. They may even begin questioning whether their efforts directed toward professional development were wasted. Second, their ego involvement and identification with their profession is probably much greater than that of those who did not go through the socialization process of graduate school or who never had the strong motivation and commitment required to embark on advanced higher education. Among employed professionals, those with Ph.D.s have been found to exhibit the least stress (Estes, 1973), probably because they were involved with work that provides great ego satisfaction. When those with advanced degrees lose their jobs they are likely to feel deprived of an essential part of their very identity.

Identification and commitment to a profession may not only be related to completion of advanced higher education, but also to the choice of a particular graduate major. In our study we found that half of the professionals whose graduate major was in engineering or science experienced high levels of stress resulting from job loss compared to only 23 percent of those who majored in a nontechnical field. Although many of the latter had technical undergraduate degrees, their involvement with a technical profession was apparently minimal, since they were very likely in the process of switching to another occupation. This career flexibility may have been accompanied by a feeling of improved employability, thereby contributing to lower unemployment stress.

Occupation

There is strong evidence that the type of occupation a professional has pursued is an important factor related to stress following unemployment. For example, it has been found that unemployed technical professionals experience higher stress levels than those working in business or in "human resource" occupations such as social work and teaching (Estes, 1973). Furthermore, the unemployed technical professionals were the only occupational group to exhibit significantly higher stress than their employed colleagues. It has been suggested that since the work of technical professionals is primarily "thing" rather than "people" oriented, they are not as developed in dealing with emotional and human types of problem solving as are those in human resource and business occupations (Estes, 1973). This explanation was further elaborated by a group of psychotherapists who identified the following personality pattern that made adjustment to unemployment stress particularly difficult for technical professionals:

1. *Little* sensitivity to other people.

2. *Difficulty* listening to another person's emotional problems.

3. *Trouble* talking about nontechnical issues or feelings.

4. *A* tendency to be obsessed about technical work problems during working hours.

5. *A* primary concern with the world of things, not people.

6. *Little* interest in family members and their problems.

7. *An* absorption in hobbies like stereo equipment, astronomy or any pursuit that is totally consuming and avoidant of people.

8. *A* childlike tendency to demand that his own needs and creature comforts be met by people around him.

9. *Little* interest in sex, preferring brief sexual encounters so he can sleep or watch television.

10. *A* fearful approach to marital fights, running away from aggression or anger.

11. *An* inability to express his anger, often classified as a passive-aggressive personality. (*Human Behavior*, 1972, p. 54).

Another explanation of why technical professionals exhibit high unemployment stress is that their education is generally quite demanding and the personal investment in becoming a professional may be perceived as much greater among engineers and scientists than among those in business and human resource occupations. Related to this is the possibility that ego involvement and identification with their work are greater among technical professionals and consequently job loss comes as a much more severe blow to their self-image. However, this may not apply to technical professionals in all functions. In our study we found that 56 percent of professionals working in R&D experience high stress following job loss compared to 21 percent of those in other technical areas, such as design or production. This has been corroborated in another study where, among a wide variety of functions in different professions, the emotional stress was clearly greatest among those who had been employed in R&D (Estes, 1973). There is also evidence that the more one is involved with R&D activities, the greater is the emotional stress following job loss. For example, we found that the number of patents produced by a professional, which can be used as an index of R&D involvement, was negatively correlated with overall adjustment ($r = -.40, p < .01$) and positively with the severity of the unemployment experience ($r = .28, p < .05$).

Several explanations have already been offered which may shed some light on why extreme stress levels are experienced by unemployed R&D professionals. One may be their lower capability of handling emotional problems since they are involved primarily with physical problem solving and are unaccustomed to dealing with human problems. It is also clear that R&D professionals are the most highly educated among the unemployed, most having completed advanced graduate study. Consequently, they are likely to be the group most identified with their work and to have made the greatest investment in developing themselves professionally. For professionals whose services had always been in great demand, involuntary job loss comes as an unexpected shock. With their highly developed knowledge and skills no longer in demand, they are likely to experience extreme frustration and stress.

It has been suggested that another reason why R&D professionals exhibit high levels of stress is that most of them were formerly employed by aerospace and defense industries, where their work was so highly specialized that their overall professional knowledge and skills had become obsolescent, thereby limiting their transferability to other industries (Estes, 1973). The evidence found in our study tends to contradict this explanation. The professionals whose work was defense oriented revealed slightly less severe effects of job loss than did those whose work was consumer oriented. Furthermore, only 22 percent of those who had been employed in the aerospace industry were severely affected by their unemployment experience which was significantly lower than that experienced by professionals who worked in other industries.

Although the evidence failed to support the contention that the highly specialized work carried out by professionals in aerospace and defense industries predisposes them to high stress levels following job loss, the results with respect to obsolescence were less clear cut. For example, it was found that more aerospace professionals (one-third) than those in other industries felt that their knowledge and skills were not sufficiently up to date for effectively transferring to new work. However, such obsolescence was relatively low among professionals formerly employed in defense industries. It is interesting that the lowest levels of obsolescence were found among non-R&D technical professionals who had been employed in industries dealing with construction or machinery. The type of work these professionals typically engage in does not require as up-to-date knowledge of technical developments as does R&D work carried out in the rapidly changing aerospace, chemical, or electronics industries (Kaufman, 1974c). Professional obsolescence was reported by almost two-fifths of professionals in nontechnical occupations, the highest rate found. This result may be attributed to the fact that almost half of those in nontechnical professions were programmers or systems analysts, fields that are continually undergoing change and hence are highly susceptible to obsolescence (Kaufman, 1974c). In addition, some of those in nontechnical specialities were changing careers and may not have become professionally up to date in their new occupations.

Career

There is strong evidence that dissatisfaction with one's career is directly related to emotional stress regardless of employment status (Estes, 1973). However, those unemployed professionals who were dissatisfied with their career choice or preferred to be in another occupation exhibited some of the highest stress levels. Added to the frustration of being in the wrong occupation, job loss may create the conflict of whether to seek work in one's past occupation or to direct efforts toward a change in career. If this is the case, it is not at all surprising that those who are unhappy in their chosen career also experience high stress.

Will stress be reduced if the conflict is resolved by a decision to switch to a career that is likely to be more intrinsically satisfying? The limited evidence we do have indicates that the answer may be in the affirmative. There is some indirect indication from our study that those who desire career change undergo less unemployment stress. For example, the few professionals who were unemployed because they voluntarily quit their job generally as a result of dissatisfaction were significantly more likely to feel that their lives were normal compared to those whose jobs were terminated. It is possible that leaving an unsatisfactory position served to restore some normalcy to the lives of these professionals. Such stability would then permit them to seek a job that could satisfy their career goals.

Other results in our study indicate that those with low ego involvement with their work who decided to switch careers did experience significantly lower employment stress than did others. These career switchers may have been less susceptible to experiencing unemployment stress because for them being out of work could be used as an opportunity to begin a new and more rewarding career. In fact, one study of technical professionals found that almost half did not view job loss as a necessarily negative experience, and the most frequent explanation was that unemployment provided an opportunity to change jobs or careers (Little, 1973, 1976). As one senior mechanical engineer in that study explained:

> I didn't like it at my last job. Maybe this is a chance to think about getting into a new career—teaching maybe. I was under a lot of stress before because I didn't like the work. Being really happy on your job means a lot (Little, 1973, p. 150).

Those who were more positive about losing their jobs experienced slightly less psychological stress and considerably less economic stress. It may be that those possessing greater economic resources were in a better position to view their job loss as an opportunity for career change. This is quite plausible since the availability of financial support is one of the most important facilitators of midcareer change (Clopton, 1972). It would appear that those possessing greater economic resources were in a better position to view their job loss more positively.

It should be noted that individual differences in professional development may affect attitudes toward career change. For example, there is evidence that those unemployed professionals who have attained higher levels of proficiency in their field are more resistant to a change in career (Powell and Driscoll, 1973). This is consistent with research that has found career change to be a less attractive coping strategy for professionals who are up to date in their fields than for those who are obsolescent (Kaufman, 1978). A greater willingness to shift careers has been found among those who have already experienced such a shift, such as engineers who have become managers (Powell and Driscoll, 1973). Apparently, having had the experience of making a career change makes it easier to accept subsequent changes.

Although professionals in their 30s who are entering midcareer are highly prone to experiencing unemployment stress, they may also be more likely than those in other age groups to view their job loss as an opportunity for change (Little, 1976). This positive attitude was found to be prevalent among technical professionals in their 30s and was explained as follows:

> Thus, a man who has been moving steadily upward in a firm at the early stages of his career may feel he is slowing down or "stalled" in his thirties. He may be convinced, from observing the career histories of his seniors and peers, that the best way to maintain upward mobility is to change jobs. In this way, it becomes possible to rationalize the "failure" of being laid off as a contingency in one's career pattern that is necessary to sustain movement toward the top (Little, 1976, p. 269).

Moreover, it was suggested that this type of rationalization "probably serves as an effective defense against some of the stress and guilt which past research has shown to be associated with unemployment'' (Little, 1976, p. 267). Thus, although unemployed professionals in their 30s may experience the most stress, they also may be most likely to cope with that stress by perceiving their job loss as an opportunity for career change.

Another interesting finding was that enforced idleness resulting from job loss was a real problem for only three-tenths of technical professionals, and these tended to be individuals who felt negative about losing their jobs (Little, 1973). Some responded to the question about extra time with exclamations such as it was ''driving me nuts'' (Little, 1973, p. 157). Idleness appeared to be a problem for the professionals who were still highly committed to their chosen profession. However, idleness was not such a great problem for those who viewed job loss more positively, since the free time may have been just what they needed to prepare for a career change. As one unemployed electrical engineer explained about his field: ''I've been wanting to get out of it anyway. Now I've got time to find out what I *want* to do'' (Little, 1973, p. 150).

It appears that the enforced idleness that was reported to be so detrimental to middle and working class alike during the Depression (Cavan and Ranck, 1938; Jahoda, Lazarsfeld, and Zeisel, 1971; Komarovsky, 1971) may not be such a great problem for most of today's unemployed professionals. As we have seen, job loss for many professionals becomes an opportunity to consider changes in job or career. Unlike the Depression years, there are now greater financial resources available as well as more career and job options open to the professional in search of work.

SOCIOCULTURAL CHARACTERISTICS

Personal characteristics that are sociocultural in nature may also influence the professional's response to job loss. These characteristics include factors related to family background and community ties.

There is some evidence that family background may have an effect on unemployment stress. For example, unemployed professionals whose fathers were in a nonprofessional occupation exhibited higher stress levels than those whose fathers were professionals (Estes, 1973). Similar stress differences were related to their fathers' education level. Furthermore, among professionals, the unemployed who were nonwhite experienced greater emotional stress than did either the jobless whites or the nonwhites who had not been terminated.

It may very well be that those who have had the greatest upward mobility are most affected by job loss. People who have worked hard to overcome numerous barriers to achieve a higher socioeconomic level are likely to feel extremely frustrated when they are suddenly deprived of the rewards expected to accompany their attainment of professional status. Therefore, it appears that professionals coming from less advantaged backgrounds are highly vulnerable to severe emotional stress following the loss of not only their job but also of a newly acquired status in which they had invested a great deal of time, effort, and money to achieve, and from which they expected so much.

This type of reaction apparently does not occur among professionals who come from families with foreign-born fathers, since their emotional stress has actually been found to be slightly lower than that of those whose fathers were born in the United States (Estes, 1973). However, what of the many professionals who are foreign-born themselves and not American citizens? The data we have, based on a small sample of professionals in our study who were not U.S. citizens, indicated that foreign born professionals were more likely than their American colleagues to be affected adversely by the unemployment experience ($r = .24, p < .05$) and to feel that it would take longer their for lives to return to normal ($r = .33, p < .05$). One might speculate that the foreign professionals experience greater stress not only because of their limited resources but also because they have uprooted themselves from their cultures. Not only can immigration create stress, but there is evidence that when resources from a support group are lacking, mental disorders are more prevalent (Kantor, 1965). But how does this account for the low stress levels exhibited by unemployed professionals who come from immigrant families? It is likely that these professionals were American born or bred and it can be speculated that they not only felt at home in the United States, but also could fall back on the cultural roots and traditions of their family and community.

There is further evidence which indicates that having ties to community and institutional life does provide emotional support in dealing with stress. For example, rural workers who were terminated received greater social support through community ties and experienced less psychosomatic illness than did urban workers (Gore, 1973). Religious ties also appear to affect unemployment stress. During the 1971 recession employed professionals without any religious affiliation were found to exhibit substantially greater stress than those who identified as Protestants, Catholics, or Jews (Estes, 1973). No such difference occurred among professionals who did not experience unemployment. These results confirm those found in studies carried out during the Great Depression. One such study revealed that among a large sample of the unemployed, many of whom were professionals, those who had no religious affiliation were significantly lower on life satisfaction than those who identified with some religion (Watson, 1942). A study of jobless engineers during the Depression found that positive attitudes toward religion were directly related to their psychological well-being and lower hostility toward employers (Hall, 1934). A further analysis of those between ages 31 and 40, a stress-prone group, revealed that being religiously oriented was very strongly associated with positive feelings toward themselves as well as employers among those in the most severe financial straits; such relationships did not exist for those who had minimal financial problems. Thus when unemployed professionals undergo financial stress, religion can serve to maintain their psychological well-being. It has been suggested that having been deprived of their traditional socioeconomic roles and financial security as a result of job loss, the professional who is not affiliated with a religion does not have a faith to turn to for emotional support as do those who identify themselves with a religious group.

It would appear that the greater an individual's community ties, the more he or she is able to deal with a personal crisis such as job loss. There is some evidence for this. For example, an index of social integration (indicating participation in social institutions such as religious groups, political parties, civic organizations, and professional societies) was highly related to stress among unemployed professionals (Estes, 1973). Those unemployed not having any ties with such institutions also had the highest stress levels, whereas minimum stress was exhibited by professionals having the greatest number of community ties. Indeed, the stress level among unemployed professionals was found to decrease significantly as the number of community relationships increased. These findings corroborate the results of a study carried out during the Great Depression which found that the stronger the unemployed professionals' ties to social groups and organizations, the greater their life satisfaction and psychological well-being (Hall, 1934).

Community ties may be important sources of social support which is not only emotional but also instrumental in nature, insofar as those ties provide a network that can help in finding a job. On the basis of existing evidence it can be concluded that professionals who are most isolated from community ties are deprived of the social and psychological support needed to cope with job loss. As a result, these socially isolated professionals may be highly vulnerable to experiencing severe stress following loss of their job.

EFFECTS OF PREVIOUS ADJUSTMENT

It is possible that adjustment of professionals prior to their job loss may affect the unemployment stress they experience subsequent to termination. We have already seen that preexisting problems were likely to affect stress responses to unemployment. For example, professionals who had marital problems prior to job loss were likely to experience more stress in the family than were those who had a good marriage to begin with. Also, career dissatisfaction may initially contribute to higher stress following job loss. Perhaps more relevant is that effectiveness in coping with stress was found to depend on psychological factors such as the individual's locus of control. We examine next how the psychological state of professionals prior to job loss, as well as previous unemployment episodes, can affect the stress experienced as a result of being out of work.

Prior Psychological State

The psychological state of workers prior to job loss can have a major effect on their reactions to unemployment. Even psychologists during the Great Depression felt quite strongly that this was true despite a lack of research evidence, as the following evaluation indicates:

> Undoubtedly the previous personality make-up of the individual plays an important role in determining his attitude during unemployment. For example, it seems very likely that the individual who was well adjusted before unemployment can face the crises better than the individual who was maladjusted (Eisenberg and Lazarsfeld, 1938, p. 376).

Recent research appears to have validated this assumption. For example, a longitudinal study of blue-collar workers whose general adjustment, as indicated by ego resilience, was measured before their plants were closed has rather convincingly demonstrated that the psychological state of the individual prior to job loss does have a major effect on subsequent stress (Kasl and Cobb, 1970; Kasl, Gore, and Cobb, 1975). Those who had low initial ego resilience showed a significantly poorer recovery, physically as well as psychologically, from the high stress associated with job loss than did those who were well adjusted. There was also evidence that those who were more rigid encountered greater stress as a result of unemployment.

Among unemployed professionals, it has indeed been found that the highest levels of emotional stress were experienced by those who had a prior history of psychiatric treatment, with 44 percent classified as having severe or moderate impairment (Estes, 1973). Such high levels of impairment were exhibited by three-tenths of the unemployed who did not have any previous psychiatric treatment or of the employed who had been psychiatric patients. Only 8 percent of the employed professionals who had no history of psychiatric disorders exhibited high levels of emotional stress. However, having had a history of psychiatric treatment was not found to predispose professionals to job loss. It is, therefore, fair to conclude that those who have had problems of psychological adjustment prior to unemployment would be more vulnerable to emotional disorders when confronted by the stressful experience of job loss. This conclusion is compatible with results which indicate that unemployment creates mental health problems more as a result of "uncovering" existing behavioral disorders than by "provocation" of new psychological problems (Catalano and Dooley, 1979). This uncovering of problems by job loss may also apply to many of those with preexisting difficulties in their marriage or career. Thus, a great deal of unemployment stress may be a result of the uncovering of adjustment problems that were there all along.

Previous Unemployment Experience

There is some indication that having had a past experience of joblessness affects the individual's reaction to subsequent unemployment. In fact, one longitudinal study found that the "greater the amount of past unemployment experience, the lower the self-confidence for the currently unemployed, suggesting a cumulative effect of unemployment on self-confidence" (Cohn, 1977, p. 164).

Other research reveals that emotional stress among unemployed professionals increased with repeated episodes of termination and was least severe among those who had no such previous experience (Estes, 1973). Even for employed professionals, stress was considerably higher among those who had experienced job loss in the past. Since the study was carried out in 1971, a recession year, it is likely that the threat of job loss created stress in those who had learned from experience that they were not immune to termination.

These findings have been corroborated among the unemployed professionals in our study. Almost three-fifths of professionals who had a previous job loss reported that the unemployment experience was at least very disturbing to them—about twice the rate among those who were jobless for the first time. Furthermore, one-fourth of the professionals who had a prior unemployment experience believed that their lives would never return to normal, which was five times the rate among those who had not been out of work before. These relationships are reflected in the significant correlations found between the number of times the professionals experienced a job loss during the four years preceding the study and the severity of their unemployment experience ($r = .25$, $p < .05$), as well as how long they felt it would take their lives to return to normal ($r = .35, p < .01$).

Although having had to deal with loss of work in the past may increase the stress level of professionals when they find themselves jobless again, prior termination experience may also help them to use more appropriate coping behaviors to deal with the realities of unemployment. Indeed, one study of unemployed professionals reported that men who had a prior history of job loss were more knowledgeable concerning what to do about being unemployed than were those who had never been out of work (Powell and Driscoll, 1973). Those who were previously unemployed had saved a greater proportion of their earnings. They also handled the reversal of roles more smoothly when their wives had to go to work and were more open and willing to talk about their unemployment experience. In seeking new jobs, they tended to begin earlier and use more appropriate search strategies than did those who had never been terminated.

In our study, half of the professionals who had previous termination experiences began looking for a job prior to their loss of work, whereas such job-seeking behavior was reported by fewer than two-fifths of those unemployed for the first time. The greater stress and the earlier initiation of job hunting among those who had been out of work before was apparently related to their stronger need for security. Almost nine-tenths of those with prior job loss experience reported a greater need to return to work to attain security, which was about three times the rate found among those experiencing unemployment for the first time. Thus it would appear that professionals who had prior unemployment experiences may react with greater stress when job loss occurs, but this stress may also be accompanied by coping behaviors that were learned during their earlier periods of joblessness. This is explained by an unemployed professor of educational psychology in his late 40s who was undergoing great stress but had learned some coping behaviors to maintain a sense of normalcy in his life:

> If this is a totally new experience, you have a lot to learn. In my case, I already knew some of the things that had to be done. I knew, for example, that it is very important to fool yourself into thinking that things are normal. You get up at the same time, shave every day, either go to the employment office or to your desk to do something–anything to make yourself believe that you are still of service to the world. . . . As the weeks drag into months, this becomes more difficult.

As noted in Chapter 4, intense efforts at coping with joblessness are likely to be accompanied by high stress. It may very well be that out-of-work professionals who had previous episodes of unemployment are better prepared to mobilize and focus greater efforts to deal with their situation than are those who had no prior experience with joblessness. Such efforts may contribute to, as well as be a consequence of, high unemployment stress.

INDIVIDUAL DIFFERENCES AND SYNDROMES OF UNEMPLOYMENT

Three syndromes among unemployed professionals were identified in Chapter 2. In an attempt to explore the relationship between individual differences and each syndrome, we turn to path analysis, a multiple regression technique that permits the testing of a sequence of relationships (see Kerlinger and Pedhazur, 1973). Thus far we have focused on how specific individual differences are related to the effects of unemployment, but little has been attempted to explore the interrelationship among the individual differences themselves. Path analysis is not only suited for such an analysis but can be used to determine the indirect as well as direct "effects" of individual differences on each syndrome of unemployment (Lewis-Beck, 1974). As in all multiple regression findings, the results of our exploratory path analysis must be considered tentative, pending replication by future research. With this cautionary note in mind, we can nevertheless arrive at some tentative preliminary models of how individual differences are related to the syndromes of unemployment.

Simplified path analyses found for each syndrome are depicted in Figures 3.1 through 3.3. A summary of the total effect coefficients are listed in Table 3.1. The

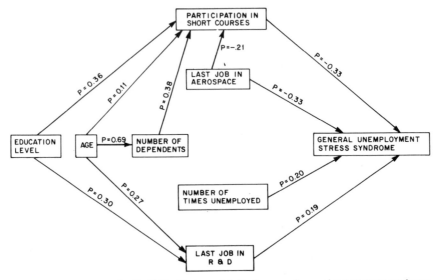

Figure 3.1.   Path analysis of individual factors related to the general unemployment stress syndrome.

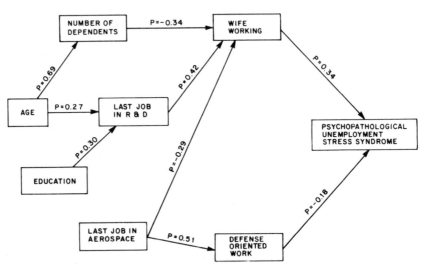

Figure 3.2.   Path analysis of individual factors related to psychopathological unemployment stress syndrome.

total effect coefficients are a sum of the direct and indirect effects of a particular individual difference on a specific syndrome. As such, they can be interpreted as correlation coefficients with effects that are not accounted for being removed (Lewis-Beck, 1974).

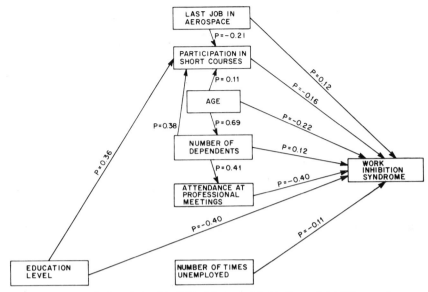

Figure 3.3. Path analysis of individual factors related to the work inhibition syndrome.

TABLE 3.1. Total-Effect Coefficients Between Individual Differences Among Jobless Professionals and Syndromes of Unemployment

	Syndrome		
Characteristic	General Unemployment Stress Syndrome	Psychopathological Unemployment Stress Syndrome	Work Inhibition Syndrome
Age	−.07	−.04	−.32
Dependents	−.13	−.12	−.11
Wife working	−	.34	−
Level of education	−.06	.04	−.46
Last job in R&D	.19	.14	−
Last job in aerospace	−.25	−.19	.17
Defense-oriented work	−	−.18	−
Short courses taken in last year	−.33	−	−.16
Professional meetings attended in last year	−	−	−.40
Number of times unemployed	.20	−	−.11

As can be seen from Figure 3.1, the number of times a professional was previously terminated has a direct effect on the general unemployment stress syndrome but no indirect effects. However, those who experienced more periods of joblessness were slightly less likely to be work inhibited (see Figure 3.3), and this too was only a direct effect. As we have already discussed, despite the higher stress among those professionals who have had a prior experience of job loss, they may be better prepared to deal with their new reality and hence would be more able to maintain their motivation to work.

Age had no direct linear association with either stress syndrome and made virtually no indirect contribution (Table 3.1). This is to be expected given the curvilinear relationship consistently found between stress and age. In a further analysis, we found that both general and psychopathological stress syndromes are most extreme among those in their 30s. However, work inhibition is apparently greatest among the younger professionals (Figure 3.3). In fact, we found that professionals at midcareer exhibited the highest motivation to work. This is a further indication that those who want or need to return to work the most are the ones more likely to experience the greatest stress by remaining jobless.

Whether or not the professional's wife was working had a strong direct effect on the psychopathological unemployment stress syndrome (see Figure 3.2). This further reinforces our finding that for some male professionals, a reversal of roles with their wives as a result of unemployment can be an important contributor to the deterioration of their psychological well-being.

The fact that a professional had more dependents did not have any direct effect on either stress syndrome. However, there was a small indirect effect, indicating that those with more dependents experience slightly lower stress. Although this relationship was very weak, it is contrary to our previous conclusions. In the case of psychopathological stress, professionals with more dependents tend not to have their wives working, and hence there would be less stress created by role reversal. With regard to general stress, those with more dependents tend to take more short courses and, as we discuss at greater length later, this contributes to lower stress. It is also this participation in short courses, as well as professional meetings, that appears to counteract the direct effects of dependents on work inhibition, with a net result that having more dependents turns out to have a slightly positive indirect effect on the motivation to work. The level of education attained by the professional did not appear to have much effect on either stress syndrome, but those with the highest education were very clearly the least likely to become work inhibited. Apparently, the professional commitment developed as a result of advanced education helps in maintaining a motivation to work while one is unemployed. However, the most highly educated in our sample were more likely to have been working in R&D, and these professionals manifested both stress syndromes, which is consistent with the results reported earlier. One possible implication of this is that it is not the level of education per se that is related to unemployment stress but the nature of the work role in which that education is utilized and the type of individuals attracted to that role.

We also wanted to determine how those who had been employed in aerospace and defense jobs fared in a very difficult job market. Interestingly, the aerospace professionals exhibited relatively lower stress than others, but they were also more work inhibited. Aerospace professionals also tended to be out of work longer than others ($r = .42$, $p < .01$), a characteristic unrelated linearly to stress.[3] As we shall see in Chapter 4, work inhibition may accompany lower stress for the long-term unemployed. However, those whose work had been defense-oriented were not among the long-term unemployed and work inhibition was not apparent; but they did tend to exhibit lower levels of psychopathological stress.

As was already mentioned, work inhibition was not a problem for those unemployed who attended many professional meetings, as well as short courses, while they were out of work. Furthermore, the general unemployment stress syndrome was slightly less apparent among profesionals who had participated in more short courses. It is likely that those who maintain contacts with their professional community or continue their professional development can maintain a motivation to work, although such motivation can also serve to stimulate professional activities. Perhaps one way of helping to diminish work inhibition is to increase involvement in a variety of professional activities. In later chapters we discuss the types of professional activities that not only can help maintain work motivation and self-esteem but also serve to attain reemployment.

CROSS-CULTURAL COMPARISONS

There is an almost complete dearth of research in other countries that has focused on the relationship between differences in personal characteristics and the stress of unemployment among professionals. One of the few such investigations involved case studies of managers in England and revealed great differences in unemployment stress (Fineman, 1979). For example, those who experienced high levels of stress following termination were likely to have had a strong involvement with their job, a spouse who was not supportive, or financial commitments that were difficult to meet. On the other hand, low-stress cases had a low involvement in their previous job, viewed job loss as an opportunity for change, or maintained a high degree of self-esteem and confidence in their own abilities. These results tend to support those found in the United States.

The impact of cross-cultural differences within a society on unemployment stress was highlighted in a study carried out in Israel among 946 professionals, many of whom were new immigrants (Bar Yosef, Shield and Varsher, 1975). That study corroborated some of the relationships between personal characteristics and stress that we found in the United States and provided additional understanding of cross-cultural differences.

With regard to age, the study did not find any linear relationship with any index of stress. However, in reevaluating the data, we revealed that the curvilinear relation found between age and stress in the United States also existed in Israel.[4] For example, economic stress reached a peak among those in their 30s, with over half of this group being unable to maintain a reasonable standard of living. In comparison, only three-tenths of those in their 20s reported that they were in such a precarious economic situation. The professionals over 40 were moderately affected by unemployment, with two-fifths reporting a high level of economic stress. A somewhat similar relationship was found between age and stress in the family. For example, only one-fifth of the professionals in their early 20s reported a negative change in the attitudes of their families toward them as a result of their being out of work, but the number of those so affected continues to climb until the late 30s, where two-fifths experience family stress. A slightly lower incidence of such stress was reported among those over 40 years old.

The published study revealed few significant sex differences in stress responses to unemployment. The only exception was that men were much more likely than women to perceive unemployment as a stigma. However, in situations where the spouse was working, family stress increased significantly. We explored this interesting phenomenon further and found that it was definitely true for males but that females tended to react in an opposite fashion. Forty-three percent of unemployed males whose spouses were employed full-time reported an increase in family stress, compared to only 30 percent among those men whose wives were not working. For unemployed women, however, the situation was completely reversed. Only 29 percent among those whose husbands were working experienced high family stress compared to 43 percent of the women in situations where both breadwinners were out of work.

Differences in economic stress reactions were not as clearcut. Somewhat over two-fifths of the unemployed males reported high economic stress whether or not their wives were working. However, among unemployed women, economic stress was most in evidence among those whose husbands were also out of work. Almost half of them reported high economic stress compared to only three-tenths of the women whose husbands were working fulltime. In fact, among the latter women, almost one-fourth reported they did not need to work to maintain a reasonable standard of living. We also found that regardless of sex, economic stress was lower among single professionals compared to those who were married. The high economic stress exhibited by the married professional women who were out of work was contrary to results found in the United States and may be attributed to the fact that most of their husbands were also out of work. When the men of the households are unemployed, the women are likely to be under great pressure to help support their families, and hence they too would experience high levels of stress.

In sum, the male professionals in Israel revealed high stress when their wives were working. As suggested by studies in the United States, these unemployed men may experience a diminished status as a result of the role reversal and consequently, many would experience high stress. Women whose husbands had jobs were least affected by being out of work. We have already attributed such a low stress reaction among females in the United States to a reduction in the conflict between work and family roles. The fact that being unemployed was considered to be much more of a stigma by men than by women in Israel may imply that work is still associated with fulfilling the male rather than the female role, even in such an ostensibly egalitarian society.

Perhaps the most interesting revelation of the research in Israel was that a professional's country of origin turned out to be one of the best determinants of his or her reaction to being out of work. For example, professionals of eastern European origin experienced the greatest economic stress, and those with the lowest stress came from Western countries. About half of the professionals who came from the Soviet Union and Rumania had extreme economic difficulties compared to about one-fourth of the Israelis and only 14 percent of those coming from western Europe or the Americas. This is understandable in light of the fact that because of severe restrictions by their countries or origin, the eastern Europeans arrived with very limited resources, whereas those from Western countries were free to bring anything with them. However, this does not completely explain why eastern Europeans, particularly those from the Soviet Union, perceived unemployment as more of a stigma than did others. Nor does it entirely explain why family stress was experienced by most of the professionals from the Soviet Union but by relatively few whose origins were elsewhere. In fact, for those who came from other countries, and for native born, more reported an improvement than a deterioration in family relationships, which is exactly what has been found in the United States. One can speculate that the extreme stress resulting from joblessness experienced by the unemployed professionals of eastern European origin, particularly those from the Soviet Union may be partly a result of having come from a highly controlled society where the individual depends on the State for work and in which unemployment generally does not occur. During the Great Depression, it was reported that in the Soviet Union, mental disease was much less prevalent since the individual did not have the pressures of job-finding responsibility (Williams, 1934). Indeed, a more recent contrast of the Soviet system of assigning jobs to university graduates and the American system of free choice found that "to many Russians, the American job market looks chaotic, and the American graduate's need to find his own job seems terrifying" (Shipler, 1979, p. 42).

Another factor affecting stress experienced by unemployed professionals from the Soviet Union is their very strong ego involvement with their former job (Hawks, 1980). This job involvement has been attributed to the emphasis in the Soviet Union on the career as the primary path for self-expression. Career socialization begins early in school and the educational system is designed to feed graduates into specific jobs. Suddenly being thrust into a society where the individual is primarily responsible for finding work can be extremely stressful to professionals with a strong ego involvement with their work who have been conditioned to be dependent on a support system provided by the state for their job security. This was apparent when those in the Israeli study identified where they placed the blame for not finding a job. The eastern Europeans said that it was primarily the fault of government agencies, whereas professionals from Western countries blamed the labor market and themselves. The latter response appears to be more reality oriented given the relatively low unemployment rates in Israel at the time of the study and the availability of government assistance in job placement if the individual requests such help. Very likely an important determinant of how individuals respond to unemployment is the degree to which they have learned to be dependent on societal institutions. This conditioned dependency may partly explain the different stress reactions to joblessness among professionals from different cultural backgrounds.

With the international migration of professionals in search of work likely to become an even more common worldwide phenomenon in the future, the stress created by not only being out of work but also having to adjust to a totally new culture (Kantor, 1965) may create widespread international mental health problems among highly educated workers. We discuss this problem at greater length in Chapter 7, but it is clear that more cross-cultural research will help to contribute a better understanding of why some professionals are more susceptible than others to experiencing high levels of stress as a result of joblessness.

SUMMARY AND CONCLUSIONS

In this chapter several personal characteristics have been identified that increase the likelihood that the professional will experience severe stress as a result of unemployment. Married men in their 30s appear to be the group prone to the greatest stress. This is probably because job loss strikes just when they are most vulnerable to the midcareer crisis. The financial burden of this group is also much greater because of family responsibilities. However, those 30-year-olds who maintain high self-esteem may be able to cope with joblessness more effectively and thereby minimize the stress.

Adequate financial resources can help to relieve stress to some degree during unemployment. However, if the wife goes out to work to ease the financial burden, it can increase her husband's stress because of the reversal of roles and his loss of status. This tends to be manifested by symptoms of the psychopathological unemployment stress syndrome. However, relatively few families appear to experience a deterioration of marital relations while the husband is unemployed. In fact, family ties may be strengthened in cases where the marriage is not based on rigidly defined roles. The wife in such a marriage can much more readily provide the financial support necessary to relieve her family's economic stress by finding employment. It appears that social support provided by the wife and others can be crucial in helping relieve stress among jobless men. However, the involvement of the wife in her husband's efforts to cope with the job loss experience can increase her stress as well. Although the wife's entry into the work force may exacerbate marital problems, remaining at home as a housewife can be detrimental to her psychological well-being.

In contrast to the potentially severe effects of unemployment on married men with dependents, job loss for married women whose husbands are working may actually serve to reduce the stress resulting from their conflict between career and family roles. However, unemployed single professionals of either sex may experience high stress probably because they lack the financial and especially the social support that those who are married can obtain from their spouse. Single people, nevertheless, do not experience as high stress as do married men, especially those entering midcareer who have family responsibilities.

With regard to educational, occupational, and career factors, job loss creates greater stress among those who have earned a graduate degree as well as technical professionals, particularly those who are involved in R&D types of work activities. However, it is those in R&D who tend to have the higher education, and perhaps it is this work role and the type of person it attracts rather than the education per se that determines their response to job loss. The high level of stress exhibited by R&D professionals may be attributed to the extreme frustration they experience after having made such a great material, intellectual, and psychological investment, not only in preparing for and developing their careers, but also in responding to the highly demanding nature of their work. For R&D as well as other technical professionals, this frustration may possibly be combined with a less developed capability for dealing with emotional types of problems, and consequently they may be more susceptible to severe stress reactions resulting from job loss. However, those whose last job was in aerospace were less likely to manifest stress reactions, and were more work inhibited, apparently because of long-term unemployment. However, maintaining a strong professional commitment or involvement may serve to avoid the work inhibition syndrome.

It seems that those dissatisfied with their career choice may experience high stress following job loss. This higher stress could result from a conflict over whether to seek work in their past occupation or to direct their efforts toward a change in career. Those who use their unemployment as an opportunity to start a new career may actually diminish their stress as a result of job loss.

The sociocultural backgrounds of professionals also influence their responses to unemployment. Those who have had the greatest upward mobility, such as minorities, are highly vulnerable to severe emotional stress. They experience not only the loss of their jobs, but also the loss of their newly acquired status in which they invested so much. Another group of professionals who may be quite vulnerable to severe stress are those who are most isolated from community and institutional ties, particularly those of a religious nature. The absence of such ties deprives them of the social and psychological support needed to cope with the traumatic experience of job loss.

The adjustment of the individual prior to job loss affects the degree of stress experienced as a result of unemployment. For example, professionals with previous histories of psychiatric treatment or hospitalization experience greater stress during unemployment, but they were not found to be more prone to job loss. Thus, a great deal of unemployment stress may be a result of the uncovering of preexisting adjustment problems.

Professionals who were previously unemployed appear to experience increased stress when job loss strikes again. However, a previous unemployment experience does prepare the individual to cope with it more realistically. Such coping and stress reactions may also depend on how long the professional remains out of work, and it is to this issue that we turn next.

NOTES

1.   The positive correlation between age and the effects of unemployment may have resulted because of a restriction in range for the age variable. There were no professionals included in the oldest age groups, which have typically exhibited lower stress levels.

2.   This curvilinear relationship was analyzed using η^2, which was significant ($\eta^2 = .37, p < .025$).

3.   Although duration of employment was not related linearly to the stress syndromes, it was positively related to work inhibition ($r = .29, p < .05$). However, duration of employment was not included in the path analyses because only individual differences present prior to unemployment were investigated relative to the stress syndromes and work inhibition. Nevertheless, duration of unemployment is an important variable and Chapter 4 is devoted to its analysis.

4.   These analyses were based on a survey of unemployed professionals in Israel carried out by the Work and Welfare Research Institute of the Hebrew University in Jerusalem, which provided me with access to the survey data. I am especially grateful to Gili Shield and Yehudit Varshar for the help they provided in my analyses of the data they collected.

CHAPTER FOUR

Stages of Unemployment

The anticipation of joblessness can create stress well before termination actually occurs. We have already noted that during the Great Depression, professionals who expected to lose their jobs exhibited lower morale than many who had already been terminated (Hall, 1934). Similarly, a longitudinal study initiated in 1969 found that job satisfaction was significantly lower among professionals who later suffered job loss in the subsequent recession than among those who remained working (Kopelman, 1977). Those who had lost their jobs apparently had anticipated termination.[1]

Longitudinal studies of blue-collar workers have found that psychophysiological stress increases during the period in which they are anticipating job loss. For example, workers in a plant that was to be closed had increases in blood pressure, serum uric acid levels, and other physical symptoms, as well as lowered self-esteem (Kasl, Cobb, and Brooks, 1968; Kasl and Cobb, 1970; Kasl, Gore, and Cobb, 1975). It should be noted, however, that when terminations are uncertain, those who do not anticipate job loss may not experience stress. In a study of a hospital whose closing was uncertain, psychophysiological stress was found to be significantly higher among the health workers who believed that terminations would occur than among those who did not (Jick and Greenhalgh, 1978). It may very well be that denial of impending terminations can be an effective defense against stress, at least under conditions of uncertainty. It has been observed that "denial is a readily available way to reassert control, to forestall threats and to maintain a favorable version of reality" (Weisman and Hackett, 1967).

It is frequently assumed that the severity of unemployment stress increases the longer one is out of work. There is evidence both for and against this assumption.[2] A study of unemployed professionals during the Great Depression indicated that psychological stress increased with length of time out of work (Hall, 1934), but more recent studies have not found this to be true (Estes, 1973; Little, 1973). It is possible that the absence or inadequacy of unemployment compensation during most of the Depression may have resulted in more serious financial difficulties the longer the professional was out of work. Even as late as 1938, only six states had unemployment insurance benefits extending beyond 16 weeks (Corson,

Nicholson and Skidmore, 1976). In addition to inadequate financial assistance, finding a job during the Depression of the 1930s was much more difficult than during the recessions of the 1970s. With no income and few, if any, job prospects on the horizon, it is understandable why professionals during the Great Depression may have experienced increased stress the longer they were out of work.

Recent evidence indicates that there may be a curvilinear association between at least some aspects of stress and duration of unemployment. For example, one study found that overall stress levels were quite high for professionals out of work three months or less, then dropped considerably among those unemployed seven to nine months, but increased again for those who were out of work between one and two years (Estes, 1973). In another study of unemployed technical professionals, irritability and self-blame were lowest among those recently out of work (one to eight weeks) as well as the long-term unemployed (33 weeks and over), although there was a tendency for depression and psychosomatic symptoms to increase with time out of work (Little, 1973). Longitudinal studies of blue collar workers whose plants were closed failed to find any significant linear correlations between time out of work and various psychophysiological measures of stress (Kasl and Cobb, 1970). However, there does appear to be a curvilinear relationship, with stress being significantly lower during the second month after the plant closing compared to that during the anticipation period. There was a significant increase occurring about half a year after termination, and, finally, another significant decline in stress one year after they lost their jobs (Kasl et. al., 1975). As we shall shortly see, this may closely parallel the stages of unemployment experienced by many jobless professionals.

In the absence of longitudinal studies of job loss among professionals, a fruitful, and probably the only approach to exploring the duration of unemployment and its effects would be to examine what happens to out-of-work professionals who are at different "stages" following their termination. The existence and importance of stages of unemployment were recognized by psychologists as far back as the Great Depression, when it was noted "that the various types of attitudes maintained among those out of work are more a function of the stage of unemployment than anything else" (Eisenberg and Lazarsfeld, 1938, p. 378). Psychologists and social scientists who studied the course of unemployment during the Depression years consistently reported the following stages:

First there is shock, which is followed by an active hunt for a job, during which the individual is still optimistic and unresigned; he still maintains an unbroken attitude. Second, when all efforts fail, the individual becomes pessimistic, anxious, and suffers active distress; this is the most crucial state of all. And third, the individual becomes fatalistic and adapts himself to his new state but with a narrower scope. He now has a broken attitude (Eisenberg and Lazarsfeld, 1938, p. 88).

This description of what happened after job loss during the Depression has been replicated to a great degree by a more recent study by Powell and Driscoll (1973) that was based on interviews with unemployed male professionals, but four rather than three distinct stages of unemployment were identified. It should be noted, however, that any description of what happens during each stage of unemployment is meant only as a guide, since not all of those who experience job loss react in the same way. For example, the initial shock of termination can continue for some professionals well beyond the first stage of unemployment, and psychological defenses may take the form of denial, with the individual behaving as if job loss never occurred. Keeping in mind that departures from the norm do exist, we attempt to identify what appears to be most characteristic during each of the four stages of unemployment. Unless otherwise indicated, the description of these four stages that follows is adapted from the research of Powell and Driscoll, augmented by the results of our investigation as well as other studies.

STAGE I: SHOCK, RELIEF AND RELAXATION

During the first stage of joblessness there is a sequence of shock, relief, and relaxation. Although the initial impact of job loss is typically one of shock, in general, this rapidly gives way to a reduction of the stress often built up during the preceding period of anticipation and uncertainty. One unemployed purchasing agent who anticpated job loss but did not know when it would happen explained: "I knew it was coming. . . .For over a year I hadn't been sleeping very well because I could see business falling off and knew they didn't need me. When I was finally laid off I stopped worrying. . .for a while anyway" (Powell and Driscoll, 1973, p. 18). Many do not even feel they are unemployed, but this may be a form of denial which can serve to keep stress levels down, as was already noted. Others protect themselves from feelings of shame by keeping their job loss a secret from neighbors and even wives (Briar, 1976). Possibly to avoid acquiring an unemployed identity, many experiencing termination use the free time suddenly thrust on them as if it were a vacation. Such reactions were reported by counselors dealing with problems resulting from job loss:

> Some clients did not initially take their unemployment seriously. They thought of it as a vacation, maintaining the idea that finding other employment would not be difficult or, as had happened in the past, they would be called back to the job from which they were laid off (United Way of King County, 1974).

A case in point of a professional taking a vacation in response to job loss is the stockbroker discussed in Chapter 3, who was expecting to be dismissed. He was stunned when it actually happened, but this feeling was short-lived and then, as he described it, "there was this sense of relief, as if somebody just got off my chest. I took some money out of the bank, rented the house for two months, piled Carole and the children into a Volkswagen camper and we were off on a vacation we always wanted to take and never had the time for" (Wilkes, 1975, p. 79).

The period of relief and relaxation was reported to last about a month, although for some it lasted over two months. During this period, the unemployed professionals described themselves as confident and hopeful of finding work as soon as they felt ready to look for it, and they maintained normal relationships with their family and friends. However, considerable bitterness toward their employer is reported during this initial stage.

It is noteworthy that relaxation was not reported in the first stage of unemployment during the Great Depression, probably because of the lack of unemployment insurance to cushion the loss of income, as well as the much greater difficulty in finding work. Following the initial shock of job loss, most of the unemployed during the Depression apparently could not afford to relax since, in order to have an income, they had to find work immediately. Even during recent recessions, behavior during stage I of unemployment may have been affected by job market factors. For example, unemployment in Seattle, Washington, during the early 1970s reached levels approaching that of the Great Depression and only a minority of those who lost their jobs took a vacation during stage I (Briar, 1976). Most started their job search immediately, as was typical in the Depression years. Thus it would appear that although shock and even relief are common during stage I of unemployment regardless of the job market (see Briar, 1976), relaxation may be considerably diminished because of poor reemployment opportunities.

The data from our study revealed that among professionals out of work six weeks or less, two-fifths did report that the unemployment experience was at least very disturbing to them, but all felt that it would take only six months or less for their lives to return to normal. This stage I group also exhibited low levels of anomie, aggression, and need to be employed in order to feel secure. They were also high in self-esteem, hopefulness, and life satisfaction. Other research has found that psychosomatic disorders were lowest during this stage (Little, 1973).

Furthermore, those in our study who were in the first stage of unemployment generally felt up to date in their profession and were most flexible about the job they were willing to accept. As noted in Chapter 2, professional obsolescence and occupational rigidity tend to occur together. Other research has also found that most professionals in stage I experience no career deterioration whatsoever (Little, 1973) and even see their job loss as an opportunity for change (Little, 1976).

Despite the fact that professionals in stage I appear to have a generally positive response to their job loss, there are some indications that beneath their calm exteriors, their unemployment experience is affecting them. For example, we found that they exhibited the highest levels of resentment about what had happened, corroborating the bitterness toward the employer reported during this stage by Powell and Driscoll (1973). As the unemployed professor of educational psychology, who we discussed in Chapter 3, explained: "My first reaction was one of utter shock. I had received no warning or notice that anything was wrong. I then went into a state of violent anger and now have some pretty good battles going [with my former employer]." Such anger may stem from a sense of betrayal or violation of the psychological contract with the employer (Schlossberg and Leibowitz, 1980).

During stage I, unemployed professionals in our study also appeared quite anxious about the future. Furthermore, they reported receiving the least amount of social support from others compared to those who were unemployed for longer periods. It was noted that neither husband nor wife openly air their concerns during stage I (Powell and Driscoll, 1973), but greater openness is precisely what the professional may require to deal with pent-up feelings of resentment and anxiety.

In general, however, the first stage of joblessness is one of low stress. In fact, our data indicate that professionals in stage I did not manifest the syndromes of either general or psychopathological unemployment stress. Neither did they exhibit the work inhibition syndrome. However, those in stage I who were low in self-esteem were significantly more work-inhibited than individuals whose self-esteem was high. It is likely that having high self-esteem can cushion the initial blow of job loss by helping the professional maintain a strong motivation to work.

STAGE II: CONCERTED EFFORT

The behavior of professionals changed dramatically when they entered stage II of unemployment, referred to as the period of concerted effort (Powell and Driscoll, 1973). During this stage professionals concentrated almost totally on finding work. Although this tended to be a time of optimism, lasting about three months, the length of time the individual was able to sustain confidence depended on such factors as financial security and social support. Indeed, this appeared to be a time of maximum support and encouragement from family and friends. The wife became especially helpful in providing both moral support and assistance in finding a job. She was often as emotionally involved as her husband in the job search and, as was noted in Chapter 3, his failures affected her as well. The wife's ability to maintain her optimism was an important influence on her husband's continuing effort to find work.

To some degree the picture presented above for stage II was verified by the data from our study. Those who were unemployed during this stage (between 7 and 16 weeks) reported the most social support and the least resentment, irritation, and anxiety. Apparently, their job-hunting efforts had reduced some of these feelings that may have troubled them during stage I.

During the period of concerted effort, the professionals' belief that they were still in control of their lives was at its height. Sometimes the need to be in control was manifested by an indiscriminate use of money, a practice noted by psychologists even during the Great Depression (Eisenberg and Lazarsfeld, 1938). The unemployed college professor explained:

> As you enter the second stage, you have an absolutely uncontrollable urge to splurge. I took my understanding and gentle wife out to expensive restaurants, using up in one meal what would have seen us through a week. I took her to entertainments which we had not attended when I was working! I think I was trying to show that I still was in control of things, and that whatever system was working did not have me beaten.

Counselors dealing with the effects of job loss in Seattle noted the dysfunctional effects of such behavior:

> These persons continued their lifestyles as if there had been no loss of income and in so doing rapidly depleted their financial resources. Some clients resisted the changes taking place, desperately clinging to the material possessions that identified their station in life. There was manifested a terrible need to maintain the expensive home, vacation property, the boat or the extra car, instead of gearing down and adjusting the lifestyle to the income (United Way of King County, 1974, p. 25).

As one remains in stage II, the inability to find work begins to take its toll on the individual's psychological well-being. Among the professionals in our study, high levels of anomie appear during this period, as do strong feelings about being burdened with responsibility and needing to return to work in order to attain security and self-esteem. The type of deterioration that can occur during the period of concerted effort was illustrated by the experience of an engineer in midcareer who had spent three months searching for work in his field:

> The family survived on money which we had accumulated for a house down payment (we lived in an apartment at the time) but the financial status deteriorated rapidly. Everything unnecessary was cut back—difficult for a family with two children—a boy 13 and a girl 5. My wife bore it stoically.
>
> The most difficult periods were those of inactivity, sitting around the house doing nothing. While ads were being answered, résumés constructed, interviews planned and engaged in, newspapers scanned, there was still hope. But with nothing to do, the feeling that the family blamed me was ever present.

Despite his deteriorated financial state, feelings of self-blame, and difficulty in dealing with idleness, this engineer tried to maintain hope. We found that whereas some professionals in stage II maintained hope, most had become dissatisfied with their lives. Furthermore, over half reported that the unemployment experience was at least very disturbing, and three-tenths felt that it would take longer than a year for their lives to return to normal. No one at this stage, however, was pessimistic enough to feel that life would never return to normal.

Negative reactions that we found during this period may have resulted from feelings of financial insecurity, which were most dominant among those in this stage. For professionals who needed to return to work to attain security, only one-fifth felt satisfied with life compared to three-fourths who were satisfied among those for whom finding work was not important to their security. The findings relating security needs to unemployment stress were even clearer. About eight-tenths of those who urgently needed a job to attain security reported that the unemployment experience was very disturbing or had changed their whole lives. Not one of those who did not have to find a job because of security needs was so affected.

It is the professionals in midcareer who appeared most vulnerable to stress during stage II. Three-fourths of those in their 30s and 40s reported that the unemployment experience was very disturbing or had changed their whole lives, compared to only one-fifth of those under 30 who felt this way. In addition, all married men whose wives were working experienced high levels of stress, presumably because of financial insecurity combined with their diminished status. It may well be that despite the social support, which was widespread during stage II, the urgency for the professional to return to work to provide for the financial needs of the family, combined with the concerted effort to find a job, resulted in the high levels of stress that we found in this period.

It should be noted that only the syndrome of general unemployment stress was manifest during stage II, with psychopathological unemployment stress remaining low. As suggested earlier, this general stress may be a normal reaction to being out of work, and the intensive job search could in itself contribute to such stress. As would be expected, motivation to work was at a peak during the period of concerted effort. Furthermore, those in stage II of unemployment exhibited the greatest initiative and highest occupational aspiration level.[3] It is clear that professionals have a strong desire to return to work during stage II and are willing to make strenuous efforts to find a position appropriate to their career aspirations.

STAGE III: VACILLATION, SELF-DOUBT, AND ANGER

After several months of unsuccesful job searching, there is a reduction in efforts to find work and a third stage begins, lasting an average of six weeks, that has been characterized by Powell and Driscoll (1973) as the period of vacillation and doubt. We have added anger as another characteristic of this period.

During stage III the unemployed professionals begin to question their ability to find a job. These self-doubts are accompanied by high levels of anxiety, with erratic job-searching efforts directed primarily at reducing that anxiety. Vacillation in their job search accompanies serious occupational identity problems and feelings of becoming professionally obsolete. There is even a tendency to allow the job market to determine their occupational identity. Many begin to consider a major career change, with some taking steps to redirect themselves toward another occupation. Those who have changed careers before, such as from engineering into management, appear most flexible regarding an occupational move. However, some still remain committed to their profession and resist any career shift.

Characteristic of the vacillation during stage III are extreme changes in mood such as those described by a young unemployed personnel manager:

> It's like being on a roller coaster of mental attitude, a yo-yo of mental attitude. Sometimes I feel depressed—I mean really depressed, and wonder if I'll ever snap out of it. After a while I begin to feel really agitated. . . you know, filled with energy. Then I'm really hyper! I spend a lot of energy, though I don't seem to get much done (Powell and Driscoll, 1973, p. 22).

High levels of frustration and anger during stage III are often accompanied by an impairment in relations with others. Strains in marital relationships appear during this period and men feel they are a burden to the family. As noted in Chapter 3, the most severe marital problems occur in families where the roles are rigidly defined. In such cases, the problems are intensified if the wife begins to work.

Although attributions of blame during this period are typically focused on the "system," inability to direct their anger against the real cause of their frustration frequently leads to displaced aggression, with the out-of-work professional striking out irrationally against any source of irritation. The unemployed college professor discussed earlier described such a reaction, which involved clashes with neighbors in the apartment complex in which he lived:

> I once conducted a completely idiotic, but to me completely rational, battle with stereos. The neighbors who were young liked to play acid rock which vibrated through the walls of my apartment. I bought a bunch of bagpipe records and put them on my own set, and we battled back and forth for days. It all seems incredible now, but they became the focus of all my troubles.

However, aggression can also be directed against oneself through internalized anger manifested by psychosomatic disorders. Such disorders have been found to start increasing during stage III (Little, 1973). In addition, feelings of despair and a sense of panic are at their height during this period and men may become more susceptible to committing suicide. Counselors dealing with problems of job losers noted that: "Because the new job did not materialize, the unemployed person often began to feel there was something *wrong* with him. He displayed feelings of inadequacy, anger, and shame'' (United Way of King County, 1974, p. 26). Such a psychological deterioration can be detrimental to the health and well-being of the individual. This is clear from the experience described by the unemployed college professor:

> My mental condition deteriorated, and began to affect my physical condition. I became prey to every anxiety symptom one can name. My heart palpitated, my breathing became difficult, muscles became paralyzed, my stomach was constantly upset, warts appeared and disappeared, I could not sleep, I broke into uncontrollable sweats. You name it and I had it. Eventually, it became necessary to control this with medication. A physician put me on a series of tranquilizers, but I soon built up a tolerance to them and new conditions arose. I began to take long, long walks and to think very seriously of ways of ending things.

Professionals in our study who were out of work during this period (between 17 and 25 weeks) exhibited the most extreme levels of anxiety, irritation, and conflict with others. The effects of unemployment became quite disruptive and, for the first time, professionals begin reporting that their lives would never return to normal. However, as bad as things were during this period, most still tried to remain hopeful.

Observations of counselors dealing with the effects of job loss reveal that the panic and anxiety resulting from not being able to find work can become quite dysfunctional:

> When the awareness that the next job was further away than originally anticipated, a sense of immediacy and/or panic in finding a job became evident. This was coupled with the anxiety created by unpaid bills and the financial inability to satisfy normal monthly expenditures. In some cases, this anxiety was so extreme, it had an immobilizing effect upon the individual and caused him to isolate himself from potentially helpful sources. Instead of calling a creditor and making an effort to explain the situation and seek financial arrangements, he was so caught up in his anxiety that he did nothing to communicate his plight to his creditors (United Way of King County, 1974, p. 25).

Drastic changes also occurred among professionals in our study with regard to work and career. For example, a noticeable upswing occurred in feelings about obsolescence, with almost one-fourth reporting they were not sufficiently up to date to effectively take on a new assignment in their profession. It is also during stage III that ego identification with their work plummets, with almost half of the professionals exhibiting extremely poor work involvement. There are also sharp drops in initiative and occupational aspirations. Unemployment finally begins to take its toll on motivation, with the work-inhibition syndrome clearly making its first appearance during this period.

STAGE IV: RESIGNATION AND WITHDRAWAL

Further dramatic changes occur as the unemployed professional reaches the fourth and last stage, called the period of malaise and cynicism by Powell and Driscoll (1973). However, we believe that resignation and withdrawal more accurately describes what occurs during stage IV, since as far back as 1930 in the classic study of the unemployed in the Austrian town of Marienthal, these have been found to be the predominant characteristics of the long-term jobless (Jahoda, Lazarsfeld, and Zeisel, 1971; Lazarsfeld, 1932–1933).

For professionals during stage IV, job seeking was infrequent, if it occurred at all. The psychological state of the individual tended to stabilize, being characterized by a loss of motivation as a reaction to the frustration of not being able to find work. Such comments as ''I've lost my drive and don't care'' or ''Not only have I lost my drive but I'm not doing much of anything. I'm just staying around the house'' (Powell and Driscoll, 1973, p. 23) were typical of the sentiments expressed by two-thirds of unemployed professionals in stage IV.

In addition to a loss of drive, most unemloyed professionals began to lose the sense that they were in control of their own lives and future. As one scientist explained: ''No matter what I do it just doesn't make any difference. It's just a throw of the dice, whether I'll get the job or not'' (Powell and Driscoll, 1973, p. 23). Feelings of powerlessness were mixed with cynicism as a defense for their reduced efforts at finding work. For example, one engineer unemployed for 15 months was counseled to teach math or science. His response was, ''Well, even if I get a job in education I'll never get one of those high-paying jobs because everything is all political anyway'' (Powell and Driscoll, 1973, p. 24).

Coping with rejection has been noted by counselors as a common problem for the individual who has suffered long-term unemployment:

> It was difficult to cope with the disappointments of being told ''no,'' for the discouragement of having his application placed upon a mountainous pile, and for the failure of not securing the job that would bring his life back to order (United Way of King County, 1974, p. 26).

Various defenses were used by the unemployed professionals to avoid being turned down for a job and to protect their self-esteem. One avoidance approach was to seek only a position that fit precisely their experience and training. The longer professionals remained in this fourth stage, the more rigid their occupational identity became. In essence, their avoidance of job seeking became progressively greater.

The psychological state of the unemployed professional stabilized during stage IV, with feelings of anxiety and desperation considerably reduced and replaced by helplessness and quiescence. In addition, social relations tended to improve but were more limited to a few very close relatives and friends. A major factor affecting outside social relationships was the drastically altered life-style, with the family prefering to stay at home rather than be with their acquaintances, whose life-styles were no longer the same as theirs. The unemployed college professor we discussed earlier noted the social isolation during this stage:

> The few friends I had made never called, for when one is unemployed one becomes a pariah. Those who are still working. . .just don't want to embarrass the jobless. I don't need them. I kept exercising, walking and giving my lectures to the trees.

As indicated in Chapter 2, studies have consistently found that the most obvious change in life-style among the unemployed was a drastic reduction in their social relations. The dysfunctional effects of this extreme change in life-style was noted by counselors assisting the longterm unemployed:

> Unemployment created for many people a dramatic change in their personal relationships. There was the loss of friends seen daily on the job and the loss of feeling productive. The family situation was altered with the interruption of the work-day routine and many times provoked friction that led to serious quarreling. Recreation and leisure activities were reduced or curtailed altogether as finances dwindled. Entertaining in the home suffered when the food budget was reduced. Invitations to dinner from friends were refused because the unemployed person could not afford to reciprocate. This caused further isolation and cut off other potentially helpful sources (United Way of King County, 1974, p. 25).

Many of these reactions described for stage IV have been verified in our study among professionals out of work for more than 26 weeks, who had an average unemployment period of over a year. One of the most striking findings among the long-term unemployed was that only one-fifth reported that they were at least very disturbed by being unemployed, compared to almost half of the professionals feeling this way who were in the previous stages of unemployment. In addition, the anxiety of those in stage IV about the future was considerably lower than it was among those in stage III. This lower anxiety accompanies a feeling of hopelessness and a sense of acceptance of their situation with about one-third admitting that their lives would never return to normal. Furthermore, the need to return to work in order to attain self-esteem, as well as growth and development, reached its lowest point among professionals in this stage and was accompanied by poor self-esteem as well as low initiative, occupational aspirations, and achievement values. This reduced motivational state was also manifested by the widespread belief that they lacked control over their lives and future. The lowest levels of personal control were also found during this stage in other research (Little, 1973). Despite the apparent outward acceptance of job loss, there is evidence that psychosomatic symptoms among unemployed professionals are most prevalent during stage IV (Little, 1973).

Although social support was lower than in stage II or III, social needs may not be as great during this period and irritation, as well as conflicts with family and friends, were considerably lower. In addition, feelings of being burdened with responsibility were at their lowest during stage IV.

Nevertheless, supportiveness from others may affect how satisfied these professionals are with their lives. Eight-tenths of those who did receive social support during this period reported a high degree of life satisfaction, compared to only one-third who felt satisfied with life among those not receiving strong support from others. It may very well be that social support plays an important role in the professional's ultimate acceptance of being in a situation of joblessness.

Professionals in our study also exhibited the highest levels of obsolescence during stage IV. One-third reported that they did not have the up-to-date knowledge and skills to take on a new job in their profession. This high incidence of obsolescence was also accompanied by the most extreme occupational rigidity. In fact, length of time out of work was correlated positively with professional obsolescence ($r = .49$, $p < .001$) as well as with occupational rigidity ($r = .43$, $p < .001$). These were the only two significant relationships we found between duration of unemployment and characteristics of the person. Although it is likely that those who are most up to date and willing to be more flexible find jobs much more easily, it is also likely that the longer professionals remain out of work, the more obsolescent and occupationally rigid they become. Some support for this was found in another study, which revealed an increased perception of career deterioration in terms of career goals becoming unattainable the longer professionals were out of work (Little, 1973). About half of the professionals in stage IV experienced a high level of career deterioration. It was explained that "as the length of time unemployed increases, a feeling of marking time or even falling behind in one's field might increase feelings of career goal loss" (Little, 1973, pp. 127–128).

It is clear that there is a continuous deterioration in the professionals' perception of their occupational capabilities the longer they remain out of work. Such a deterioration would probably affect how professionals view the instrumentality of returning to work in order to attain certain goals. In an attempt to investigate this, the instrumentality of reemployment to attain goals related to Maslow's need hierarchy was examined for each stage of unemployment.[4] As can be seen from Figure 4.1, during stage I the instrumentality of reemployment is greatest for attaining growth and development followed by self-esteem, security, and social goals, in that order. By stage II, however, the need to return to work for security ranks second, exceeding that of self-esteem. After stage II the instrumentality of reemployment for attaining all goals falls rapidly. By stage IV, security ranks as the most important reason for returning to work. However, the instrumentality of

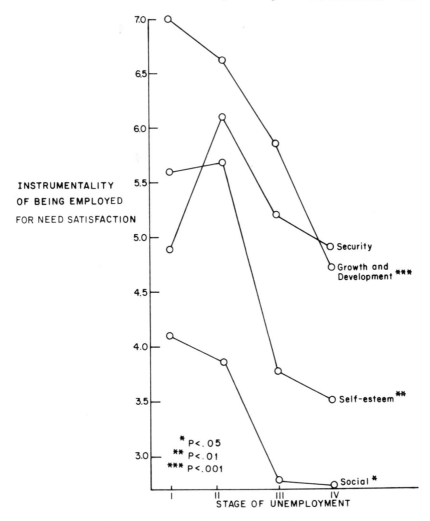

Figure 4.1.   Instrumentality of being employed for satisfying specific needs during each stage of unemployment.

reemployment is relatively low, even for attaining security. Thus the implication is not only that there is a reversal in the need hierarchy from growth to security by stage IV, but also that a great reduction in the motivation to return to work occurs among the long-term unemployed. Indeed, unemployed professionals during stage IV were most characterized by an extreme manifestation of the work-inhibition syndrome.

The psychological state of the professional who has suffered from long-term unemployment appears remarkably similar to that of those who are most work-inhibited—the hard-core unemployed. The latter not only have low levels of self-esteem, doubting their own worth and having little confidence in themselves, but also strongly believe that there are external forces over which they have no control which will determine their future (Tiffany, Cowan, and Tiffany, 1970). In fact, it appears to be the lack of success in finding work that contributes to a loss of esteem and increased dependence among welfare recipients (Goodwin, 1972).

The notion that some professionals can come to resemble the hard-core unemployed is not far-fetched. The terminated stockbroker discussed earlier (Wilkes, 1975) is an example of a jobless professional who turned to welfare assistance and acquired the characteristics of those receiving such aid. He did not appear to experience great emotional stress, but did report a reduction in motivation and a withdrawal into a "welfare mentality" after being out of work for over a year. As he explained:

> You eventually get into a state of mind: Why do it today? There's no hurry. I can do it tomorrow, tomorrow comes, and it's the same thing (p. 84).

> We've become a lot more sympathetic to people on welfare. . .Now I feel a crazy kinship with black guys, Puerto Ricans, poor whites. . .maybe I've gotten into a welfare mentality, but I don't really think about months and months ahead. It's this month and how many days does it have, how far will the food stamps go, what do we have to make it through? (p. 98)

Such a welfare mentality was found to be a common adaptation among jobless workers in the hard-hit Seattle area during the 1970–1971 recession (Briar, 1976). Counselors assisting in Seattle noted that the work inhibition common among welfare recipients was typical for the long-term unemployed person:

> With his confidence and energies depleted, the unemployed individual rapidly moved toward a point of becoming virtually unemployable and un-saleable on the job market (United Way of King County, 1974, p. 26).

The counselors referred to these individuals who were experiencing long-term unemployment and the need for public assistance for the first time in their lives as the "new poor." Perhaps the number of unemployed professionals needs to reach a "critical mass," as happened in Seattle, before their withdrawal into a welfare mentality becomes a widespread and acceptable adaptation to long-term joblessness.

There is evidence that less-effective job-seeking behavior is exhibited by those who have become passive-dependent (Stevens, 1973). Thus professionals who develop a welfare mentality would have difficulties in finding work created by the very psychological defenses erected as a result of their failure to find a job. Professionals whose self-esteem, personal control, and motivation have been impaired as a result of long-term unemployment may be permanently inhibited from seeking work. Work inhibition does, in fact, accompany adjustment to long-term joblessness. A study during the Depression by Eli Ginzberg (1943) found that: "The better adjusted the unemployed man became, the more difficulties he had fighting his way back into private employment" (p. 76). Such a conclusion certainly appears to be applicable to the long-term unemployed professionals; they are able to adjust through a maladaptive coping process that results in work inhibition.

DURATION OF UNEMPLOYMENT AND FINANCIAL RESOURCES

It is clear that the relationship between duration of time spent out of work and the psychological state of the unemployed professional is quite complex. Although the stages of unemployment do appear to be related to the process of adjustment to job loss, there is consistent evidence that the financial resources of professionals may be a more important determinant of their emotional stress than is the length of time they are out of work (Estes, 1973; Hall, 1934; Jacobson, undated). It appears likely, however, that while time out of work would have the greatest effect on the unemployed professionals with the most limited financial resources, eventually even those possessing greater resources could be affected by long-term joblessness. Terminated professionals who have adequate financial resources must still cope with the loss of self-esteem, social isolation, enforced idleness, and other consequences of unemployment, as the following case illustrates:

> Jim Beeker, age 49, has been out of work for three years. He worked as a hygienist for 23 years. His previous $15,000 a year salary enabled him to invest so that he was able to fall back on at least $7000 when he lost his job. He probably intended to put this money toward more luxurious uses than simple sustenance. He has already cashed in his life insurance policy, and if necessary is prepared to sell one of his two houses. He still owes $10,000 in mortgage fees for one house. One new expense since his unemployment is a $5000 hospital bill, a direct result of his loss of health insurance. This loss complicated his hardships; continuing medical needs incur new debts. He still has $2000 in the bank and can sell his other house, for about $14,000. He has been able to "make do," and probably will continue to for some time. He has been "coasting" on his resources, using them in ways never planned for. He has been very dissatisfied with the way he has been spending his time. Work was his one major source of self-esteem. The one activity that has relieved some of the tensions and dissatisfaction of idle day to day living is his newly developed interest in beekeeping. This hobby will not become a career. It keeps him occupied, and has been a source of new friendships. Jim's previous friends rejected him when he lost his job.

Relatively speaking, Jim's financial situation is stabilized, and has not required irreparable sacrifices as others have experienced. Yet Jim still complains about financial worries and says he is having trouble paying bills (Briar, 1976, pp. 68–69).

It is noteworthy that stress attributable to financial problems has been found to be minimal not only among professionals recently out of work but also among those experiencing long-term unemployment (Little, 1976). As the duration of joblessness increased, these professionals were more likely to cope with their financial problems in several ways. Some took temporary or part-time nonprofessional jobs that provided an income but left them underemployed. Among most married professional men, financial adjustment was attained by their wives starting to work. It was noted that for the long-term unemployed professionals, such "financial adjustments and an altered life style may increase acceptance of joblessness with a more resigned attitude" (Little, 1976, p. 269). Thus although an infusion of financial resources may serve to reduce unemployment stress, it may also contribute to the resignation and withdrawal common to stage IV. The implication is that adapting financially to job loss without meaningful reemployment contributes to the adjustment of professionals but probably at a high cost to their work motivation.

The motivational state of the individual appears closely affected by time out of work and limited financial resources. For example, in our study about two-thirds of those who did not have a great need to work to attain security maintained high achievement values during all four stages of unemployment. But among those who had to work in order to satisfy strong security needs, only one-third had high achievement values during the first three stages, and this rate plummeted to only one-eighth of those in stage IV.

Somewhat similar results were obtained in an analysis we conducted of the achievement drive among young graduates who were part of a nationwide study carried out during the recession of 1971.[5] We found that the longer these young professionals were out of work, the more likely they were to report a below-average drive to achieve. However, this was most evident for those who had a total income of less than $7,000 per year (see Figure 4.2). Such a relationship was much less noticeable among professionals whose annual family income had been over $7,000. Among those out of work for over a year, 40 percent in the limited income group rated themselves below average in achievement drive compared to only 17 percent among the higher-income group. For males, the disparity was even greater—50 percent and 23 percent, respectively. However, for those out of work for less than a year, the difference in achievement motivation between the two income groups was not significant. Among the implications of these results is that those possessing greater financial resources tend to maintain their achievement motivation, even after a period of long-term unemployment. On the other hand, professionals who lack financial resources would be more likely to reduce

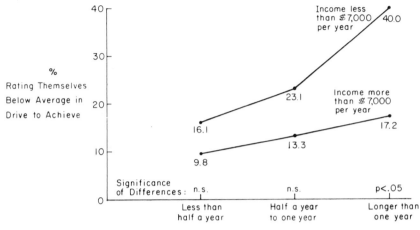

Figure 4.2.   Percentage of young college graduates seeking work who rate themselves below average in drive to achieve as a function of length of unemployment for groups at different annual income levels.

their drive to achieve after having been unsuccessful in their efforts at finding a job. Of relevance here are the findings reported in Chapter 3 that those possessing financial resources are more positive about their job loss and may even welcome the opportunity to change their careers.

Although having financial resources can and does serve as a cushion to absorb at least some unemployment stress, it does not provide complete protection. In our study we found that regardless of how secure they were, professionals among the long-term unemployed felt that they lacked control over their lives and exhibited an occupational rigidity which would tend to eliminate consideration of jobs they might otherwise take if they were more flexible. It would thus appear that even among professionals who are economically secure, long-term joblessness erodes their occupational identity and brings about a loss of control, which eventually can lead to the psychological deterioration characteristic of those with more limited financial resources.

CROSS-CULTURAL COMPARISONS

Cross-cultural studies that have dealt with the duration of unemployment and its effects on the well-being of the individual provide limited evidence supporting the existence of stages of unemployment. In fact, the earliest evidence comes from the classic study of the unemployed in the Austrian town of Marienthal during the Depression, which examined the impact of joblessness on the worker and his family and found that "the incidence of illness increased with the duration of unemployment. Only with children below the age of six, the relation is reversed; their state of health is better in the families of unemployed parents" (Jahoda et al., 1971, p. xi). These results are in accord with the onset of psychosomatic illness found by more current studies among jobless workers and their wives in the United States. In addition, as noted in Chapter 2, young children react positively to having their fathers at home. It was also observed at Marienthal that the long-term jobless "kept almost obsessive order in their own rooms while they neglected their backyard and lost practically all contact with the larger community and its concerns (Jahoda et al., 1971, p. xi). This phenomenon was referred to as a reduction of the psychological life space or effective scope of the person. Such rigidity of behavior and social isolation are defenses characteristic of the basic suicide syndrome discussed in Chapter 2.

Perhaps of greatest interest are the more recent studies carried out in developing countries. One study of jobless engineers in India found that functional disorders involving maladjustment were lowest among engineers unemployed for less than six months, but increased significantly for those out of work between 7 and 12 months, and then stabilized at this high level for the longer-term unemployed (Shanthamani, 1973). Another study of Indian college graduates in a variety of fields found that anxiety was quite high for those out of work less than six months and reached a peak among those unemployed between half a year and a year (Santhanam, 1973). The explanation for the latter finding was that during the first six months the professionals "make an intensive search for a job and failing to get a job results in the increase in the anxiety" (Santhanam, 1973, p. 265). It would appear that these professionals were going through stages II and III in their unemployment experience. For those out of work between one and two years, there was a reduction in anxiety to normal levels. A further drop in anxiety occurred among those unemployed longer than two years. It was suggested that the reason for this was that the professionals "get used or conditioned to this situation of unemployment and they begin to take things as they come" (Santhanam, 1973, p. 285). Such a conclusion is supported by the study of unemployed professionals carried out in Israel (Bar Yosef, Shield and Varsher, 1975). It was found that those out of work the longest felt the least family stress. The researchers suggested that the long-term jobless had adjusted to their situation and that this contributed to a reduction in tension at home.

The evidence and conclusions provided by the few studies carried out in other countries seem rather consistent across cultures regarding what happens to long-term unemployed professionals. As we had found in the United States, professionals in other cultures apparently accepted their jobless state and thereby reduced some of their stress. Although the evidence is rather limited, it would appear that unemployed professionals, even in developing countries with quite different labor market problems, may go through stages of adjustment similar to those of their colleagues in the United States.

RELATIONSHIP TO THEORIES OF STRESS

The stages of unemployment described in this chapter have some relationship to current theories relevant to stress. Therefore, to examine the parallels between the stages of unemployment and those of stress reactions in general, a brief excursion into a somewhat more theoretical realm is in order.

The reactions associated with the stages of unemployment are consistent with the most widely accepted physiological theory of stress—the general adaptation syndrome of Hans Selye (1956), which has also been applied to social–psychological stress (see Dohrenwend, 1961). The adaptation syndrome of Selye basically occurs in three stages; (1): the alarm reaction—the initial shock followed by mobilization of the bodily forces and defenses to meet the stress—comparable to what happens in stage I of unemployment; (2) the stage of resistance in which the mobilized forces and defenses attempt to cope with the stress—which is what occurs in stages II and III of unemployment; and (3) the stage of exhaustion—which occurs when the stress is prolonged or the forces of resistance cannot cope with the stress—comparable to the final unemployment stage of resignation and withdrawal. It should be noted that during the period of resistance some of the initial symptoms disappear but the adaptation itself is stressful and prolonged mobilization can result in psychosomatic disorders. As will be recalled, many of those in stage II of unemployment experience high stress, and by stage III somatic and psychological problems occur. Hence the adaptation to unemployment may itself be quite stressful and if prolonged, potentially damaging to the individual.

The variety of stress responses experienced during each stage of unemployment can be viewed from the perspective of the theory of coping evolved by Richard Lazarus (see Lazarus and Launier, 1978). Of particular relevance is that this theory recognizes that coping responses to stress involve changes that occur in stages.

> When stress occurs, and for effective coping with it, either the person changes as emotion ebbs and flows, or the environment must change, or both. This means that it is necessary to observe stress-related transactions as they take place over time, often in sequences or stages (Lazarus and Launier, 1978, p. 321).

Although coping with unemployment can be effective through transactions associated with environmental changes, such as an improved job market, much of the coping has to do with the individual changing. The theory does not attempt to detail the types of individual changes that occur during each stage, but there is a classification scheme suggested for the different types of coping that is relevant. Fundamental to this coping classification scheme is that there are essentialy two functions to coping. One function involves direct action focusing on "the *instrumental* or problem-solving aspects of a stressful person–environment transaction. If coping as problem-solving is ineffective, the threat will not go away" (Lazarus and Launier, 1978, p. 315). It would appear that instrumental or problem-solving coping reaches a peak during stage II of unemployment, when a concerted effort to find work occurs. If this type of coping proves to be ineffective, it will very likely cease by the end of stage III. The second function of coping with stress is that of palliation or efforts at regulation of the emotions through defense mechanisms or physiological mobilization. Whereas physiological mobilization probably reaches a peak during stages II and III of unemployment, as would be predicted by the general adaptation syndrome, defense mechanisms appear to become most predominant during stage IV, when they serve to protect the individual from feelings such as rejection and anxiety but are dysfunctional to becoming employed. In terms of adaptation to stress, instrumental as well as physiological mobilization during stage II are adaptive responses to job loss, whereas efforts at regulation of the emotions following stage II become increasingly maladaptive (see Dohrenwend, 1961).

The two types of coping functions in Lazarus' classification scheme may occur in response to work stress (Kahn, Wolfe, Quinn, Snock and Rosenthal, 1964) as well as to loss of one's livelihood (Anderson, 1976, 1977). Furthermore, research has demonstrated that instrumental, task-oriented behaviors predominate at moderate levels of stress but that at high stress levels the coping mechanisms dealing with emotional responses are most in evidence (Anderson, 1976). This suggests that if the task-oriented coping behaviors are not effective in dealing with unemployment, the stress increases and maladaptive coping responses take over to deal with the emotional reactions to unemployment. It would appear that these coping responses do serve to reduce emotional stress reactions among the long-term unemployed but very likely at the cost of their becoming work-inhibited.

The coping responses that occur during each stage of unemployment are relevant to the theory described by Ezra Stotland in *The Psychology of Hope* (1969). Strictly speaking, this is not a theory of stress since it focuses on hope, the expectation of success in attaining goals. However, hopelessness can be viewed in terms of stress and coping. The theory predicts that the unemployed during stage I would have a very high hope of attaining a very important goal—an appropriate job. This hope leads to action during stage II in terms of a concentrated job search. However, an unsuccessful job search would lower the expectation of success in finding work. This increased hopelessness in turn increases anxiety, which is "a negative subjective state as well as a state of physiological arousal" (Stotland,

1969, p. 28). As we have seen, following an unsuccessful job search, those in stage III experience high anxiety and even manifest psychosomatic disorders. The theory then predicts that to escape anxiety, the individual may reduce the importance of the goal, but by so doing "he then tends to become depressed, apathetic, withdrawn; goals do not matter to him. At the overt level, he does not act; covertly, he may disavow interest in the goal" (Stotland, 1969, p. 34). This is comparable to the resignation and withdrawal that occurs in the final stage of unemployment.

The dynamic changes in coping during each stage of unemployment are comparable to those predicted by the model of Cofer and Appley (1964), which involves four "thresholds" of psychological stress. First comes the instigation threshold, when new coping responses emerge that are primarily task-oriented, problem-solving behaviors. Such coping responses emerge most prominently following stage I of unemployment, when efforts are focused on the job search. If the situation is perceived as likely to be beyond the capacity of the individual's coping behaviors, a second threshold is reached—that of frustration. It is at this point that anxiety-related responses and ego-protective coping behaviors emerge. This is precisely the situation reached at the end of stage II of unemployment, when job search efforts have not succeeded and anxiety and ego-defensive reactions are observed. When both task- and ego-oriented behaviors have persisted without any effective change, a stress threshold is reached in which there is an exclusive preoccupation with ego protection. This threshold is reached at the end of stage III of unemployment. Finally, the cessation of ego-defensive behaviors leads to an exhaustion threshold characterized by "*the perception of helplessness or hopelessness. . .and a drop in activity occurs*" (Cofer and Appley, 1964, p. 452). This is typically what happens during stage IV among the long-term unemployed who have become work-inhibited.

As we have seen in Chapter 2, helplessness is also predicted by the theory of Seligman (1975) as being a response to a loss of control. Attempts to integrate the learned helplessness model with reactance theory (Wortman and Brehm, 1975) are relevant to the stages of unemployment. Reactance is comparable to the task-oriented or instrumental coping behaviors that are integral to the theories of stress we have already discussed. The integrative model suggests that when people experience an uncontrollable outcome their motivation to exert control over that outcome (reactance) increases if they expect such control but do not attain it initially. The more important the outcome, the greater the reactance. Thus, when professionals become unemployed, it is extremely important for them to find a job, and they typically begin their job search at the end of stage I with high expectations. According to the integrative model, the intensity of reactance would increase with continued exposure to uncontrollable outcomes (e.g., not finding a job) until they begin to feel that they may not be able to control the outcomes, at which time their reactance begins to diminish. This is typically what occurs at the end of stage II of unemployment. When they feel a lack of control over the outcomes, they will stop trying, and that is when they enter a state of helplessness. This is in essence what occurs during stage IV of unemployment. Thus it appears that the changes that occur during the stages of unemployment are in accord with the integrative model of reactance and learned helplessness.

What occurs during each stage of unemployment may parallel the reactions to other traumatic events. For example, this appears to be true for what is probably one of the most extreme forms of trauma—learning about the imminence of one's death. The stages of dying have been explicitly described by Kubler-Ross (1969). Denial may occur in the first stage of dying, which "functions as a buffer after unexpected shocking news, allows the patient to collect himself and, with time, mobilize other, less radical defenses" (Kubler-Ross, 1969, p. 39). After the initial shock of job loss, some among the unemloyed actually deny that they are out of work but many buffer the impact by behaving as if they are on vacation—which may be a disguised form of denial. Denial of impending death gives way to resentment and anger. For those experiencing job loss, resentment occurs during stage I after the shock has worn off, and anger manifests itself in stage III after all efforts have failed. No efforts on the part of the dying can reverse their impending death, so finally there is acceptance of the inevitable. The final stage of acceptance "is almost void of feelings. It is as if the pain had gone, the struggle is over. . . He wishes to be left alone. . . Visitors are often not desired" (Kubler-Ross, 1969, p. 113). This reaction is remarkably similar to the resignation and withdrawal of the final stage of unemployment. We can thus see that the reactions to unemployoment for many professionals are comparable to what occurs in the stages of dying—and in many respects job loss can be the death of an important part of themselves.

This very brief exploration has demonstrated that the empirical findings pertaining to stages of unemployment are consonant with current theories related to stress and coping. Hence the dynamic nature of the coping reactions to the unemployment experience do not appear to be essentially different from those occurring during adaptation or adjustment to major life stresses in general. However, the responses described as occurring during each stage of unemployment should be considered time bound—that is, tied to socioeconomic conditions or values prevalent at a particular time. For example, stage I of unemployment was apparently more stressful during the Great Depression than it is today, probably because the environment was not as supportive then as it is now and values toward work may have changed. This lends credence to those theorists who note that "relationships that hold in the 1970's may not be generalizable ten years later" (Korman, Greenhaus and Badin, 1977, p. 180). Hence future changes in the environment (e.g., a guaranteed income, full-emloyment legislation) or in individual work values may further modify the stages of unemployment that we have described. Indeed, changes in work values have already occurred among some professionals (Lindsey, 1975; Sarason, 1977) and unemployment may not be detrimental to their well-being. Therefore, to the degree that work values decline in importance among professionals, the less likely is it that they will pass through the stages of unemployment when they are out of work.

SUMMARY AND CONCLUSIONS

Stress generally begins to increase when job loss is first anticipated. However, once termination occurs, severity of stress does not necessarily increase the longer one is out of work. Rather, it has been suggested that there may be a curvilinear relationship between stress and time out of work. This has been explained by four stages of unemployment through which many jobless professionals progress. The stages of unemployment are supported by existing theories dealing with the developmental stages that individuals experience in response to prolonged stress. Since what happens during the stages may be rather complex the stages have been summarized in Table 4.1.

When job loss occurs, there is a very short-lived initial shock accompanied by extreme resentment of the employer responsible for the decision. However, the stress that may have arisen during a period of anticipation and uncertainty is now considerably reduced, with a sense of relief that can last up to approximately two months and even longer in some cases. The psychological state of the individual is generally good and, despite some anxiety, the newly acquired free time is used by many to relax and even take a vacation. This latter reaction may be a way to deny the fact that one is out of work. This should be differentiated, however, from more extreme defenses involving overt denial, such as an unwillingness to accept or reveal that one is unemployed, which occurs in some cases.

After the initial period of relaxation, the professional begins to make a concerted effort toward reemployment that generally lasts several months. This effort helps reduce the initial resentment and anxiety and may help reinforce the belief that one is in control of one's life. However, it is during this period that increased stress and psychological deterioration begin to occur, particularly for those lacking financial security and social support. Professionals in midcareer are especially prone to high stress during stage II. The job search itself, which is very intense during this period, contributes to this stress.

If the professional is still out of work by stage III, high stress may continue, but the frustration of not being able to find a job manifests itself in vacillation about career choice, doubt concerning ability to find work, erratic job searching, very high anxiety, moodiness, extreme anger, and aggressive behavior directed toward others and possibly against oneself. This period is relatively short lived, lasting about one and a half months.

The last period, stage IV, is of indefinite duration during which time profes-

TABLE 4.1 Stages of Unemployment Summary

Duration:	Stage I: Shock, Relief, and Relaxation	Stage II: Concerted Effort	Stage III: Vacillation, Self-Doubt, and Anger	Stage IV: Resignation and Withdrawal
	Approximately 1–2 months	Approximately 3 months	Approximately 1½ months	Indefinite

Psychological effects	1. Initial shock; reduction in stress following period of anticipation and uncertainty
	2. Low need to return to work to attain security
	3. Positive mental state in terms of:
	  a. Self-esteem
	  b. Life satisfaction
	  c. Hopefulness
	  d. Low Anomie
		1. Stress dependent on financial security and social support; those in mid-career most affected
		2. High motivation to work, including:
		  a. High initiative
		  b. High occupational aspirations
		3. Mental state improved in terms of:
		  a. Low anxiety
		  b. Personal control
		4. Mental state begins to deteriorate in
			1. Frustration and questioning of ability to find a job
			2. Lower motivation to work, including:
			  a. Low initiative
			  b. Low occupational aspirations
			  c. Occupational identity problems
			3. Some hope still remains
			4. Mental state deteriorates in terms of:
			  a. High anxiety
				1. Resignation to being in a jobless state
				2. Work inhibition accompanied by:
				  a. Low initiative
				  b. Low occupational aspirations
				  c. Occupational rigidity
				  d. Professional obsolescence
				3. Mental state improves in terms of reduced:
				  a. Anxiety
				  b. Feeling of desperation

	4. Some negative reactions in terms of: a. Resentment of employer b. Anxiety	terms of: a. Anomie b. Life dissatisfaction c. Being burdened with responsibility	b. Extreme anger	c. Feeling of being burdened with responsibility 4. Mental state deteriorates in terms of: a. Low motivation b. Low self-esteem c. Loss of control d. Helplessness e. Hopelessness
Possible behavioral and physical manifestation	1. Behaves as if on vacation 2. Normal social relationships; lack of openness about job loss 3. Hostility against employer	1. Concentrates almost totally on finding work 2. Receives social support 3. Attempts to be in control	1. Job search becomes erratic; attempts to change career or occupation 2. Conflicts with family and friends 3. Psychosomatic disorders and suicide proneness begin	1. Avoidance of searching for a job 2. Social relations limited to a few close relatives and friends with activities centered at home 3. Increases in psychosomatic disorders, suicide proneness, and susceptibility to premature death

sionals become resigned to being without work and enter a state of withdrawal. This final acceptance of unemployment as a way of life apparently results in a diminished anxiety with the professionals no longer feeling desperate and burdened by responsibility. However, this stress reduction is accompanied by a sense of not being in control and a loss of motivation manifested by the work inhibition syndrome. A return to work is not required for self-esteem or to attain higher-order growth needs; security needs become most important, but even these are relatively weak. Various defenses are erected to avoid rejection by prospective employers, including an occupational rigidity that excludes many potential jobs. A state of extreme passivity is characterized by a lack of job search activities, staying close to home with family and acceptance of what might be labeled a "welfare mentality" in which the person focuses on surviving from day to day with little concern for the future. For those with the most limited financial resources, the impact of long-term joblessness may be considerably exacerbated. The deterioration among some long-term unemployed professionals can be manifested by psychosomatic illness and even premature death from suicide or disease.

It is clear that if the psychological deterioration resulting from unemployment is to be kept at a minimum, professionals should become reemployed before the end of stage II, the period of concerted effort. This means that they have up to about five months in which to direct their efforts toward finding work. Although this may be enough time for some professionals to secure a job, others encounter barriers that keep them unemployed well into stage IV. In Chapter 5 we examine the individual facilitators and barriers to successful reemployment.

NOTES

1. It is also possible that satisfaction is lower among those professionals who are poorly adjusted to their job and hence more prone to termination. Indeed, there is longitudinal evidence that professionals who get fired are more likely to be dissatisfied with their jobs and have below average performance than are their colleagues who remain working (Hinrichs, 1979). Thus dissatisfaction and poor job adjustment may contribute to termination. Although there is evidence that this may, in fact, occur (e.g., Cohn, 1977; Thompson, 1973), it does not preclude that impending termination results in increased stress and poorer job adjustment.

2. A major problem in comparing the results of studies that have investigated the relationship between the duration of unemployment and stress are the different indices used to measure stress. Not only are there a variety of stress indices that have been used in studies of the unemployed, but also various psychological measures that may or may not be indicative of stress. Thus when the results from different studies of unemployment stress do not agree, that lack of agreement may be a result of differences in the way stress was measured in each study. On the

other hand, when results of different studies do agree, we can be that much more confident in their validity.

3. These characteristics were measured by the initiative and perceived occupational level scales from the Ghiselli Self-Description Inventory (Ghiselli, 1971).

4. The scales used to measure instrumentality of employment in attaining goals related to Maslow's need hierarchy appear in note 9 in Chapter 2.

5. The survey was carried out by the American Council on Education (Bisconti and Astin, 1973) and we analyzed the responses of those college graduates in the ACE sample who were unemployed.

CHAPTER FIVE

Finding Work: Individual Barriers and Facilitators

The success of unemployed professionals in finding appropriate jobs is related to factors that serve as barriers or facilitators to reemployment. One important factor is the nature of the job market. Others, however, involve individual differences that may inhibit or enhance employment opportunities, such as the nature of a professional's education, experience, or career expectations. In this chapter we examine some of the factors related to the individual that serve as either barriers or facilitators in attaining successful reemployment.

BARRIERS TO REEMPLOYMENT

Job Scarcity

The major barrier encountered by out-of-work professionals seeking jobs in their field is the scarcity of such jobs, particularly during recessions (Battelle Memorial Institute, 1971; Brown, 1972; Langway, 1966; Leventman, 1974; Loomba, 1967). This not unexpected finding is substantiated by the results of our study (see Table 5.1) which compared three matched groups of professionals who had been out of work during the recession of 1970–1971: one group that remained unemployed, another group that had been reemployed in their field, and a third group that had become "underemployed" by taking a job that was either part time or outside their field.[1]

A large majority in all three groups reported that a lack of jobs was a major barrier to reemployment.[2] However, only among the unemployed group was a perception of job scarcity strongly related to time out of work ($r = .45$, $p < .001$). Those who remained jobless were not significantly more likely to point to a lack of jobs as a barrier to finding work than were professionals who were able to find work. But this was not true for other barriers. For example, the

122

TABLE 5.1.   Percentage of Professionals Rating Barriers as Extremely or Quite Important in Causing Difficulty in Finding a New Job

Barriers	Employment Status		
	Unemployed (N=48)	Underemployed (N=45)	Reemployed in Field (N=44)
Lack of jobs	72	62	60
Inappropriate experience	30	29	11
Overqualified	23	14	7
Reluctance to relocate	21	11	11
Previous salary too high	19	5	14
Age	4	5	7
Inappropriate education	4	5	5
Unemployed for too long	4	0	0

unemployed compared to those reemployed in their field were more likely to attribute the difficulty in finding work to their inappropriate experience or overqualifications.

Despite the numerous barriers to finding work, unemployed professionals more frequently blame their difficulties on the external factor of job scarcity than on personal inadequacies or barriers attributable to their own situation. The direction of this blame, however, may be related to specific individual differences. For example, among the unemployed group, those who perceived a lack of jobs as an important barrier to reemployment were less flexible in the type of position they were willing to accept ($r = -.38, p < .01$) as well as more likely to have an external locus of control ($r = .27, p < .05$). This lack of personal control, as well as flexibility, may very well be a developmental phenomenon, since the likelihood that professionals view a lack of jobs as a major barrier to reemployment increased among those who had been out of work the longest, as noted above.

For professionals experiencing long-term unemployment, the attribution of blame to external causes for not being able to find work may become a defense to protect their self-image. As we have seen in Chapter 4, professionals who have been unable to find work after a long job search may use various defenses in an attempt to protect themselves against rejection by potential employers. These defenses apparently include a reduced flexibility in the type of work they are willing to take or attribution of their situation to external events over which they have little control. The unemployed professionals with opposite attributes had a greater reluctance to relocate—relocation was more of a barrier to those who were less rigid in the type of job they would accept ($r = .27$, $p < .05$) or had greater personal control ($r = -.24$, $p < .05$). Professionals may be able to resist a change in location in order to find work by maintaining flexibility in the type of job they are willing to accept as well as a strong belief that they can control events affecting their lives. Reluctance to relocate as a barrier to reemployment, unlike a lack of jobs, does not change the longer the professionals are out of work. This has been corroborated by other research (Gutteridge, 1978). Since relocation may be the only option in facilitating reemployment for some professionals, it is discussed more extensively below as well as in Chapter 7.

Age

Perhaps the most surprising results in our study were the factors that were *not* considered by professionals as important in preventing reemployment. Few regarded their age, education, or length of unemployment as major difficulties in finding a job. However, these results may be somewhat misleading with regard to age, because the older professionals comprised a relatively small segment of our sample. In fact, age was considered a barrier to reemployment by the older group.

Outright discrimination in hiring older professionals because of age has been identified as the major barrier to their reemployment, with other factors being less important (Loomba, 1967). Even during severe recessions, being too old has been found to rank second only to a lack of jobs as the most important barrier to reemployment among jobless professionals (Battelle Memorial Institute, 1971). As one 44-year-old securities analyst, who was terminated after 15 years with a major investment counseling firm, explains: "I've been told by a number of recruiters and agencies that I have the job skills but that companies are looking for someone younger. I just want a job, not a lawsuit, but it is discouraging that you do have the skills, but that employers set up artificial barriers" (Goodwin, 1975, p. 2).

The difficulties encountered by the older professional have been documented in many studies. For example, an investigation of engineers and scientists unemployed in the San Francisco Bay area during 1963–1965 found that age was the most significant factor in determining how long they remained out of work (Loomba, 1967). Forty-three percent of those over age 45 were unemployed over 18 weeks compared to only 26 percent who were jobless that long among those age 35 or younger.

A more precise analysis of age and unemployment among technical professionals was carried out in the greater Boston area during the same period (Mooney,

1966). In that study, those under the age of 30 were found to have the least difficulty in finding new jobs, returning to work after an average of seven weeks of
unemployment. Difficulties in finding work were greater after age 30 but, interestingly, the duration of joblessness was about the same for professionals in their
30s as for those in their 40s—12 weeks on the average. For those over age 50,
difficulties in finding work again increased, to an average of over 16 weeks of
unemployment.

Somewhat similar results were reported among a more heterogeneous sample
of unemployed professionals who had lost their jobs in California during the early
1970s (Estes, 1973). The major difference in the results of this study was that the
leveling off of average time spent out of work occurred for those in their 40s and
50s, 10 years later than for the technical professional group in the Boston area
study. We can speculate as to why such a discrepancy occurred. It is likely that the
knowledge and skills of the older professionals are perceived to have become obsolescent, and consequently, would be less marketable. Engineers and scientists
may experience obsolescence at an earlier age than those in other professions
(Kaufman, 1974c). This could explain why, when the job market contracts, technical professionals appear to encounter difficulties in finding reemployment at a
younger age than those in other fields.

Although professional obsolescence among the unemployed group we have
been studying was found to be related to perceived reemployment barriers such as
inappropriate experience, $(r = -.27, p < .05)$, it was not directly correlated with
perception of age as a barrier. If anything, those who felt they were professionally
up to date reported greater problems with barriers such as being overqualified $(r = -.26, p < .05)$ or their previous salary being too high $(r = .28, p < .05)$. Indeed, more of those in their 30s and 40s felt they were up to date in their profession
than did their younger colleagues. It may be that, at least until midcareer, professional obsolescence may decrease with age, mostly as a result of accumulated experience and self-learning (Kaufman, 1974c, 1975). Obsolescence may be used
by employers as a convenient excuse for hiring younger and less experienced professionals at salaries considerably lower than those which older professionals have
attained.

It has been demonstrated that older terminated professionals do experience the
greatest salary reductions when reemployed (Kaufman, 1980). Such losses were
attributed primarily to high termination salaries and not age per se. There is some
indication that professionals with higher pretermination salaries do have greater
reemployment difficulties (Thompson, 1972). However, other research found that
the most highly paid professionals tended to have the shortest duration of
unemployment, but they also accepted the greatest salary reductions in their new
jobs (Kaufman, 1980). Thus, employability may have been enhanced by an increased willingness to accept a reduction in pay.

Generally, the older the unemployed professionals, the greater a reduction in salary they are willing to accept to improve their employability (Brown, 1972; Gutteridge, 1978). Indeed, lower salary aspirations appear to facilitate reemployment (Gutteridge, 1978). A reduction in aspirations, not only for salary but for the type of work professionals are willing to accept, is apparently directly related to the reality of age discrimination. An older forecasting specialist who was terminated after a lifetime with one firm explained: "None of the excuses I heard during my job interviews was hiding one factor. Being sixty years old and unemployed is a mighty poor combination. However, I want to be constructive, and productive again, even in a more modest way" (Drucker, 1975, p. 36). A similar flexibility was shown by the unemployed 50-year-old college professor we discussed earlier. He had already gone through several consecutive job losses and noted that "it was not a situation in which I could be at all choosy. My age and unemployed condition were definitely against me, so I had to aim for a situation in which hardly anyone else would fit—or one that hardly anyone else would tackle."

In contrast to their older colleagues, the youngest professionals can often afford to be more selective and remain out of work until they find an appropriate position. When this attitude among young professionals is combined with the increasing competition from new graduates, they are apt to experience long-term unemployment comparable to that of their older colleagues. This may have occurred during the recession of the early 1970s, when terminated engineers in their 20s were likely to be out of work as long as those over 40 (Kaufman, 1980). Long-term joblessness tended to be least prevalent among engineers in their 30s, who typically were under the greatest unemployment stress because of family responsibilities and career growth needs.

The experience of age discrimination can affect not only level of aspiration but also other psychological characteristics. For example, age discrimination was found to be widely experienced by unemployed middle-aged workers and became associated with their belief that they are controlled by the external environment (Andrisani and Abeles, 1976a). Thus, when age becomes a barrier to reemployment, it can create far-reaching changes in an individual's motivation with respect to work as well as life in general.

Acceptance of the realities of their situation, together with diminished levels of aspiration as well as personal control, may help explain why older professionals often experience lower stress than did their younger colleagues following job loss. This low stress may also be indicative of a greater susceptibility among those experiencing age discrimination to enter stage IV of unemployment. Indeed, one can speculate that age as a barrier to reemployment may serve to compress the stages of unemployment stress, so that older professionals would move through the stages more rapidly than their younger colleagues. It is clear that, despite a willingness to reduce their expectations in order to return to work and remain useful, age nevertheless remains a very real barrier to reemployment for older professionals.

Barriers Related to Age

Not only did the older professionals in our study identify age as a barrier to reemployment, but they indicated that other barriers to finding work became more likely with increasing age (see Table 5.2). Older professionals tended to perceive that their previous salary level, being overqualified, and the length of time they were out of work were barriers to reemployment. It should be noted that being overqualified among the unemployed was related to their having attained a higher level of education ($r = .38, p < .01$). Thus being overqualified can mean having *too much education*.

Reluctance to relocate was associated with age for those who were able to find reemployment (see Table 5.2). Other research also indicates that older unemployed professionals will relocate only as a last resort (Gutteridge, 1978). Nevertheless, among those in our study who remained unemployed, there was a weakening of the relationship between age and reluctance to relocate. Perhaps for some of the older professionals, an inability to find jobs in their local area increased their willingness to relocate.

TABLE 5.2. **Correlations Between Chronological Age and Degree to Which Barriers Cause Difficulty in Finding a New Job**

	Employment Status		
Barriers	Unemployed (N=48)	Underemployed (N=44)	Reemployed in Field (N=44)
Lack of jobs	.07	−.20	.07
Inappropriate experience	−.18	−.51***	−.11
Overqualified	.30*	−.22	.42**
Reluctance to relocate	.11	.28*	.31*
Previous salary too high	.46***	.29*	.57***
Age	.46***	.23	.51***
Inappropriate education	.14	−.02	.31*
Unemployed for too long	.26*	.10	.40**

*p < .05.
**p < .01.
***p < .001.

Older professionals are likely to resist relocation because of deeper roots in their communities involving attachment to home, relatives, and friends (Langway, 1966; Loomba, 1967). In our study, those with more dependents also reported a greater reluctance to relocate among both the unemployed ($r = .24$, $p < .05$) and the underemployed ($r = .28$, $p < .05$). Although this has not been corroborated by some research findings (Gutteridge, 1978), the desire to avoid taking children out of school has consistently been found to be an important determinant of resistance to relocation (Langway, 1966; Loomba, 1967; Perline and Presley, 1973). This factor would most likely affect professionals in their 30s, who are more apt to have school-age children.

Given these findings, the greatest reluctance to relocate would be expected to occur among older professionals who have children in school. Such individuals may attempt to overcome the barriers to reemployment by reducing their aspirations and future expectations. Illustrative of this situation is that of a 47-year-old quality control engineer, who had a series of relocation experiences following both voluntary and involuntary terminations. After over a year of unemployment, he described his limited aspirations and reluctance to relocate:

> I'm living for the present now. God willing, if a good job comes along then it may be that I'm going to want to stay with it for the rest of my life. . . . I feel as though I'm a little too old right now to go from one job to another in a short time. This has happened in the past three or four years. I don't like that feeling because I'm not only upsetting myself but I'm fouling up the well-being and the harmony of family life. I'm making my wife a nervous wreck by going from one job to another, by moving to a different area, maybe two, three times a year. And my son, of course, good Lord! His education right now is more important than a lot of other things. If I keep moving him around, his education is going to suffer, and I don't want that to happen (Levinson, 1978, p. 290).

Our results indicate that younger professionals who became underemployed reported inappropriate experience as a barrier to reemployment, whereas inappropriate education was considered a problem by the older professionals who were reemployed in their field (see Table 5.2). It would appear that deficiencies in experience affect the youngest professionals, who, as a result, may become underemployed, whereas deficiencies in education may become a barrier for those who are older. In general, however, our data indicate that professionals who are older perceive greater barriers to finding work, regardless of their success in obtaining a new job.

Barriers and Syndromes of Unemployment

Several barriers were found to be related to the syndrome of general unemployment stress, but not to psychopathological stress. Age as a perceived barrier to reemployment (but not chronological age) turned out to be related to general stress ($r = .36, p < .01$), as was a lack of jobs ($r = .37, p < .01$) and being unemployed too long ($r = .31, p < .05$). Furthermore, job scarcity and age barriers were related to being out of work too long and, hence, may have contributed to general stress indirectly as well as directly. Once again it is the factors beyond the individual's control that are most crucial. Job scarcity and age discrimination can have a detrimental effect on jobless professionals by lengthening their unemployment and increasing their general stress. However, such barriers may not be sufficient by themselves to create the more extreme symptoms of the psychopathological stress syndrome.

Oddly enough, those jobless professionals who had become most work inhibited were also *less* likely to report that they perceived barriers to reemployment as stemming from their overqualifications ($r = -.45, p < .001$) or previously high salary level ($r = -.36, p < .01$). However, as we have already seen, the most work-inhibited professionals were those who were not only out of work the longest, but also the younger, less-educated individuals with the most limited professional involvement. Hence they would be less likely to have had a high salary or to have been overqualified.

Reluctance to relocate was also less of a barrier to those who were more work-inhibited ($r = -.27, p < .05$). This is understandable since we have also seen that relocation is less acceptable to those who are more flexible in the type of work they are willing to accept or who feel they have greater personal control over their lives. Such individuals are also less likely to experience work inhibition. Thus it appears that some barriers may be perceived as relatively unimportant to those who become work inhibited.

DISCRIMINATION AS A BARRIER TO REEMPLOYMENT

Discriminatory practices of employers have been identified as a major barrier to reemployment (Briar, 1976). Although age is clearly a barrier for many professionals, there is fairly consistent evidence that hiring decisions have often been biased not only because of age, but also because of sex, race, or disability (e.g., Dipboye, Fromkin, and Wiback, 1975; Fidell, 1970; Haefner, 1977; Rickard, Triandis and Patterson, 1963). In these sections we examine briefly various types of discrimination in hiring.

Sex Discrimination

Despite equal employment opportunity legislation and widespread affirmative action programs, sex discrimination still appears to be a prevalent hiring practice (see Fidell, 1970; Haefner, 1977). It is noteworthy that during the recession of the early 1970s one study of unemployed professionals found that men were out of work longer than women (Estes, 1973). However, these findings may result from the fact that many of the men were technical professionals, a group that experienced great difficulty in finding work at the time. Among scientists and engineers terminated during that period, women were found to experience significantly longer unemployment than were men (Kaufman, 1980). Marital status for these women made no difference in the amount of time they spent out of work. This implies that even the women most in need of working—those who were single—may have experienced job discrimination in hiring. Such discrimination does not appear to have been diminished as a result of affirmative action programs. Indeed, the contrary may be true. In 1977 one-fifth of women professionals reported sex discrimination, double the rate in 1969 (Quinn and Staines, 1978).

According to a female educational psychologist who had been out of work for over three years, many of the unemployed professional women with whom she was acquainted "became so discouraged at the beginning of their job hunt that they have either given up entirely or else have acquired typing, secretarial or other positions which are far below their training and education" (Maxwell, 1977, p. 3). She suggests that it is best not to think "about situations pointing to discrimination. Dwelling on these matters will make a job hunter become bitter and bitterness can, in turn, cause depression" (Maxwell, 1977, p. 8).

The problems that female professionals encounter in finding work have undoubtedly been exacerbated by women reentering the labor force in ever-increasing numbers. Earlier we indicated that unemployed married women whose husbands are working can more readily wait out a recession. However, reentry into their profession after a lengthy period of being out of the work force may be quite difficult. As the unemployed educational psychologist notes:

> The homemaker whose children are all in college, and whose husband travels most of the time, would like to return to work. But she finds that at her age it is difficult to reenter the work force. She may also want to add financial support to the family budget with the strain of teen-agers in college. Therefore, her needs may be three-fold: emotional, economical and intellectual. Because of the difficulty in obtaining a professional position, she may be unable to satisfy these needs and as a result may become discouraged (Maxwell, 1977, p. 8).

In fact, there are indications that older women professionals who have been terminated experience the greatest discrimination in finding work (Kaufman, 1980). One can speculate that older women encounter the most extreme barriers to reemployment since they are confronting discrimination because of age as well as sex.

Racial Discrimination

Discrimination in hiring because of race has long existed even among professionals. This appeared to be true during the recession of the early 1970s when minority scientists and engineers who were terminated experienced significantly longer unemployment than their white colleagues (Kaufman, 1980). Nevertheless, as a result of job market breakthroughs in equal employment (Freeman, 1977a, 1977b), professionals who are members of minority groups may be encountering diminished racial discrimination (Quinn and Staines, 1978). In fact, there is evidence that race has ceased to be an important factor in hiring decisions (Haefner, 1977). Moreover, black professionals are reported to be making more rapid salary progress than are their white colleagues (Magarrell, 1977). However, there is still widespread skepticism among black professionals, particularly with regard to management advancement (Freeman and Fields, 1973). Thus although "access" discrimination has declined for minorities, "treatment" discrimination may still exist, particularly with regard to promotions (Stevens and Marquette, 1978). Although it may be too early to tell, it would appear that equal employment opportunities have begun to evolve for minority professionals, at least in hiring. Nevertheless, as was noted in Chapter 3, minorities may be more prone to unemployment stress, and thus any barriers experienced in their search for work could be quite detrimental to their well-being.

Discrimination against the Handicapped

Perhaps one of the most neglected groups with regard to equal employment opportunities is the handicapped, who are generally not even protected by law against discrimination, as are women, minorities, and older workers (except in the case of federal contractors). Only about six-tenths of disabled professionals were working in 1965 (German and Collins, 1974) and it is likely that a smaller ratio were employed during the recession of the mid-1970s (Ruffner and Sale, 1975). In fact, an evaluation of existing data pertaining to the work status of the disabled points to "a very substantial drop in employment over the 1970s" (Levitan and Taggart, 1977, p. 10). However, the unemployment of the handicapped is not always a result of discrimination. Also relevant are problems of mobility and access related to the physical limitations of the individual (Falcocchio, Kaufman, and Kramer, 1976). Federal efforts to improve access should go far to remove at least the architectural barriers to the employability of the handicapped. However, even with improvement of access, the handicapped still face many barriers to employment, including psychological ones which may require special approaches to overcome (see Davis, Johnson, and Overton, 1979).

"Reverse Discrimination"

Before we leave this all too brief discussion of barriers due to discrimination, mention should at least be made of the controversial question of "reverse discrimination." Generally, such reverse discrimination has been said to have an adverse affect on white males because of affirmative action program aimed at the hiring of women and minorities.

Discrimination because of personal characteristics unrelated to competence can have the same detrimental effect on white males as it has on other groups. One young white male Ph.D. sociologist describes his experience:

It was very upsetting to me that everyone was looking for blacks, chicanos, or women—nobody wanted to hire a white male. After completing my doctorate I applied at a number of universities with no success—most did not even answer my letter of inquiry. At a convention in Chicago it seemed virtually every dean I talked to, after asking about a position, said they had none and then I would often overhear the dean talking to another dean saying, 'Do you have any bright women or any bright blacks? We have several positions in our. . . .' I finally got so upset applying for positions that evidently didn't exist that I asked several deans, 'Why are you here then?' and they answered, 'To help place *our* graduates.' It was especially upsetting in that a number of my female colleagues who earned their doctorate the same time I did had a number of offers—at least they stated they did. I drove home from Chicago extremely depressed and continued to apply—nothing. After sitting home for month after month I became more and more bitter—no money, no job, no prospects. I started going and applying every place I could—machine shops, drafting shops and anywhere else I felt I could get a job—they all said the same thing: 'We're not hiring—we just laid off several of our workers.' I became angrier and angrier, experiencing depression with alternate moods of aggression.[3]

In addition to such anecdotal evidence, reverse discrimination in the hiring of professionals has been reported to exist and may be widespread in certain fields (Kryger and Shikiar, 1978; Ornstein, 1976). White male professionals have begun to file legal suits charging employers with reverse discrimination (Roberts, 1977), and the Supreme Court decision in the Bakke case is likely to increase such legal actions.

It is certain that with an increasingly difficult market for professionals, discrimination will act as a barrier for some and a facilitator for others. Paradoxically, there may even be some reverse discrimination because of age as a result of an increased demand for older experienced managers as was reported during the recession of the mid-1970s (Barmash, 1977). Retrenchment and avoidance of risks led many organizations to prefer hiring older, more experienced managers with a proven track record. Therefore, at least for some older managers, their experience combined with organizational needs during a recession may have served as facilitators of reemployment. On the other hand, a lack of experience was a barrier to the hiring of younger managers. Such a situation illustrates not only the changing nature of discrimination but also the interaction of personal characteristics with employer bias. This bias creates a barrier to finding work for particular groups of people applying for certain kinds of positions, and each of these factors may change at different time periods with changing legal requirements, economic conditions, labor market forces, and societal values.

FAMILY RESPONSIBILITIES AS A FACILITATOR OF REEMPLOYMENT

Evidence indicates that family responsibilities may stimulate the drive to find a job and, hence, facilitate reemployment. With regard to the male professionals who remained unemployed in our study, considerably more were single (53 percent) than was found to be the case for those who had become underemployed (38 percent) or who were reemployed in their field (26 percent). The number of dependents they had was also related to reemployment success. Fewer of the unemployed had two or more dependents (44 percent) than did the underemployed (58 percent) or those reemployed in their field (67 percent). The differences in marital status as well as number of dependents between the unemployed and those reemployed in their field were highly significant. Since the groups were closely matched in age and other characteristics, these results are all the more striking.

There is other evidence that married male (but not female) professionals with greater family responsibilities are more likely to become reemployed (Dyer, 1973; Gutteridge, 1978; Kaufman, 1980). However, the job taken may only be a stop-gap measure to provide income, as indicated by the following findings in a study of unemployed professionals:

> In all cases, lower family responsibilities lead to lower probability of employment, either at layoff or after some unemployment. Single men . . . are not under the same pressures to find employment for family support and so can afford to wait for employment opportunities to develop, rather than having to take whatever job might be available. The larger the family, the greater the need for continuing income. This in turn, explains the higher turnover rate which is also associated with large family heads; since they are apt to take deadend jobs to assure continuing income, they are also the ones most vulnerable to new cutbacks and employment terminations (Allen, 1972, pp.172–173).

It would appear that financial responsibility for others increases the motivation to find work. Indeed, for professionals in our study who did find a job, regardless of its nature, the need to return to work to attain security was significantly greater than for those who remained unemployed. The latter group, characterized by fewer dependents and lower motivation to return to work for reasons of security, could more easily afford to wait until they found the right job. It is interesting to note that the need to be working in order to have self-esteem was greater for those unemployed who had more dependents ($r = .35, p < .01$). The diminished status of the unemployed male professional in the eyes of his family may be at least as important as financial security in motivating him to find work. The results of our study reveal that among married men who found jobs that left them underemployed, those whose wives were working accepted positions that they rated as much worse than their previous job ($r = -.52, p < .01$), particularly with respect to security ($r = -.54$, $p < .01$) and salary ($r = -.34$, $p < .05$).[4] In light of our earlier discussions concerning role reversal, it appears that when unemployed male professionals lose their breadwinner role to their wives, they are driven to find a job at all costs in an attempt to restore their status in the family and their own self-esteem.

EDUCATIONAL AND OCCUPATIONAL BARRIERS AND FACILITATORS

Numerous studies have shown that educational and occupational characteristics of unemployed professionals may facilitate[5] or hinder their return to work. The specific characteristics examined include the professionals' level of education and areas of specialization. In addition, the relationship of such characteristics to the difficulties of young college graduates in their search for work is investigated.

Level of Education

How long it takes professionals to become reemployed has generally been related to their educational level, although some research has failed to find a strong relationship (Kaufman, 1980). Professionals without college degrees, who had attained professional status primarily as a result of experience, not only have been highly prone to job loss, they also have the greatest difficulty in becoming reemployed. In the study cited previously of unemployed technical professionals in the Boston area, persons without any degree were out of work for an average of 11.9 weeks, while those who had completed an associate's degree were out of work for practically the same period as the 8.8 weeks of joblessness experienced by the professionals with a bachelor's degree (Mooney, 1966). Individuals with at least a master's degree fared best, experiencing an average of only 6.6 weeks of unemployment. It should be noted that professionals without degrees tend to be much older than their colleagues with degrees. For example, in the Boston area study, not one of those professionals without a degree was under 30.

Being older and without a degree definitely creates a major barrier to reemployment. This has been found to be true for professionals in various fields (Horowitz, 1968). In fact, one study found that "for nondegree individuals age is the most important factor in determining their period of unemployment" (Loomba, 1967, p. 52). Among those with a bachelor's degree, the relationship between age and length of unemployment was not as strong but was still significant. However, for those at the master's level, age had no effect on the length of unemployment. The study concluded "that one way of combating old age is to obtain a higher degree" (Loomba, 1967, p. 53). Indeed, those who had such degrees cited their formal education as the most helpful factor in finding a new job. Moreover, other research has indicated that advanced education among professionals is instrumental in attaining reemployment regardless of age (Brown, 1972; Conner, 1973).

Professionals who have a graduate degree are generally perceived as being most up to date and there is evidence that this is in fact the case (Kaufman, 1974c, 1975). Therefore, the excuse of employers in not hiring older professionals because they are obsolescent is not valid when advanced education is added to experience. In fact, on the basis of the research carried out in Boston, it was concluded: "If enrollment in a master's or doctor's program can be regarded as an attempt to stave off obsolescence and thereby improve reemployment opportunities, it seems to be working very well" (Mooney, 1966, p. 525).

However, as we have already mentioned, those with more advanced education also reported that being overqualified was a barrier to their finding work. In fact, having a doctorate may actually handicap some job seekers. We have seen in Chapter 1 that a surplus of Ph.D.s has become a reality in some fields. Thus, possessing a Ph.D. may actually create barriers to finding work.

This is further illustrated in a study of aerospace professionals terminated in California during the early 1970s, which found that those possessing a doctorate had a higher unemployment rate than did their colleagues with bachelor's or master's degrees (Allen, 1972). Those with an M.S. degree had the lowest unemployment rate and spent the least time out of work. Apparently, some employers preferred the more general knowledge and the more moderate salary requirements of aerospace professionals with master's degrees compared to those with doctorates. It was further observed that: "Employers fear that men with too much skill will quickly leave less challenging jobs for better positions as they become available. The fear is justified, for men with doctorates also demonstrate the highest turnover of any education group" (Allen, 1972, p. 175).

In addition, holders of doctorates may be less flexible in the type of work they are willing to accept because of a commitment to their field. The reluctance to change fields was explained as follows:

> These men have devoted the greatest amount of time and energy to developing their skill and therefore stand to lose the most by shifting into other fields. At the same time, the greater training investment was also the result of a real commitment to their particular specialty. The higher satisfaction of utilizing this education in an occupation to which they have demonstrated deep commitment makes them all the more reluctant to change their preferences for their field. A greater amount to lose makes for a longer and more intensive search within the specific specialty (Allen, 1972, p. 175).

Our data show that when professionals found work in their own field, the jobs of those with a higher level of education were better than their previous position with regard to both salary ($r = .36, p < .01$) and skill utilization ($r = .37, p < .01$).

Hence advanced education can pay off with a better job, but this is most likely to occur when the job is in the professional's field. Although professionals who hold a doctoral degree are more likely to be up to date than others in their field, their more limited flexibility and overqualification for most positions can slow their progress in finding work.

However, being up to date may be affected by recency as well as by level of education. Studies of technical professionals reveal that the more recently they had completed their education, the more apt they were to find work (Conner, 1973) and the shorter their period of unemployment was likely to be (Allen, 1972). Recency of education appeared to be independent of age, since many professionals "continued college credit work while on the job, finishing bachelor's degree requirements and completing higher degrees after prolonged experience in the field. As a result, the findings suggest strongly that those who do not keep current with technological developments in their own field through continued education are less likely to be acceptable in new engineering positions" (Allen, 1972, p. 176). In fact, our data show that the new positions found by those who were most up to date in their field provided an even greater utilization of their skills than did the jobs they had lost. This was true among professionals who became underemployed ($r = .37, p < .05$) as well as for those who were reemployed in their own field ($r = .41, p < .01$).

Area of Specialization

In addition to the level and recency of education, it would appear likely that one's degree major or occupational specialization would influence reemployment success. Unfortunately, what little research is available that can provide answers to this question tends to be inconsistent and even contradictory. Evidence from a study of terminations in aerospace companies during 1963–1964 indicated that professionals holding degrees in business or the social sciences were out of work longer and were much more likely to be reemployed in a subprofessional position than were those with degrees in engineering or science (Eaton, 1971). These results tend to be supported by a study of aerospace industry terminations during the early 1970s in southern California (Allen, 1972), which found that those with an M.A. or M.B.A. averaged a longer period of unemployment (28.4 weeks) than did those with an M.S. (21.8 weeks). Even within the engineering and science group, success in gaining rapid reemployment varied greatly according to specialization. For example, civil engineers and nuclear specialists were most successful, whereas industrial engineers and metallurgical specialists encountered the greatest difficulty (Allen, 1972). A national survey of engineers and scientists terminated during this period revealed more extensive data (Kaufman, 1980). In addition to civil engineers, R&D managers and computer specialists found new jobs rapidly. On the other hand, those most likely to experience long-term unemployment included aeronautical, industrial, electrical, mechanical, and metallurgical engineers, as well as chemists, physicists, and the formerly underemployed in areas outside engineering or science.

In another study that investigated various types of professionals in the Boston area during the mid-1960s it was found that artists, writers, administrative specialists, and educators had the greatest difficulty in finding new jobs, whereas engineers and the life science specialists experienced the least difficulty (Horowitz, 1968). Seemingly contradictory results were found in a study of professionals terminated in California in the early 1970s, which showed that technical professionals, particularly those in R&D, experienced the longest unemployment; those in human resource specialties, such as social work and teaching, had the shortest time out of work (Estes, 1973). The difference in the findings of these studies may be attributed to the better market for technical professionals during the mid-1960s compared to the early 1970s.

During the recession of 1970–1971, large numbers of unemployed aerospace professionals probably encountered more barriers to finding work than did other professionals who were jobless. Indicative of such barriers is the evaluation provided by one unemployed engineer in our study, who reported that having his background in aerospace "is a cross between being a leper and an Edsel dealer. The employment opportunities are about the same." The major employment barrier such professionals encountered was their lack of nonaerospace experience (Ware, 1974). This was clearly indicated by both the professionals and prospective nonaerospace employers. In total, about three-fifths of aerospace professionals pointed to reemployment barriers involving some aspect of their aerospace background (e.g., lack of other types of experience, bias against ex-aerospace personnel, or lack of cost-consciousness). In fact, the duration of unemployment among such professionals was found to be significantly reduced if one had a previous job outside the aerospace industry (Conner, 1973). Here we see a good example of how a high degree of specialization can actually block the professional's career. It is noteworthy that despite the barriers to finding work in other industries, almost half of the unemployed aerospace professionals said they would reject an offer to return to an aerospace firm and most of the rest would return only under the condition that permanent work was guaranteed (Ware, 1974). Indeed, among those who actually received an aerospace job offer, over half rejected it. Such a reaction is not unique to aerospace engineers. For example, only about one-third of laid-off New York City teachers were willing to return to the school system when openings became available (Goldman, 1977; Shanker, 1977). Job security was the chief reason that the majority of teachers refused to return. Thus it appears that the trauma of mass terminations suffered by professionals creates drastic changes in career committment, with the need for security becoming central in their search for a new position.

The job market for all professionals is subject to the vicissitudes of supply and demand. Hence it would be hazardous to state any conclusions regarding any particular field or area of specialization as a barrier to finding work. Although the market for some fields may be more sensitive to government funding or cyclic recessions, our conclusions in Chapter 1 make it quite clear that most professional occupations will continue to suffer from an oversupply well into the future. This problem will, of course, be exacerbated by periodic recessions.

The Young College Graduate

It may be informative to evaluate briefly the situation of unemployed young college graduates during a recession period. The data we report are from a sample of college graduates in their late 20s who were unemployed and seeking work in the 1970-1971 recession.[6] Among male professionals who attained only a bachelor's degree, 22 percent were out of work over a year compared to 11 percent of master's degree holders and one third of the Ph.D.s. These results are consistent with those of most studies which have found master's degree recipients least likely to experience long-term joblessness. However, the high incidence of long-term joblessness among young Ph.D.s indicates that barriers to their employment were already quite prevalent in the early 1970s. About one-fourth of women professionals were out of work over a year, but this was very likely a result of their concentration in liberal arts and social sciences. In fact, 71 percent of these women had an undergraduate major in the arts, humanities, or social sciences and over one-fourth of the women in these majors were out of work over a year. Among the men, a comparable percentage were jobless more than a year only among those with undergraduate majors in social science, a group that comprised 22 percent of the male sample.

Although the sample sizes were small in each occupation, some indication of the relative difficulty of finding work in different fields can be assessed. As can be seen from Table 5.3, among the males, engineers remained out of work the longest. Men who had worked as technicians also experienced long-term unemployment during this period. These results would reflect the poor market for graduates with a technical background during the 1970–1971 recession. Among those who had been salespersons, most were out of work less than six months, but many also experienced over a year of unemployment. In times of recession, sales positions become popular among the college-educated (Oser, 1975), and the findings may reflect increased competition for such jobs. In fact, one study found that about one-fourth of aerospace professionals unemployed in California during the recession of the early 1970s were reemployed in sales positions—only a third of which were identified as technical sales (Conner, 1973). Relatively few secondary school or college teachers among the males were unemployed over a year, but many had already been out of work more than six months, a portent of the difficul-

TABLE 5.3. Time out of Work and Attitudes toward Reemployment among Young Unemployed College Graduates as a Function of Last Occupation

Sex and Occupation	N	Percentage Out of Work: Less Than 6 Months	Between 6 Months and 1 Year	Over 1 Year	Percentage Reporting Good Prospects to Find Job Fitting Training	Percentage Considering Changing Field or Type of Work
Male						
Engineer	18	50	28	22	17	61
Salesperson	15	60	20	20	53	67
Teacher (secondary)	16	44	50	6	13	38
Teacher (college)	12	50	42	8	25	67
Administrator, manager	9	67	33	0	44	33
Industrial technician	7	43	57	14	0	71
All occupations	181	56	25	19	33	52
Female						
Teacher (elementary)	13	23	39	39	23	31
Teacher (secondary)	10	20	50	30	30	40
Teacher (college)	8	25	50	25	13	50
Social worker	12	42	50	8	42	42
Writer, journalist	8	50	25	25	38	25
Librarian	7	0	71	29	71	43
Administrative assistant	7	45	57	0	29	43
Secretary	7	43	29	29	0	71
All occupations	114	40	37	24	39	46

[a]Based on data from the American Council on Education.

ties that lay ahead in the field of education. Men who had been administrators or managers seem to have had the least difficulty, since most had been unemployed less than six months and none had been out of work for longer than a year.

Among the male graduates, those who had been employed as managers were least likely to consider changing fields and tended to feel that they had good prospects for finding a job appropriate to their training (see Table 5.3). The former sales personnel were also optimistic about their prospects, but most of them were considering changing their work, which may have been temporary to begin with. Few of the engineers or male teachers expected to find a job to fit their training, and with the exception of secondary school teachers, most were considering changing their fields. Faring worst of all among the men were those who had been technicians, none of whom believed they could find a job to fit their training. Most were planning to change the type of work they had been doing. It is very likely that their involvement with the subprofessional work at which they had been employed previously was not very strong to begin with.

In accord with most studies, young women college graduates tended to be out of work longer than males. Despite their generally longer period of unemployment, women were more likely than men to feel that they had good prospects of finding a job that fit their training and were less likely to consider changing fields. This may, in part, reflect the attitudes of married women with home responsibilities, since they had the financial support of their husbands and could more readily afford to wait out a recession until they found the job they desired. In fact, almost half (48 percent) of the women who were out of work over one year attributed their unemployment to involvement with home or child care. Since these women were looking for work, they apparently perceived their domestic role as temporary and continued to maintain their optimism about returning to work. Staying out of work too long, however, may create career reentry problems for women professionals (Kaufman, 1974a).

The time spent out of work among women may also be related to their occupation. As can be seen from Table 5.3, librarians and teachers were most likely to experience long-term unemployment, with many, particularly elementary school teachers, remaining jobless for over a year. Few social workers and no administrative assistants were out of work that long.

The librarians were most optimistic about finding a job fitting their training, although many were considering changing fields. Relatively few of the women college teachers felt that prospects were good and they, too, were considering changing their fields. Those who had worked as secretaries reported that they had no prospects of finding a job appropriate to their training, but most were considering changing their occupation. It is likely that these women had become secretaries because they could not find work that would utilize the knowledge they had acquired in college, but they clearly desired a different type of job.

The women college graduates who had become secretaries may be similar to the men who were working as technicians insofar as both had been underemployed and strongly desired a change in occupation. As discussed in Chapter 1, the problem of the underemployed professional is becoming increasingly prevalent. Settling for underemployment is an attempt to cope with the problem of being out of work and we have more to say about it in later chapters.

Prior Adjustment and Reemployment

It would appear reasonable that adjustment problems prior to job loss could serve as barriers to finding work. Unfortunately, there is very little direct evidence concerning the role of individual differences in adjustment prior to termination on subsequent job search success.

The best way of determining the impact of prior adjustment on reemployment is by collecting data before termination and following up the jobless individuals in a longitudinal study. There is only one study that has done this, but it was carried out with blue-collar workers and investigated only a limited number of individual differences in adjustment prior to termination (Cobb and Kasl, 1977). Nevertheless, that study provides some indication of whether or not prior adjustment can be a barrier to reemployment. For example, general adjustment, as indicated by ego resilience before job loss, was not at all related to the amount of time workers were unemployed or the number of job changes experienced subsequent to termination. Ego resilience, as we saw in Chapter 3, is related to lower levels of stress following job loss. We concluded in Chapter 3 that professionals who had a history of psychological problems prior to unemployment would be more vulnerable to stress following job loss. However, whether preexisting adjustment problems actually affected job-finding success so far has not investigated. Thus it appears that although prior psychological adjustment affects unemployment stress, its impact on reemployment remains to be demonstrated.

There does not seem to be any doubt that some professionals begin their career possessing psychological characteristics, such as passive-dependency, that results in their failure to obtain desired jobs (Stevens, 1972, 1973). Such characteristics are associated with the work inhibition of the long-term unemployed and thus may be reflective of poor adjustment in job-search behavior. Indeed, possessing psychological characteristics associated with work inhibition prior to termination may be related to subsequent reemployment as well as stress. For example, we have noted in Chapter 3 that rigidity affects unemployment stress. In addition, workers who were initially more rigid experienced a greater number of job changes after termination and such rigidity also contributed to a longer period of unemployment—but only for those who received a high degree of social support (Cobb and Kasl, 1977). We can speculate that individuals who lack flexibility prior to termination may be more selective in the type of job they are willing to accept, especially when they receive the social support that permits them to remain out of work until they find the right job. Therefore, rigidity may be both a cause and an effect of long-term joblessness and unemployment stress.

Although it has yet to be demonstrated that psychological adjustment prior to job loss affects reemployment, the evidence is rather clear that physical health can be a major barrier to finding work (Cobb and Kasl, 1977; Ferman, 1979). Poor health occurs more frequently among older workers, as do other barriers to reemployment, such as inadequate education. Such was the case with a 47-year-old quality control engineer who had been out of work over a year after suffering a cerebral hemorrhage and described his experience as follows:

> Although local newspapers have a lot of jobs, these companies don't want to touch people like myself.
>
> They won't take you on and you can't get a reason as to why. Well, there are three things I can think of: I don't have the background, I don't have the degree, or I'm too old. You tell them you had cerebral hemorrhages and enjoyed full recovery, but all they see is cerebral hemorrhage. Recovery is way to heck over here to the side, but they can't even see it. They don't want to take a chance. I don't know what the hell I'm going to do.
>
> I'm running into a big blank wall. I feel that I'm useless, no good to anybody. I realize that that's wrong, but even so I get that feeling. I get into these depressed moods. I don't talk to anybody. It's almost like I was a clam and just closed up and the heck with anybody else who is around. This is wrong, but it's exactly the way I feel because I can't find a decent job. I'm absolutely useless because I can't support my family the way they should be. This is foremost on my mind. The idea that I can't provide the necessities, that the money is not there and that we cannot get my son what he needs, it makes me feel like a dope, like an asshole (Levinson, 1978, p. 289).

Although this man attributes his difficulties to several factors, he seems to feel that his previous health problem was the major barrier to reemployment. In many respects the unemployed who have a history of health problems encounter discrimination barriers similar to those experienced by the handicapped. The case cited above is illustrative of the barriers to reemployment, such as prior health problems, that are beyond the control of the individual and thus serve to create the resignation and withdrawal commonly found among the long-term unemployed.

We have already described in Chapter 3 how job loss can uncover preexisting adjustment problems. Such uncovering may also apply to prior difficulties related to marriage and career. The extent to which problems uncovered by joblessness become barriers to reemployment is virtually unknown. Thus one area of future research is to determine to what degree adjustment problems prior to job loss interfere with finding work.

DIFFERENCES IN INITIATION AND INTENSITY OF THE JOB SEARCH

Unemployed professionals generally go through a time-consuming and often frustrating job search before they find work. However, there are many differences in the way individual professionals approach their search for work. We investigated two such differences: the time of initiation and the intensity of the job search. How such differences facilitate finding work as well as their relationship to psychological characteristics of the unemployed professionals is the focus of our investigation.

Time of Initiation of the Job Search

One obvious approach to help facilitate reemployment is to initiate the job search as early as possible. In fact, our study indicates that professionals who begin looking for a job in anticipation of being out of work may be more successful in finding work. For example, among those who returned to work in their field, 57 percent had begun looking for new jobs before losing their old ones.[7] This was significantly more than the 41 percent of those still unemployed who had begun an early job search. Among the underemployed, 48 percent had been similarly inclined. Moreover, the earlier professionals began to look for work, the shorter was their duration of unemployment ($r = .34, p < .05$), regardless of the type of work they found. This corroborates the results of other research (Dyer, 1973; Gutteridge, 1975; McKenna, 1973; Reid, 1972). In fact, among professionals who found work in their field, those who began their job search earlier tended to end up in positions that were better than the ones they lost ($r = .26, p < .05$).

Although embarking on an early job search appears to facilitate reemployment success, many professionals do not begin to look for work until after they lose their jobs, even when termination in imminent. Indeed, one study of a plant closing found that almost one-half of the white-collar workers did not search for a job before the shutdown, even though they all had received advance notice of their termination (Foltman, 1968). This is not all that surprising if we recall that even after termination actually occurs, many professionals relax for some weeks before they begin to engage in a strenuous search for work.

Differences in personality and motivation may explain why some begin their job search early and others delay it. Among professionals in our study who became reemployed in their own field, those possessing greater self-esteem were more likely to seek work before being terminated ($r = -.28, p < .05$). It could very well be that those with high self-esteem have a strong need to be working in their profession in order to maintain a cognitively consistent self-concept. Thus they begin looking for work as soon as possible.

As for professionals who remained unemployed, those whose desire to find work was most motivated by security needs began looking for work quite early ($r = -.40, p < .01$). For this group, an early job search not only failed to help them find work but it would appear that this lack of success, combined with a strong need for security, was also detrimental to their psychological well-being. In fact, among professionals who remained out of work, those who had begun their job hunt early were more severely affected by their unemployment experience ($r = .37, p < .01$). As one might expect, no such relationship was evident for those who had found work. On the contrary, professionals who were reemployed in their field were more likely to have their lives return to normal the earlier they began their job search ($r = .37, p < .01$). It appears that beginning to look for work prior to job loss can help the adjustment of professionals only if they become reemployed in their field. If they do not find work, having begun the job hunt early could aggravate their sense of frustration and thereby increase their stress.

Intensity of the Job Search

Unemployed professionals in our study who began their job search early also used more methods to look for work ($r = -.51, p < .001$). This certainly makes sense since those who allowed themselves more time to look for work had more opportunities to try a greater variety of job-search methods. However, the evidence is not at all clear as to whether an intense job search is related to reemployment success.

It has been found that among unemployed blue-collar workers, those who have the highest achievement motivation engage in a more intensive job search, as measured by number of job-finding techniques used; and the greater this intensity, particularly among the younger workers, the more likely they were to become reemployed (Sheppard and Belitsky, 1966). The intensity of the job search may be related to the individual's knowledge about the existence of the various job-hunting techniques. In fact, it has been concluded that "for many job-seekers, ignorance about job-seeking techniques is a barrier to success in finding a job" (Sheppard and Belitsky, 1966, p. 215).

With regard to professionals, there is somewhat contradictory evidence concerning the relationship between an intensive job search and reemployment. For example, one study of unemployed engineers and managers found that those who contacted more employers each week experienced a shorter period of joblessness (Dyer, 1973). Similarly, unemployed professionals who carried out a more intense job search, as indicated by the number of résumés sent out or the number of interviews one had, experienced a shorter period of unemployment (Conner, 1973). However, another study found that not only was there no difference in the number of job search methods used between professionals who found work and those who did not, but the more intense the job search, the longer the length of unemployment was likely to be (Gutteridge, 1975). Using a similar measure in our study, we found no difference in the number of job search methods used by professionals who remained unemployed and those who found work. Out of a possible 11 job search methods, the average number used by the unemployed group was 5.6 compared to 5.7 for those who were reemployed, regardless of the nature of their new job. However, we found a positive correlation between intensity of job search and the number of weeks out of work among professionals who became underemployed ($r = .26$, $p < .05$). No such relationship was found for those who did find work in their field. Other research has found that professionals who use more methods to find a job end up with higher salaries (Stang et al., 1976), but in our study the opposite result was found among those reemployed in their field ($r = -.40$, $p < .01$).

Perhaps the most obvious explanation for the discrepancies in results is the differences among, and inadequacies of, the various techniques used to measure job search intensity. First, the number of job search methods used may not be an adequate measure of intensity. One who occasionally uses many methods may engage in a less intensive job search than the person who frequently uses only a few techniques. The professional who contacted many employers directly could have engaged in a more intense but focused job search than those who used many methods. Second, using a rate such as number of employers contacted per week may not be adequate either since those who are out of work the longest are likely to have the lowest average weekly rate of contacts. Hence, the relationship between such a measure of job search intensity and duration of unemployment is likely to be spurious. These examples are sufficient to help explain the discrepancy in the results of different studies.

Although the number of job search methods used may be inadequate as an index of intensity, it nevertheless indicates that there is motivation, or perhaps desperation, to find work. For example, among professionals who found work in their field those who perceived a lack of jobs as a barrier tended to use more job search methods ($r = .26$, $p < .05$), as was the case for those who became underemployed ($r = .39$, $p < .01$).

Regarding professionals reemployed in their field, those who tried more job search methods had a greater drive to return to work in order to satisfy their needs for security ($r = .23$, $p < .05$), self-esteem ($r = .33$, $p < .01$), and self-actualization ($r = .31$, $p < .05$). However, the reemployed professionals who used more methods were also more likely to perceive that their being out of work too long was a barrier to their reemployment ($r = .30$, $p < .05$) and to feel more depressed ($r = .26$, $p < .05$). It may very well be that for professionals who have a strong need to return to work, the use of many different methods to find a job can enhance their chance of reemployment. But having to turn to additional methods may imply a lack of success in finding work by means of methods already used and hence may be detrimental to their psychological well-being by reinforcing their feelings of hopelessness. Thus the more intense the job search, as well as the earlier it is initiated, the greater is unemployment stress likely to be among those who experience difficulty in finding work.

CROSS-CULTURAL COMPARISONS

The paucity of cross-cultural evidence concerning individual differences that serve as barriers or facilitators in finding work among unemployed professionals creates a problem in attempting to arrive at any generalizations. Discrimination as a barrier in hiring, particularly among those who are older, was found in a study carried out in Greece, but it was noted that this bias may have resulted from the existing pension laws, requiring relatively high compensation at the time of termination of employment (Triandis, 1963). Furthermore, many Greek firms had government-approved constitutions specifying the characteristics of those eligible to be hired. Such a "practice essentially institutionalizes discrimination because of race, religion, nationality and age in a manner that is unknown in the United States" (Triandis, 1963, p. 95). Barriers to employment because of either overt or covert discrimination does not exist solely in Western countries. One need only consider anti-Semitism in the Soviet Union (e.g., Freiman, 1979) and ethnic antagonisms in some developing countries to realize that barriers to employment because of official or covert discrimination are practically universal.

Perhaps the only study outside the United States that has attempted to investigate relationships between individual differences among unemployed professionals and their job search is the one carried out in Israel that was discussed previously (Bar-Yosef, Shield, and Varsher, 1976; Bar Yosef and Varsher, 1977). In that study it was found that women and older professionals, as well as liberal arts graduates, encountered greater difficulties in their attempt to find work. Apparently, barriers similar to those found in the United States exist elsewhere.

Furthermore, those who were from eastern Europe reported a longer period of unemployment than either native Israelis or those who came from other countries. Ironically, eastern Europeans generally had not anticipated a problem finding work in their professions, whereas most of the native Israeli job seekers were less optimistic. Such high expectations may help explain, in part, why those who came from the Soviet Union reported that they engaged in a less intensive job search than did others.

Another possible reason for the lower intensity in looking for a job among those of eastern European origin was that they had the least knowledge of the methods used to find work. The native Israelis, as would be expected, were most familiar with the job-hunting methods available. This may help explain why professionals of eastern European origin spent a significantly longer period of time looking for work than did their native Israeli colleagues. It would appear that the amount of knowledge professionals have about the methods available to them for finding a position not only affects the intensity of their job search but also how long it takes them to find employment. This tends to support conclusions arrived at in research carried out in the United States, and thus points to the importance of having a good knowledge of appropriate job search techniques as a facilitator of reemployment, regardless of culture.

The more methods used to search for work by the professionals in Israel, the longer they were likely to have been looking for a job. Moreover, the longer they spent in their job search, the more likely they were to become underemployed. It was suggested that the number of job search methods used was not a measure of intensity but rather of failure to find a job by means of any single method, thereby requiring the use of other methods. This is precisely the explanation we suggested for similar results found in our research. However, the study in Israel did find that the greater the degree to which the methods used to look for work involved personal initiative, the shorter the duration of the job search and the less likely underemployment would occur. Thus the specific job search methods used are apparently more important in finding appropriate work than are the total number of methods tried.

One important characteristic found among the professionals who were seeking work in Israel was that a lack of jobs did not appear to be as important a barrier to reemployment as in the United States. Of those who did experience problems in finding work, most attributed the difficulties to their own attributes involving either inadequacies (e.g., language, professional knowledge, experience) or personal characteristics (e.g., age, sex, immigrant status). Therefore, it would appear that even when a society does not have a lack of professional-level jobs, individual characteristics still remain important as barriers or facilitators in the search for work.

SUMMARY AND CONCLUSIONS

It is quite clear that the major barrier encountered by out-of-work professionals in finding work in their field is the lack of available jobs. Personal inadequacies or barriers attributable to their own situation were less likely to create problems in finding work. However, it appears that the direction of blame may be related to individual differences. Those who attributed their difficulties in finding work to the job market were more likely to be rigid in the type of positions they were willing to accept, as well as to have an external locus of control. Such an orientation may have developed to serve as a defense in protecting the self-image of the long-term unemployed professionals. An opposite orientation tended to characterize those who attributed blame to barriers they themselves created, such as reluctance to relocate. This reluctance may have been possible precisely because these professionals had a greater flexibility toward accepting jobs and felt they were in control of what would happen to them.

Older professionals tended to experience greater barriers in finding work not only because of their age, but also because of associated factors, such as previous high salary, overqualification, and duration of unemployment. However, deficiencies in experience worked against the youngest professionals. Those with more dependents were less willing to relocate, indicating that this barrier would be most prevalent among professionals in their 30s with children in school. Unwillingness to relocate was also a barrier for those who were oldest, apparently because of their more established roots in the community. However, older professionals tended to be more flexible in the salary and type of work they were willing to accept. This flexibility among the older professionals is very likely a result of their greater difficulty in finding work compared to their younger colleagues as well as their reluctance to relocate. Those who perceived age, job scarcity, and their being out of work too long as barriers were more likely to manifest the general unemployment stress syndrome. However, the barriers we investigated did not appear to contribute to either work inhibition or symptoms of the psychopathological stress syndrome. In fact, the work-inhibited tended to perceive fewer barriers.

Discrimination in hiring not only because of age but also because of sex, race, or handicap has been quite prevalent. However, equal employment opportunity legislation and affirmative action programs appear to have resulted in a reduction of barriers in hiring, especially for minority groups. Women may still be encountering discrimination in hiring, particularly those who are older or are reentering the labor market. Worst off appear to be the handicapped, who are generally not protected by the law. With attempts on the part of employers to comply with legal requirements, some reverse discrimination against white males may exist. Regardless of the type of bias, discrimination in hiring can create frustration, anger, and depression and, hence, contributes to the psychological deterioration of the individual.

Family responsibilities did serve as a facilitator of reemployment success. However, for males with greater family responsibilities, a return to work may only be a stopgap measure to provide an income. The need to return to work, regardless of its nature, was not only to attain better security but also apparently to restore the status of the male in his role as breadwinner. Nevertheless, by taking whatever job was available, the professional may be highly vulnerable to new cutbacks and terminations. Single men as well as married women with family responsibilities seem most likely to experience long-term unemployment. Apparently, those who do not need to support others can afford to wait until they find a job they really want.

In general, professionals with more advanced education may have an easier time finding a job. Education can even serve to counteract age as a barrier to reemployment. However, holding a doctoral degree in some fields may turn out to be a barrier to reemployment. Jobless professionals with a Ph.D. may not only be overqualified for most positions but they also may be less flexible in the type of work they are willing to accept because of a strong commitment to their field. Nevertheless, if professionals with advanced education do manage to find work in their field, their new job is likely to be better than the one they lost. For experienced professionals, recency of advanced education may be an important facilitator of finding a job since they would be seen as being more up to date in their field. Indeed, it is the most up-to-date professionals who find the best jobs in terms of skill utilization, regardless of the type of work they find. The vicissitudes of supply and demand affect the job market for any particular profession, hence how such market barriers would affect employment in a specific field is difficult to predict.

Little is known about the effects of adjustment prior to job loss on subsequent reemployment success. However, preexisting psychological characteristics, such as rigidity, do appear to be detrimental to effective job search behavior. Previous health problems do serve as a barrier to finding work, and such problems are more prevalent among older professionals, thereby adding to their reemployment difficulties. However, the extent to which pre-existing adjustment problems that are uncovered by joblessness become barriers to reemployment remains to be demonstrated.

Early job search has definitely been found to be a facilitator of reemployment. Professionals who began their job search prior to becoming unemployed were more likely to have a shorter duration of joblessness and to find a position in their field which was better than their previous one. Those who successfully engage in an early job search tend to be higher in self-esteem. However, beginning to look for work prior to job loss appears to help the adjustment of professionals only if they become successfully reemployed. Otherwise, having begun an early job search could aggravate their sense of frustration and result in increased stress.

Although we found that unemployed professionals who began their job search earlier also used more methods to look for work, the evidence is not at all clear as to whether a more intense job search is related to reemployment success. Rather, it was suggested that intensity of job search was a response to difficulty in finding work, and was stimulated by the motivation to return to work in order to satisfy needs for security, esteem, and self-actualization. Ignorance of job-hunting techniques may be a barrier to success in finding work. Having a knowledge of the available techniques is important since the specific methods used to find work may be more related to reemployment success than is the number of methods used. We turn next to an extensive examination of those job search methods.

NOTES

1. All groups were selected and matched by the methods described in notes 2 and 5 in Chapter 2. A total of 53 underemployed and 54 who were reemployed in their field returned completed questionnaires. The groups were matched on age,

occupation, education, and other salient characteristics. Statistical analyses showed that the groups did not differ significantly in the characteristics used for matching. Both groups that were reemployed (i.e., either in their field or underemployed) experienced somewhat over 11 weeks of joblessness on the average.

2. Barriers to reemployment were measured by the following scales:
How important were the following factors in causing you difficulty in finding a new job?

	Not at All Important		Somewhat Important		Moderately Important		Quite Important		Extremely Important
Inappropriate education	1	2	3	4	5	6	7	8	9
Inappropriate experience	1	2	3	4	5	6	7	8	9
Overqualified	1	2	3	4	5	6	7	8	9
Age	1	2	3	4	5	6	7	8	9
Previous salary too high	1	2	3	4	5	6	7	8	9
Lack of jobs	1	2	3	4	5	6	7	8	9
Unemployed for too long	1	2	3	4	5	6	7	8	9
Reluctant to relocate	1	2	3	4	5	6	7	8	9

3. I am indebted to Jerry Bergman of Bowling Green State University for providing this case study.

4. See Table 7.3 for the items used to rate the new job.

5. Since the professionals in our study who were unemployed, underemployed, or reemployed in their field were matched as closely as possible on educational and occupational characteristics, comparisons among these groups on such factors would not be meaningful. Therefore, in this section we focused primarily on the results of other studies.

6. The data were obtained and analyzed from a survey carried out by the American Council on Education in 1971 from a representative sample of college graduates who had entered college as freshman 10 years earlier (Bisconti and Astin, 1973).

7. The following scale was used to determine when the job search was begun: When did you begin looking for a job?

1. Well before	2. Shortly before	3. At the time	4. Shortly after	5. Well after I became unemployed

CHAPTER SIX

Job Search Methods
Utilization, Effectiveness, and Efficiency

There are numerous ways to look for a job, each of which has unique characteristics. In examining how unemployed professionals attempt to find work, we take a labor economic approach in looking at the utilization, effectiveness, and efficiency of the various job search methods. However, unlike the typical analyses of labor economists, we also investigate how individual differences among professionals may influence their choice of a particular job search method, as well as their success in finding work by means of that method. In order to examine the question of reemployment success, we explore the methods used to find work by professionals in our study who were reemployed in their field in addition to those who became underemployed or who remained jobless.

Utilization, effectiveness, and efficiency of various job search methods were determined using the following definitions:[1]

1. *Utilization* of a job search method is the percentage of respondents who reported that they tried using that method to find a job.

2. *Effectiveness* of a job search method is the percentage of respondents who identified that method as most effective in finding a job.

3. *Efficiency* is a percentage determined by dividing the number of respondents who found their job by means of a particular method by the total number who used that method. Thus, efficiency is essentially effectiveness divided by utilization, and the larger the value the more efficient is the job search method.

The utilization, effectiveness, and efficiency of the job search methods investigated are reported in Table 6.1. Each of these methods is evaluated below.

TABLE 6.1. Percent Utilization, Effectiveness, and Efficiency of Various Job Search Methods

Method	Utilization[a]			Effectiveness[b]		Efficiency[c]	
	Unemployed (N=51)	Underemployed (N=53)	Reemployed in field (N=54)	Underemployed (N=53)	Reemployed in field (N=54)	Underemployed (N=53)	Reemployed in field (N=54)
Direct application to employer	78	79	85	19	23	24	26
Newspaper ads	78	81	74	21	9	28	13
Personal contacts	75	79	72	26	19	33	22
Professional colleagues	65	74	65	11	17	15	23
Friends and relatives	57	66	48	15	2	23	4
Private employment agencies	73	74	70	11	21	15	26
College placement service	33	44	50	8	21	15	41
State Employment Service	49	36	39	2	4	5	10
Professional journals	53	38	59	0	2	0	3
Professional societies	33	19	22	2	2	10	8
Outplacement service of former employer	22	15	15	4	0	25	0
National computer placement service	20	34	26	0	0	0	0
Self-employment	16	19	15	6	0	30	0

[a]Utilization = (number of job seekers using method/total number of job seekers) × 100.
[b]Effectiveness = (number of job seekers reporting method was most effective in finding a job/total number of job seekers) × 100.
[c]Efficiency = (effectiveness/utilization) × 100.

DIRECT APPLICATION TO EMPLOYERS

Unsolicited direct application, typically by sending résumés or contacting prospective employers without being referred by others, was the job search method most utilized by the professionals in our study (Table 6.1). This finding is consistent with the results of other studies (Allen, 1972; Azevedo, 1974; Battelle Memorial Institute, 1971; Bradshaw, 1973; Brown, 1965a; Loomba, 1967; U.S. Department of Labor, 1975a). Among professionals who found work in their field, direct application to employers was clearly the most effective method in obtaining their job, and it was among the most efficient (Table 6.1). Other studies have also found that applying directly to employers generally ranks first or second as the strategy that most frequently leads to a job for professionals (Allen, 1972; Azevedo, 1974; Brown, 1965a,b; Horowitz, 1968; Loomba, 1967; U.S. Department of Labor, 1975a; Thompson, 1972).

Direct application has been found to be particularly effective during periods of high unemployment (Azevedo, 1974), when employers depend more on this source of applicants than on other more formal methods (Malm, 1954). Furthermore, during recessions professionals must exert greater efforts in their job search, which would probably include a more intensive campaign directed at specific employers. However, there is some evidence that when professionals switch jobs voluntarily, relatively fewer find their new jobs through direct applications, although this is still the most frequently used method (Granovetter, 1974; Rosenfeld, 1977). Those job seekers who are working probably do not need to make as intensive an effort to find a job as do the unemployed. Consequently, their job search is likely to be more casual and lacking in an organized campaign to contact employers directly.

Among those in our study who found jobs but were underemployed, direct application ranked second in frequency of use, third in effectiveness, and fourth in efficiency (Table 6.1). But as was the case for those reemployed in their field, direct application turned out to be a highly effective way for persons to obtain a full-time permanent professional-level job outside their field (Table 6.2). Among the underemployed, professionals who were successful in using direct applications, compared to those who found their jobs by other methods, reported that their new job tended to be better on the whole than the one they had lost ($r = .31$, $p < .05$). However, direct application may be less effective for older professionals, who have been found to get a disproportionately larger share of lower-paying jobs using this method as compared with other methods (Dyer, 1972). It could be that age discrimination in placement is more likely to occur if professionals contact employers without being approved or referred by some intermediary such as a personal contact or agency.

Studies of unemployed engineers during the recession of the early 1970s have found that direct application was more effective for obtaining jobs outside their

TABLE 6.2.   Percent Reporting Method Was Most Effective in Finding Various
Types of Underemployment

	Time Allocation/Permanence		Level of Work	
	Part-time and/or Temporary (N=21)	Full-time and Permanent (N=32)	Subprofessional (N=19)	Professional (N=31)
Personal contacts	29	25	21	26
Professional colleagues	10	13	0	16
Friends and relatives	19	13	21	10
Direct application	14	22	11	26
Newspaper ads	29	19	37	16
Private employment agencies	14	9	11	13
College placement service	5	9	0	10
Self-employment	0	9	5	7
State Employment Service	0	3	0	3
Outplacement of former employer	5	3	11	0
Professional societies	5	0	5	0

field than in it (Allen, 1972; Thompson, 1972). This apparently reflects the extreme difficulty of finding work in a field that had suddenly become glutted with a surplus of professionals. Furthermore, R&D professionals who found work through direct application were generally the poorest performers (Thompson, 1972.) It was suggested that the better performers found jobs through other means and hence did not have to resort to strategies such as the mass mailing of résumés.

As for professionals who remained unemployed, our study found that direct application was used more frequently by the professionals who were older ($r = .31$, $p < .05$), had more experience ($r = .26$, $p < .05$), and worked in R&D ($r = .29, p < .05$). Perhaps professionals with greater barriers to reemployment (because of their age and work experience) are more apt to make an effort to contact potential employers directly. Although unemployed R&D professionals tended to use direct applications, such an approach paid off with reemployment in their fields for those who had not previously been working in R&D ($r = -.29$, $p < .05$). Therefore, the efforts unemployed R&D professionals made in a direct application campaign may have been better spent using other job search methods.

This may apply to engineers in general, since they utilize direct applications moreso than other professionals but are less likely than others to find a job in this way (U.S. Department of Labor, 1975a).

Professionals who obtained positions in their field by direct application to employers were less apt to be working in order to satisfy their needs for security ($r = -.23, p < .05$) or esteem ($r = -.36, p < .01$). It may be that the professionals who do not have as strong a need as others to be working can afford the greater effort and time entailed in an organized campaign directed to prospective employers. Such would be the case for many married women. This could explain why female professionals are much more successful finding jobs through direct application than are males (U.S. Department of Labor, 1975a). It is noteworthy that this sex difference does not apply to elementary or high school teachers, who are predominantly women. Although such teachers tend to look for and find their jobs by direct application more often than other professionals, males more frequently obtain their teaching positions in this way than do females (U.S. Department of Labor, 1975a). Very likely it is the younger teachers of either sex who, because of their more limited responsibilities for others, can more easily devote the time and effort necessary to carry out a direct application campaign to schools. This may help explain why many entry- and junior-level faculty also obtain their positions by applying directly to colleges (Brown, 1965a,b; Marshall, 1964). Another reason for this is that educational institutions are more willing to hire the less-experienced teachers who apply directly for positions. As we shall see, senior-level teaching positions typically are filled through other means, such as personal contacts.

Direct application by professionals from minority groups is generally less effective and efficient in finding work than it is for whites (U.S. Department of Labor, 1975a). We have noted that professionals who come from minority groups have a strong need to be working. This may militate against their allocating the great amount of time and effort required to mount an effective direct application campaign. Moreover, as we shall see, minorities prefer using intermediaries such as friends to help them find professional jobs rather than the more impersonal direct application approach. As was suggested in the case of older professionals, discrimination may be more frequent when there is a lack of an appropriate intermediary to establish contact with an employer.

Our evidence indicates that although the most strenuous efforts in using the direct application approach may be among professionals with greater barriers to reemployment, such efforts may pay off more for those who are not so desperate to return to work. It could very well be that applying directly to employers is most effective and efficient when the pressure to return to work is not great and when the individual's background does not serve as an employment barrier. In general, however, direct application to employers does appear to be a highly effective strategy for obtaining professional level jobs either within or outside one's field.

NEWSPAPER ADS

On the whole, almost as many professionals in our study turned to newspaper ads as to direct applications in their quest for work (Table 6.1). Other research also finds that utilization of want ads in newspapers ranks second or third among job search methods available to professionals seeking work (Allen, 1972; Azevedo, 1974; Battelle Memorial Institute, 1971; Bradshaw, 1973; Loomba, 1967; U.S. Department of Labor, 1975a). However, as a means for actually acquiring a job, such want ads have been found to rank, at best, third in effectiveness as well as efficiency (Allen, 1972; Azevedo, 1974; Horowitz, 1968; Loomba, 1967; U.S. Department of Labor, 1975a).

The effectiveness and efficiency of job advertisements for unemployed professionals may depend on the type of work they are seeking or are willing to accept. For those in our study who found jobs in their field, newspaper ads proved fairly ineffective and inefficient (Table 6.1). On the other hand, those who became underemployed not only tended to use newspaper ads more frequently than direct applications, but also found the ads to be more effective and efficient in leading to a job. Compared to jobs found by other means, these placements through ads were likely to lead to subprofessional work that was either temporary or part-time, rather than to permanent professional positions (Table 6.2). Even among the professionals who became underemployed, those who found work through want ads tended to end up with jobs that were lower in salary ($r = -.42, p < .01$) and skill utilization ($r = .38, p < .01$).

Other research also found newspaper ads to be the best source of information about jobs outside a technical professional's field (Allen, 1972), and these ads tended to result in actual placement in such jobs (Thompson, 1972). In fact, almost one-fifth of terminated engineers and scientists who found new jobs through want ads accepted positions that were subprofessional or outside their field (Kaufman, 1980). Moreover, the jobs found via want ads required salary reductions.

Even from the perspective of employers, want ads have been found to be most helpful in filling clerical, sales, and service jobs and least helpful for professional and managerial positions (Walsh, Johnson, and Sugarman, 1975). Since want ads are the only means for announcing job openings by almost half of the employers who use them, they become a major source of information on job availability in a local area. However, it is primarily the larger companies that use want ads, since they have more openings than small employers and are more willing to conduct a widespread geographic search to attract adequate numbers of applicants.

Certain types of professionals appear to depend more on newspaper ads for finding work. The most clear-cut finding in our study was a consistent tendency for older professionals to use newspaper ads regardless of reemployment success. Among the professionals who actually found work in their field, those who did so through newspaper ads were also older ($r = .31$, $p < .05$), and they acquired jobs that were lower in skill utilization ($r = -.30$, $p < .05$). They also felt less up to date in their profession ($r = -.31$, $p < .01$) and reported that they more frequently encountered barriers to reemployment because their salary had been too high ($r = .32$, $p < .05$) or they were overqualified ($r = .28$, $p < .05$). These findings were further reinforced by the results found for the underemployed group. For example, those in this group who found jobs through newspaper ads not only tended to be older ($r = .24$, $p < .05$), but were also out of work longer ($r = .37$, $p < .01$).

Other research tends to substantiate our findings. For example, among older professionals, newspaper ads were not only found to be the most frequently used job search method, but they also resulted in the greatest number of job placements (Dyer, 1972). Furthermore, there is evidence that professionals who find work through answering want ads were more likely to have been among the poorer performers on their previous job (Thompson, 1972) and to have experienced long-term unemployment (Kaufman, 1980). Indeed, the long-term unemployed were likely to turn to ads as a defense against being rejected by employers. This was found to be typical for the male professional who is in stage IV of unemployment:

> He protects his self-esteem by responding mostly to blind ads which ask for applicants to send their résumés, but don't require a personal contact. In this impersonal exchange, no response is the worst thing that can happen. There isn't much of an investment in getting the job—and not much chance of getting it either (Powell and Driscoll, 1973, p. 23).

The ads themselves may also be contributing to problems of placement. For example, the major complaint from job seekers is that ads are often misleading, overstating either the qualifications or the kind of work to be performed (Briar, 1976). In light of such findings it is not difficult to understand why professionals who found their positions through want ads were more highly susceptible to subsequent termination (Shapero, 1969). When professionals, whose employability may already be limited by numerous barriers, find a new position in which their knowledge and skills are grossly mismatched with job requirements, their psychological well-being and performance are likely to suffer. Thus they become prime candidates for termination, which for some may turn into a vicious cycle of job loss and underemployment.

In general, there is consistent evidence that newspaper ads are widely used by professionals to search for work but they are more effective and efficient in helping them find jobs outside their field that leave them underemployed. This may be the reason why Ph.D.s, who tend to be strongly committed to their specialties, use newspapers much less frequently than those with more limited education (Kaufman, 1980; Loomba, 1967). In addition, not only do male professionals use want ads more frequently than do women professionals, but they also find them more effective and efficient (U.S. Department of Labor, 1975a). However, this may result from the fact that the utilization and effectiveness of want ads is greater for engineers and managers, who are generally male, than for noncollege teachers, who are more likely to be female (U.S. Department of Labor, 1975a). Thus it would appear that men turn to newspaper ads to find their jobs more than do women because the professions listed in those ads tend to be male-dominated.

The picture is rather clear that newspaper ads are a primary vehicle through which the more difficult-to-employ older professionals look for and find work. For professionals who have greater reemployment difficulties because of the age barrier, such ads may be useful in finding work outside their field. However, it appears that the jobs they do get may leave them not only highly underutilized with respect to their knowledge and skills, but also underpaid. Even when professionals do find jobs in their field through want ads, they are still likely to end up doing work that is below their capabilities. The fact that these professionals are poorly utilized in their new jobs indicates that they may have lowered their aspirations about the type of work they were willing to take. Indeed, such flexibility among older professionals was noted in Chapter 3. This flexibility, combined with the fact that newspaper ads are a prime source of information about various types of positions that employers actually need to fill, improves the chances that the professional will find a job by responding to these ads. However, by taking work that does not fit one's qualifications or capabilities, a professional may just be creating a situation that will lead to another job loss experience.

PERSONAL CONTACTS

Personal contacts through professional colleagues, friends, and relatives was the third most utilized job search approach found in our study (Table 6.1). This tends to confirm other studies, which have typically found such contacts to rank second or third in frequency of use among job search methods tried by professionals (Allen, 1972; Azevedo, 1974; Battelle Memorial Institute, 1971; Loomba, 1967; U.S. Department of Labor, 1975a). However, one investigation found that among a representative sample of professionals unemployed during the recession of 1970–71, personal contacts ranked in fifth place among all job search methods used (Bradshaw, 1973). As we shall discuss later, when professionals are out of work during recessions, many turn to job search methods that they would not ordinarily use to find a position when they are less desperate. Thus, although the utilization of personal contacts does not necessarily change in absolute terms during recessions, the relative ranking may be lowered because more professionals are forced to try other job search methods.

Those in our study who used personal contacts turned to professional colleagues more frequently than to friends and relatives. This tends to corroborate other research findings (Dyer, 1972). Professional colleagues would be much more likely than friends and relatives to be aware of job openings where they work as well as elsewhere, and may even have entrée to such openings, as we will shortly see.

Research has found that personal contacts typically ranked from first to third place as the most effective means by which professionals obtained their positions (Allen, 1972; Azevedo, 1974; Dyer, 1972; Horowitz, 1968; Kaufman, 1980; Loomba, 1967; U. S. Department of Labor, 1975a; Thompson, 1972), but as low as seventh place in terms of efficiency (U.S. Department of Labor, 1975a). For those in science and engineering occupations, personal contacts have been found to be the most effective way of finding a job, particularly at the places where these contacts are employed (National Science Foundation, 1975a; Kaufman, 1980; U.S. Department of Labor, 1975a). Personal contacts have also been found to be effective for members of minority groups (U.S. Department of Labor, 1975a). Acquaintances may help overcome barriers from discrimination that could be encountered when a direct application approach or more formal job search methods are used.

It was those who performed better in their previous job who tended to find work through personal contacts, since "one would expect a friend or former work associate to be more willing to recommend a high performer for a job than a low performer" (Thompson, 1972, p. 69). Furthermore, professionals who were recruited with the help of personal acquaintances were much less likely to be terminated than those who found the job by some other method (Shapero, 1969). Most employers have indicated a strong preference for personal referrals. This is particularly true with referrals from current employees, since they "usually provide good screening for employers who are satisfied with their present work force. Present employees tend to refer people like themselves, and they may feel that their own reputation is affected by the quality of the referrals" (Rees, 1966, p. 262).

Among employers, family and friends were reported by one study to be the most frequently used source of professional recruitment, particularly during periods of high unemployment (Malm, 1954). However, for the job seeker, friends and relatives have been found to be more effective when unemployment is low (Azevedo, 1974). This is not necessarily a contradiction. We already noted that during recessions professionals are more likely to use a greater variety of job search methods than when positions are plentiful. Thus, even if there is an increased dependency of employers on referrals from friends and relatives during recessions, the likelihood of professionals finding a job through other channels increases during such periods.

For professionals in our study who found work that left them underemployed, personal contacts were clearly the most effective and efficient means of acquiring jobs (Table 6.1). Although they more often turned to professional colleagues, it was family and friends who usually came through with jobs that resulted in underemployment, typically in part-time subprofessional jobs (Table 6.2). However, professional positions in another field were more frequently obtained through colleagues (Table 6.2). Since personal contacts often lead to lower-level types of jobs, it is understandable why professionals without degrees are much more likely to use such contacts (Loomba, 1967). Friends and relatives apparently provide the best leads to these lower-level jobs, with friends being more effective than relatives (U.S. Department of Labor, 1975a). Not surprisingly, both friends and relatives were somewhat more effective in helping to provide jobs where they worked than elsewhere.

For those reemployed in their field, the effectiveness of personal contacts in finding a job ranked only in fourth place, with almost all such jobs obtained through professional colleagues (Table 6.1). Friends and relatives were used much less frequently by professionals reemployed in their field than among those who became underemployed, and few actually obtained work in their field through such personal contacts. The use of colleagues by professionals to find work in their field was just as efficient as having friends and relatives locate a job that resulted in underemployment (Table 6.1). Other research has also found that although friends and relatives, as well as professional colleagues, provide entrée into jobs, the best positions, in terms of utilization and salary, found through personal contacts are obtained with the help of colleagues (Dyer, 1972).

The contacts provided by teachers and professors have also been found to be effective and efficient in helping professionals find work (U. S. Department of Labor, 1975a). Such professional contacts are the most usual channel that Ph.D.s use to find jobs (Solmon, 1978; Solmon and Hurwicz, 1978) and to obtain positions in the academic marketplace (Brown, 1965a; Caplow and McGee, 1958; Marshall, 1964). Although the younger academic job seekers are most likely to consult former professors, having personal contacts in colleges and universities is significantly more important for placement of senior faculty and for positions in the more prestigious schools and departments. The assistance of colleagues is especially important for academics who lose their positions, a common occurrence among nontenured faculty. In fact, about half of those who found positions in educational institutions subsequent to their termination, did so with the help of personal contacts (Kaufman, 1980).

It is interesting that although black educators also tend to find their positions through personal contacts, these are most likely to be friends (Moore and Wagstaff, 1974). It appears that the informal job information network for black professionals depends more on personal friendship than does that of their white colleagues, at least for academic positions. Despite the federal government's call for affirmative action in hiring faculty by expanding recruitment activities beyond the informal network, all indications are that not only does dependence on the colleagial network remain strong, but it can also be effective in the hiring of minorities and women (Marcus, 1977; Solmon, 1978). Thus it appears that under the pressure of affirmative action, minorities and women are becoming part of the informal colleagial network in the hiring of faculty.

Professionals who turn to colleagues in their job search tend to be very different in their personal characteristics from those who focus on friends or relatives. For example, among the underemployed group in our study, those who found work through friends and relatives tended to have fewer dependents ($r = -.25$, $p < .05$) and to be younger ($r = -.25$, $p < .05$), whereas those who obtained their job through professional colleagues had more dependents ($r = .25$, $p < .05$) and pointed to their age more often as a barrier to reemployment ($r = .25, p < .05$). Furthermore, professionals whose friends or relatives helped find them jobs in their field tended to be lower in self-esteem ($r = -.29$, $p < .05$), as well as in decision-making ability ($r = -.23, p < .05$), than did those using other methods. However, professionals who obtained positions in their field from contacts provided by their colleagues were generally higher in self-esteem ($r = .30, p < .05$) and decision-making ability ($r = .24, p < .05$), as well as in initiative ($r = .30$, $p < .05$), than individuals obtaining such reemployment through other means. In addition, they tended not to have worked in R & D ($r = -.43, p < .01$), aerospace ($r = -.39, p < .01$) or defense work ($r = -.35$, $p < .01$), possibly indicating that even professional colleagues have limited usefulness in obtaining certain types of jobs during periods when such jobs are extremely difficult to find.

It appears that, in general, professionals who find work through their colleagues are older and have more positive motivation and personality characteristics than do those whose friends and relatives help them find a job. Moreover, these older professionals may be superior to their contemporaries who are more likely to be reemployed through newspaper ads. Younger professionals, with fewer years of work experience, have had more limited opportunities to develop useful contacts among colleagues, and it is understandable that they should turn to friends and relatives. They are also likely to be in lower-level positions and thus more open to the kinds of jobs that friends and relatives can typically provide. This might also be true of those possessing lower motivation and less positive personality traits. In particular, their self-concept may be related to the status of their personal contacts. What is being suggested is that those with a more positive self-concept seek out higher-status professional colleagues for help. Those with lower self-esteem may feel more comfortable with friends and relatives and hence turn to them for assistance. Professional acquaintances generally lead to better jobs than do friends and relatives, but this may result in part from the likelihood that those who find jobs through their colleagues have superior qualities to begin with.

PRIVATE EMPLOYMENT AGENCIES

Private employment agencies, which have long been available as a formal method of job placement (Martinez, 1976), were found in our study to be the fourth most utilized job search method (Table 6.1). This is in accord with the results generally found in other investigations (Allen, 1972; Azevedo, 1974; Bradshaw, 1973; Loomba, 1967; U.S. Department of Labor, 1975b). Such agencies are more likely to be utilized by the most highly educated and less likely by professionals without a degree (Loomba, 1967; U.S. Department of Labor, 1975a). This is understandable in light of the fact that employers use private employment agencies much more extensively to recruit higher-level personnel than other workers (Bureau of National Affairs, 1969). Many firms apparently find it desirable to have applicants for high-level positions screened by such agencies. This practice is much more prevalent among smaller firms, since they lack the extensive recruiting and hiring staff maintained by the larger companies. While private agencies tend to be utilized to a greater degree by the highly educated, they are more likely to place those with less education and a more limited professional orientation (Kaufman, 1980). The reasons for this are probably related to the inadequacies of private employment agencies, an issue that is discussed later.

Private employment agencies are apparently more effective and efficient in placing professionals in their own fields than outside them. As indicated in Table 6.1, such agencies fall just behind direct applications as the method by which professionals reemployed in their own field acquired their jobs. Private agencies also rank second in efficiency for this group. Although at least one other study has also found that private employment agencies were effective in placing professionals in their field (Thompson, 1972), research generally finds that they rank, at best, in third or fourth place in overall effectiveness and even lower in efficiency (Allen, 1972; Azevedo, 1974; Horowitz, 1968; Kaufman, 1980; Loomba, 1967; U.S. Department of Labor, 1975a). In fact, for older unemployed professionals, private employment agencies were found to be the third most frequently used method in their job search, but few actually obtained positions through such agencies (Dyer, 1972).

The discrepancies between the results we reported and those found in other studies may, in part, be a result of geographic differences in the availability and effectiveness of private employment agencies. Our data are based on a sample obtained in the New York metropolitan area, which has the most extensive network of private employment agencies in the United States (U.S. Department of Commerce, 1970). The other studies were carried out either nationwide or in California and Boston, where fewer such agencies exist. Indeed, reemployment of terminated technical professionals via private employment agencies was most predominant in the mid-Atlantic states, which include New York (Kaufman, 1980). Another explanation for the discrepancy is that many of those in our sample were engineers. A nationwide survey has found that when engineers look for work, private employment agencies rank second as the method used and third in effectiveness (U.S. Department of Labor, 1975a). This, plus the fact that our sample was from the New York metropolitan area, very likely accounted for the differences between our results and findings from other studies.

For those in our study who became underemployed (typically in nonengineering jobs), private employment agencies ranked only fourth in effectiveness and even lower in efficiency, which is more comparable to the results of other studies. In any case, professionals who used a private employment agency to find jobs that left them underemployed tended to have begun their search later than those using other methods ($r = .29$, $p < .05$). The underemployed who found their jobs through private employment agencies perceived that they had several barriers to reemployment, including being overqualified ($r = .27$, $p < .05$), overpriced ($r = .28$, $p < .05$), and out of work too long ($r = .53$, $p < .001$). Apparently, those who experienced greater difficulties in finding work turned to the private employment agencies to obtain jobs regardless of their nature.

Professionals who found work in their own field by using private employment agencies also felt that having been unemployed too long was a barrier to finding a job ($r = .38$, $p < .01$), and they tended to have less initiative ($r = -.28$, $p < .05$). In general, relatively few professionals use private employment agencies during the initial period of their unemployment. However, at a later stage, when they begin to realize that they are unable to find a job through their own efforts, they are likely to turn to the assistance of a private agency. Similarly, professionals who are searching for work while they are employed, and therefore are not so desperately in need of a job, are much less likely to use private agencies than are those who are unemployed (Bradshaw, 1973; Rosenfeld, 1977). In addition, those professionals who have lower initiative may depend less on their own efforts to find work in their field and thus would be quite willing for a private employment agency to take on the responsibility of placing them in a job.

Other evidence indicates that private agencies are more likely to be used by professionals who come from minority groups, but such agencies are more effective and efficient in finding jobs for white males than for women or minorities (U.S. Department of Labor, 1975a). The most obvious explanation for this is that women and minorities have not yet acquired the experience necessary for the managerial or technical positions available from private employment agencies. However, discriminatory practices were not found to be unusual in private employment agencies (Johnson, 1973). Thus, there still may be some race or sex discrimination in the screening practices among some private agencies that would make them less attractive for minorities and women to use in their job search.

There have been numerous inadequacies identified in the services provided by private employment agencies. Although such agencies charge fees that are paid by either the job seeker or the employer, personnel managers report that employees hired through these agencies are not better qualified than those recruited through other sources (Dennis and Gustafson, 1973). Moreover, personnel managers feel that private agencies are not only more expensive than other recruiting services but also that they do not adequately screen or counsel their clients. Such inadequacies in screening or counseling may explain why professionals who acquire their jobs through such agencies may be more highly susceptible to termination (Shapero, 1969; Kaufman, 1980). Nevertheless, many employers do indicate satisfaction with private employment agencies, particularly those that serve the specialized needs of their clients (Rees, 1966).

Another criticism leveled against private employment agencies is the way in which they use newspaper advertising to acquire pools of job applicants. Many of these ads have been found to be for jobs that were either not available or nonexistent (Cerra, 1977). In fact, one study showed that among professionals who contacted agencies in response to an ad, not one "experienced a positive response from the agent concerning his chances of obtaining the job advertised" (Martinez, 1976, p. 126). Reportedly typical of such encounters was the experience of a 23-year-old black applicant:

> I asked about that particular job (junior accountant), but the interviewer never answered me about that particular job. He tried to line me up. First, he said I didn't have education qualifications. By the ad in the paper I did, but when I got down there I didn't. He asked me if I was interested in being a field representative, which was just a fancy name, but all it was was knocking on people's doors asking them to pay their bills (Martinez, 1976, p. 126).

In defense of the private employment agency that advertises such a position, investigations have found that the position was usually either filled from within by the employer or that it was listed with several agencies, one of whom had already filled it (Cerra, 1977).

Probably the most damning evidence against many private employment agencies concerns the possible psychological damage they may inflict on applicants. A study of such agencies described this process:

> Individual agents vary in method, but the goal is always the same: to instill in the applicant a sense of dependency in order to control him. The degree of dependency is measured by the extent of compliance. In my agency, the process even had a name "conditioning." The agent seeks (1) to establish his authority and (2) manipulate, or at least profoundly influence, the applicant's image of himself. The agent must accomplish both of these goals; if he does not, he cannot properly control the applicant.

> Probably the most important factor that influences conditioning is brought to the agency by the applicant himself: his self-image, his belief in what he is and what he is worth. Most of the applicants at my agency were professional and technical workers with a lot of formal training. They therefore tended to regard themselves highly

and to consider their skills valuable. They would not take just any position. They strongly resisted such ideas as a possible cut in pay or moving to another city. So the agent's first job was to psychologically cut these applicants down to size . . .

One very successful agent specialized in placing highly trained structural engineers and designers. Yet he would systematically tear down each new applicant, ripping apart his self-image piece by piece. Applicants often became angry, voices rose and politeness disappeared. But after the applicant was sufficiently frustrated and depressed, the agent would indicate that there might still be hope—and start to put the image back together again into a more acceptable, controllable form. In effect he said: ''You aren't worth much to industry, but I may be able to do something for you anyway.'' For him this approach worked, and he wouldn't change it. He said that he couldn't afford to ''lose a placement'' (have an applicant refuse a job offer) because of inadequate conditioning (Martinez, 1976, pp. 110–112).

Professionals whose self-esteem is most vulnerable are those who turn to an agency after having exhausted other available means of getting a job. These have been called the frustrated applicants, who typically have the following experience:

The greatest blow to self-esteem is felt by frustrated applicants. It is characteristic of the frustrated applicant to harbor a self-image of self-reliance, which partially accounts for his personal attempts to find a job, before turning to an agency. It is usually this aspect of the self that suffers the most damage among frustrated applicants. A process of redefining has already started when the frustrated job-seeker decides to become a frustrated applicant.

The frustrated applicant's self-esteem is quite damaged from fruitless job-searching before he goes to the agency. Once inside the agency, the agent often tries to enhance the frustration in order to let the applicant know that his frustration is both recognizable and perhaps justified. This is done in order to seize control over the applicant quickly, since it is often necessary to try to ''counsel'' the frustrated applicant into accepting another kind of job in a more accessible line of work (Martinez, 1976, pp. 118–119).

It should be obvious that not all private employment agencies are culpable of the practices described above. Some, in fact, do provide a useful service for certain professionals, particularly in specialized job markets (Rees, 1966). For example, in the academic marketplace, commercial agencies that specialize in college faculty appear attractive to teachers who are difficult to place since ''there is a tendency in most fields for only the weakest candidates to use the services of a placement agency'' (Caplow and McGee, 1958, p. 121). Furthermore, there is evidence that some faculty positions are filled with the help of commercial agencies, which tend to be used by smaller colleges (Marshall, 1964). Although relatively few academicians use commercial teachers agencies—primarily because they are considered either worthless or unprofessional—many of those who do are successfully placed in faculty positions at poorer-quality schools (Brown, 1965a). Thus, such agencies may be highly effective, particularly in the placement of weaker candidates in the less attractive academic positions.

As we already noted, private employment agencies were relatively effective and efficient in finding work for technical professionals who were terminated. Moreover, the jobs in which such professionals were placed appear to be relatively good ones. For example, the new positions were relatively high on utilization, requiring minimal change in occupation or specialization, and the salaries were considerably higher than in their terminated jobs (Kaufman, 1980). However, the agency placements more often required relocation and, as was already noted, were less secure than jobs found through other methods.

In general, private employment agencies have many drawbacks because they operate on a financial incentive to place people in jobs rapidly, often without regard for adequate matching of applicants with positions. It appears that despite their limitations, some private agencies do provide effective assistance to certain professionals. These include individuals who have encountered greater difficulty in finding work, particularly in specific fields such as teaching and engineering. Thus for those who need to use the services of a private employment agency, the caveat would be to select one with great caution.

COLLEGE PLACEMENT OFFICES

Colleges and universities typically offer job placement services to their graduating students and alumni. As can be seen from Table 6.1, many, but not most, of the unemployed professionals in our study took advantage of their college placement office. Relative to other job search methods, the college placement office ranked seventh, eighth, and ninth, respectively, in frequency of use by professionals reemployed in their field, those who found work that left them underemployed, and the group that remained unemployed. The few studies that have included college placement offices in their lists of job search methods used by unemployed professionals have come up with comparable rankings (Allen, 1972; Azevedo, 1974). However, a nationwide study of job seekers, which also included new entrants into the labor market, found that the school placement office ranked fourth among the methods most frequently used by professionals to find work (U.S. Department of Labor, 1975a).

It was the youngest professionals in our study who most frequently used the college placement office. This inverse relationship with age was strongest for those reemployed in their field ($r = -.48, p < .001$), somewhat less for the underemployed ($r = -.35, p < .01$), and lowest for those remaining unemployed ($r = -.27, p < .05$). Similar relationships were found for work experience. It would appear that those who had earned their degrees recently were more likely to maintain contact with their college than were those who had been out of school for many years. However, difficulty in finding work may bring back some of the older alumni to their college placement office. This could explain the somewhat weaker relationship found in use of this method among younger compared to older professionals in our study who remained jobless.

There was a clear tendency for those who were out of work longest to seek assistance from their college placement office, particularly among professionals who remained unemployed ($r = .38, p < .01$) and who became underemployed ($r = .41, p < .01$). It would appear that alumni turn to their college placement office when other job search methods prove unsuccessful. Interestingly, of all the professionals who returned to work, it was those who scored highest in decision-making ability who most often made use of their college placement office ($r = .28, p < .05$), regardless of the type of job they obtained. These professionals tend to consider carefully all aspects of their situation before coming to a decision. Apparently, this decision-making approach led them to their college placement office.

Once professionals turned to their college placement office, they experienced very positive results. In fact, this method was tied for second place with private employment agencies for effectiveness in finding a job among those who returned to work in their field (Table 6.1). Furthermore, it was clearly the most efficient method for those professionals.[2] Two-fifths of those who used their college placement service actually found a job in their field through its assistance, well above the efficiency of any other method. As would be expected, it was those with less work experience who were more likely to find jobs in their fields through the college placement office than through other methods ($r = -.39, p < .01$).

Other studies have generally found that as a method for actually finding a job, the college placement office ranks between second and sixth place (Allen, 1972; Azevedo, 1974; U.S. Department of Labor, 1975a). In line with this range of results, college placement ranked fifth in effectiveness for those in our study who became underemployed (Table 6.1). These professionals also found this method to be relatively inefficient.

Among the underemployed, it was clearly the youngest who found the college placement service most effective in finding them work ($r = -.47, p < .001$). Moreover, those in this group who used the placement office at their college pointed to their inappropriate experience as a barrier to reemployment ($r = .39, p < .01$). Despite the lack of experience of these recent graduates, all who found work outside their fields through their college placement offices were able to obtain professional-level positions (Table 6.2). It is noteworthy that a study of unemployed aerospace professionals found that the college placement office was most effective in providing jobs outside their field (Allen, 1972). Although this may have been a result of the professionals' aerospace background (for which there was only a limited market at the time of that study), other research has revealed that career change and underemployment is prevalent among the positions found by terminated scientists and engineers through college placement (Kaufman, 1980).

Jobs found via college placement that resulted in underemployment provided higher salary increases than did similar types of jobs that were found by other means ($r = .27$, $p < .05$). This has been corroborated by other research (Kaufman, 1980). However, there is a high likelihood that recent graduates had been working in entry-level jobs which paid low salaries and, when reemployed, they were able to receive relatively higher increases in pay than were their older, more experienced colleagues.

The evidence tends to favor college placement services as a means by which recent graduates can find work. Large companies use college recruiting more frequently and more successfully than other methods for hiring employees with degrees (Bureau of National Affairs, 1969). In fact, not only do firms hire more college graduates through school placement offices than all other recruiting sources combined, but they also feel that the placement offices on campus are the best sources for young professionals (Dennis and Gustafson, 1973). A high degree of success in matching the best applicants with appropriate jobs could explain why professionals whose positions were obtained through their college placement office are less likely to experience termination. (Kaufman, 1980). However, when professionals find reemployment in this manner following termination, the likelihood of their becoming unemployed again is about the same as the overall average rate.

Elementary and secondary school teachers are much more likely than other professionals to use their college placement office, and for them it ranks behind direct contacts in effectiveness for finding a job (U.S. Department of Labor, 1975a). It is especially effective for female teachers. College faculty, particularly those with education degrees, have also been found to use their school's placement office, which for academic positions has been reported to be only slightly better than using a private placement agency (Brown, 1965a; Caplow and McGee, 1958). This has been attributed to the fact that the college placement offices "are mostly patronized by aspirants with degrees in education, a discipline, which, in the view of many academic men, occupies a special Siberia of its own" (Caplow and McGee, 1958, p. 121).

Other research has also indicated that terminated scientists and engineers who found reemployment through their college placement office were more likely to be young females and have experienced long-term joblessness (Kaufman, 1980). Furthermore, of those scientists and engineers who found positions in educational institutions, almost three-tenths did so via their college placement office.

Despite the efficiency and effectiveness of college placement offices found in our study, their use by unemployed alumni remains relatively limited, and those who do turn to them tend to be the younger, less experienced graduates or the professionals for whom other job search methods have not worked. It remains to be seen whether college placement offices can respond effectively if larger numbers of unemployed alumni, particularly those who are older and more experienced, begin to use their services.

STATE EMPLOYMENT SERVICES

Professional placement offices that operate within the State Employment Service were first established on a pilot basis in 1952 (Adams, 1969). From an initial experimental program in five cities, a professional office network was expanded to 109 centers by 1960. Placement services for specific professional groups, such as teachers, were also initiated.

Despite the availability of professional placement assistance at no cost, most of those in our study did not take advantage of the State Employment Service, which ranked sixth or seventh in utilization (Table 6.1). Other studies have found such assistance to rank between third and seventh among job search methods utilized by professionals (Azevedo, 1974; Bradshaw, 1973; Dyer, 1972; Loomba, 1967; U.S. Department of Labor, 1975a). As in the case of private employment agencies, certain professionals, such as engineers, are more likely to turn to the assistance of the Public Employment Service (U.S. Department of Labor, 1975a).

State professional placement services appear to be utilized more by those who have difficulty finding a job (Table 6.1). The more the professionals in our study perceived a lack of jobs as a major barrier to their reemployment, the more likely they were to use the Employment Service, and this was most evident for those who remained unemployed ($r = .32, p < .05$). In fact, we found that use of such services reaches a peak among those who have been out of work for over half a year. These professionals may be assumed to have tried other methods and, after repeated failure, turned to the Employment Service as a last resort. Indeed, professional placement help from the state was perceived as one of the least probable paths to locating a job among all groups in our study, regardless of reemployment success. This may help explain why so few professionals use the Employment Service to look for work while they have a job (Rosenfeld, 1977) and are presumably not so desperate in finding a new one.

Among those in our study who were reemployed, few actually found their job through the Employment Service, and therefore, the method also ranked low in efficiency (Table 6.1). These results have been corroborated by other studies (Azevedo, 1974; Brown, 1965a,b; Dyer, 1972; Horowitz, 1968; U.S. Department of Labor, 1975a).

A somewhat limited picture of the types of jobs professionals find through the State Employment Service is available from a longitudinal study we carried out with the National Sample of Scientists and Engineers (Kaufman, 1980). These professionals had been terminated at some time between 1969 and 1972, and therefore, most were looking for work during a recession. The positions they found through the Employment Service resulted in a salary decrease relative to the job they lost. Moreover, one-fourth of the placements were not in professional-level positions in science or engineering, the highest rate of underemployment resulting from use of any of the formal job search methods. Most of those underemployed acquired jobs as technicians or as clerical, sales, or blue-collar workers. It seems clear that many of the placements found by professionals through the Employment Service left them both underpaid and underutilized.

The poor success of the Employment Service in professional placement can be understood if examined from the perspective of employers. Although the larger employers tend to use the Employment Service, professional-level jobs are highly underrepresented in the openings they list (Camil Associates, 1976). The greater likelihood of finding a lower-level job may be the reason why professionals with the least education tend to turn to public job placement services (Loomba, 1967). Employers have been quite reluctant to list professional job openings with the Employment Service or hire professional applicants who were referred by such public agencies (Thompson, 1972). Some studies have concluded that employers avoid hiring professionals referred by the Employment Service, since they view such applicants as inferior to those from other sources (Allen, 1972; Roderick, 1970). Indeed, firms who use the Employment Service find that it is much less satisfactory than even private employment agencies (Rees, 1966).

Although only a few professionals may be ignorant of the Employment Service's assistance in finding jobs (Brown, 1965b; Katz, Gutek, Kahn, and Barton, 1975), almost all appear to be aware of its inadequacies. Thus they do not seek out the professional placement assistance provided by the Employment Service even when they are out of work, although such help is available at no cost. Even in cases where the Employment Service's assistance has been sought, many would not use it again primarily because of the poor treatment they received (Camil Associates, 1976). An example of such treatment is the following experience reported by a female professional:

> There must be something wrong with the system. I recently lost a very good job in the managerial circulation field because of the sale of my company. When I reported to the local employment office, I was given a date of a few days later to appear at the professional placement center. This is as it should be.
>
> However, when I reported, the receptionist stamped the card and advised that my next reporting date would be approximately three months hence. It was not possible to be interviewed; I could not even leave a résumé. This is a most discouraging situation for a bona fide job seeker.
>
> It seems to indicate that the State Employment Service is not functioning for the professional-level applicant. If someone were to place a job offer for an administra-

tive spot in circulation or related areas, nobody would have any information about who might be available. This system is really not helping the employee or the employer. There must be a better way to bring applicant and employer together (Silverman, 1977, p. A20).

It seems clear that the Employment Service is neither very effective nor very efficient in placing professionals in jobs of any type. Despite limitations such as those described above, the widespread availability of professional placement offices in the Employment Service indicates a potential that has yet to be effectively utilized. This potential is discussed in greater depth in Chapters 8 and 9.

PROFESSIONAL SOCIETIES AND JOURNALS

Frequently, professional societies provide job search assistance to their members. Such assistance is typically available at professional meetings, where employers can interview prospective candidates, or in professional society publications, which list position openings as well as job seekers. Attempts to provide such assistance became widespread during the Great Depression (Kotschnig, 1937). By the early 1960s at least 112 professional associations provided placement services (U.S. Office of Education, 1961).

Those in our study utilized professional journals to a much greater degree than the societies themselves, which ranked near the bottom of all the job search methods investigated (Table 6.1). Similar results have been reported by others (Allen, 1972; Azevedo, 1974; Loomba, 1967). However, for some professionals, such as college teachers, the professional societies rank relatively higher as a method used to search for work (Brown, 1965a,b). On the other hand, advertisements in journals appear to be a good source of employment information for technical professionals (Hoyt, 1962; U.S. Department of Labor, 1975a).

Professional journals were most frequently used by those in our study who had attained a higher level of education, and this was consistent for all groups regardless of reemployment experience ($r = .24$, $p < .05$ for the unemployed; $r = .23$, $p < .05$ for the underemployed; and $r = .33$, $p < .01$ for those reemployed in their field). This corroborates other research which found that professionals with higher levels of education (especially Ph.D.s) make more use of their journals, as well as societies, to find work than do those with less education (Loomba, 1967).

Interestingly, we found that the number of journals professionals read was more strongly related to their utilization of professional societies in their search for work than it was to the utilization of the journals themselves. This was consistent for all three groups. For example, among those reemployed in their field, the correlation between the number of journals read and the utilization of societies was higher ($r = .41$, $p < .01$) than that with the utilization of journals ($r = .26$, $p < .05$). This may indicate that the most professionally oriented are more likely to use their societies to find work. We have other data to support this. For instance, those among the unemployed who turned to their professional societies for assistance tended to have had more published papers ($r = .28$, $p < .05$) and patents ($r = .45$, $p .01$), as well as to have attended a greater number of short courses ($r = .35$, $p < .05$) and professional meetings ($r = .38$, $p < .01$). No such relationships were found with utilization of professional journals. Even among college teachers, who typically possess Ph.D.s, it is the more professionally oriented who tend to utilize their associations to find a position (Brown, 1965a).

Despite the use of professional societies or journals by those in our study, few actually found work through them (Table 6.1). This corroborates the findings of others (Allen, 1972; Azevedo, 1974; Brown, 1965a; Loomba, 1967; U.S. Department of Labor, 1975a). Although professional societies may be less effective than journals (Azevedo, 1974), they appear to be more efficient (Allen, 1972; Loomba, 1967). Interestingly, there is some indication that ads in professional journals may be more effective during periods of low unemployment (Azevedo, 1974). It is likely that during such periods, employers are more dependent on advertising to fill vacancies. However, when professionals are searching in a difficult job market, the work they find through journals may be in other fields and subprofessional in nature (Allen, 1972).

Many professional societies attract those with advanced education to their placement services because they list academic positions requiring a doctorate. Indeed, jobless professionals who are reemployed with the help of so-called "slave markets"—the formal placement activities organized at regional or national professional society meetings—are more highly educated than are those acquiring their positions by other means (Kaufman, 1980). However, the limited evidence indicates that professional societies play a relatively small role even in academic placement, helping only about five percent of college teachers to secure a faculty position (Brown, 1965a). In a nationwide survey, comparable percentages of biologists, psychologists, and social scientists, who typically have Ph.D.s, found a position through their professional society (National Science Foundation, 1975a). Yet there is clear evidence that the positions found by job losers through their professional society meetings were more likely to be in educational institutions than in any other type of organization (Kaufman, 1980). Professionals who find positions through such placement services may be relatively secure since they were not as likely to be terminated as those who used most o ther methods to find a job (Kaufman, 1980). However, this greater security may come at the cost of having to relocate.

Although playing a relatively small role in the academic job market as a whole, placement services of professional associations that are separate from those at conventions and journal ads may be a significant factor in the market for experienced college faculty, particularly those at the full-professor level (Brown, 1965a). Senior-level college teaching positions were somewhat less likely to be found through professional journal ads (Brown, 1965a), but the effectiveness of such ads appears to depend greatly on the particular academic discipline (Marshall, 1964).

It is the "slave markets" at professional meetings that attract students and recent Ph.D.s to apply for the predominantly entry- and junior-level positions that are listed (Brown, 1965a; Stang, McKenna, Kessler, Russell, Sweet, Rosenfeld, Peleg, and Kafton, 1976). Thus the relatively small number of placements made at the "slave markets" are primarily in vacancies at the instructor and assistant professor levels, but these tend to be in the higher-quality schools (Brown, 1965a). Although such academic placements were reported to be superior to those of both private and college placement services (Caplow and McGee, 1958), the informal contacts established at professional meetings have been found to be among the best methods of securing a college teaching position (Marshall, 1964).

Although the placement services provided at professional meetings appear most useful to the younger, more recent graduates, some older professionals also use them. However, there is evidence that among academic psychologists who find their jobs through professional meetings, the older job seekers are more likely to be placed in the less prestigious positions (Stang, 1976; Stang et al., 1976). Although older candidates may have weaker qualifications, it could also be possible that, because of the preponderance of junior-level vacancies listed at such meetings, there is a bias toward youth. This bias may preclude experienced academicians from employment in the more prestigious positions.

The older academician is not the only one who may encounter bias at professional meetings. It was found that women psychologists who secured academic placements by using the services provided at a professional meeting were less likely to receive a position that represented a promotion than were men (Stang et al., 1976). It could be that despite the establishment of affirmative action programs in institutions of higher education at the time of a shrinking job market, the charge of "reverse discrimination" may not be as widespread in placements at professional meetings as some believe.

In Chapter 3 we demonstrated that those unemployed who attended more professional meetings were much less likely to be work inhibited. Although these unemployed may be more professionally oriented to begin with, it may very well be that it is the informal contacts made at their society meetings that help sustain a motivation to work. Professional meetings can provide social support which may also open channels to securing a position. In fact, there is evidence that merely attempting to find a job by actively participating in placement activities at professional meetings may serve to relieve stress (Levy, 1977). It would appear that such meetings provide an opportunity to obtain job contacts and social support from colleagues, particularly those sharing similar employment problems, thereby helping professionals cope more effectively with their unemployment. However, with regard to the more formal activities of professional societies, one can only conclude that they generally are not providing adequate job placement assistance to the majority of their members who are seeking work.

OUTPLACEMENT SERVICES OF THE PREVIOUS EMPLOYER

Some employers provide outplacement services to assist their terminated personnel in finding work elsewhere, a practice that became common with the mass dismissals of professionals during the 1970s. However, relatively few professionals in our study utilized such services (Table 6.1). This tends to corroborate the results found by others (Allen, 1972; Azevedo, 1974; Battelle Memorial Institute, 1971; Loomba, 1967). Outplacement services did not appear to be very effective for the professionals in our study, as few found work through this method.

The fact that so few professionals use outplacement services probably reflects the limited availability of such employer-sponsored services. Although surveys indicate that a majority of companies that have terminated employees for economic reasons reported offering some type of outplacement services, these services may be quite informal and provide only limited assistance (Miner, 1978).

More formal and extensive services would be expected in industries such as defense and aerospace, which have experienced cyclic mass terminations of their professionals. However, most terminated aerospace workers reported that no such services were provided by their company (Battelle Memorial Institute, 1971). Nevertheless, when aerospace firms did set up outplacement services, their utilization was relatively high (Allen, 1972; Battelle Memorial Institute, 1971). Professionals in our study who did use such services tended to have been employed in R&D or defense work. This was especially evident among those reemployed in their field ($r = .32, p < .05$). Moreover, terminated defense and aerospace professionals seem to have fared somewhat better than others in their use of outplacement services. For these professionals, studies have found that outplacement ranked between third and fifth place in effectiveness as well as efficiency (Allen, 1972; Loomba, 1967; Rollins, 1970). Outplacement in aerospace firms was useful to over one-fifth of workers who used such services (Battelle Memorial Institute, 1971), and appeared to be particularly effective for finding work in a professional's own field (Allen, 1972). For professionals from nonaerospace industries, however, outplacement services rank near the bottom among job search methods that lead to reemployment, which is in accord with our results.

Despite the fact that few unemployed professionals find their jobs through outplacement, such services do appear to be somewhat more effective during periods of high unemployment (Azevedo, 1974). During such periods, more vigorous employer efforts to place terminated personnel would be expected. With an increasing number of civil service professionals losing their jobs in a difficult job market, outplacement services have been established at the local government level, such as New York City's Job Referral Center (Gerston, 1974). This even occurred at the highest levels in Washington, where for the first time a "job bank" was established in the White House by the outgoing Ford administration to assist staff members in finding positions (Shabecoff, 1976).

Although most employers who have had separations because of economic reasons claim to provide outplacement services, their success in helping terminated professionals find work appears to be quite limited. Nevertheless, when there is employer commitment to serious job search assistance, outplacement would appear to have the potential of being effective and efficient in attaining reemployment. It is a hopeful sign that employers have begun to accept responsibility for providing job search assistance to their terminated employees. Some employers who lack the appropriate personnel resources have even hired outplacement consultants. The services provided by such consultants may be useful in helping the victims of mass terminations not only to find work but also in their overall adjustment, as we shall see in a more extensive analysis of outplacement in Chapter 8.

NATIONAL COMPUTER PLACEMENT SERVICES

Computerized services which attempt to match professional applicants with appropriate jobs were first developed during the 1960s. Private employment agencies pioneered such services, with fees charged to their clients (Dear, 1970). By the onset of the recession of the early 1970s, noncommercial systems had already been developed for use by professionals. The most ambitious of these systems attempted to carry out computer matching on a national basis. One was the National Registry for Engineers supported by the U.S. Department of Labor and administered by the California Department of Human Resources Development in cooperation with several professional societies. The National Registry was created primarily for unemployed technical professionals. Another system, the Grad computerized résumé service, was sponsored by the College Placement Council to tie together the college placement offices throughout the country for use by their alumni. Despite the fact that such computer placement services were available at no cost, relatively few unemployed professionals in our study actually made use of them (Table 6.1). This has been found to be true in other studies as well (Allen, 1972; Azevedo, 1974).

Professionals who use computer placement services often do so after other methods have proven unsuccessful. Among professionals in our study who had not found a job, those who experienced long-term unemployment were more likely to turn to computer placement ($r = .41, p < .01$). This is corroborated in a study of the National Registry, which found that professionals turned to the computerized system after being out of work an average of six months (Gutteridge, 1975), and, typically, as a consequence of using the State Employment Service (Ullman and Gutteridge, 1973). Professionals did not use computer services except as a last resort, probably because they did not feel they were very useful. This is indicated by those in our study, who felt that such services had the lowest probability of any search method in helping them find a job. In fact, none of those who used computer placement found a job through such a service (Table 6.1). Other studies have also found that very few professionals obtained their jobs through a computerized placement service (Allen, 1972; Azevedo, 1974; Ullman and Gutteridge, 1973). Some of the systems, such as the National Registry, had several blatant weaknesses in their design resulting in an inability to properly match employers with job applicants (Bain, 1974; Ullman and Gutteridge, 1973).

The poor results using elaborate computer placement systems to place unemployed professionals may help explain why they were discontinued. The demise of these systems has been attributed to the fact that too few employers listed too few jobs and hired too few people through them (Alden, 1973). Even among employers using the National Registry, only 4.5 percent considered it as one of the four main sources for hiring experienced professionals (Ullman and Gutteridge, 1973). Also, it may very well be that too many systems were competing simultaneously for the placement of a large number of professionals in relatively few available jobs. The National Registry had over four applicants for every job listed (Bain, 1974).

Professional societies have not fared too well when they tried to venture into computer placement of their members. A good case in point is the American Bar Association, which introduced Juriscan, a computer service designed to match young lawyers with jobs (Goldstein, 1977). It was swamped with law students about to complete their studies, but since few employers had listed positions, the service was discontinued within two years.

Not all computerized professional placement systems have been failures. In fact, they can be very effective when there is a high participation rate for employers as well as candidates. One of the few examples of this is the National Intern Matching Program (NIMP), a highly successful computerized system for matching physicians about to begin their internship with hospital vacancies (Arnstein, 1965). The success of NIMP could be attributed to the fact that practically all hospitals and interns participated in the program. Indeed, a system based on NIMP as a prototype was suggested for college teacher placement by the National Education Association (Arnstein, 1965).

Although most computerized professional job-matching systems have met their demise, government efforts to establish such systems for a broad range of occupations has been accelerating. The Employment Service first introduced computer-assisting job matching on an experimental basis in the late 1960s and all state agencies are expected to have such capabilities by the early 1980s (Stevenson, 1976). These computerized job-matching systems include a listing of employers' job openings that is updated daily in local job banks as well as a file of applicant characteristics in the Applicant Data System (*ETA Interchange, 1977*). Job matching uses both systems to either find job openings for an individual applicant or applicants for a particular job on the basis of classifications using Dictionary of Occupational Titles (DOT) codes. Once all the state computerized job-matching systems are established, a national linkage among the systems is expected to follow, with the use of communication satellites providing coast to coast tie-ins for computer placement, a very real possibility (Barnes, 1977).

It is doubtful that the highly sophisticated computerized job-matching systems being developed by the government will be of much use to professionals, given the ineffectiveness of the Employment Service in assisting the placement of highly educated workers. In fact, early evaluations of these job-matching systems indicate that the Employment Service's emphasis on job placement of the disadvantaged via computer comes at the expense of others, including professionals (Ullman and Huber, 1973). This is unfortunate since terminated professionals feel that there is a need for centralized job banks to provide them with information channels about job openings (Briar, 1976).

It is noteworthy that local self-help groups, established with the help of the U.S. Department of Labor, involved unemployed professionals as volunteers to match individuals with jobs in their geographic areas and were relatively successful without using computers (Alden, 1973). A major ingredient in the success of the volunteer group was their job development activities, in which they found or created appropriate job opportunities for their members. Perhaps integrating such job development services with less ambitious, and more localized, computerized professional placement systems would enable them to fare better than the elaborate systems which had failed. Such an integration is discussed further in Chapters 8 and 9.

RETURN TO WORK THROUGH SELF-EMPLOYMENT

When there is a scarcity of jobs, some unemployed professionals consider starting their own business. This was found in our study (Table 6.1) and has been corroborated in other research (Allen, 1972; Kaufman 1980; Palen and Fahey, 1968; Thompson, 1972). Although such an approach in not strictly a job search method, when professionals are faced with bleak employment prospects, some are willing to try their luck in their own business. In fact, there is evidence that most individuals who become private entrepreneurs do so because of negative events in their career, such as job loss (Shapero, 1975). The surge in the registration of such businesses reported during the recession of the mid-1970s attests to this (Levy, 1975).

Perhaps the most comprehensive picture of the professional who becomes self-employed subsequent to job loss comes from an analysis of the National Sample of Scientists and Engineers (Kaufman, 1980). Of those who experienced involuntary termination between 1969 and 1972, about five percent became reemployed by establishing their own business. This was about the same order of magnitude found among the underemployed in our study, but although relatively ineffective, this approach to reemployment may be efficient (Table 6.1).

In the National Sample, engineers, as well as physical and life scientists, were found to be more likely to go into business for themselves than were chemists, computer specialists, mathematicians, psychologists, or social scientists. Few had previous experience with establishing their own business. Apparently, a strong professional commitment was an important factor in the decision to seek self-employment. For example, compared to professionals who were reemployed in salaried positions, those who went into business for themselves were more likely to possess a doctoral degree, to be a professional society member, and to have acquired professional licensing, certification or registration.

It would also appear that midcareer engineers and scientists who had become well established in their field were most likely to become entreprenuers. For instance, those going into business for themselves tended to have had higher salaries and greater managerial responsibilities in the job from which they were terminated than did those reemployed in salaried positions. Moreover, almost half of those who established their own business were in their 40s, about twice as many as would be expected given the age distribution of the terminated sample. In addition, for the over-55-year-old scientists and engineers, becoming an entrepreneur was among the most likely paths to reemployment. On the other hand, few under age 30 became entrepreneurs, despite the fact that almost one-fourth of the sample was in this youngest age bracket. Other studies of terminated workers have also found that it is the middle-aged who are most inclined toward self-employment (Palen and Fahey, 1968). Those who reach midcareer and beyond have probably acquired both the expertise and financial resources necessary for venturing into their own business.

Among terminated professionals in the National Sample, those who became entrepreneurs were more likely to have school-age children than were those who were reemployed in salaried positions. As noted in Chapter 5, the desire to avoid taking children out of school is an important determinant of resistance to relocation. If attempts at self-employment were motivated in any way by a resistance to relocation, they were apparently successful. Almost none of those who established their own business relocated, compared to one-third among the terminated professionals who did relocate when reemployed.

By becoming self-employed, most terminated engineers and scientists were able to remain working as professionals, typically by providing consulting or other technical services. However, their work was somewhat more likely to be on a part-time basis compared to those who found positions as salaried employees. Moreover, those who went into business for themselves typically experienced a substantial reduction in income, whereas most reemployed professionals were able to improve on their pretermination salary. It could very well be that being able to return rapidly to professional-level work without a need to relocate was sufficient compensation for any initial loss in income. By becoming self-employed, these professionals helped assure the stability and continuity of their family life as well as of their own career. Indeed, terminated professionals who go into business for themselves are more likely to remain in their new career than are those who switch fields after job loss (Allen, 1972).

Although those well into midcareer have been most inclined to enter business for themselves as a result of termination, the increasing number of new college graduates who cannot find appropriate jobs appears to be stimulating the entry of young professionals into entrepreneural ventures. Indeed, by the mid-1970s a sharp increase in the number of businesses started by those under 30 had been noted (Levy, 1975). One government official involved with the registration of small businesses observed that "the youngsters just out of college, who are talented and well educated seem frustrated. Many don't feel like sitting around collecting unemployment or doing unskilled labor. So now gutsy ones have been coming in quite a lot more than any other age group" (Levy, 1975, p. 15).

In our study, attempts at self-employment appeared to be attractive to single professionals, particularly among those who remained unemployed ($r = -.34$, $p < .05$) or who became underemployed ($r = -.31, p < .05$). Apparently, professionals who are younger or have no family responsibilities are quite willing to take the risks involved in entering their own business venture. Furthermore, since younger college graduates have not yet established a strong commitment to an occupation, they should be more flexible toward entering into self-employment that requires a career change than would older, established professionals. Perhaps what younger entrepreneural aspirants lack in experience and financial resources, they compensate for with a greater willingness to take risks and be flexible in their entry into new ventures. As professional opportunities diminish for college graduates, entrepreneural careers will become an increasingly attractive alternative to joblessness or underemployment.

PLACEMENT OF GROUPS EXPERIENCING DISCRIMINATION

Various organizations have devoted their efforts to trying to place individuals who, because of their age, race, sex, or physical disability, may encounter discrimination in hiring. As we have seen in Chapter 5, such groups have encountered barriers to employment because of employer bias. Unfortunately, there is almost a complete dearth of research that has focused on the role of organizations that help provide professional placement assistance to groups experiencing discrimination.

One of the exceptions is research carried out at Forty Plus, a voluntary self-help organization with independent chapters throughout the United States and Canada, whose purpose is to provide job search and placement assistance for professionals and managers who are likely to encounter discrimination because of age. In one study carried out at Forty Plus of Southern California the assistance provided by the organization turned out to be the most effective of the job search methods and one of the most efficient (Dyer, 1972). However, the salaries of those placed through Forty Plus tended to be somewhat below the average salary of the older professionals who found employment through other methods. So, although Forty Plus may be a highly effective and efficient means for older professionals to attain reemployment, it may lead to underpaid positions. With the increased growth in the number of older professionals, organizations such as Forty Plus may become even more important in the future.

With regard to minority groups, there is evidence that more than one-fourth of black and other minority professionals seek work through their local organizations, such as the Urban League or community groups (U.S. Department of Labor, 1975a). For minorities, local organizations were even more effective than either private employment agencies or the State Employment Service. Thus despite the breakthroughs made by minority professionals as a result of equal employment legislation, they may still need special placement assistance, especially given their susceptibility to unemployment stress when they are out of work.

Women professionals also appear to have a need for their own placement organizations. As women have been increasingly breaking out of their traditional family and occupational roles, there has been a burgeoning of organizations assisting female professionals in job placement. These organizations have ranged from voluntary self-help groups to private employment agencies dealing exclusively with the placement of professional women. Some have dealt with the special problems of women seeking reentry into their professions after having been out of the labor force for some years because of family responsibilities. Although specialized organizations would appear to be useful in providing placement assistance to women professionals, their effectiveness and efficiency remain to be demonstrated.

Placement assistance to the handicapped is provided by the State Office for Vocational Rehabilitation, as well as by some private nonprofit agencies. It is noteworthy that the number of college graduates seeking such assistance has increased at an alarming rate (Bozza, 1975). This increase is likely to continue given federal regulations that institutions of higher learning provide access to the handicapped. Thus it would appear necessary for organizations responsible for job placement of the handicapped to devote more time to locating professional-level positions.

The success of the Forty Plus groups can be used as a model for other organizations that are attempting to overcome bias in hiring. Since some groups, such as the handicapped, do have great barriers to overcome in terms of employer bias, turning to an organization which has developed contacts with firms that have strong social responsibility commitments may turn out to be a highly effective and efficient method of finding work for these groups.[3]

CLASSIFICATION OF JOB SEARCH METHODS

In attempting to classify job search methods, labor economists have generally identified them as either formal or informal (Reid, 1972). Formal methods include private employment agencies, the State Employment Service, and advertisements. Informal methods involve use of personal contacts of any kind and direct application to employers. Some researchers have elaborated on these somewhat simplistic classifications. For example, one approach used three job search classifications: (1) formal methods in which the job seeker used an impersonal intermediary such as a newspaper ad, public or private employment agency, and placement services provided by universities or professional societies; (2) personal contacts; and (3) direct application to employers (Granovetter, 1974). The latter two categories typically had been classified by others as informal. However, even the three-way classification is impressionistic and has not been empirically validated. As we have amply demonstrated, each job search method tends to be used by particular groups of professionals and often leads to certain types of jobs. Thus, existing classifications of job search methods may be too simplistic.

In an attempt to provide a more meaningful empirical basis for classifying and understanding the ways in which professionals look for jobs, we used factor analysis to investigate the dimensions of job search behavior.[4] A total of five dimensions emerged from the factor analysis of the job search methods used by the unemployed professionals in our study, and these are classified in Table 6.3.

The job search dimension classified as formal (accounting for 32 percent of the variance), includes methods that others have also classified in the same way. Professionals who turned to formal methods tended to use private employment agencies and the State Employment Service as intermediaries and, in addition, were likely to have followed up ads in newspapers and professional journals. This is understandable, since private employment agencies often use ads to announce the positions they have available.

However, there were those who may have used newspaper ads as a means to reach employers directly and, as can be seen from Table 6.3, such ads were classified under the direct-methods dimension (accounting for 27 percent of the variance). In this case, professionals may not be responding to private employment agency ads but rather directly to employer want ads. It could be that some profes-

TABLE 6.3.   Job Search Dimensions among Unemployed
Professionals based on Factor Analysis

Dimensions	Factor Loading
Formal Methods	
Private employment agencies	.74
Newspaper ads	.67
State Employment Service	.57
Professional journals	.38
Direct Methods	
Direct application to employers	.98
Newspaper ads	.48
Personal Contacts	
Friends and relatives	.78
Professional colleagues	.59
Professional Sources	
Professional societies	.75
Professional journals	.42
Professional colleagues	.35
No-Fee Services	
National computer placement service	.50
Former employer's outplacement service	.47
College placement service	.39
State Employment Service	.30

sionals who follow up newspaper ads are oriented more toward using a direct approach in contacting employers rather than a formal intermediary such as a private employment agency.

A third dimension turned out to be personal contacts (accounting for 17 percent of the variance). It is interesting that professionals who seek assistance in finding work from their friends and relatives are also likely to turn to their professional colleagues, despite the differences we found in the characteristics of those who use each type of contact. However, these differences may be explained by the fact that professional colleagues also emerge as part of a fourth job search dimension we called professional sources (accounting for 12 percent of the variance). Those who use such sources were more likely to turn to their professional societies or journals for job information. We can speculate that among individuals seeking work through professional colleagues, some may be oriented toward a more impersonal formal approach and would be likely to use their societies and journals, whereas others may prefer making personal contacts and turn primarily to people they know.

Finally, the fifth dimension includes all the placement services whose common denominator is that they are available at no charge (accounting for 11 percent of the variance). It is possible that those who used a national computer placement service did so because it was made available by either their former employer, college placement office, or State Employment Service. Although all such methods would have been classified as formal by others, we see that these job-finding techniques mostly differ from the methods we included under the formal dimension. The most apparent difference is that the professional who uses these methods need not pay a fee for any of the services provided. This is an important consideration for unemployed professionals with financial burdens. It also appears that, with the exception of employer outplacement, these services tend to be more frequently used by long-term unemployed professionals. They are not only likely to be under more financial pressure, and hence attracted to a free service, but they also probably have already tried other job search techniques and turned to the free services as a last resort.

It is clear from this brief exploration that previous classifications of job search methods are somewhat simplistic. We have demonstrated empirically that job search behavior is not only multidimensional but is also quite complex, with some methods overlapping two dimensions. It would appear that each unemployed professional is likely to have an orientation toward using specific types of job search methods that possess common characteristics. There is evidence that unemployed professionals rely primarily on job-finding strategies which they have found to be successful in the past (Kaufman, 1980; Powell and Driscoll, 1973). Thus, although professionals may have an orientation toward using specific job search methods to begin with, differences in the strategies they use to find work may become firmly established as a result of learning experiences that reinforce the use of particular methods.

CROSS-CULTURAL COMPARISONS

The dearth of cross-cultural research on the job search methods used by unemployed professionals limits our ability to make comparisons with other countries. Fortunately, the study carried out in Israel that we have discussed at length previously (Bar-Yosef, Shield, and Varsher, 1975), does examine cross-cultural differences in the use of job search methods within one country. In that study it was found that native Israelis concentrated on the informal methods, such as friends and relatives, as well as on direct contacts with employers. However, immigrants from eastern Europe focused more on personal contacts, whereas those who came from Western countries were more familiar with contacting employers directly or using newspaper advertisements. Nevertheless, for all groups the single most likely method utilized for finding work was the Government's Bureau of Professional Employment, which provides services free of charge to native Israelis and immigrants alike.

Although job search techniques used by professionals in Israel appear similar to those used in the United States, there are nevertheless some differences. For example, although contacting employers directly is also important in Israel, personal contacts and "proteksia"—receiving privileges based on knowing the right people in the right places—rank relatively higher. Indeed, it is the personal contacts that ranked highest in effectiveness and efficiency for finding work (Bar-Yosef and Varsher, 1977). However, contrary to results in the United States, relatively few jobs were found by applying directly to employers. One may speculate that obtaining jobs on the basis of "who you know rather than what you know" is more prevalent in the traditional cultures found in smaller or less developed countries than in large highly industrialized societies. This speculation is supported by studies of college graduates in India, which found personal contacts to be the most frequently utilized of all job search methods (Asher, 1972). About half of these graduates felt that a lack of personal contacts contributed to failure in finding a job. Indeed, for college graduates in India, personal contacts frequently provided the only access to jobs in the private sector.

Clear-cut differences with respect to public employment assistance were found between professionals in Israel and those in the United States. In Israel the government's Bureau of Professional Employment was ranked in first place among the methods used for finding work (Bar Yosef et al., 1975) and in second place with respect to effectiveness and efficiency (Bar Yosef and Varsher, 1977). This is in sharp contrast to the relatively low utilization and performance of the State Employment Services found for professionals in the United States. This great difference is understandable, since the State of Israel has centralized private and public sector job placement to provide all its citizens with the opportunity to work. Indeed, the Israeli government has such a widespread responsibility in job placement that private employment agencies are quite rare. In some countries, such as West Germany, private employment agencies are banned by law, thereby giving the federal employment office a monopoly on professional placement (Tagliabue, 1980). It is noteworthy that in the study of Indian college graduates, the widespread availability of on-campus placement offices resulted in their being ranked third in utilization, whereas the government Employment Exchanges were the least frequently used (Asher, 1972). In contrast, university graduates in Israel do not have college placement services to turn to since that function is the responsibility of the Bureau of Professional Employment.

Despite its relatively high effectiveness and efficiency, the Israeli Bureau of Professional Employment, like its American counterpart, initially was perceived as less likely than other job search methods to help in finding work. Although immigrants generally had more positive attitudes toward the Bureau of Professional Employment than did native Israeli professionals, those of eastern European origin tended to be most dissatisfied with the service they received. This is understandable in light of the unrealistic expectations among eastern Europeans. As will be recalled from our discussions in Chapters 3 and 5, those from eastern Europe apparently had expectations that the state would provide them with jobs in their respective fields. When their high expectations were not met, they blamed the government and its agencies for their unemployment difficulties.

The situation is similar among Soviet Jewish immigrants to the United States. As one of them explained:

> The job hunting was really something we were not ready for. . . . In Russia, when you finish university or some other institution of higher education you are assigned to a job. Preparing résumés, selling your skills to an employer and having to compete is very strange to us (Kass and Lipsit, 1980, p. 112).

Those who did not perceive difficulties in finding work in their field or whose job search was less intensive were more satisfied with the service they received from the Bureau of Professional Employment. Such satisfaction was also highly related to their perception of how well the placement officer provided them with assistance. As will be recalled, in the United States a major reason why those who used the State Employment Service would not use it again was the poor treatment they received.

It is interesting to contrast the placement of professionals in India with respect to public employment assistance. Despite the fact that all employers are required to report all vacancies to the Employment Exchange, they are not compelled to fill them through the Exchange (Asher, 1972). Indeed, private employers frequently refuse to consider candidates referred by the Employment Exchange. This bias is similar to that reported in the United States. When placements are made through the Employment Exchange in India, they are typically in public sector jobs. Furthermore, the Employment Exchanges have been criticized because they place candidates more on the basis of how long they had been registered at the Exchange rather than on the basis of individual qualifications. These factors, together with the widespread availability of on-campus placement for new graduates and newspaper ads for experienced professionals, help to explain why educated workers in India typically do not choose the Employment Exchanges among the formal job search methods available to them.

From the very limited evidence we have, it is reasonable to speculate that job search behavior among professionals in a particular country is dependent to a great degree on the characteristics of its job placement resources, in addition to cultural factors. For example, the greater the centralization of formal job placement procedures for all positions, the less likely that other methods would be used to find work. The results we have found with respect to the job search for professionals in the United States may, therefore, be similar to those in other countries to the degree that the characteristics of the job placement resources are comparable. Such speculations await future research.

SUMMARY AND CONCLUSIONS

Unemployed professionals utilize a variety of methods to look for work. Some methods are used more than others, and they vary in their effectiveness and efficiency for securing work. Each method also differs in terms of the characteristics of the professionals who utilize it or find their jobs by means of it. Consequently, differences in job placement depend to some degree on the particular job search method used for securing the position. To clarify these differences, we have attempted to integrate the disparate findings from various studies and have summarized them in Table 6.4. It should be noted that this integration is very tentative and is meant merely as a guide to some of the more interesting findings which require confirmation by future research. With this caveat in mind, we attempt to summarize some tentative conclusions about each job search method.

1. *Direct application* to employers is often the most popular method of job hunting among professionals, especially older and more experienced ones. Many do find a job by direct application, but this approach appears to be more effective for professionals who are not under pressure to find work and can spend the time on an intensive organized campaign, such as younger professionals or married females. Although R&D professionals have been found to apply directly to employers more often than do others, they less frequently found their jobs by this approach. R&D professionals who do find jobs through direct application tend to be the poorer performers—the better ones may feel they do not need to carry out such a campaign. Nevertheless, the jobs generally found through direct application tend to be either in the professional's field or in better positions outside their field. Older professionals, however, may not secure positions as good as their younger colleagues through direct application, possibly because of age discrimination. Applying directly for jobs appears to be more effective during recession periods, when employers reduce their more formal recruiting programs. In general, direct applications to employers appears to be most effective and efficient for professionals who are under less pressure to return to work or who do not experience barriers to reemployment as a result of their background or personal characteristics. Those who need to overcome employment barriers may require an intermediary for entry to a position; thus direct applications would not be the best job search strategy for such professionals.

2. *Newspaper ads* rank just under direct applications in utilization, but they are not very effective or efficient, particularly for attaining reemployment in one's

TABLE 8.4. Characteristics of Users, Finders, ...

Job Search Method	Utilization	Characteristics of Users	Characteristics of Those Who Found Jobs Using Method	Characteristics of Positions Found Using Method
Direct application to employer	High	Older R&D professionals Engineers Teachers	Younger Female White Teachers Not under pressure to find job Poorer performers in R&D Junior level college faculty	In professional's field Better jobs outside professional's field Poorer jobs for older professional Found during recessions
Newspaper ads	High	Older Less education Engineers Managers	Older More obsolescent Greater barriers (i.e. high previous salary, overqualified) Engineers Managers Poorer performers	Subprofessional Temporary outside professional's field Underutilized in professional's field Termination more likely Lower salary
Personal contacts	High	Minorities	Minorities Engineers Better performers	Permanent job Termination less likely
Professional colleagues	High	College faculty	Age as a barrier More dependents Higher self-esteem Better decision-making ability Greater initiative Senior-level college faculty	In professional's field Professional level work outside field Better teaching positions

TABLE 6.4. (continued)

Job Search Method	Utilization	Characteristics of Users	Characteristics of Those Who Found Jobs Using Method	Characteristics of Positions Found Using Method
Friends and relatives	High	Less education	Younger Fewer dependents Lower self-esteem Poorer decision-making ability	Outside professional's field Part-time work Found when unemployment is low
Private employment agencies	High	Higher level More education Engineers Managers Minorities	Greater barriers (i.e., high previous salary, overqualified) Unemployed longer Began job search later Less initiative Less education White Males Engineers Managers	In professional's field In smaller organizations In poorer quality colleges Terminations more likely
College placement service	Moderate	Younger Unemployed longer Better decision-making ability Teachers	Younger Less experienced Female Teachers	In professional's field Better positions outside professional's field

Source	Effectiveness	Characteristics	Who	Outcomes
State Employment Service	Moderate	Less education Unemployed longer Lack of jobs a barrier Engineers	Engineers	Lower salary In larger organizations Subprofessional Termination more likely
Professional journals	Moderate	More education Engineers	Engineers	Found when unemployment is low
Professional societies	Low	More education (Ph.D.s) More professionally oriented College faculty	More education (Ph.D.s) Junior level college faculty	Higher-quality positions for junior-level faculty Relocation more likely Termination less likely
Outplacement services of former employer	Low	R&D professionasls Defense-oriented work Aerospace industry		Found during recessions
National computer placement service	Low	Unemployed longer		
Self-employment	Low	Midcareer Recent graduates	Midcareer More educated Professionally oriented Managerial experience Higher salary School-age children	No relocation Lower income

field. However, such ads are very useful in finding jobs outside the professional's occupation. Regardless of whether or not the new position is in the professional's field, a job found by means of an ad is more likely to result in underemployment than one found by other methods. In general, it appears that professionals with the greatest barriers to reemployment, most typically associated with their age, turn to newspaper ads. However, since these ads lead to work that does not fit their qualifications or capabilities, they may be setting themselves up for another job loss experience.

3. *Personal contacts* to locate jobs generally ranks almost as high as newspaper ads in utilization, with professional colleagues turned to for help more frequently than friends or relatives. For professionals likely to experience discrimination, such as minorities, this may be an attractive approach that can pay off with jobs. Personal contacts can serve to overcome barriers resulting from discrimination and gain entrée to a potential employer where other methods would be less successful. Professional colleagues generally lead to better jobs than do friends and relatives. However, this may result not only from the greater awareness of job availability by those working in the field but also from the fact that the unemployed who turn to professional colleagues tend to be more mature and have superior individual qualities than those who depend on friends or relatives. In general, however, jobs found through personal contacts may turn out to be permanent and provide greater protection against termination.

4. *Private employment agencies* tend to rank just below personal contacts in utilization, but they are used more by higher-level and more educated professionals. However, it appears that those professionals with greater barriers to reemployment and less initiative depend on private employment agencies to find work. Such agencies appear successful in placing engineers as well as managers in their chosen profession, but these may be professionals with more limited education. Females and minorities do not seem to fare too well with private agencies, possibly because of their limited numbers among professions in demand by agencies (e.g., engineering) or because of outright discrimination. The screening that private employment agencies provide has been highly criticized. This may not only be a factor in discrimination but also inappropriate job placement that could contribute to a higher likelihood of future termination for professionals who find their jobs through private agencies.

5. *College placement services* are ranked below private employment agencies, and in terms of utilization they were classified as only moderate. All methods discussed above were rated as high in utilization. The lower rate of use for the college placement service is very likely a result of its attractiveness primarily to the younger, less experienced professionals. However, even the younger unemployed professionals tended to come to their college placement service only when they were unsuccessful in using other methods to find work. Nevertheless,

this service was both efficient and effective in helping these professionals to find jobs in their fields or good positions in another occupation. This positive record probably results from the fact that employers view the college p lacement office as the best source for recruiting young professionals. It remains to be seen whether this record could be maintained if larger numbers of older, more experienced alumni began to use their college placement services.

6. *State Employment Service* assistance has a moderate rate of utilization, but it helped very few professionals to find work. Those who turned to the Employment Service had less education and had been out of work longer. These professionals very likely tried other methods and, after repeated failure, turned to the Employment Service as a last resort. Not only are professional-level jobs underrepresented at the Employment Service, but employers may perceive those professionals who use the Service as being inferior. When such factors are combined with the poor treatment professionals sometimes encounter when they seek public employment assistance, it is understandable why the Employment Service has had such a poor record. However, it may have a potential that has yet to be fully realized for professional job placement.

7. *Professional journals* have a moderate rate of utilization, particularly by engineers and the more highly educated. Relatively few professionals actually find a job through their journals, but engineers are likely to do better than others. Professional journals appear to be more effective in finding positions when unemployment is low and employers are more likely to advertise job openings.

8. *Professional societies* have a low rate of utilization. As was the case for journals, it is the more highly educated who use their professional societies, but few jobs are actually obtained through such channels. Positions found by academicians through the placement services of their professional societies are generally at the entry or junior-level. The better positions secured by means of such placement services may go to the younger academicians. It appears that professional societies are not providing adequate job placement assistance to most of their members who are seeking employment.

9. *Outplacement services* provided by former employers are utilized by relatively few unemployed professionals probably because of a lack of availability. Outplacement has been concentrated in industries that have experienced cyclic mass terminations of professionals, such as aerospace and defense. Although few find jobs through outplacement, the use of this approach is likely to grow in the future, with specialized consultants providing such services to organizations that do not possess in-house capabilities.

10. *National computer placement services* to find work are utilized by very few jobless professionals, and those who do, tend to be the long-term unemployed. Despite their availability at no cost, professionals apparently did not use computer services except as a last resort. Professionals did not feel that such ser-

vices would help them, and they were essentially correct. Where the more elaborate national computer placement systems have failed, perhaps more carefully developed, less ambitious, and localized job matching systems may fare better.

11. *Self-employment* is considered by some professionals when faced with a bleak job market. These entrepreneural types tend to be in midcareer and professionally oriented. Although they may experience reduced income by going into business for themselves, this loss may be offset by the continuity of their career and the avoidance of relocation. They, therefore, may avoid much of the stress resulting from disruption of family life as well as career. The entry of younger professionals into entrepreneural ventures is likely to be stimulated by the increasing number of college graduates who cannot find meaningful work.

Various organizations have been established to help find jobs for those who because of their age, sex, race, or physical disability may encounter discrimination in hiring. It appears that turning to an organization which has developed contacts with firms that have strong commitments to social responsibility in their hiring practices would be a highly effective and efficient method of finding jobs among groups that have encountered bias in their search for work.

It was demonstrated that previous classifications of job search methods by labor economists were much too simplistic. Job search behavior was found to have five dimensions, with professionals selecting methods characterized as either formal, direct, personal, professional, or involving no fee. It would thus appear that each unemployed professional is likely to look for work using particular job search methods that have characteristics and strategies in common.

We have seen that some job search methods are clearly better than others. However, aside from adopting a superior job search strategy, there are other changes in themselves that out-of-work professionals can implement which can improve their job opportunities and the likelihood of reemployment success. It is to these individual change strategies that we now turn our attention.

NOTES

1. There is no universal agreement on the definition of effectiveness or efficiency of job search techniques (see Stevens, 1972). Indeed, the ratio we have defined as efficiency—the number who found their job by means of a particular method divided by the total number who actually used that method—is often referred to as effectiveness. The measure we used for effectiveness—the percentage of unemployed who find their job by means of a particular method—is frequently used but often without being associated with a concept such as effectiveness.

2.   The high efficiency found for the college placement service in our study could be partly attributed to the fact that there were a large number of younger professionals in our sample.

3.   Lists of organizations providing placement assistance to professionals who had experienced discrimination in the past have recently begun to appear (Vetter, Babco, and McIntire, 1978).

4.   The factor analysis used the varimax orthogonal rotation available in the Statistical Package for the Social Sciences (SPSS).

CHAPTER SEVEN

Improving Employability and Adjustment:
Strategies for Individual Change

Since the job search process can be long and fruitless, unemployed professionals frequently attempt to develop and carry out a strategy that will change their situation or themselves and enhance their employability and adjustment. Some will decide on geographic relocation to overcome the lack of jobs in their community. Others, attempting to overcome certain barriers to reemployment created by limitations in their background, adopt such strategies as continuing their education or retraining for a new career. A relatively recent strategy is participation in counseling programs that focus not only on the practical techniques of job hunting but also on bolstering the morale and self-esteem of unemployed professionals. In this chapter we examine individual change strategies to determine how useful each strategy is in helping the professional cope with unemployment. The experience of joblessness can be so disruptive to the well-being of professionals that some of its effects may not entirely disappear even upon finding satisfying work. We close this chapter with an examination of the relationship between reemployment and adjustment.

GEOGRAPHIC RELOCATION

Some jobless professionals try to improve their employment prospects by seeking work outside their geographic area where there may be better job opportunities. As was seen in Chapter 5, relocation does not appear to be attractive to many, if not most, unemployed professionals. We found that regardless of reemployment experience, only about one-fourth of those in our study attempted to relocate elsewhere in the United States, and one-tenth abroad. Despite the fact that professionals, particularly the more highly educated, have the highest rates of migration of any occupational group, they are less likely than other groups to relocate because of unemployment (Ritchey, 1976). Moreover, although professionals travel farther to look for work than those in other occupations, they are much more likely than other workers to reject a job because of its location (U.S. Department of Labor, 1975a). We examine next the factors that affect the unemployed professional's attitudes toward relocation as well as the impact of relocation when it occurs.

Willingness to Relocate

A professional's willingness to relocate is affected by situational as well as personal factors. Some important situational factors appear to be associated with the geographic area in which the professionals reside when they become unemployed. For example, studies of jobless defense and aerospace industry professionals terminated during 1963–1965 reveal that relocation to other geographic areas ranged from a low of 19 percent on Long Island (Langway, 1966), to about one-third in Denver and San Francisco (Fishman, 1966; Loomba, 1967), to as much as one-half of those in Seattle (Brandwein, 1966). The variation in relocation rates may be tied to the job market in each locality, with the greatest mobility occurring in communities with the worst unemployment problems. Perhaps more important, though, are the roots established in the community. There is clear evidence that professionals who had already experienced migration were much more likely to relocate again following job loss (Gutteridge, 1978; Kaufman, 1980). This may explain the relatively high relocation rates found among professionals terminated on the West Coast, where many professionals had already migrated in search of job opportunities.

We have seen in Chapter 5 that reluctance to relocate is a barrier to reemployment among professionals who have deeper roots in their community. These include those with more dependents and with greater attachments to home, relatives, and friends. Professionals who are willing to relocate tend to be younger and have fewer dependents and attachments which would limit their mobility. Moreover, demographic studies have consistently found the highest rates of migration to be among the youngest workers (Ritchey, 1976). Unemployed professionals who did relocate to find work were found not only to be younger and have fewer teenage children than those who did not relocate but were also more likely to be males or noncitizens (Kaufman, 1980). Thus actual relocation to find work appears to depend, in part, on the degree to which attachments with family and community limit one's mobility.

In addition to a lack of attachments, there are psychological differences that appear to be associated with professionals who had attempted relocation in order to find work. For example, in our study there was a general tendency for professionals who tried to relocate to have an external locus of control, and this was most evident among those who remained unemployed ($r = .37, p < .01$). This is consistent with the conclusion in Chapter 5 that professionals who feel they are more in control of their lives may be better able to resist changing locations in order to find work. Since relocation can serve to improve the external conditions affecting reemployment, it would be most attractive as a way of coping with joblessness for individuals who feel their return to work is more dependent on environmental conditions than on their own capabilities.

Relocation also appears to be affected by factors related to one's profession. For example, professionals who are in fields that have rigid licensing requirements without interstate reciprocity are less mobile than those who are not affected by such constraints (Holen, 1965; Kleiner, 1977). Some professionals may have to relocate because their high degree of specialization may be in demand only in specific locations. This may explain why metallurgists and physical scientists are much more likely to relocate than are other professionals following job loss (Kaufman, 1980). Furthermore, it appears that those who have become strongly committed to their profession are the least reluctant to relocate in order to have the opportunity to utilize their knowledge and skills. In this regard, it is the most highly educated unemployed professionals who have been found to have the greatest likelihood of relocating (Kaufman, 1980; Loomba, 1968; Gutteridge, 1978).

In general, relocation appears to be more attractive to whose who are professionally oriented. For example, members of professional societies are more likely than nonmembers to be reemployed by relocating after job loss (Kaufman, 1980). Among the unemployed in our study, those who tried to find work by relocating elsewhere in the United States contributed more professional papers ($r = .34$, $p < .05$) and read a greater number of professional journals ($r = .34$, $p < .05$) than did those who had not attempted moving. Demographic studies have also found that those in the most highly professional salaried occupations are more likely to migrate in national rather than local labor markets (Ladinsky, 1967). Those who are highly committed to their profession need to utilize their knowledge and skills and, therefore will,seriously consider any opportunity to do so, even if it involves relocation.

Needs Satisfaction and Relocation Abroad

Willingness by professionals to work anywhere in order to utilize their knowledge and skills has resulted in migrations to other countries where greater work opportunities may exist. Among those in our study, the desire to satisfy self-actualization needs through a return to work was related to relocation attempts, both in the United States ($r = .27$, $p < .05$ for the underemployed; $r = .28$, $p < .05$ for those reemployed in their field) and elsewhere in the world ($r = .25$, $p < .05$ for the underemployed; $r = .34$, $p < .01$ for those reemployed in their field). Seeking domestic relocation was not related to security needs, although other studies have found relocation to be conditional on its providing job security

(Briar, 1976). In our study, professionals who were most in need of work to attain security were more likely to attempt relocating abroad ($r = .30$, $p < .05$ for the underemployed; $r = .26$, $p < .05$ for those reemployed in their field). Hence, for some professionals to even consider relocating abroad, there must exist strong needs to return to work to attain security as well as self-actualization.

When unemployed professionals in California were asked for solutions to their problem, the most frequent response—from almost six out of ten—was that professionals should be encouraged to work in the international community (Estes, 1973). Indeed, with a tight professional job market in the United States, a reverse brain drain has emerged, with American professionals migrating to countries where they can better utilize their knowledge and skills (*The New York Times*, 1975b). The desire to emigrate had become relatively widespread among professionals in the United States, particularly younger ones. Opinion polls have shown that by the early 1970s three-tenths of college-educated Americans under the age of 30 desired to settle in another country (Gallup Opinion Index, 1971). However, with most countries suffering from a surplus of highly educated workers, the effectiveness of migration abroad as a strategy to attain reemployment is considerably curtailed. Therefore, migration to other countries is likely to remain a realistic alternative for only a relatively small number of American professionals.

Relocation and Reemployment Success

Flexibility with regard to relocation typically enhances reemployment success. Just the willingness to relocate, especially abroad, appears to increase the likelihood of reemployment in general, as well as more specifically in the professional's field (Thompson, 1972). Studies of domestic migration among out-of-work professionals usually have found that relocation is likely to lead to better jobs. One exception was a study of unemployed professionals listed in the National Registry for Engineers, which revealed that those who found a job by relocating—about one in five—were not significantly different in the time they spent out of work from those who did not relocate, although individuals who relocated were able to come closer to their pretermination salary than those who did not move (Gutteridge, 1978). Although the study concluded that in terms of reemployment success, geographic relocation had only a modest payback for the unemployed professional, this may be true primarily for those with reemployment problems who were more apt to use a computer placement service such as the National Registry.

When jobs are scarce in a particular locality, migration is an especially effective response to unemployment. In a study during the early 1970s of unemployed technical professionals in the Wichita, Kansas, area—where unemployment rates were over 10 percent—more than two-fifths relocated; they were less likely to be unemployed or to have changed their occupation and more likely to have received a higher salary after migration than were those who remained (Perline and Presley, 1973). Several other studies carried out during the same period found similar results on a national basis. One investigation revealed that among technical professionals terminated in various parts of the United States, those who relocated to find work generally did end up with higher salaries because it was the pay that induced them to move in the first place (Thompson, 1972). An analysis of the National Sample of Scientists and Engineers found that placements following job loss that required relocation—about one out of three—not only paid more but also were less likely to result in underemployment or another termination compared to placements that did not involve a geographic move (Kaufman, 1980).

It would thus appear that unemployed professionals who are reluctant to uproot themselves might be willing to accept a pay cut, underemployment, or less job security as a trade-off to avoid relocation. In fact, location is the most important factor in the rejection of job offers by job-hunting professionals (U.S. Department of Labor, 1975a). Apparently, some unemployed professionals would rather remain without work or become underemployed than relocate. For jobless professionals who do relocate, however, the evidence indicates that they become reemployed in their field at a higher salary and with greater job security than do those who find work that does not require that they move.

Relocation and Adjustment

It is clear that unemployed professionals who relocate to find work generally end up in better positions than do those who remain in their community. However, the relationship between relocation and psychological adjustment is not clear.

In our study those who attempted relocating were also more severely affected by their unemployment experience, and this was most evident for those reemployed in their field ($r = .40$, $p < .01$ for domestic relocation; $r = .26$, $p < .05$, for relocation abroad). Since these were mostly attempts at relocation, it would appear that professionals may become more flexible with regard to where they live as one way to cope with unemployment stress. Nevertheless, studies in the United States and elsewhere tend to show that migration may be a contributing factor to mental disorders (Murphy, 1965; Sanua, 1970). There is even evidence indicating that suicides among white males are more likely to occur when job loss or other types of "work failure" are combined with migration (Breed, 1966; 1967). Because of the possible negative effects of migration, policies emphasizing relocation as a method of coping with unemployment are open to question. As Harold Sheppard, a noted researcher who has studied problems of unemployment, asserts:

> Geographic mobility as a successful adjustment technique has severe limitations and can be over-rated by policy makers as a remedy. It cannot be repeated too often that

we know very little about the human factors involved in the mobility behavior of unemployed or displaced workers (Sheppard, 1965, p. 172).

Given the possibility that relocation can result in further stress as a result of the need to adjust to additional major life changes associated with migration, other strategies of change may be more appropriate for most professionals who encounter severe reemployment problems.

CONTINUING EDUCATION

To improve their chances of finding a job, unemployed professionals sometimes return to school to continue their education (Briar, 1976). This education may be directed to upgrading or updating their knowledge and skills in their field, typically by taking postgraduate courses to enhance their employability in their own or a related profession, or by enrolling for a degree in another field.[1] As shown in Chapter 3, taking courses can be one way not only to reduce unemployment stress but also to avoid work inhibition. Moreover, continuing education after job loss appears to help facilitate career change (Kaufman, 1980).

Despite the fact that the professionals in our study were mostly engineers, their participation in graduate-level technical courses was less frequent than in continuing education oriented toward either business or some other field (Table 7.1). Those who became reemployed in their profession were most likely to enroll in graduate business courses, which tended to be rated as more useful than technical courses in finding work. It should be noted that technical professionals frequently moved into management positions and many enrolled in graduate business programs to help them make this transition (Kaufman, 1974b; 1975).

There were indications that among those who found jobs in their field, the least professionally oriented tended to seek out the business courses. For example, individuals reemployed in their profession who enrolled in graduate business courses were less likely to have read journals ($r = .31$, $p < .05$) or to have attended professional meetings ($r = -.28$, $p < .05$) than those who did not take such a path. Among professionals finding reemployment in their field, those who turned to graduate technical courses exhibited a much greater need to find work in order to attain esteem ($r = .43$, $p < .001$). One can speculate that enrolling in graduate courses related to one's field is an attempt at maintaining self-esteem while looking for a job. In addition, graduate technical courses are useful for keeping abreast of one's field (Kaufman, 1974c, 1975, 1977). Indeed, those who remained most professionally up to date found work in their field that utilized their skills to a much greater degree than had their previous job ($r = .41$, $p < .01$).

Professionals who became underemployed by accepting jobs outside their field or part-time positions also tended to enroll more often in business than in technical courses, but the two types of education were rated equally useful in finding work.

TABLE 7.1.   Percentage Reporting That They Tried Using Continuing
Education and Training to Assist Their Reemployment

	Employment Status		
Type of Continuing Education or Training	Unemployed ($N = 51$)	Underemployed ($N = 53$)	Reemployed in Field $N = 54$)
Other degree or graduate courses[a]	43	38	39
Degree in another profession	28	19	15
Graduate business courses	22	21	28
Graduate technical courses	22	15	20
Government retraining program***	10	2	4

[a]Includes a degree in another profession or graduate courses, either technical or business.

The underemployed who enrolled in business courses, compared to those who did not, exhibited greater job flexibility ($r = .26$, $p < .05$), initiative ($r = .25$, $p < .05$), decision-making ability ($r = .24$, $p < .05$), and personal control ($r = .31, p < .05$). With such positive qualities among the underemployed who took business courses, it is not surprising that the jobs they obtained tended to be better than the one they lost, particularly in the type of work they were doing ($r = .41, p < .01$) and in the use of their skills ($r = .40, p < .01$). On the other hand, those among the underemployed who enrolled in graduate technical courses revealed greater self-esteem ($r = .29, p < .05$). This lends further support to our speculation that enrolling in courses related to one's field may serve to maintain self-esteem. Such courses, however, did not appear to influence the type of work they obtained, at least among those who became underemployed.

We found that for professionals who were reemployed in another field or in part-time jobs, enrolling for a degree in another profession was rated as the most useful continuing education approach to finding work. It is likely that such enrollment enhanced mobility out of one's field. It is of interest that in this group, those who enrolled for a degree in another field scored higher on perceived occupational level than did those who did not ($r = .33, p < .01$). These professionals could very well view the degree in another profession as a means toward attaining their higher occupational aspirations.

Among those who remained unemployed, a degree program in another profession was the type of continuing education most commonly used. The younger unemployed professionals were more likely to take graduate business courses or a degree in another profession ($r = -.28$, $p < .05$). This tended to support other studies which have found older professionals more reluctant to go back to school (Kaufman, 1974c; Thompson, 1973). This reluctance of the older professionals to get involved with continuing education, combined with their unwillingness to relocate, indicates that it may not be easy to improve their job opportunities thorugh such change strategies.

Although younger professionals are most likely to continue their education, great resentment may result if their upgraded credentials overqualify them for the job market. Such was the case for an aspiring young teacher who was unemployed and went back to school for a master's degree:

> I loved school and wanted to stay there as long as I could but was looking forward to working—I had to work someday. I was quite disappointed in not being able to find a teaching job and was somewhat bitter at being forced to go back to school—but once I got back in school my hopes went up. Maybe with another degree I would be able to find a job easily. I became quite bitter when I realized that I had educated myself out of a job.

Not being able to find a job after completing his master's degree, he went on to finish a doctorate in sociology. Experiencing the same frustration again, including the reverse discrimination described in Chapter 5, this time he rebelled by turning against society, as we shall see in Chapter 8.

Such cases notwithstanding, continuing education generally appears to enhance employability and may even help overcome some of the barriers associated with age or a lack of experience, as noted in Chapter 5. There is some evidence that many of those professionals who faced bleak employment prospects in the mid-1970s returned to colleges and universities, thereby contributing to the greatest enrollment increase in higher education since the 1960s (Maeroff, 1975a,b). A good deal of this increase has undoubtedly occurred in career-directed studies at the graduate level. For example, graduate schools of business were swamped with applications during the 1970s (Singular, 1975). However, we have also begun to witness large numbers of college graduates coping with unemployment by returning to school to complete either a second baccalaureate, an associate's degree, or just courses at a community college in order to acquire more marketable knowledge and skills (Briar, 1976; Cummings, 1976). Such enrollments, however, may occur primarily as a last resort to cope with the problems of long-term unemployment, as is illustrated in the following case of a 45-year-old unemployed methods analyst:

He optimistically thought that it would only take him two weeks to find a job after he lost his job with the phone company. Now after 15 months of unemployment he believes it will only take him two more months to find work. He is also enrolled in a community college where he is taking accounting and computer programming courses. He believes these courses will enable him to get a job. Vernon already has a B.A. degree, but is using the community college to provide himself with additional marketable skills. Even if he doesn't complete these courses or use them to become employed, schooling offers him the appearance of attempting to do something about the joblessness. His status as a student may also help him with the "misery" of being at home all the time. He probably would not have been able to seek schooling had he been solely responsible for his family finances. His wife's working, has rescued him from the burden of providing for his family (Briar, 1976, pp. 67–68).

Career-oriented continuing education serves a dual purpose in helping jobless professionals become more employable as well as cope with stress while they are out of work. As already noted, course taking appears to reduce unemployment stress and enhance work motivation. Although professionals may return to work in a new field, the effect of such a career change on their overall adjustment may depend on whether or not the change was voluntary. Insofar as continuing-education can serve to socialize the individual into another career, such course taking may well enhance adjustment to reemployment in a new field. However, if attempts at reemployment are still unsuccessful after having completed additional education, further psychological deterioration is likely to result. We return to the important issue of continuing education in Chapter 8 when we examine the role of colleges and universities in dealing with unemployment.

RETRAINING

Retraining programs have been specifically designed to prepare the unemployed to transfer into new careers, typically through intensive formal courses which can last from several weeks to over a year.[2] Retraining of the unemployed generally has been carried out under contract with government funding. Of course, some training may occur subsequent to reemployment in a new job. Indeed, it appears that such employer-sponsored training helps facilitate career change for professionals (Kaufman, 1980). However, the focus here is on retraining that occurs prior to reemployment.

As can be seen from Table 7.1, few among the professionals in our study participated in any type of government sponsored retraining program. Those who tried such retraining were concentrated in the unemployed group, and they were more likely to have had a greater number of job-loss experiences ($r = .33$, $p < .05$). This suggests that the experience of recurring bouts with unemployment may motivate professionals to seek entry into another career that offers greater stability. But since those who enrolled in retraining programs were still unemployed, the effects of the retraining on their employability may be quite limited. Even among the few who had found work after retraining, none felt that the retraining had contributed to their reemployment. However, because of the small number involved, conclusions about effectiveness are unwarranted.

Willingness to Retrain

The limited participation in retraining programs does not seem to result from a professional's unwillingness to participate in retraining or to change fields (Briar, 1976; Rittenhouse, 1967; Thompson, 1972). In fact, in our study many more felt they could adapt or convert their knowledge and skills through retraining than had actually participated in such programs (Table 7.2). Although unemployed professionals have been found willing to retrain, many would not do so unless financial assistance were provided and a job assured at completion (Thompson, 1972). Therefore, the desire to retrain exists, but unemployed professionals may be unwilling to risk their scarce resources in an investment that may not pay off with a job.

There is certainly no lack of specialties in which professionals can be retrained. For example, we selected the specialties listed in Table 7.2 because they were oriented toward solving some of society's most pressing problems at the time of the study (1971). Transportation and pollution control turned out to be the most likely areas where conversion of skills would be most effective for those in our study, but the other areas were also considered appropriate for retraining by a smaller

TABLE 7.2. Percentage Indicating That Their Knowledge and Skills Are Extremely or Quite Adaptable for Conversion to Different Areas of Specialization

Area of Specialization	Employment Status		
	Unemployed (N=51)	Underemployed (N=52)	Reemployed in Field (N=54)
Pollution control	37	35	46
Public administration	26	29	37
Transportation	51	37	45
Health care	16	25	17
Law enforcement	12	10	13
Urban development	35	19	32

number of professionals. The popularity of transportation and pollution control may reflect the technical backgrounds of many in the sample.

The willingness to retrain seems to be concentrated among those who did not want to relocate. For example, the unemployed professionals who were more reluctant to relocate tended to be more adaptable to retrain for careers in pollution control ($r = .30, p < .05$), public administration ($r = .27, p < .05$), transportation ($r = .38, p < .01$), and urban development ($r = .60, p < .001$). Apparently, professionals who have limited their job options to a particular geographic area attempt to improve their employability by a greater willingness to redirect their career.

There were also some individual differences consistently associated with the degree to which professionals felt their skills were adaptable. Those among the unemployed who were more willing to take risks in the type of job they wanted indicated greater adaptability toward such areas as pollution control ($r = .29$, $p < .05$), transportation ($r = .55, p < .001$), and urban development ($r = .42$, $p < .001$). Similar but slightly lower relationships were found between personal control and adaptability in these fields. Hence a willingness to retrain may be determined to a large extent by the professionals' venturesomeness and openness toward change, as well as belief in their own capabilities to effect change. Since these characteristics tend to be most prevalent among those who have been out of work less than six months, the intervention of retraining may be most effective during the earlier stages of unemployment.

It should be noted that defense industry professionals who had lost their jobs felt that they could more easily retrain or adapt their skills than did their colleagues who were still working (Gannon, Foreman and Pugh, 1973). A willingness to change fields has been found to increase the longer professionals remain out of work (Gutteridge, 1978). Apparently, the experience of losing a job accompanied by the need to be employed can serve to unfreeze identification with an occupational specialty. Certainly, when there are no jobs available in a professional's field, there would appear to be no choice but to become more flexible in the type of work one is willing to accept. However, as we have noted, such flexibility may not last for those experiencing long-term unemployment, since professionals who have been out of work for an extended period of time can develop an occupational rigidity as a defense. Nevertheless, our data indicated that the length of time professionals spent out of work was not linearly related to their willingness to retrain. But there does appear to be a curvilinear relationship with the maximum retraining adaptability exhibited by those in stage III of unemployment. As we have seen, it is during this period that career change becomes a serious option.

The professionals' willingness to retrain was related not only to personality factors but also to the versatility of their technical knowledge and skills. For example, the unemployed who remained more up to date in their profession felt that their knowledge and skills were more adaptable in areas such as transportation

($r = .26$, $p < .05$) and law enforcement ($r = .28$, $p < .05$). In addition, the number of professional journals read by individuals was related to how adaptable they believed their skills were for jobs in public administration ($r = .35$, $p < .01$), law enforcement ($r = .43$, $p < .01$), and urban development ($r = .27$, $p < .05$). Professionals who keep abreast of new developments are those who are better able to maintain a versatility and openness to change (Kaufman, 1974c) and hence would be more prepared to go through the retraining required for working in another field.

Factors Related to Retraining Adaptability

In an attempt to explore more extensively the factors affecting professionals' willingness to retrain, we again turned to path analysis (see Chapter 3). We computed an individual index of retraining adaptability for every unemployed professional by summing the ratings of how adaptable their knowledge and skills were for conversion to each field.

As is evident from Figure 7.1, retraining adaptability among the unemployed men in our study was greatest if their wives were not working. At first this seems

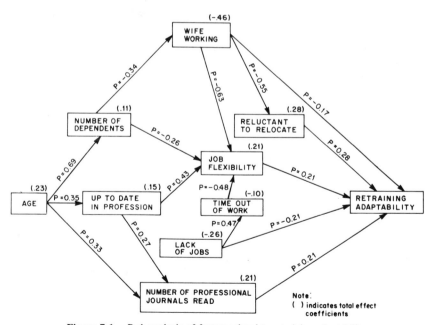

Figure 7.1.   Path analysis of factors related to retraining adaptability.

contrary to what one would expect since if one's wife is working there is at least a family income that could permit the husband to take the time to retrain. However, on further inspection of the path analysis, we see that the wife is probably not working because of the need to take care of her children. Men with more dependents and whose wives are not working would have a strong need to find employment that provides security and this could explain why they are not attracted to jobs involving a high degree of uncertainty and change. Those who lacked this flexibility were also less adaptable to retraining. In addition, men whose wives were working were more willing to relocate, which in turn was related to a lower retraining adaptability. Relocation not only may be a more attractive option to those not tied down by children, but it also could serve to restore the breadwinner status of the husband, especially if the wife ceased to work when the family moved. On the other hand, retraining is likely to help the husband find reemployment without relocation, in which case the wife may be more apt to continue working than if they had moved. Whatever the case, it seems that there are trade-offs between retraining and relocation, so that resistance toward one is compensated for by flexibility toward the other.

Barriers to reemployment resulting from a lack of jobs serves to increase the professional's retraining adaptability. However, it is those who stay most up to date, especially by reading professional journals, who are more open to retraining. Interestingly enough, these individuals tend to be somewhat older. Upon further analysis, the highest adaptability turned out to be among midcareer professionals. In contrast to older professionals' reluctance to relocate or continue their formal education, it appears that at least among those in midcareer who have remained broadly knowledgeable, retraining is quite attractive. In fact, as mentioned in Chapter 3, many may have just been waiting for the opportunity to carry out a career change. Thus, for the professional in midcareer, retraining to improve employability appears to be more desirable than either relocation or formal continuing education.

Retraining and Reemployment

A major barrier to skills conversion has not been the professionals' reluctance to participate but rather the scarcity of appropriate retraining programs. Almost all government-sponsored job training activities have been directed toward the unskilled, the economically disadvantaged, and the hard-core unemployed. Among the exceptions were several small-scale programs initiated during the early 1970s to deal with the reorientation and conversion of out-of-work aerospace and defense industry professionals. The specific problem of retraining such specialists was recognized well before it became critical (Rittenhouse, 1967), yet little was done to prepare for it. Since on-the-job training was considered an adequate path to skills conversion, formal retraining programs for professionals were not greatly stressed. It would appear that the responses developed, including the on-the-job training offered by the government's Public Employment Program (PEP) established under the Emergency Employment Act (EEA) of 1971, were not adequate to deal with the large numbers of unemployed professionals who became eligible for retraining *(Manpower Report of the President,* 1975). Although such government responses are discussed in Chapter 8, an analysis of the impact of retraining on reemployment is appropriate here.

The relatively few retraining programs that were developed for professionals apparently had some success, albeit on a small scale. One such program, the Aerospace Employment Project (AEP), was carried out by the National League of Cities and U.S. Conference of Mayors under a grant from the Department of Housing and Urban Development and the Department of Labor. Its purpose was to determine whether professionals formerly employed in aerospace and defense industries could effectively help to meet the needs of local government (DiNunzio, 1972; Ventre and Sullivan, 1972; Wheaton, Jones, and Fox, 1972).

A total of 376 such professionals selected from 7000 applicants in the 10 areas most stricken by high unemployment attended 30-day courses given at Massachusetts Institute of Technology and the University of California at Berkeley. This program could more accurately be called reorientation rather than retraining, since it was designed to introduce participants to the terminology and problems of local government and to acquaint them with the types of jobs that would be available. The teaching techniques used in this program included lectures and panel discussions by civic authorities, simulation games, field trips, and informal group discussions. Simultaneously, attempts at job development were carried out which included a promotional campaign by the project staff to inform prospective employers about the availability of their pool of skilled manpower, and the establishment of a system to bring together employers and participants. One of the most effective aspects of the program was the organization of participants into self-help groups which maintained close communication with the 10 target areas and the project centers, found jobs in each area for other participants, and generally helped sustain morale. The importance of such group support during the job search cannot be underestimated and is discussed more extensively later in this chapter.

The combination of reorientation and job development paid off; almost eight out of ten were placed in jobs within seven months of completing the course. Of those placed, 65 percent were in local government and the rest were employed in private industry. Only one-fourth felt that substantially different skills were required in their new jobs, indicating a relatively high utilization of prior skills. Over half were reemployed in administrative positions, with most of the others returning to technically oriented work. Money was not a key factor in accepting a position in local government; the salaries of these professionals in their new jobs were generally lower than in their previous positions. Rather, their choice was apparently influenced by anticipated security and advancement in a public service career and a reluctance to relocate.

Participants who entered public service generally felt that the program was helpful, particularly in giving them understanding of the new environment in which they were planning to work (Ventre and Sullivan, 1972). Furthermore, the courses contributed to clear-cut attitudinal and cognitive changes, especially with respect to urban problems. Apparently, the reorientation program succeeded in sensitizing the unemployed aerospace professionals to the unfamiliar types of work they were preparing to enter. The greatest value of such reorientation programs may be the socialization of the participant in a new career.

A more varied retraining program was sponsored by the Department of Labor and carried out by the National Society of Professional Engineers (NSPE) under their Technology Utilization Project (TUP). In terms of goals, TUP was similar to the AEP discussed above, but it was designed to reorient and convert aerospace engineers toward technologies which research had already identified as being in demand by industry. Furthermore, the content of the courses generally involved very intensive training in the technical knowledge and skills required for each area.

Courses in 11 different fields, lasting up to 12 weeks, were provided to 329 unemployed engineers and scientists at universities scattered throughout the United States (National Society of Professional Engineers, 1973). Some 96 percent of the participants were reemployed within 28 weeks after the courses were completed, six out of ten in the fields in which they had received their retraining. In some courses, such as traffic engineering, forest service engineering, and residential construction engineering, all participants found new jobs and almost all were placed in the fields for which they had trained. Their salaries on the whole were lower than those in their previous jobs, but as was the case in the AEP, reluctance to relocate apparently resulted in a willingness to accept lower pay in their local community.

One reason for the success of TUP was the rapport established with potential employers. Job development is crucial to the success of such retraining programs. One program administered by the California Department of Human Resources was designed to train "environmental managers" but failed to place its graduates because the jobs for which they were prepared did not exist (Hammer, 1974). A program with a similar orientation set up by a consortium of Florida educational institutions was highly successful because "job vacancies were lined up *before* the potential job holder was trained" (Hammer, 1974, p. 407). Similarly, the involvement of private corporations in the support of a New York State Regents' sponsored seven-week program to retrain humanities Ph.Ds for careers in business apparently helped assure successful placement of participants (Harrison and

May, 1978). There is no question that professionals who experience difficulty in the job market are willing and able to be retrained. However, unless they are matched with appropriate jobs following retraining, all that will have been accomplished is the creation of unemployed or underemployed retrainees.

Retraining and Adjustment

It is often assumed that retraining of unemployed professionals will improve their adjustment. This is not necessarily true. Retrainees who remain unemployed may be worse off than before. Indeed, jobless professionals who had difficulty finding work after being retrained became depressed since their high expectations of being reemployed were not met (DiNunzio, 1972). Retrainees who are placed in positions in which they must take a salary reduction may also have problems of adjustment. This was found to be the case among aerospace professionals who were retrained for positions in local government. It was observed that if the retrainee's "civil service salary is substantially lower than the salary he received in aerospace, his ability to find ways of adapting his skills may be impaired because his own self-esteem is reduced, thus impairing his professional functioning" (Ventre and Sullivan, 1972, p. 105). A considerably lower salary may be associated with a loss of status. Thus reemployment in such a case may not contribute to adjustment but rather to a greater likelihood of psychological deterioration.

Lest we conclude that successful placement following the retraining of professionals is all that is necessary to assure a positive adjustment, let us take heed from the following observations of a public administrative officer about a group of local government retrainees who were hired: "The rather desperate unemployment situation was obviously a traumatic experience for some of these people. Several of them have so far remained quite unsure and reticent, and have a tendency toward anonymity which will have to be overcome" (DiNunzio, 1972, p. 145). For these professionals the retraining was instrumental in their reemployment, but it apparently did little to repair the psychological damage resulting from job loss.

Researchers who have investigated the psychological impact of unemployment have explained: "For a person who has worked for many years in a particular line of work, and whose self-concept is centered in that job, retraining for an entirely new occupation is extremely difficult, particularly in retraining programs that fail to focus on the personal adjustment problems of the trainees" (Tiffany, Cowan, and Tiffany, 1970, p. 29). Although counseling was part of the retraining programs we have discussed, it apparently was not effective for many in dealing with their adjustment to a new work role. In view of the importance of this problem, we turn our attention next to job counseling and its effects on reemployment and adjustment.

JOB COUNSELING

For many professionals, suddenly having to search competitively for a job in the tight labor market of the 1970s was a completely new experience, and some simply did not know how to go about finding work. In fact, it was observed that for most of the TUP retrainees, "there was a definite deficiency in the student's ability to engage in job-seeking activities on his own behalf" (National Society of Professional Engineers, 1973, p. 22). In addition, the inability of professionals to find work can lead to a reduction in their job search efforts. Indeed, some professionals who get turned down after several job interviews lose confidence in their ability to present themselves and may even cease going to interviews (DiNunzio, 1972). As we have already seen, this is a common characteristic of the long-term unemployed professionals who have become work inhibited.

The early intervention of job counseling can "inoculate" jobless professionals in an attempt to "immunize" them to the psychological deterioration associated with long-term joblessness. Crucial to such immunization is maintenance of the belief that one is still in control (Seligman, 1975). When jobless professionals learn not only to understand what is happening to them, but also how to cope more effectively with being unemployed, they are more likely to remain in control. It will be recalled that those professionals who had previous job loss experiences generally knew better how to cope with the problems encountered when they were again unemployed. As Seligman (1975) explains: "A past history of experience with controllability over a given outcome will lead to an expectation that the outcome is controllable. . . . A past history of uncontrollability will make it difficult to believe that an outcome is controllable, even when it actually is" (p. 60). Hence, one major objective of any intervention for enhancing the adjustment of unemployed professionals would be to help them maintain the belief that they are still in control. This could be accomplished by means of stress inoculation, a cognitive therapy approach that has been applied to a variety of problems, including anxiety, anger, and depression (Meichenbaum, 1975; Novaco, 1977). Stress inoculation involves developing the individual's cognitive, affective, and behavioral coping skills and then providing for the practice of these skills. Such skill development directed toward dealing with unemployment stress would appear to hold much promise in enhancing the employability of those who suffer job loss.

Counseling directed toward career change may be useful not only to professionals who view job loss as an opportunity to leave an occupation in which they were dissatisfied, but also to those who try to cope with their reemployment difficulties by attempting an involuntary career change. The latter professionals should be counseled with caution, since they very likely have reached stage III of unemployment, when career change becomes a typical coping response accompanying the psychological deterioration that has already begun. For such individuals, evaluations and tests used for career counseling can be very misleading. Illustrative of this is the case of a 42-year-old rising executive who had lost his position in a major company involved in the space program (Seligman, 1975). He took a job in which he was so unhappy that he quit after six months. His psychological state then deteriorated rapidly. He turned to professional counseling in response to the urging of his wife, and completed some vocational guidance tests to help direct him toward a satisfying job. Reaching this goal, however, became doubtful, as the following assessment indicated:

> When the results of the tests came back, they revealed that he had a low tolerance for frustration, that he was unsociable, that he was incapable of taking on responsibility, and that routine, prescribed work best fit his personality. The vocational guidance company recommended that he become a worker on an assembly line.
>
> This advice came as a shock . . . since he had twenty years of high executive achievement behind him, was usually outgoing and persuasive, and was much brighter than most sewing-machine operators. But the tests actually reflected his present state of mind: he believed himself incompetent, he saw his career as a failure, he found every small obstacle an insurmountable barrier, he was not interested in other people, and he could barely force himself to get dressed, much less to make important career decisions (Seligman, 1975, p. 76).

This case illustrates the questionable value of certain types of career assessment techniques for counseling jobless professionals whose employability may be greatly impaired by an advanced state of psychological deterioration. It also argues in favor of interventions, such as counseling, as early as possible after job loss has occurred. Unfortunately, counseling is typically sought by those who have encountered rejection and frustration in their job search and feel like giving up (Briar, 1976). Thus, most unemployed professionals who seek counseling do so as a last resort, when it may be too late for some.

Since job-seeking behavior has been found to be related to reemployment success, professionals should benefit from counseling designed to help promote a more successful job search. Indeed, it has been found that the employability of hard-to-place professionals increased as a result of such intensive individual counseling (Horowitz, 1968). However, with masses of professionals looking for work, group counseling would appear to be better able to handle the problem than the individual approach. In fact, there is accumulating evidence that group counseling can be highly effective not only for improving job search techniques but also in dealing with problems of adjustment. Therefore, we examine next how some group-oriented approaches have attempted to deal with unemployment stress.

Employment Workshops

In 1970, a major attempt at providing group job counseling to large numbers of unemployed professionals was initiated in California by the American Institute of Aeronautics and Astronautics (AIAA) in the form of Employment Workshops. The enormous popularity of this program was indicative of the need for such counseling. With support from the U.S. Department of Labor and the National Aeronautics and Space Administration, the program eventually spread throughout the country and involved the participation of other professional societies. By the end of 1971, a total of 175 workshops had been held in 43 cities, attended by 14,600 out-of-work professionals.

According to the AIAA (1972), the Employment Workshops prepared professionals to be competitive in their job search and taught them effective techniques of presenting themselves to a potential employer in an ''employers market''. An additional objective was to bolster morale and improve attitudes. The workshops consisted of three sessions of several hours' duration, spaced one week apart. Participants split into small groups guided by trained counselors, who generally were peer volunteers. The sessions focused on developing a systematic job search, writing letters and résumés, and improving interview techniques. The methods used ranged from self-analysis of professional skills to role playing and group criticism. One innovation involved a separate workshop for wives of the unemployed to help them deal with the types of stress experienced in their families.

Only about one-tenth of the professionals in our study took part in Employment Workshops, despite the fact that most were in technical fields and had access to the workshops through their professional societies. Although professionals who used the workshops tended to be among those who became reemployed, few rated them as very helpful in finding work. Unfortunately, the sample was too small to arrive at any conclusions about the effectiveness of the workshops.

A follow-up study (AIAA, 1972) of 459 workshop participants who were unemployed indicated that the workshop did contribute to the improvement of their job search techniques, particularly the writing of résumés as well as letters and the development of interview skills. To a lesser degree, the workshop also helped the participants learn how to research job prospects and improved their awareness of employment trends. One of the weaker areas was the defining of personal goals, although even here most felt that the workshops were of at least some value. However, only slightly over one-tenth of the participants attributed improved morale to the workshops. Furthermore, of those who found work within two months after attending the workshop, only 15 percent felt that what they gained from the workshop was mainly responsible for their acquiring a new job. Although there was no evidence that attendance at the workshops increased a participant's chances of finding work, most of those who became reemployed did feel that the workshops had been of some value in helping them get their job. There was even some indication that attendance at the workshop diminished the likelihood of underemployment. Practically all participants gave positive recommendations about the workshops to their colleagues.

To determine whether the workshops had any effect on attitudinal or motivational characteristics, we administered questionnaires to participants in the New York City area before, as well as after, they participated in the workshops. Among the 24 who provided useable responses, we found a significant improvement in attitudes toward the importance of job search techniques, such as researching job prospects, writing various types of résumés, and varying one's strategy for each prospect. No significant changes were found in such characteristics as self-esteem, initiative, or job interview anxiety, although there was some indication that the workshop could serve to reduce some of the stress resulting from unemployment. Before beginning the workshop over half of the participants reported that their unemployment was either very disturbing or had changed their whole life; after completion of the workshop only about three out of ten felt this way. Because of the small sample size this result was not significant, but the trend was clear. It appears that the Employment Workshops were effective primarily in stimulating the development of job search techniques, but their usefulness in improving psychological adjustment may be limited, at best, to alleviating some of the stress of the unemployment experience. We must remember that the workshops involved only three sessions and expecting any major change beyond the learning of new job search techniques would be unrealistic.

Intensive Group Counseling

By increasing the number of group counseling sessions, it should be possible to improve the psychological adjustment as well as the employability of jobless professionals. One experiment investigated the effectiveness of 10 group meetings which focused on improving job search skills as well as enhancing the self-esteem of 22 unemployed professionals (Powell, 1973). Ninety days after the last group meeting, those who had participated were significantly more likely to have returned to work than were those in a control group. The participants also were more active in utilizing placement agencies and college job banks, as well as in scheduling more interviews; and they showed an improvement in self-esteem, an indication that such group sessions can have an effect on the overall adjustment of unemployed professionals. The participants responded most positively to the didactic and situational role-playing aspects of the group experience but were less enthusiastic about the self-analytic features. Group leaders, however, felt that the greatest benefit was derived from sessions where self-analytic and didactic features were integrated.

There is evidence that even more intensive small group counseling sessions that utilize behavior-modification techniques can further improve the effectiveness of job hunting. Such an approach, which deals with the skills of finding employment in the framework of a social reinforcement process, has been described as follows:

> Job-finding was viewed as requiring a number of complex skills which should be learned best in a structured learning situation that emphasized such learning factors as motivation, maintenance of behavior, feedback, imitation, and practice. Job counseling was considered as a learning experience which should be taught in a structured and continuing manner until the job was obtained. In addition, the present program was a systems approach oriented to the perspective of the job-seeker: the program assisted the job seeker in every area that was believed to be influenced in obtaining a job. Assistance was provided for such diverse problems as discouragement in job-seeking, need for family understanding, transportation, peer assistance, professional advice, job leads, preparation of a résumé, interview skills, techniques for approaching friends, practice in obtaining interviews, scheduling of one's time and expanding one's vocational choices (Azrin, Flores, and Kaplan, 1975, pp. 17–18).

An experiment which applied this group counseling approach in a job-scarce area demonstrated that 90 percent of the unemployed, many of whom were college-educated, who had been randomly assigned to attend a daily "job club" found work within two months from the time the club began, compared to 55 percent of those in a control group which did not receive counseling (Azrin et al., 1975). Furthermore, those who participated in the club found their jobs much more rapidly than did the controls, and club members' jobs were superior both in salary and in utilization of knowledge and skills. Interestingly, regular daily attendance was highly correlated with early success in finding a job. Club members who did not find work had attended irregularly or had ceased coming at an early stage in the program, whereas those who found jobs attended regularly and continuously. Apparently, the continuous social reinforcement provided by the job club was instrumental in providing both the skills and motivation to carry out a successful job hunt. As the psychologist who developed this approach, Nathan H. Azrin, explains: "It is not only a matter of learning what to do. Motivation is an important part of it. I created a situation in which job seekers worked together to find a job, and I used social contact to provide the motivation" (*The New York Times,* 1975c, p. 30). Why the group effort approach is a crucial factor in the success of the job club is elaborated on further in an interview with Azrin:

> The group effort approach, says Azrin, is a crucial factor in the program's success. Having the reassurance that there are others "in the same boat" generates a feeling of camaraderie among the job-seekers as they provide one another with mutual encouragement and advice. Job-seekers, he explains, frequently become so discouraged by their failure to obtain a job that they abandon all efforts. In order to over-

come this discouragement, Azrin enlists the support and encouragement of family members, as well as former job club members who have already obtained employment. It works almost like an Alcoholics Anonymous or Weight Watchers group with those who have been through the same painful process providing examples of "I did it. You can do it too".

"People who are unemployed tend to stress their limitations and what they can't do," says Azrin. "It's important to reverse the negative opinions these people have about themselves and instill a heightened self-image to get them to emphasize their positive attributes" (Schaar, 1976, p. 6).

The evidence certainly favors this group-based behavior modification approach to help the unemployed professional pursue a successful job search. In order for any group approach to be truly effective in dealing with psychological adjustment, the focus should be on enhancing the motivation and self-esteem of participants as well as on the skills and knowledge necessary for finding work. Insofar as a group approach, such as the job club, helps to develop cognitive, affective, and behavioral coping skills to deal with job loss, it can provide unemployment stress inoculation to many more than could be reached through individual counseling. As we shall see in the next section, reemployment may help adjustment to some degree, but for many a return to work may not be sufficient to repair the psychological damage caused by the job loss experience. The group counseling approach, with its social support and reinforcement mechanisms, holds much promise in enhancing a more complete adjustment to job loss in a highly cost-effective way.

Peer Counseling and Self-Help Groups

Thus far we have focused on job counseling from the perspective of jobless professionals who may be in need of such assistance to improve their employability and adjustment. However, some professionals have responded to their own job loss by volunteering as counselors to help others who are "in the same boat." Although at first this may seem a very altruistic gesture, becoming a peer counselor can contribute greatly to the well-being of the professional who volunteers for such a role. Such volunteer work can be motivated by many factors, even guilt, as the following case illustrates:

Ralph, a 42 year old researcher, has been out of work for a year. He has kept busy and active by organizing and working with groups of unemployed men in the same situation. He claims that his motivation for helping these other jobless workers is so that he can better understand the experience of what it means for people to be thrown out of work. Before he was laid off, he had the task of laying off people at Boeing. Two tragedies occurred after he terminated some workers—one committed suicide and another became an alcoholic. He felt responsible for these events and believed that he lessens his guilt by helping others who are jobless (Briar, 1976, p. 45).

We have already noted that the Employment Workshops were staffed largely by unemployed professionals who volunteered their services. Another example of a predominantly volunteer effort was that of Start-Up, a community program that brought together a variety of services to help the large number of unemployed in the Seattle area during the early 1970s (United Way of King County, 1974). The one criterion counselors had to meet was that they had been unemployed. Such a selection criterion for counselors was considered both an asset and a burden, for the following reasons:

> The counselor in training could readily relate to waiting in lines, having one's phone disconnected, not having enough money to pay bills, applying for food stamps and the built-up family tension and anxiety created by unemployment. His own experiences allowed him to possess accurate empathy for his client's situation. This essential ingredient was to become one of the unique qualities in Start-Up's counseling program.
>
> The burden was whether the formerly unemployed person could maintain objectivity in the face of circumstances that had created recent personal pain. The new counselor had before him not only the task of learning interviewing techniques, communication skills, crisis intervention theory and process, and community resources, but the task of dealing with his own feelings regarding unemployment and his own newly healed unemployment wounds as well.
>
> The Start-Up counselor, by his own experience, was keenly aware of the effects of unemployment upon an individual's self-esteem, dignity and self-confidence. This awareness coupled with the training enabled the counselor and client to mutually examine the client's situation. Together, client and counselor sorted out feelings and events and moved toward the process of problem solving (United Way of King County, 1974, p. 14).

Each counselor received 265.5 hours of training that included therapeutic psychology, group work, and dealing with problems such as low self-esteem, depression, anger, and suicide. The combination of this training together with their own unemployment experience was essential for providing effective counseling, although there were some initial difficulties. As one woman, who was unemployed for three months after losing her position as a high school teacher and counselor, explained:

> My own unemployment experience was such that I had very strong feelings for people in trouble. I did not expect people to open up so quickly, in terms of discussing their own hurts. The training that we received from the Crisis Clinic was very essential for learning how to cope with people in trouble.
>
> I found that I became as distressed as the clients in the beginning of the program because I didn't have the answers either. It was very hard for me to deal with client

depression. After a couple of months, I started to feel much better about finding resources quickly and advocating for clients. Each week and month that went by
strengthened us all. The counselors were very supportive to each other with special
problems that one person couldn't solve. One of my counselor supervisors was
indispensible to me personally in dealing with difficult people. I really learned a lot
about handling emotions and how people interact.

My most important job here has been to discern what the client's real problems are
and how it is affecting their employability. Learning to refer people for counseling
for emotional problems or to constructively guide them about some behavior that
may be effecting their getting a job I developed a lot of confidence in my own judg-
ment, and it was gratifying to see a client zero in on his own problem and have a
place to work on it. It has been very important to me to have actually helped other
people, and also learn to cope with not being able to help.

The services that Start-Up offered were so diverse, depending on the needs of the
client, that the ability to respond to a broad range of problems in itself was the
greatest service. I don't know of any other place that a person could walk in and get
help, tailored to their particular situation. I am struck by the terrible isolation in a
large city of people floundering because of unemployment, family break-down and
the absence of community feeling. People fall through the cracks in a large city into a
spiritual void, but no matter how down or depressed they are, they are most eager to
help others, when they have the chance. The Job Readiness Workshop has been a
fantastic service for people to pull employment and personal difficulties together. I
think that Start-Up's greatest service has been a place to help end the isolating factors that occur in a time of crisis, and to help people find a place to grow.

Start-Up has been the greatest work experience of my life. It has been like reading
four books a day, sharing the lives of so many different types of people. The training
sessions have really been enlightening. It has been fascinating to work with a staff of
such different ages and life styles and witness how very close they have become. I
have really learned about the problems of this city, which have become flesh and
blood issues, rather than abstract newspaper items. I am a changed person from what
I was 18 months ago. (United Way of King County, 1974, pp. 20–21).

There does not seem to be any doubt that volunteering as a peer counselor to assist
others who are unemployed can also help professionals acquire the skills and self-
confidence to enhance their own employability and adjustment. Although counseling programs such as Start-Up have been the exception rather than the rule, especially since many volunteers became paid counselors, many opportunities for
unemployed professionals to provide peer counseling were created by the self-
help groups that were established throughout the country in the early 1970s. For
example, within the framework of Start-Up were several self-help groups for professionals. These included SEA-VEST (Seattle Volunteer Engineers, Scientists
and Technicians), Teachers Without Students, and Talent Plus, a self-help group

for professionals in all fields. In addition to peer counseling, such groups also involved unemployed professionals in job development and placement activities. Moreover, these self-help groups provided the unemployed professionals with social support from those who shared their problems as well as a "cloak of dignity" to conceal their jobless state from others, as the following description indicates:

> Daily the men would congregate to plan or discuss job finding strategies. Most wore business clothes, some appeared in their regular professional work garb, with attaché case and all. It was possible because of these organizations to leave home with the work hour crowd and arrive with the crowd in the evening after spending an eight hour day at the self-help office. And this also permitted one to conceal his unemployment from neighbors and friends (Briar, 1976, p. 55).

Self-help groups clearly have an important role to play in enhancing the employability and adjustment of unemployed professionals. Therefore, we discuss them further in our evaluation of societal responses in Chapter 8.

CROSS-CULTURAL COMPARISONS

In attempting to find cross-cultural evidence regarding strategies of change that unemployed professionals use to cope with their situation, we are again faced with a paucity of data. Even the widespread international migration of professionals in search of work has not been adequately investigated. However, it does seem clear that one of the most important motivational factors which stimulated the "brain drain" of highly educated workers to the United States was the need to utilize their professional knowledge and skills. According to a National Science Foundation study, almost one-fourth of immigrant scientists and engineers who settled in the United States reported that they did so because there just were no jobs in their country of origin which could utilize their professional background (National Science Foundation, 1973). One researcher who focused on the brain drain of highly educated workers from England to the United States explained that "like most professionals they seem to express themselves as persons most vitally in their work, and it appears that in the deepest sense, they are vested in their work, and want to be allowed to get on with it. . . . Migration is seen as a means toward this end—towards the best use of their talents, and not as a means to an easier life, more money, leisure, or the like" (Wilson, 1969, p. 446). Such migration does appear to improve professional utilization. For example, three-fourths of immigrant scientists and engineers in the United States reported that their professional opportunities did indeed become better after migrating to the United States (National Science Foundation, 1973).

A special case related to migration involves the many Soviet Jewish scientists who requested permission to emigrate but were denied such permission and lost their positions as a result of their request. These unemployed professionals formed a self-help group which since 1972 has organized scientific seminars to keep up to date in their fields despite government attempts to stop such gatherings (Austin, 1980a,c).

There is a limited amount of research on relocation of unemployed professionals within their own countries. One such study focused on India (Asher, 1972). As was the case in the United States, professional commitment may strongly influence geographical mobility in India. For example, it was the better educated Indian job seekers who were more willing to take jobs away from home. Furthermore, those in certain professions, such as engineering or medicine, were much more mobile than others. Although job opportunities in India may be somewhat better for engineers or doctors than for other professionals, their greater willingness to be employed outside their own states may be attributed to a professional commitment manifested by a strong desire to utilize their knowledge and skills, even if it requires relocation.

Perhaps the most extensive cross-cultural data concerning strategies of change that jobless professionals use to improve their employability comes from Israel. As was found to be true in the United States, having roots in a community was also an important factor in the willingness to relocate among unemployed professionals in Israel. For example, almost half of the native-born Israelis were unwilling to relocate, compared to only one-third of recent immigrants (Bar-Yosef, Shield, and Varsher, 1975). The latter group had migrated from abroad and most had not yet established roots in the country. However, regardless of origin, only about one-tenth were willing to relocate without preconditions. The most important of these preconditions—for over half the sample—was that relocation would be acceptable only if the job was especially good. Two-thirds of the native-born Israelis, as well as those who came from Western countries, endorsed this precondition for relocation. In this situation we see that the desire to be reemployed in a good position can overcome a reluctance to relocate. However, the situation is not comparable to that in the United States since Israel is smaller than most of the 50 states. Relocation from one part of Israel to another would be comparable in distance to an intrastate migration in the United States. Hence, relocation in Israel is likely to be much less disruptive of attachments to family and friends than it would be in the United States.

Attitudes toward relocation in Israel were also related to sex differences. As was found in the United States, male professionals in Israel were more willing to relocate than their female colleagues. For men, the major precondition was that the position be a good one, whereas women were willing to move only if there was a good job for their husbands. In a further analysis of sex differences we found that for men, the greater the difficulty they had in finding a job in their profession, the more willing they were to relocate without preconditions. Women, on the other hand, were more willing to relocate unconditionally if their husbands were out of work. We thus see that it is the problem of reemployment for the male in the family that is crucial in creating a willingness to relocate on the part of both men and women. It is interesting that only among women was a lack of personal control clearly related to a willingness to relocate. Our earlier conclusion, that professionals who feel that they are more in control of their lives may be better able to resist changing locations in order to find work, also applies to Israel, at least for women. However, the feeling of personal control among unemployed Israeli women professionals is probably related not only to external job market conditions but also to their husbands' work status. Unemployed women professionals whose husbands were also out of work would be expected to have much less control than their male colleagues over the decision to relocate. Whether or not this holds for unemployed women professionals in the United States remains to be demonstrated.

The limited evidence we have indicates that when retraining of professionals is carefully planned and implemented, high success can be achieved in placement. Unfortunately, such retraining has not been carried out in the United States on a large scale encompassing many types of professionals. However, Israel has attempted retraining of college graduates for a wide range of occupations, and all indications are that they have been quite successful in placement (Bar-Yosef, 1977; Globerson and Baram, 1971). Of particular interest is that the Israeli retraining programs, which have been going on since 1966, have found that the greatest willingness to retrain, as well as the most successful placement following retraining, occurred among humanities, social science, and natural science graduates (Bar-Yosef et al., 1975; Globerson and Baram, 1971). In fact, a majority of unemployed humanities graduates were willing to retrain without the precondition that work in their own field could not be found. Those who had prior professional education, such as in engineering or law, were most resistant to retraining or working in their new occupation if they had completed retraining. However, engineers in Israel who had become underemployed following a period of joblessness appeared more willing to retrain and exhibited greater occupational flexibility than did those reemployed in their field (Bar-Yosef and Varsher, 1977). Apparently, underemployment following job loss can serve to unfreeze one's commitment to a profession.

Since the most serious employment problems of the highly educated are likely to occur among liberal arts graduates without career-oriented skills, retraining would hold much hope for them. However, retraining of those with a strong professional identification is likely to be more successful if their new occupation is related to their old one. In fact, three-fourths of the unemployed professionals in Israel were prepared to accept retraining when it was related to their field (Bar-Yosef et al., 1975). Only 5 percent were willing to retrain in an area totally different from their own occupation. Furthermore, the amount of work experience was found to be related to successful completion of retraining (Bar-Yosef and Weinberger, 1975). This lends further support to our conclusion that retraining would be highly appropriate for professionals in midcareer.

Although professional background was clearly the most important determinant of a willingness to retrain, there were other individual differences that had an effect as well. Over half of the unemployed men were unwilling to undergo retraining under any circumstances, whereas less than a third of the women were so resistant (Bar-Yosef et al., 1975). This could be explained only partly by the greater professional orientation among the men, since even within the same profession, such as engineering, women were found to be more willing to retrain than were their male colleagues (Bar-Yosef and Varsher, 1977). In a further analysis of the data we found that educational level was strongly related to a reluctance to retrain, regardless of sex. Furthermore, the greater the difficulty in finding a job in their profession, the more willing both men and women were to accept retraining. However, we did find that single women were more willing to retrain than were those who were married, but no such relationship was evident for the men.

Among professionals who were married, a willingness to retrain was clearly greater for those whose spouses were working. However, this relationship was considerably stronger among women. Apparently, it is professionals who do not have a great burden of financial responsibilities, such as women whose husbands are employed, who can more easily afford to take the time to retrain. In fact, we found that professionals in Israel under the greatest economic stress were more reluctant to retrain, regardless of sex. However, stress in the family was related to a willingness to retrain only among males. This may be a result of their wives working, which we have already seen is also associated with a greater willingness to retrain among male professionals in Israel. In contrast, our study in the United States found that male professionals whose wives were working were least willing to accept skills conversion, but this was in part a result of their greater willingness to relocate. This may indicate some trade-off between relocation and retraining, with an increased willingness to accept one strategy compensated for by an increased resistance toward the other. There was no evidence for such a trade-off in Israel, possibly because the group under study consisted largely of immigrants, many of whom were living in temporary quarters and who expected to relocate.

Although we found inconsistencies between results in the United States and those in Israel with respect to retraining, one factor appears to hold true in both countries: that under the right conditions most unemployed professionals are willing to be retrained and that retraining can lead to successful placement. It would appear that, regardless of culture, careful screening and counseling to determine individual readiness and ability to be retrained for a new occupation would be an important determinant not only of successful course completion and placement following retraining, but also of better adjustment to work following the disruption to career and life created by joblessness.

For unemployed professionals who are reluctant to retrain, continuing education to upgrade competency in their field would seem to be more appropriate. The potential effects of continuing education were revealed in a longitudinal study carried out in England which involved jobless managers who enrolled in a course designed to increase management competency (Hartley, 1980). The course participants showed a significant increase in self-esteem, whereas no such an increase was found among nonparticipants. As was the case in the United States, course taking cannot only upgrade the competency of jobless professionals in their field but can also improve their psychological well-being. Although the data are limited, continuing education holds much promise in contributing to the overall adjustment of unemployed professionals.

REEMPLOYMENT AND ADJUSTMENT

All the strategies we have discussed in this chapter have been directed at improving the employability of jobless professionals. Although reemployment may contribute to the adjustment of professionals who have been out of work, the job loss experience appears to have long-lasting effects which even a return to work cannot completely alleviate.

Many of the jobs obtained by terminated professionals resulted in their underemployment. A longitudinal study of a representative sample of displaced workers indicated that the major long-term impact of job loss was a substantial deterioration in occupational status (Parnes and King, 1977). This deterioration was clearly a result of professionals being reemployed in subprofessional jobs, which left them underemployed.

In examining the effects of reemployment in our study, it was found that more than one-fifth of the professionals who took a position that left them underemployed reported that their whole life was changed as a result of their job loss. On the other hand, such a drastic change was reported by only one-twentieth of the professionals who remained out of work or who were reemployed in their field. Furthermore, only 47 percent of the underemployed compared to 72 percent of those reemployed in their field reported that their lives had returned to normal. Although the underemployed were more than twice as likely to report normal lives as the unemployed (only 20 percent of whom did so), 29 percent still felt that a return to normalcy would occur in over a year or not at all, a rate comparable to the 27 percent found among the unemployed. In sharp contrast, only 9 percent of those reemployed in their field reported that it would take over a year for their lives to return to normal, and not one was so hopeless as to feel that it would never occur. It could very well be that the greatest amount of life stress occurs among professionals who take a job that leaves them underemployed, because many of them may be undergoing an involuntary career change. This could help explain why retraining does not appear to enhance the adjustment of some professionals.

Most professionals who found reemployment in their field considered their new jobs at least as good as their previous positions in every way (Table 7.3).

TABLE 7.3.   Comparison by Respondents (Percent) of Their New Job With the One
Held Prior to Unemployment on Various Characteristics

	Underemployed (N = 38)			Reemployed in Field (N = 42)			Significance of Difference[a]
	Worse	Same	Better	Worse	Same	Better	
Salary	50	13	37	10	31	60	$p < .001$
Job security	24	16	60	2	36	62	$p < .01$
Use of skills	68	11	22	17	41	43	$p < .001$
Type of work	51	19	30	12	41	49	$p < .001$
Working conditions	32	24	33	14	43	43	n.s.
Fringe benefits	32	30	38	10	57	33	$p < .02$
Chances of promotion	28	14	58	21	33	45	n.s.
Supervison	29	34	37	17	45	38	n.s.
Commuting conditions	29	42	29	41	33	26	n.s.
Job as a whole	40	5	55	12	19	69	$p < .01$

[a]Significance of difference between underemployed and reemployed in field; n.s., not significant.

Other research has also found this to be true for terminated professionals who were reemployed in permanent jobs (Brown, 1972). It would appear that job loss can lead to a positive career change and, as was indicated above, successful placement is associated with a more rapid return to a normal life.

Although those who became underemployed found positions that generally were inferior to their former jobs in salary, type of work, and use of skills, their new jobs tended to provide them with greater security and better chances for promotion (Table 7.3). This stability and growth potential apparently led to a majority of the underemployed rating their new job as better than their previous one. It is interesting that for the underemployed, the degree to which their life had returned to normal was strongly related to the job security of their new position relative to their last one ($r = -.61, p < .001$), but it was not at all related to other job characteristics. After professionals have undergone job loss, a position that provides them with greater security and a future may be more attractive to some than one offering a higher salary and utilization of their professional skills. Although most aerospace professionals who lost their jobs had to change their occupation as well as industry (Kaufman, 1980; Conner, 1973), their need for security may help explain why they were better adjusted in their new jobs than they were in their former ones (Ware, 1974). As one terminated aerospace professional who was reemployed in a nonaerospace job explained: "I took a $34.00 a week cut in pay. . . . I find the job interesting because it gives me security, which rests my mind.'' Apparently, for professionals who work in fields where job security is lacking, a career change that provides stability can contribute to their overall adjustment, even in cases of underemployment.

Despite the fact that the underemployed in our study tended to feel that they have a better job and that it is more secure, they may be paying for that security in psychological terms. Further evidence for such a conclusion is found by comparing the groups on the index of overall adjustment discussed in Chapter 2. Whereas professionals who were reemployed in their field were significantly higher in overall adjustment than the group remaining out of work, those who became underemployed were no better adjusted than the jobless. Similar results appeared for some of the specific scales making up the overall adjustment index. For example, compared to those who could not find work, the underemployed were no less resentful of what happened to them, but those reemployed in their field did exhibit significantly less resentment. It would thus appear that although a return to work in one's field does contribute to individual well being, taking a job that leaves a professional underemployed is far from effective in promoting psychological adjustment.

The use of professional skills among the underemployed in our study was considerably diminished in their new job. This has also been found to be true in other research (Briar, 1976; Brown, 1972). There is evidence that such a lack of utilization is a major contributing cause of obsolescence (Kaufman, 1974c). In fact, we found that the underemployed not only exhibited a significantly greater degree of professional obsolescence than those who were reemployed in their field, but also tended to be less professionally up to date than those who remained unemployed. Although it is possible that the more obsolescent would have greater difficulties finding successful reemployment, it is just as reasonable to attribute the inability to stay up to date among the underemployed to poor utilization of professional knowledge and skills in their new job. In addition, the underemployed may have undergone a career change, in which case they would still be learning about their new field. Nevertheless, we found that although few professionals who became reemployed in their field were underutilized in their new jobs, they too reported being significantly less up to date than those who had continuous employment. Although the most obsolescent may be more prone to termination, it is also likely that a lack of utilization during the period that professionals remain out of work can serve to exacerbate obsolescence or, at the very least, diminish feelings of competence when taking on a new job.

There is evidence that poor utilization can contribute not only to obsolescence, but also to job stress and poor adjustment to work (Caplan, Cobb, French, Harrison, and Pinneau, 1975; Ritti, 1971). Professionals who take temporary part-time jobs following termination become highly discouraged and anxious about their career (Briar, 1976). Indeed, among terminated professionals who accepted temporary positions, a lack of skill utilization was the only aspect of the job that was related to poor work adjustment, as indicated by a desire to leave their positions (Brown, 1972). Poor pay or job security were not at all related to adjustment in their new positions. This supports the evidence already presented that underemployment is likely to be detrimental to the psychological well-being of professionals. Since the problem of underemployment will continue to grow into the foreseeable future, the damaging effects of poor utilization on the mental health of professionals could rise to staggering proportions.

Underemployment has already become a stigma for some, particularly among recent college graduates. A university placement director discussing underemployment observed that many employers "don't understand what's happening, and they look on it as a very negative characteristic in a résumé that a graduate has taken a marginal job. They want to know what's wrong with him that he wasn't good enough to get a job in his field in the first place" (Shaffer, 1976, p. 16). Thus, becoming underemployed can evolve into a self-perpetuating situation. To break out of it will likely become more difficult as underemployment among the highly educated continues to increase. Therefore, although taking a job primarily to provide security may serve as a temporary stopgap measure to cope with joblessness, underemployment is likely to be damaging to the professionals' long-range career growth and ultimately, to their mental health.

Although professionals who become underemployed may do so to attain security, they can, in fact, increase their chances for job loss (Kaufman, 1980). We have already noted that professionals who have multiple episodes of job loss tend to experience the greatest stress. Studies of blue-collar workers have also indicated that repeated terminations can lead to extremely poor mental health (Ferman, 1979). Thus, if underemployment was perceived as providing security but in fact it did not, further psychological deterioration would be expected.

Perhaps the situation most likely to lead to psychological deterioration occurs when the jobless professional finds a superior job, only to be terminated again. Although data on professionals are lacking, studies of unemployed blue-collar workers revealed that "apathy and alienation tend to increase. . .even more acutely in the case of those workers who lose a new job which was considerably above the skill or pay level of the old, regular job" (Sheppard, 1965, p. 172). Therefore, reemployment in a better position in one's field is not sufficent to protect against further stress—job security must also be present.

In general, the evidence indicates that the more successful the reemployment experience, the greater the likelihood of adjustment. Yet even among professionals who were successfully reemployed in their field, the job loss experience may have a long-lasting influence on the individual which is not immediately obvious. Aside from detrimental effects, such as increased obsolescence, job loss apparently results in a loss of self-esteem, regardless of success in reemployment (Kaufman, 1973). All professionals experiencing joblessness, including those reemployed in their field, were significantly lower in self-esteem than the matched group of professionals who were continuously employed. In addition, the self-esteem of professionals reemployed in their field was not significantly higher than that of the underemployed or unemployed. It appears that a diminished self-esteem caused by job loss may not be fully restored even among those professionals who were successful in obtaining work in their field.

There is some evidence from other research which supports our findings on reemployment and psychological adjustment. For example, a study of laid-off blue-collar workers who found work in lower-level positions reported that "reemployment in such positions may restore some of the financial deprivation, but it does not necessarily restore the individual to his previous level of self-esteem, morale, and general psychological state" (Sheppard, 1965, p. 171). This conclusion would certainly apply to professionals who become underemployed. The case of the terminated aerospace executive described earlier in this chapter is illustrative of the psychological deterioration that can follow poor placement following job loss (see p. 211).

Perhaps the clearest evidence that reemployment does not necessarily remove the effects of job loss comes from several longitudinal studies. One such study that investigated terminated blue-collar workers over a two-year period found that despite the fact that the men eventually acquired new jobs, their evaluations of their life situation continually deteriorated "as if their experiences had permanently uprooted optimistic evaluation of their life and of their future" (Cobb and Kasl, 1971, p. 171). It is noteworthy that among jobless women workers, who were studied over a one-year period, reemployment did not have any discernible impact on their mental health (Fidell, undated). However, reemployment brought with it an increase in the use of alcohol, cigarettes, caffeine, aspirins, and other substances. This may indicate increased stress resulting from the conflict between home and work roles. With respect to out-of-work professionals, a study that investigated their psychological health for over a year arrived at a conclusion remarkably similar to that for blue-collar males: that reemployment "did not serve to reintegrate these workers into the milieu at their previous high levels of emotional or social functioning" (Estes, 1973, p. 277). The study of the professionals reported further that the "displacement effects following reemployment is somewhat troublesome since it confirms that the previously unemployed harbor chronic, if not permanent, scars from their unemployment experiences" (Estes, 1973, p. 277). In that study, half of the formerly unemployed professionals had changed to a different line of work and presumably many had become underemployed.

Career disruption and underemployment can have permanent debilitating effects not only on the individual professional but also on the society as a whole, whose well-being is so dependent on the commitment and contributions of its highly educated citizens. The potentially disruptive effects on society of widespread unemployment and underemployment among professionals calls for societal responses to deal with the problem. In Chapter 8 we will examine some of the possible responses on a societal level that can serve to promote the utilization and well-being of this country's professional resources.

SUMMARY AND CONCLUSIONS

We have examined several strategies that jobless professionals have used to enhance their employability as well as their adjustment. These strategies include the following:

1. *Geographic relocation* does not appear to be attractive to most unemployed professionals, particularly when they have established roots in their community such as those involving school-age children or attachments to a home, relatives, and friends. Thus, most likely to relocate are the youngest professionals or those who have already experienced extensive migration. Professionals who feel that they are more in control of their lives appear to be better able to resist relocation in order to find work, whereas a change of location becomes more attractive to those who feel that their reemployment is more dependent on environmental conditions than on their own capabilities. Migration is also more appealing to the most highly educated and professionally oriented. For these individuals, the need to utilize their professional knowledge and skills is of utmost importance, and to satisfy this need they would be willing to migrate practically anywhere. This has been one of the prime causes of the "brain drain" to the United States, but with a difficult job market a "reverse brain drain" has developed, with American professionals moving abroad in search of job opportunities.

Relocation appears to be most effective as a change strategy for professionals unemployed in areas where job opportunities are limited. Although those who do relocate may do better in terms of salary, job security, and skill utilization, it may be that such factors induced them to move in the first place. On the other hand, unemployed professionals who are reluctant to relocate appear to be more willing to accept a pay cut, underemployment, or less job security as a trade-off to avoid uprooting themselves or their families.

Although professionals may be more willing to relocate if they experience high unemployment stress, the additional life changes created by migration itself may actually contribute to an exacerbation of stress rather than its reduction. Given this possibility, other strategies of change may be more appropriate for most professionals who encounter severe reemployment problems.

2. *Continuing education* is another change strategy that unemployed professionals use to improve their employability. This typically involves enrolling for courses or a degree directed either toward self-improvement in their field or an actual career change. Business- or management-oriented courses are highly at-

tractive, particularly for technical professionals, and appear to be effective in enhancing reemployment. Those enrolling in business courses appear to be less professionally oriented, but they tend to have motivational and personality characteristics appropriate for management roles. Continuing education in the professionals' field may serve to maintain self-esteem as well as to update their knowledge and skills. On the other hand, enrolling for a degree in another profession appears to be highly effective for carrying out a career change.

Although continuing education may help to overcome some of the barriers associated with age or experience, it appears that older professionals are the most reluctant to enroll in formal courses. Since they are also less willing to relocate, such change strategies do not hold too much promise for improving the employability of older professionals.

Career-oriented continuing education generally appears to help professionals become not only more employable but also to cope better with being out of work. Insofar as continuing education can serve to socialize the professional into another career, it may very well enhance adjustment to reemployment in a new field.

3. *Retraining* programs are generally designed to prepare the unemployed to transfer into a new career. Most unemployed professionals appear willing to retrain, but this willingness is dependent on factors such as financial support, relevance of the training to their existing knowledge and skills, and perhaps most important, the assurance of a job on completion of the retraining. Professionals who have limited their job options by being unwilling to relocate may attempt to compensate for this and improve their employability by a greater willingness to retrain for another field. A willingness to retrain may also be determined by the professionals' venturesomeness and openness toward change as well as by their belief in their own capabilities to effect change. Since these characteristics tend to be most prevalent among those who have not experienced long-term unemployment, the intervention of retraining may be most effective some time before the end of stage III, when career change is most likely to become a serious option.

The professionals who keep abreast of new developments apparently develop the versatility and openness to change that makes retraining highly attractive to them. For older professionals, paticularly those in midcareer, retraining appears to be more desirable than either relocation or formal continuing education. Many may have just been waiting for the opportunity to change careers, and retraining would certainly be one of the best strategies to accomplish such a change.

The few retraining programs in the United States specifically directed toward professionals have been on a small scale, but they appear to have been largely successful, with job development being a crucial factor in their success. There is no question that jobless professionals are willing and able to be retrained, but unless they are matched with appropriate jobs, all that would be accomplished is the creation of unemployed or underemployed retrainees. For such individuals, psychological deterioration is likely to occur since their high expectations of reemployment is not met. However, even for some of the retrainees who become reemployed, severe problems may occur related to adjusting to the new field. This would be true especially for professionals whose self-concept had been based on their former occupation.

4. *Job counseling* for unemployed professionals is a relatively new phenomenon. The need for such assistance became clearly apparent in the early 1970s, when having to hunt competitively for a job become a new experience for many professionals, some of whom just did not know how to go about finding work. Since unemployed professionals who get turned down after several job interviews begin to lose confidence and may even become work inhibited, a counseling approach would be necessary at an early stage of joblessness to prevent this from occurring. Such intervention is also important in helping jobless professionals maintain a belief that they are still in control, thereby ''inoculating'' and ''immunizing'' them against unemployment stress and the psychological deterioration that is likely to occur the longer they are out of work.

Individual counseling has been found to improve the employability of even hard-to-place professionals, but group counseling appears to be a better approach not only because large numbers of professionals are in need of appropriate jobs, but also because the group can provide the much needed social support to maintain self-esteem and the motivation to work. The demand for such types of counseling was indicated by the enormous popularity of the Employment Workshops established in the early 1970s by some technical societies with government assistance. The Employment Workshops appear to have been effective primarily in stimulating the development of job search techniques, but because they were of short duration (three sessions held once a week) their usefulness for improving adjustment was limited.

However, there is evidence that by increasing the number of sessions, psychological adjustment in terms of enhanced self-esteem can be accomplished. Perhaps the best approach developed to date combines intensive group counseling with behavior modification. Continuous social reinforcement was apparently instrumental not only in developing the skills and motivation to carry out a successful job hunt but also in providing the mutual reassurance and encouragement for a more complete adjustment.

Although reemployment does contribute to the adjustment of professionals who have been out of work, experiences of job loss may have long-lasting effects which even a return to work cannot completely overcome. This is particularly true of jobless professionals who accept work that leaves them underemployed. In many respects they are no better adjusted than those remaining without work. Some of the underemployed may be experiencing a greater disruption in their life because of an involuntary career change. However, the lives of the underemployed were much more likely to return to normal if their new position provided job security. After undergoing the trauma of joblessness, a position that provides security is apparently more attractive to many professionals than one offering a higher salary or greater utilization of their knowledge and skills. Although taking a job primarily to provide security may serve as a temporary stopgap measure to cope with joblessness, underemployment is likely to be damaging to the professionals' long-range career growth and ultimately to their mental health. However, the importance of job security cannot be overestimated. Indeed, it seems that a situation in which termination occurs again after reemployment in a better job may be at least as psychologically damaging as if reemployment had not occurred.

Finding a better, as well as a more secure, position in their field helps professionals' restore normalcy to their lives. Yet even among those successfully reemployed in their field, the job loss experience can have a long-lasting influence on the individual that may not be outwardly visible. Not only do they feel less competent in taking on new assignments in their profession, but the diminished self-esteem caused by job loss may not be fully restored even by successful reemployment in their field. Of course, this has implications for society as well as for the individual, and we discuss these further in Chapter 8.

NOTES

1.   There is no universal definition for continuing education. However, a definition of continuing education used by the National Science Foundation will be adopted: "It is education that occurs or is taken after beginning full-time employment as a professional. . .and is usually addressed to such purposes as updating and diversification for maintaining competency of a professional. . .or develop competency in a new field but not necessarily on a higher level" (National Science Foundation, 1977, p. 1). For the purposes of this book only formal types of continuing education, such as graduate courses and degree programs, were investigated, although it should be clear that other modes are possible.

2.   Retraining is often included under continuing education, but we have treated it separately. For the purposes of this book, retraining pertains to any type of program that is specifically designed to accomplish a transfer of skills from one occupation to another. Although various types of continuing education may be used by participants to help them in changing their careers, such programs were not considered as retraining unless they were designed intentionally with career change as their primary goal.

CHAPTER EIGHT

Societal Responses:
Options for Institutional Change

In previous chapters we concentrated on the manner in which individual professionals cope with joblessness. However, the disruptive effects of widespread unemployment and underemployment of highly educated workers is clearly a societal problem, the solution of which—if one is possible—would require the active involvement not only of the government, but also of employers, professional associations, and educational institutions. Hence in this chapter we explore how professionals experiencing joblessness or underemployment view various societal responses to alleviating their problem as well as how the institutions themselves have responded. We also consider various options for institutional change that may alleviate the plight of future generations of the highly educated in their quest for meaningful work.

SOCIAL AND POLITICAL CHANGE

Although self-blame is prevalent among unemployed professionals, most have been found to attribute the problem of unemployment among their ranks to external factors such as governmental policies, societal priorities, or the "system" (Briar, 1976; Estes, 1973; Leventman, 1976; Little, 1973). Such widespread resentment by professionals toward a system perceived to be responsible for problems in finding appropriate work may create a greater willingness to support political extremism and radical change. This can be one type of response to the high levels of frustration and loss of self-esteem experienced by unemployed professionals. Others have arrived at similar conclusions, as is clear from the following evaluation:

> By virtue of the specialized and prolonged training and the high level of commitment associated with professional occupations, professionals are more likely to feel frustrated when faced with limited job opportunities and to express their frustration in

political protest. . . . For example, studies of the Nazi movement in Germany suggest that a disproportionate percentage of the leadership came from professionals who had been unemployed for long periods of time, or could not find satisfactory employment commensurate with their own self conceptions (Lipset and Schwartz, 1966, pp. 301–302).

Similar types of frustrations and threats to the self concept afflict the growing number of educated unemployed in the less developed countries for whom appropriates jobs are not available. The "brain drain" to highly developed countries has served as a safety valve but is becoming less of an option as unemployment and underemployment among professionals becomes a worldwide problem.

Asia provides some of the most striking examples of widespread unemployment among the college educated, who have been in the forefront of attempts at radical change. A major factor in the 1971 armed uprising in Sri Lanka (formerly Ceylon) was widespread unemployment, particularly among "well-educated youths unable to find jobs equal to their qualifications" (*The New York Times,* 1971, p. 4). Although this revolt was suppressed with widespread bloodshed and arrests, the symptoms that ignited it had not been dealt with adequately and unrest erupted again five years later as a result of "growing student frustration over lack of employment opportunities" (Rangan, 1976, p. A14). As unemployment among the college educated spread to the Western countries, the poorest and less stable ones began to experience similar student protests. A case in point is the widespread student riots in Italy during 1977. An analysis of these uprisings indicates that the "rapid increase in the numbers of students and the tight job market are regarded as the root of the problems and frustrations" (*The New York Times,* 1977a, p. 6).

The United States has never experienced the kind of economic chaos that doomed Weimar Germany, and the present prospects of young American professionals cannot be compared to the situations faced by college graduates in countries with unstable governments, limited resources, or underdeveloped technology. It may, however, be hasty to conclude that these situations have no relevance to the problem of professional unemployment in highly developed countries or, for that matter, in the United States. Indeed, unemployment has been found to be related to political violence, such as riots, political demonstrations, and politically related deaths and assassinations, with this relationship strongest in the most highly developed countries (Gupta, 1977). Concern over growing unemployment among university graduates became a factor in student protests even in relatively stable and well-developed countries such as West Germany (*The Chronicle of Higher Education,* 1977a). Indeed, a German psychologist, Curt Donig, who has studied the impact of unemployment in his country, attributes the growth of the neo-Nazi movement as well as radical left terrorist groups such as the Baader-Meinhof gang largely to frustration among educated youth over the lack of job opportunities (Donig, 1978). Increased intergroup conflict and racism may be additional consequences of the increased competition for professional-level jobs. Indeed, racism has been reported on the increase in Canada as a result of the continuing flow of educated immigrants from the less developed countries, which has exacerbated an already competitive professional job market (Trumbull, 1977). Similarly, aliens have been accused of threatening the jobs of professionals in the United States (e.g., Feerst, 1977). As the highly educated in the United States become increasingly frustrated because of unemployment and underemployment, it is not too far fetched to imagine a greater radicalization and extremism among their ranks, with jobs becoming the *cause celèbre* of the 1980s or 1990s, comparable to the Vietnam war of the late 1960s and early 1970s.

It is noteworthy that in the past unemployment has in fact served to radicalize American professionals. One study found that unemployed engineers in the United States during the Great Depression tended to be more radical and support more extreme political solutions than did their colleagues who were still employed (Hall, 1934). For example, almost one-fourth of unemployed engineers favored revolution, as compared to 6 percent of those working. Moreover, among the engineers who had lost their jobs, one-third felt that what this country needed was a strong dictator, and 15 percent were in favor of communism, which was about twice the rate of support for such political change among those still employed. However, these results should not be taken as being indicative of all professionals since "as members of a very conservative profession, engineers, when pressed to reject the status quo, opt for a movement of the radical right, rather than the radical left" (Lipset and Schwartz, 1966, p. 306).

The professionals in our study, most of whom were engineers, rated the usefulness of several political approaches to solving the problem of unemployment (Table 8.1). Changing society's priorities was endorsed by a majority of the jobless and underemployed as well as by many of those who had been reemployed in their field or who had not lost their jobs. Precisely what the new priorities would be was not specified, but a desire for change was obvious. It is interesting that the unemployed, who most strongly favored this less radical solution, tended to be less willing to take risks in the type of job they wanted ($r = -.35, p < .01$) and to have an external locus of control ($r = .27, p < .05$). Changing society's priorities appears to be most acceptable to those who were more dependent on external events than on themselves and less willing to put themselves into a situation involving uncertainty and change. Clearly, these are not the revolutionaries, but their passive acceptance of change could be a danger signal, depending on the type of change they would support.

The majority of professionals in our study did not consider the more extreme political approaches, such as radical social change or activism involving picketing and mass demonstrations, to be useful in dealing with the unemployment problem. However, the relationships that we found are quite revealing. Among unem-

TABLE 8.1.   Percentage Indicating That Specific Changes or Activities Would Be
Useful in Resolving Unemployment Problems Among Professionals

	Employment Status			
	Unemployed (N = 51)	Underemployed (N = 52)	Reemployed in Field (N = 54)	Continuously Employed (N = 54)
Changing society's priorities	57	56	46	43
Radical social change	26	31	15	17
Peaceful activism	22	35	17	15
Temporary work in government projects	68	60	59	48
Government aid for staying up-to-date	51	60	63	69
Political lobbying by professional societies	59	46	56	59
Unionizing of professionals	55	67	52	54

ployed professionals, those who were most pessimistic about when their lives
would return to normal were most willing to endorse radical social change
($r = .24$, $p < .05$), as were the more obsolescent individuals who expected to
experience difficulty in being able to carry out new assignments in their profession
($r = .40$, $p < .01$). In addition, out-of-work professionals who manifested the
general unemployment stress syndrome were more likely to support radical social
change ($r = .24$, $p < .05$). However, only among those low in self-esteem was
this general stress syndrome related to their support for activism ($r = .35$,
$p < .05$) and changing society's priorities ($r = .36$, $p < .05$). It appears that
professionals who have not maintained their self-esteem are willing to strike out
against society in a variety of ways when they experience unemployment stress.
This is certainly in accord with Korman's model of societal aggression described
in Chapter 2. In general, the evidence indicates that professionals who have been
the most adversely affected by job loss are also the most susceptible to supporting
political extremism and societal change.

Further analyses revealed that it was the long-term unemployed who were most
extreme, with more than seven out of ten wanting to change societies priorities
and about two-fifths supporting activism and radical social change. In contrast,
those who were in stage II of unemployment, the period of concerted effort, were
least likely to be extreme, with fewer than one-fourth desiring a change in society's priorities and only 15 percent supporting activism or radical social change.

Professionals in stage II of unemployment are still involved with their job search and apparently believe that their efforts will result in reemployment. Many of the long-term unemployed, however, no longer believe this and have given up seeking work. But their acceptance of being in a state of joblessness, with its concomitant loss of self-esteem, appears to be accompanied by a greater willingness to strike out against society. Although these tendencies toward societal aggression may be passive and disorganized, they could be used and manipulated by others. For example, in describing the deterioration of the long-term unemployed during the Great Depression, the noted psychoanalyst Abram Kardiner pointed out the following:

> To themselves they are a total loss, and to the state a menace. The menace is not, however, a serious one. These people have lost the capacity for initiative, and their aggression tends to be disorganized and sporadic. . . . That these individuals are easy meat for demagogues. . .goes without saying (Kardiner, 1936, pp. 194–195).

A worldwide analysis of unemployed professionals during the Great Depression took an even more extreme view, noting that; "Revolutions are born of helplessness. If the avenue which rightly or wrongly they believe to lead to success is closed to them, they are likely to revolt" (Kotschnig, 1937, p. 283). Similar warnings have been expressed during the 1970s with regard to jobless professionals in the United States. Typical of such sentiments are those expressed by one analyst of the problem of jobless professionals.

> An unemployed elite is politically dangerous. . .;they have been *pushed* out of the system, not left out. It is important to remember that such groups have the potential for affecting political and social events far out of proportion to their numbers, and have fueled ugly politics (Shapero, 1972).

Although there is a demonstrated relationship between unemployment and political violence, the evidence that unemployed professionals actually resort to such actions is primarily anecdotal or impressionistic in nature. Perhaps more typical is the reaction to frustration caused by lack of career growth and long-term unemployment of a 46-year-old electrical engineer who described himself as very conservative:

> "I was in a rut—going 'round and 'round. It was hard to move up in that situation. I'm devoting my life right now to working to implement my political philosophy. . . . I'm spending my time lobbying for bills in the state legislature. I want to deal with bigger issues than I could in the engineering job" (Little, 1976, pp. 265–266).

Although the case described above may represent a relatively benign attempt to replace a lack of career growth with the development of political activities, other cases are more extreme. There are even some in which jobless professionals vent their anger against society by displacing their aggression through not only political extremism but also antisocial behavior. For example, the young Ph.D. sociologist described initially in Chapter 5, who experienced frustration because of reverse discrimination in his field and a lack of jobs even in subprofessional work, described how he directed his aggression against society:

> I began to feel that this society was rotten—and had to be changed. I began to feel the only way was violent overthrow of the government. I guess it was really more a symbolic gesture then out of real need that I began to steal things from stores—I pocketed hundreds of things and finally one day I got caught. When the policeman asked me what I did for a living, I told him nothing—after all it was the truth. When he took me down to the police station he cursed me out most of the way. From this experience I could understand how the people I studied about in school felt. I felt I myself was a criminal and was proud of this identification. At least I was something! I began to feel elated at taking advantage of society.
>
> As I had no previous record this first case was dismissed—the next case of shoplifting (by which time I was more skilled) I got 90 days but ended up spending 15 days in the jail with time off for good behavior. I began to think more and more of revolution—I even plotted to murder Nixon, although the plotting was more in my thoughts of anger than any real direct action towards this goal. I began to read as much communist literature as I could find—feeling this must be the only way.

Not only had this unemployed professional struck a blow against society by turning to crime but at the same time was able to acquire an occupational identity—he was now a criminal. His political change is even more dramatic if we consider that he came from a relatively conservative background and as a student in the 1960s totally rejected the campus demonstrations and violence against the system. This case may be extreme but it is illustrative of the type of radical behavior change involving societal aggression that can occur as a result of joblessness.

Occupation and Political Orientation

Although the evidence presented thus far indicates that unemployment can serve to radicalize professionals, it should be noted that not all research has found a greater propensity toward political extremism and radical change associated with joblessness, at least for some types of professionals. For example, a study of a heterogeneous group of unemployed professionals found that, in general, they did not differ significantly from those who had been continuously employed in their willingness to support political activism (Estes, 1973). Regardless of employment status, between one-fourth and one-third supported picketing, marches and other mass protest demonstrations. The unemployed also did not differ significantly from the employed in their participation in political activities. However, among the more conservative occupational groups such as business and technical professionals, the attitude toward political activities tended to become more positive after they experienced long-term unemployment. On the other hand, attitudes of the most highly politicized professionals—the social workers, teachers, and lawyers—hardly differed at all with time out of work but they remained significantly higher in their support of political activities than the business or technical professionals. It is possible that those professionals who are more conservative to begin with undergo the greatest disruption of their beliefs, which is accompanied by greater stress, and therefore may be the most likely to change. This can help explain why investigations of unemployed technical professionals have generally found them more willing to strike out against the system than are their employed colleagues, whereas no such differences were found when more heterogeneous samples of professionals were investigated.

In the study reported above (Estes, 1973), it was found that, contrary to our findings, those who most strongly supported political activisim exhibited low emotional stress. It is likely that these results were artifacts of attributes associated with particular occupational groups. For example, technical professionals, who experienced the greatest unemployment stress, were also more conservative in their political attitudes than were the human resource professionals, a group that experienced relatively low stress. It is possible that the greater change in political attitudes among the technical professionals was a reaction to their greater stress and that the negligible change in the attitudes of human resource professionals was a result of their relatively lower stress. That is, the stress created by unemployment may effect a *change* in political attitudes, and the greater the stress, the greater the shift. As we have already suggested, it may be that the more conservative professionals are most prone to stress to begin with and, hence, most likely to experience a greater shift toward supporting political activism and social change.

The Underemployed and Political Activism

Professionals who were reemployed were found in one study to have more positive attitudes toward political activism than did those remaining unemployed (Estes, 1973). Why should reemployment be associated with a shift toward political activism? One possible explanation is that many of those finding work were actually underemployed. In fact, those who were reemployed part time in nonprofessional jobs exhibited a high propensity toward political activism (Estes, 1973). Therefore, their situation was comparable to that of the underemployed in our sample, who, of all the groups, were the most in favor of activism and radical change (see Table 8.1). As discussed in Chapter 7, the underemployed tend to experience high levels of stress, apparently as a result of their inability to utilize their professional knowledge and skills, and the desire to take more extreme action to alleviate their situation may be one manifestation of their frustration.

There is evidence that propensity toward political activism among the underemployed may be a result of the frustration generated by insurmountable barriers to reemployment in their field. For example, we found that only among the underemployed was support for activism related to barriers such as a lack of jobs ($r = .46, p < .001$), being overqualified ($r = .39, p < .01$), having inappropriate experience ($r = .30, p < .05$), being out of work too long ($r = .30, p < .05$), and age ($r = .31, p < .05$). It has been observed that professionals "who have been forced to enter a second choice occupation are more likely to show higher degrees of discontent than those who have reached their original aspirations and this is revealed in a propensity to back radical parties" (Lipset and Schwartz, 1966, p. 302).

Researchers have suggested that for professionals "the development of militancy may require a minimal level of job security" (Fox and Wince, 1976, p. 58). It is likely that when professionals are out of work, they are concerned primarily about their own security needs and those of their dependents. However, if they take a job that leaves them underemployed, they no longer are struggling with the day-to-day needs of economic survival; but with the fulfillment of their esteem and growth needs blocked, they are likely to direct the resentment and hostility resulting from their career frustrations against society. In fact, the underemployed who supported changing society's priorities were less likely to feel that they needed to return to work in order to attain self-esteem ($r = -.33, p < .01$) or self-fulfillment ($r = -.36, p < .01$), with similar relationships found for those who favored activism ($r = -.30, p < .05$, and $r = -.23, p < .05$, respectively) and carrying out radical social change ($r = -.24, p < .05$; and $r = -.32, p < .01$, respectively). When work no longer can provide professionals with esteem or fulfillment, they must look elsewhere to satisfy these needs, and political activism would certainly be one path they could take.

Since underemployment will definitely be a major problem facing professionals in the future, we should therefore expect growth in support for societal change and political activism concomitant with the increase in the numbers of underemployed professionals. However, if there is an appropriate societal response to the challenge of unemployment and underemployment, it is unlikely that radical political change will receive wide support among professionals. Let us now turn to a closer examination of some possible societal responses.

ROLE OF GOVERNMENT

Although only a minority of professionals believe that political activism and radical social change are useful in resolving the unemployment problem, a somewhat different question is how they feel about the role of government in alleviating joblessness. Certain types of governmental control appear to be more acceptable than others, but still only to a minority. For example, in one study a limitation on the number of professionals entering the country was endorsed by more than one-third of unemployed professionals, whereas a limit on every family to the equivalent of one full-time job was supported by only one-tenth (Estes, 1973). These responses may indicate a willingness by some to allow the government to protect the jobs of professionals, but not at the cost of personal freedom. Controls of a voluntary nature (e.g., reduction in their own work schedule) were clearly preferred to the imposition of involuntary governmental controls that limit work activities.

There is some evidence that terminated professionals have been more resistant to direct governmental intervention to help them keep their jobs or to assist them in finding new ones than were other unemployed workers (Palen, 1969). However, the difficulties experienced in the tight job market of the 1970s may have resulted in a greater acceptance of such intervention. Indeed, subsequent to the recession of the mid-1970s about three-fourths of all Americans felt that it is the government's responsibility to assure that everybody who wants a job can get one (Clymer, 1978). Professionals terminated during that recession appeared even more in favor of such government responsibility. For example, nine-tenths of the professionals terminated from civil service jobs in New York City's fiscal crisis strongly supported the Humphrey-Hawkins full-employement bill (Guyot, 1976).

Job Creation

Despite an apparent aversion to some types of government controls in dealing with unemployment, there is widespread support for federal responsibility in assuring the availability of jobs. Indeed, surveys indicate that professionals are positively disposed toward the government providing or creating alternative employment to colleagues displaced by cessation of government-sponsored programs (e.g., *Industrial Research*, 1971). In our study we also found a generally positive attitude toward such governmental intervention. For example, a majority of professionals who had been out of work felt that temporary jobs in government projects would be useful, with this attitude most prevalent among those who were still unemployed (Table 8.1). However, fewer than half the professionals who did not experience unemployment felt that temporary work was a useful approach. Although the differences in attitudes between the groups were not significant, there is a clear tendency which indicates that the experience of being out of work makes professionals more positive toward direct governmental assistance in the form of jobs. Among the unemployed, those feeling that such assistance was most useful tended to experience greater difficulty with job scarcity ($r = .27, p < .05$) and inappropriate experience ($r = -.27, p < .05$). They were also less willing to take a new job involving risks ($r = -.24, p < .05$). Temporary government jobs are apparently most attractive to those encountering a poor demand for their experience and who need the stability provided by work. However, only for those low in self-esteem was the need to return to work in order to attain security related to their positive attitudes toward temporary work ($r = .49$, $p < .01$).

Having neither security nor self-esteem apparently creates a strong enough drive to accept any type of work. But this may be true primarily for those who are not yet work inhibited. In fact, the greatest support for temporary jobs came from those in stage II, the period of concerted effort, where almost nine-tenths endorsed such government work projects. Since these professionals were still highly motivated to work, the less radical solution of federal job creation was congruent with their needs and, hence, quite attractive to them.

Government programs have, in fact, provided unemployed professionals with jobs in their own fields. One of the earliest was the federal arts projects of the Works Progress Administration (WPA) during the 1930s, which provided work to unemployed creative artists in their fields (Barnes, 1975). Under the Comprehensive Employment and Training Act (CETA), artists, who constitute a chronically underemployed sector of the labor force, were among the many professionals who have benefited from public works jobs. Despite its focus on disadvantaged groups among the long-term unemployed, CETA has had almost as great an impact on the employment of the college-educated as it has had on minorities (Wiseman, 1976). In fact, an analysis of public employment programs through 1975 has revealed that "more than one-ninth of all recession unemployment among college-educated workers was absorbed by CETA" (Wiseman, 1976, pp. 99–100). Although CETA has clearly served to reduce unemployment among professionals, it is not known to what degree the CETA jobs resulted in underemployment, which, as we have seen, can be more detrimental in some ways than remaining jobless. However, CETA may cease to be a significant program for employment of professionals. Revisions of regulations governing the conditions and the length of employment of workers hired under CETA would not only eliminate almost all professional-level positions from the program but would create undue hardships on already financially hard-pressed municipalities (Quindlen, 1979). This would certainly be a major blow to those who anticipated that CETA "could effectively alleviate the unemployment problem, eliminate the waste of highly skilled human resources, and reduce technological lag" (Hammer, 1974, p. 408).

In Chapter 7 we discussed the federally sponsored retraining programs for scientists and engineers displaced from aerospace and defense industries. Such professionals were specifically included in the Public Employment Program (PEP) established under the Emergency Employment ACT (EEA) of 1971, although unemployed professionals in fields such as education, social services, and health were also hired under PEP (*Manpower Report of the President*, 1975). In fact, almost a third of all EEA participants had some college education (Wiseman, 1976).

The success of the Aerospace Employment Project's (AEP) retraining programs in moving former aerospace and defense professionals into local government jobs was largely because almost half of the jobs were made available under EEA (Ventre and Sullivan, 1972). This emphasizes the necessity of coordinating retraining with the creation of jobs. Unfortunately, AEP was a small-scale program and whether it could be effective on a larger scale remains to be demonstrated.

The plight of those displaced from the aerospace and defense industries was taken directly into account when the Technology Mobilization and Reemployment Program (TMRP) was launched by the U.S. Department of Labor in 1971. In addition to providing grants to eligible individuals for job search activities, relocation costs in the United States, and training grants, TMRP also tried to stimulate job openings by encouraging employers to engage in on-the-job training programs, with nonproductive time reimbursed up to a maximum of $2000 per individual. This training subsidy to the employer apparently increased the likelihood of an applicant being hired (Bain, 1974). In total, TMRP had 52,667 registered in the program, among whom 4864 received job search grants, 2027 obtained relocation grants, and 4511 became eligible for training subsidies (Bain, 1974). An analysis of TMRP found that it fell far short of its goals (Comptroller General of the United States, 1973).

It should be noted that TMRP was a unique venture which focused on reemploying a specific group of displaced professionals through the use of various types of assistance provided by the Employment Service, including the help of volunteers from the ranks of the unemployed. As with any new venture hastily put together in response to a crisis, many mistakes were made, and some of these were identified as follows:

Concentrating job development activities in areas where job openings were scarce, and not adequately using nationwide job development tools which provide additional opportunities for obtaining jobs, which would have permitted greater use of job search grants and possibly job relocation grants, both of which appeared under-utilized;

A lack of follow-up to determine why participants on job search grants did not obtain employment, and a lack of additional efforts to fill the job openings for which the grant was made;

The lack of posttraining placement assistance, combined with insufficient job development activities necessary for identifying areas where institutional training could have resulted in meaningful employment for participants. (Comptroller General of the United States, 1973, pp. 15–16).

The shortcomings as well as the accomplishments of TMRP can serve as a guide for similar programs in the future. Perhaps one of the most important lessons to be learned, at least in terms of policy, was that "during periods when the economy is in a slump, consideration could be given to some type of temporary job creation activity, such as a public employment program. If the economy is fairly strong and if only one segment of it is affected by a decline, then a program, such as TMR[P], might prove more successful'' (Comptroller General of the United States, 1973, p. 13).

A direct, albeit modest approach to public job creation was the Presidential Internships in Science and Engineering administered by the National Science Foundation. This program provided up to 570 unemployed technical professionals possessing advanced degrees with one year's work in federally funded projects around the country (Aun, 1973). The participating agency received $7000 as a stipend for each intern, which the agency matched with an equivalent sum to supplement the stipend and meet overhead costs. The interns served in research projects involving pressing societal problems related to pollution, nuclear power, crime, and health. Although the participants were apparently a select group, it would appear that creating public jobs to utilize the talents of unemployed and underemployed professionals in work dealing with societal problems is the most direct way in which the government can contribute to the overall adjustment of the individuals involved while helping to cure the ills of the nation.

Although some of the joblessness among professionals can be characterized as ''deficient-demand unemployment'' attributable to recurring recessions, much of it has been ''structural'' if we consider the massive shifts in demand that occured for aerospace and defense industry professionals as well as for teachers (Guyot, 1976). Thus not only will antirecessionary measures be necessary to deal with jobless professionals, but also structuralist approaches to cope with the ever-increasing number of college-educated in the work force who will experience difficulties in finding appropriate jobs.

The limited evidence we have indicates that the government can deal with unemployment and underemployment among professionals to some degree by the direct creation of public jobs. Moreover, professionals have demonstrated their willingness to participate in such programs in order to get back to work. However, public employment projects that are temporary in nature have a built in danger to the well-being of the individual. A case in point is the experience of the counselors in Start-Up (see Chapter 7), who initially worked as volunteers but then received salaries under the Emergency Employment Act:

> Exactly eighteen months after Start-Up began, its door was closed. This had been planned. Unemployment rates had dropped from 15% to 8%; Seattle's depression was receding. Start-Up's counselors again faced job insecurity. Their jobs had been Public Employment jobs, continued only through federal funding. With the loss of the funds went the loss of the job. Some were phased into city agency jobs. One attempted suicide. Some became. . .supplicants seeking work (Briar, 1976, p. 93).

In order to avoid problems associated with work that is temporary or results in underemployment, a stimulation of demand for permanent professional jobs in the private sector should complement direct public job creation. For example, a relatively modest increase in R&D funding can have a manyfold impact on job formation, providing work for professionals, as well as other workers, while dealing with problems confronting our society (Vanderslice, 1976). Therefore, for the formation of professional jobs to be a success on a large scale, it would very likely have to be a joint enterprise between government and the private sector. All indications are that the private sector is ready and willing to cooperate with the government in dealing with unemployment (Silk, 1978). The limited evidence that exists shows that government-sponsored training and employment programs in which the private sector has played the key role have been highly successful. In fact, in one such CETA-supported program carried out by the Chicago Alliance of Business-Manpower Services resulted in 1122 on-the-job training slots, of which 23 percent were for professional and technical occupations (Sheppard, 1978). This could be a model for future cooperation between government and the private sector.

Centralization of National Policy and Programs

The limitations of existing public employment programs in providing work for jobless professionals have been noted by such groups as the Engineering Manpower Commission, which also criticized the decentralization of unemployment assistance programs at the state and local levels as making it impossible to focus adequately on professional employment problems. To overcome this handicap, they recommended the following:

> A policy office should be established within the appropriate governmental department to work through appropriate professional groups to deal with the special problems of professionals on a nationwide rather than on a local basis (Engineering Manpower Commission, 1975, p. 2).

Such a suggestion to centralize government efforts to assist unemployed professionals is supported not only by professional societies. The Department of Labor, noting the limitations of programs to assist out-of-work professionals, made the following suggestion:

> A federal role is necessary in such activity, and the role need not be contrary to decentralization, under manpower revenue sharing. Only a national effort can focus on broader concerns that affect the nation's labor force and cross regional boundaries (Comptroller General of the United States, 1973, pp. 30–31).

Unemployed professionals overwhelmingly pointed to a lack of federal government planning as the primary cause of the employment crisis and were strongly in favor of such long-range planning to deal with it (Leventman, 1976). Pivotal to any national planning effort attacking the problem of a surplus of highly educated workers would be policy and programs directed toward skills conversion. Indeed, in responding to the deteriorating professional job market of the early 1970s the U.S. Department of Labor concluded that

> skill conversion studies should be an ongoing function of the Department in order to better utilize the nation's skills. Not only are engineers, scientists and technicians a surplus commodity, but so are language specialists and a variety of teachers with special expertise. In the absence of job creation efforts like the Public Employment Program, alternative means of integrating skilled professionals into the work force are a necessity (Comptroller General of the United States, 1973, p. 30).

Perhaps the closest the federal government has come to establishing centralized efforts to deal with unemployment among professionals were a series of bills introduced in 1971 by Senator Edward M. Kennedy that were almost enacted into law (U.S. Senate Committee on Labor and Public Welfare, 1972). Although the bills were directed primarily at dealing with widespread unemployment among defense-oriented engineers and scientists, they included some well-thought-out policies which could be incorporated into future legislation focusing on employment problems among a broader spectrum of the highly educated. For example, the aborted Conversion Research, Education and Assistance Act of 1971 required that the vast potential of underutilized American talent "be converted not simply to serve civilian, consumer ends, but that it be specifically aimed at aiding the resolution of our besetting social ills" (U.S. Senate Committee on Labor and Public Welfare, 1972, pp. 2–3). The Federal Government would have been responsible for assuring continuing opportunities for socially useful employment in positions commensurate with one's professional capabilities. Provisions were also made for federal investment in civilian-oriented research and development activities to maintain future growth. Under the act, financial, technical, and educational assistance would have been provided to communities, companies, and individuals. Unemployed professionals would also have been eligible for placement and relocation assistance, as well as for reorientation and on-the-job retraining. Activities and programs supported by the act would have been centralized in the National Science Foundation and an Advisory Commission on Research and Development Conversion was to be established consisting of representatives from civilian-oriented private industry, the relevant professions and educational institutions. Thus for the first time in American history an attempt was made to establish a full-employment policy for an identifiable group of professionals who were considered to be essential to the nation's well-being. Although the effort was an abortive one, some of the principles established could serve as models for future legislation.

It is clear that any new legislation dealing with the unemployment and underemployment of professionals will be effective only insofar as it provides a centralized mechanism for stimulating the creation of appropriate jobs in the private as well as the public sector (see Mottur, 1971). Although the private sector may not see that it has a major role in the shaping of federal employment policy in general (National Commission for Manpower Policy, 1975), business and industry appear willing to become involved in planning related to problems of unemployment and the inbalance of supply and demand in professional occupations (Culhane, 1971; Silk, 1978). Policy and programs that are developed should be based on the premise that if professionals are to be kept from joining the ranks of the work-inhibited or turning their anger against society, they must be provided with meaningful work with as little delay as possible following job loss or entry into the labor market after completion of their education.

Unemployment Insurance and the Employment Service

Although rapid reemployment in meaningful jobs should be the top-priority goal in dealing with the adjustment of out-of-work professionals, the government has been relatively ineffectual in its efforts at attaining that goal. Perhaps both a symptom and a cause of these ineffectual efforts is the widespread reluctance of professionals to use government assistance as it currently exists. The extent of this reluctance was indicated in one study which found that only 54 percent of out-of-work professionals applied for unemployment benefits and they waited an average of seven weeks before doing so, although they were eligible to apply immediately after job loss (Estes, 1973). Some of the reasons for the reluctance to apply for help, including placement assistance from the Employment Service, were noted:

> Many professionals attached a type of generalized stigma to using the agency, an attitude characteristic of their distaste in using any public service (food stamps, welfare, etc.). . . .Almost all of the professionals agreed that the agency's primary interest lay in serving the needs of lower skilled workers and was not adequately prepared to help professional workers in their search for work (Estes, 1973, p. 328).

Professionals who were not receiving unemployment insurance in that study had a significantly higher propensity toward political activism than did those not receiving such compensation. Whether unemployment insurance reduces political activism or whether those who accept such compensation are less politically oriented, possibly because of their greater security needs, was not determined. However, the study did indicate that stress increases appreciably as unemployed professionals become more dependent on public support, but that appeared to be a result of the financial pressures that required them to accept food stamps or welfare assistance.

Other research indicates that receiving unemployment benefits may actually contribute to work inhibition among professionals experiencing long-term joblessness (Horowitz, 1968). Although it is possible that those who are work-inhibited to begin with are more willing to accept unemployment benefits, it also may be that being paid not to work reduces motivation to find a new job. Indeed, some professionals accept unemployment compensation in order not to work, but the psychological damage may just not be worth it, as one female TV commerical producer discovered:

> What we may not know is the damage to the whole person, the real price of dishonestly being on the dole. It took me a couple of years to feel and recognize the price I paid.
>
> Physically, my energy was never lower. I felt listless much of the time.
>
> The afternoons were the worst; people were working and I was watching the "soaps" and eating. Mentally, I was in a fog, confused and wandering, not wanting to focus on what was happening in my life. Emotionally, I felt vaguely disturbed, unworthy, generally uncomfortable, very anxious and very guilty. I was half alive, unable and unwilling to fulfill my responsibilites as an adult, to take care of myself, to give to my community. Worst of all, I was lying to myself and justifying my position.
>
> Now, when I think back, it's so clear, but then it was so insidious.
>
> There were so many rationalizations for taking the money: "The Government allows it." "I've worked 10 years; I've earned it." "I really am an animation commerical production manager. It's not my fault that there isn't a job in that field." "Everyone else is doing it." And finally, "I really am looking for a job," which simply was not true except for a cursory glance now and then at the want ads. None of these justifications ever made a dent in the gnawing guilt and sense of worthlessness.
>
> Finally, I did allow myself to feel the pain of it all and stopped the downhill run in my self-esteem by accepting (in the eyes of my glorified self-image) a very simple, humble job. I discovered that in the simplicity of doing a job, any job, I began to feel self-respect for the first time in two years.
>
> Taking money from unemployment is difficult; it hurts even when you legitimately need it and don't abuse it. But it's deadly, insidiously deadly, when you abuse it and lie to yourself about it (Knack, 1978, p. 17).

There is also evidence that accepting unemployment compensation may have a positive effect on some professionals. For example, among terminated engineers it was found "that individuals who received unemployment insurance were much more active in locating new jobs than their counterparts" (Loomba, 1968, p. 46). Probably, the least financially secure professionals depended on both unemployment insurance and an intensive job search to help restore their security.

Perhaps unemployment insurance, by cushioning the financial blow of job loss, also permits the professional to engage in a more intensive job search. But if the search is not successful, work inhibition can set it. Therefore, it is possible that unemployment compensation for the long-term jobless professionals actually may be counterproductive, in that it can serve to reinforce their work inhibition. If this is, in fact, what happens, it is certainly an argument against the way in which unemployment compensation is currently dispensed. An overhaul of the unemployment insurance system is long overdue and one objective could be to redirect the funds to encourage continuous employment (Henle, 1976; Lynton, 1975).

The contribution rates of employers to unemployment insurance could be reduced if they used alternatives to terminations. In addition to such an incentive (as well as the disincentive of higher rates based on the number of terminations), unemployment compensation can be used to subsidize work-sharing approaches, such as a shortened workweek. Judging from such public supported work-sharing programs in some European countries, they appear to be a highly cost-effective alternative to terminations, at least from the government's perspective (Levitan and Belous, 1977). Such alternatives are examined more closely when the role of the employer is addressed later in this chapter.

We have already discussed some of the reasons why the State Employment Service is ineffectual in helping unemployed professionals. Perhaps a key to the problem is a lack of services that can help job seekers cope effectively with their unemployment. An examination of the limited role played by the employment counselors is most instructive:

> The employment counselors are not permitted to probe into personal adjustments of the client, nor are they by their own admission trained to identify the despondent, possibly suicidal individual. The client type who presents the most problems for the counselors is the hostile, persistent applicant who attempts to *fully* utilize the services of the counselor. This client may go out on numerous job interviews, returning each time to blame the counselor for his failure to be hired. The frustrations may mount with increasing frequency as the employment counselor continues to steer him to job leads. In the end it is the employment counselor who is blamed and victimized as the symbol of the inefficient labor exchange. To the counselor, this applicant is a threatening menace; to the client, the employment counselor is doing a poor job (Briar, 1976, p. 87).

Even with respect to job referrals, the State Employment Service lacks an individualized approach that forces its clients to seek such assistance elsewhere, as the experience of Start-Up illustrates:

> The sources of pressure on Start-Up to provide job referrals can probably be traced to the ineffectiveness of the employment agency. The service at Start-Up was more

personalized and tailored to the individual situation. Assessing personal problems, and relieving these while taking steps to improve the employability of the client were service gaps that Start-Up was forced to fill. Few agencies could be as flexible as Start-Up in its service development, which improved the effectiveness of Start-Up and pointed out the deficits of the Employment Service. Finally, the Employment Service sent one of its counselors to Start-Up. This full time representative performed counseling and job referral services. . . . The agency as a whole began to focus more specifically on the job seeking problems of its clientele (Briar, 1976, pp. 92–93).

The success of Start-Up may have forced the State Employment Service to pay more attention to the needs of its clients. This case indicates that despite its generally poor image, the State Employment Service does have the potential to help unemployed professionals. One way this potential can be realized is to provide services directed specifically toward the unique problems of professionals who are seeking work. In a demonstration project carried out at the Professional Placement Office in Boston, individualized intensive services provided to hard-to-place unemployed professionals served to increase significantly their employability over what it would have been if only the normal services had been provided (Horowitz, 1968). The services provided to this experimental group included individual career counseling, guidance in job search techniques, and intensive efforts at job development and job referrals. Not only did these services lead to more rapid employment in higher-level jobs, but the Professional Placement Office turned out to be the chief means by which those in the experimental group found their job. This remarkable accomplishment is all the more striking since for a control group the Professional Placement Office ranked in last place as a method of obtaining professional-level work. Perhaps most important in the long run is the way in which the image of the Employment Service was changed, which was described as follows:

In a variety of ways, there are clear indications that those professionals who had been selected for the experimental group now have a favorable view of the Employment Service. The services rendered to this group were sufficiently impressive that the vast majority are no longer likely to consider the Professional Placement Office as the "last resort." If an acceptable or favorable image is a goal of the Employment Service, this project has succeeded in attaining this goal, at least insofar as the professionals in the experimental group are concerned (Horowitz, 1968, p. 70).

It is apparent that the image of the Employment Service among professionals is tied directly to how effective it is in job placement. When a Professional Placement Office has an intensive employer relations program, there is apparently a greater willingness to have professional-level jobs listed (Johnson, 1973). Indeed, one of the key elements in the placement success of professionals is job development, an activity typically not carried out by the Employment Service. This deficiency accounts for the inadequacy of computerized job banks for professional placement, which has long been advocated (Adams, 1969). In discussing job banks, Eli Ginzberg noted that "such advances depend finally on the success of the Employment Service in eliciting more cooperation from employers in listing jobs and accepting their referrals. Hence, a major challenge confronting the Employment Service is to free competent personnel for more job development efforts" (National Manpower Advisory Committee, 1974, p. 13). Without effective job development, it is questionable whether it is worth applying even more sophisticated techniques to job matching, such as those using a communications satellite (Barnes, 1977).

Perhaps the Employment Service need not free many of its personnel for job development directed at professional-level positions. Highly effective volunteer self-help groups of unemployed professionals have assisted the Employment Service in carrying out various specialized functions, including job development. One critic of the job bank system, explains why self-help groups such as Volunteer Engineers, Scientists and Technicians (VEST) have succeeded in job development:

> Should we be surprised then if job bank information systems haven't been particuarly successful, since they ignore how men really find work? The importance of the informal social networks becomes even more apparent when we consider the effects of the cooperative placement activities. VEST requires real scientists and engineers to go out and help place others like themselves. Two good things happen in the process: (1) It takes on the form of a personal validation system that professional headhunters seldom achieve and (2) it gets an unemployed man out into the community representing others, broadening his perception of what is available and what technical people can do (Shapero, 1972, p. 46).

Introducing other innovations, such as providing rewards to self-help groups for effective job development activities (Jones and Azrin, 1973), is likely to enhance further the stature of the Professional Placement Office. Thus, cooperation with self-help groups could serve to change the image of the State Employment Service as the option of "last resort" for professionals in search of work. We have more to say about this cooperation in our discussion of the professional societies in the next section.

ROLE OF PROFESSIONAL SOCIETIES

Professional societies have an important role to play as representatives of constituencies affected by unemployment and underemployment. Unfortunately, many of the societies do little more than provide placement services at annual meetings or publish lists of positions and applicants. Even those efforts are often ineffective, as was shown in Chapter 6. Nevertheless, the professional societies can play a key role not only as advocates of their constituencies rights but also in developing cooperation among employers, government agencies, and educational institutions for the benefit of their present and future members.

Cooperation with the Employment Service

Probably the best example of professional societies cooperation with the government is that involving their projects with the Employment Service. Such cooperation goes back to the 1950s, when the Employment Service inaugurated placement services at professional meetings (Adams, 1969). Changes in location of the annual meetings have worked against the continuity of these services. Typically, professional societies are now responsible for their own placement activities.

A highly innovative project with the Employment Service was an outgrowth of the voluntary self-help groups established by the American Institute of Aeronautics and Astronautics to help their unemployed members (AIAA, 1972). This project, carried out by the AIAA under contract from the U.S. Department of Labor, became Volunteer Engineers, Scientists and Technicians (VEST) and ultimately included the Employment Workshops described in Chapter 7. The major task of the VEST volunteers, most of whom were themselves unemployed professionals, was first to locate and develop job openings, then to catalog the skills and backgrounds of members and match them with the jobs. The Employment Service provided the VEST group with office space and clerical support, including telephone and mail franking privileges. In turn, the Employment Service received the benefit of a volunteer professional group that provided expertise in the placement of technical professionals and served to legitimize the Employment Service as a source of such jobs. In fact, as a result of their program, good relationships were developed between the Employment Service and individual professionals as well as with employers. These relationships apparently paid off, since a total of 32 VEST chapters were established between June 1971 and February 1973 and almost 9000 of their members were returned to work (Bain, 1974). Several conclusions emerged from the VEST experience; these included:

Self-help reemployment effort on this national scale was unique among occupations and was spurred by the idea that those in professional occupations could aid themselves in finding new work.

Because of their voluntary and temporary nature, chapter efforts were sporadic. Cooperation and assistance from the State Employment Service offices and the AIAA were often important to the continuation of chapter activities.

A considerable part of the benefits of the VEST program cannot be measured solely in the traditional labor market terms such as ''jobs developed'' and ''unemployed placed.'' The availability of a structured peer group provided emotional support to the unemployed (Bain, 1974, p. 39).

Professional societies can take advantage of the willingness of their unemployed members to volunteer their services for self-help groups that carry out employment counseling, job development, and job placement activities. As we noted in Chapter 7, such volunteerism may be motivated, in part, by self-interest. Not only did the unemployed volunteers receive emotional support from their colleagues but their activities were instrumental in locating positions that they themselves could fill. As we noted earlier, the Employment Service, by actively cooperating with the professional societies, can have its stature enhanced and thereby lose its image as the option of ''last resort.''

Skills Conversion and Retraining

Some professional societies, such as the American Chemical Society, took the intiative in offering free short courses to their jobless members (Shapero, 1972). Such courses may be useful for teaching new knowledge or skills in a professional's field as well as maintaining the psychological well-being of the individual. However, there may also be a need for concerted efforts at skills conversion through retraining for other fields, and professional societies have already demonstrated that they can provide the expertise to accomplish this. For example, the federally sponsored Technology Utilization Project (TUP), discussed in Chapter 7, was administered by the National Society of Professional Engineers (NSPE).

Prior to setting up the TUP retraining programs, NSPE carried out a Skills Conversion Project, funded under the Technology Mobilization and Reemployment Program. This project identified the industries offering the greatest possibilities for reemploying technical professionals as well as the skills required and the retraining needed. Research was conducted, primarily by volunteers, and reports on 16 industries prepared which summarized each industry's products, technology, skilled tasks by occupation, and forecasts of future employment. It was on the basis of this Skills Conversion Project that the areas of retraining were selected for TUP. The approach used by this project could serve as a model for developing retraining programs for various types of professionals. It would appear that professional societies are capable of mobilizing their expertise when necessary to carry out skills conversion studies for developing more effective retraining programs in cooperation with government efforts or on their own intiative.

Forecasting Future Supply and Demand

Professional societies can also make a major contribution by carrying out studies to forecast future supply and demand in their respective fields. Here again cooperation with government agencies such as the Department of Labor would be appropriate. One such program was established by the Engineering Manpower Commission, representing all the technical societies. According to the Commission, it initiated "a series of experimental surveys to measure occupational trends to identify areas of both strong and weak demand, and is prepared to expand its survey efforts in cooperation with government agencies as a supplement to national professional manpower data programs" (Engineering Manpower Commission, 1975, pp. 2–3).

Information on future supply and demand would not only be useful for current members of a particular profession but could also be disseminated to high school and college guidance counselors to see that they have the most up-to-date information to help students enter careers that offer them the best opportunities. This would fit in with the efforts of the Department of Labor to assist in career guidance through its National Occupational Information Service (Ausmus, 1977). Such career information, widely distributed among guidance counselors and publicized among students, might have reduced the glut of teachers and doctoral graduates which began in the 1970s. The professional societies have an obligation to their current and future members to limit the numbers in their ranks if the job market for them looks bleak. One method of accomplishing this is for the societies to provide accurate information on future prospects in their profession and to ensure that it is disseminated widely. In fact, academically oriented societies in the humanities, such as the American Historical Association, the American Philosophical Association, and the Modern Language Association, have intiated a number of efforts to redirect their younger members toward nonacademic positions (Coughlin, 1978). These efforts include providing information on the job market and career counseling that focuses on nonacademic placement. Thus not only can the professional societies contribute expert knowledge to help improve the quality of job forecasts in their field, they can also play a key role in assuring that the information is used effectively.

Professional Licensing

Another way that the societies can control the number of members entering or remaining in their profession is to require, in conjunction with state laws, professional licensing to practice. This already exists to varying degrees in professions such as medicine, pharmacy, law, accounting, and psychology, just to name a few. There are strong movements to require licensing in other fields such as teaching (Buder, 1976a; Goldman, 1979).

Renewal of licenses could be made subject to the requirement that professionals maintain a certain level of competence in their field (Phillips, 1978; Watkins, 1975, 1977). Although such control over professional workers is not yet widespread, it is likely to grow, especially if increasing numbers of professionals, as well as the public, make demands on the societies to protect their interests. Indeed, one study has found that a third of unemployed professionals supported stricter licensure laws as a solution to the unemployment problem, and this was partcularly evident for engineers, among whom such control is limited (Estes, 1973).

Political Lobbying

Professionals are also demanding more political lobbying on the part of their societies. As can be seen from Table 8.1, most professionals supported such lobbying—the only exception being the underemployed, who, as we have seen, tend to prefer even more activist approaches. Among the unemployed, political lobbying was most widely supported by those in stage II, the period of concerted effort, with seven-tenths feeling that this approach would be useful. It should be remembered that those in stage II are least likely to opt for more radical solutions, but instead turn to more traditional means of resolving the unemployment problem. Hence, their overwhelming support for political lobbying.

However, the desires of professionals may clash with those of their associations on issues such as lobbying. A good case in point is the petition submitted by members of the Institute of Electrical and Electronics Engineers (IEEE) to amend the constitution of the IEEE to include activities to promote and improve the economic well-being of its membership. Despite the initial opposition of the IEEE board of directors to this petition, it was approved by over two-thirds of the members voting (IEEE, undated; *New York Times*, 1972).

Professional Unions

It is clear that the professional societies must serve the needs of their constituencies if they are to be effective in dealing with problems such as unemployment. A more militant alternative to the professional society is unionizing to protect the interests of members. Whereas blue-collar unions have experienced declines in membership, white-collar and professional unions have been growing (Shamot, 1976; Oppenheimer, 1975). The growth of professional unions is, in part, a result of the new economic insecurity experienced by the college-educated. In offering solutions to their employment problem one-third of professionals who were out of work suggested that they unionize to protect their interests (Estes, 1973).

Our data indicate that a majority supported unionizing as a useful way to deal with the professional unemployment problem (Table 8.1). The underemployed, in keeping with their more militant stance, were most strongly in favor of unionizing, particularly among those who had become professionally obsolescent ($r = .33$, $p < .01$) and who were more willing to take a job involving risks ($r = .37$, $p < .01$). Among the unemployed, more favorable support for unions was evident among those who attended fewer professional meetings ($r = .30$,

$p < .05$), and who manifested the work-inhibition syndrome ($r = .46$, $p < .001$). Moreover, unions were most popular among the long-term unemployed, with over seven-tenths supporting such a collective approach to deal with job insecurity. Here again, we see the greater militancy among those who have been most affected by joblessness. They not only may withdraw from work but also from identification with their profession. Hence, their willingness to support unionization.

As others found (e.g., Fox and Wince, 1976), support for unions was widespread among younger professionals. The inverse relationship between age and union support was particularly evident among the unemployed ($r = -.43$, $p < .001$). In this group three-fourths of those under 26 advocated unionization. As an increasing number of young college graduates enter their professions facing uncertain careers and as the older members continue to be threatened by economic insecurity we are likely to see a greater pressure on the professional societies to adopt the more militant tactics of unions. A good example of this is the American Association of University Professors, which has evolved from being primarily a professional association into a bargaining agent to protect the job interests of its constituency (Semas, 1976), even to the extent of organizing strikes among traditionally conservative professionals such as engineering faculty (Constance, 1977). Indeed, by the mid-1970s three-fourths of all faculty members supported a collective-bargaining agent and one-fourth of the professoriate were already represented by such agents (Ladd and Lipset, 1978). As would be expected, the greatest support for collective action came from junior faculty, the group most threatened by job insecurity.

Indicative of the frustration among professionals, a survey of IEEE members in southern California found that almost half would not choose engineering as a career, primarily because of a lack of security, and favored transforming their society into a union (Gaynor, 1971). Many who preferred a union cited the American Medical Association as a model; others preferred the teamsters. As already noted, the membership of the IEEE overwhelmingly voted to amend their society's constitution over the objection of its board of directors. A major change in the constitution was that the primary purpose of the IEEE is to promote and improve the economic well-being of its membership (IEEE, undated).

Despite the increasing militancy of professional society members in protecting their rights, the limited evidence we do have indicates that actual strikes by professionals, such as teachers, is *less* likely to occur during periods of high unemployment (Weintraub and Thornton, 1976). Thus, the effectiveness of the militant professional society in protecting its members' job security in times of economic decline is open to question. Nevertheless, even if professionals do not strike, the mere act of attempting to deal collectively with the threat of unemployment and underemployment may be an effective coping mechanism for establishing a social support system to help reduce individual stress.

Investigations of Employer Compliance with Termination Guidelines

Although many professional societies have established guidelines on employer responsibility in dealing with terminations of their members, few have attempted to investigate and identify employers regarding their compliance with termination guidelines (Ross, 1973). Investigations that identify those employers possessing deficiencies in their termination policies and practices could serve to attain compliance with guidelines on terminations, if only to avoid the publicity that could damage an employer's image with professionals and the public at large. Such a practice has long been followed by the American Association of University Professors and has served to protect the position of tenured faculty members.

The most extensive efforts at investigating terminations by nonacademic employers have been carried out by the American Chemical Society (ACS). Since 1970, the ACS has been the pacesetter among societies in such investigations, reporting on mass terminations among 99 employers of chemists and chemical engineers just in a period of six years (Heylin, 1976). A target for investigation by the Committee on Professional Relations of the ACS is an "employer that has fired three or more chemical professionals, other than for cause or incompetence, within about a six month period" (Heylin, 1976, p. 57). The termination guidelines established by ACS include the following conditions (American Chemical Society, 1975):

1. *Placement assistance.*   Efforts should be made to place the individual in another position within the organization, including retraining for a new position if necessary. When such internal transfers are not possible, assistance should be provided to find employment elsewhere.

2. *Advance notice.*   A minimum of four weeks' advance notice should be given to an individual who is to be terminated.

3. *Employee service.*   Those with a minimum of ten years of service should not be terminated except for continued evidence of previously documented inadequate performance or cause. If the latter is claimed, the individual's case should be reviewed by two levels of management above the immediate supervisor as well as by professional peers.

4. *Pension plan vesting.*   Those with a minimum of ten years of service should have fully vested pension rights with survivor benefits.

5. *Severance pay.*   The individual should receive two weeks' salary for every year of service as severance pay. Additional notice in lieu of severance pay may be provided by mutual consent of both parties.

6. *Employee protection plans.*   Life insurance and medical care plans should be continued by the employer for a minimum of one month follow-

ing termination at the same rate of contribution as before. The employee would have an additional 31-day grace period.

7. *Rehire privileges.* The employer should follow a policy of rehiring those terminated in a retrenchment before simiarly qualified new employees are recruited. Rehire privileges should be carefully explained to terminated employees.

8. *Involuntary retirement.* Any individual who is involuntarily retired by an employer should be treated at least as well as an employee dismissed for economic reasons.

Information about specific terminations is collected from the employers responsible as well as from the terminated employees (Heylin, 1976). The Committee on Professional Relations of the ACS then judges the evidence regarding the employer's performance against the termination guidelines. Their investigation results in a listing that identifies the degree of compliance by each employer with every termination condition specified in the guidelines. Such listings are published regularly in *Chemical and Engineering News*, thereby publicizing the names of employers carrying out terminations, together with their degree of compliance with the guidelines. An analysis of 41 employers who were investigated found that they met the guidelines only 49 percent of the time. However, compliance varied sharply among the specific guidelines, ranging from 80 percent for employer placement assistance to a low of 12 percent for the recommended level of severence pay.

Although most employers surveyed by the ACS have agreed with the concept of professional guidelines on employer-employee relations, only 3 percent were actually willing to endorse them (Heylin, 1976). There is also an apparent growing reluctance of employers to supply details on their terminations to the ACS. Many employers apparently fear that such professional society pressure could serve as a prelude to unionism and blacklisting, charges that the societies strongly deny (Ross, 1973). Whatever the case, it does seem clear that by investigating terminations of their members, the professional societies are looking after the interests of the constituents they purport to represent. To counter charges of blacklisting, professional societies should emphasize a "white list" of employers exemplary in their policies and practices in avoiding terminations. Such policies and practices could then serve as models for other employers to follow when faced with the need to reduce professional personnel costs.

Cooperation with Employers

Professional societies can also cooperate with employers in providing assistance to terminated employees. A good example of this was the Cooperative Placement Center (CPC), a voluntary effort organized in 1969 by members of the Cape

Kennedy Personnel Associaton (an affiliate of the American Society for Personnel Administration), to deal with the large-scale space program reductions in force and to provide assistance to terminated employees (Babec and Lee, 1970). Thus, under the auspices of a professional society, competing firms were able to band together and pool their resources to help their terminated employees. The participating organizations donated facilities and clerical assistance, as well as funds to operate the CPC. The center's primary responsibility was to publicize their service, contact potential employers, collect and process résumés, and arrange for interviews by visiting recruiters. The CPC had processed 2380 résumés and within several months 523 job offers were made by recruiters, who had conducted a total of 3733 interviews at the center. Not only had this cooperative effort led to job offers in a relatively short time, but employers who had come to the center continued their recruiting in the area through local newspapers.

Cooperative efforts such as the CPC can go well beyond job placement. There is no reason why the resources for a full range of employment assistance could not be provided by a consortium of employers. As we shall see in the next section, extensive outplacement services have been established by individual employers. It would appear that the costs of such services could be shared by several employers through a cooperative effort under a professional society umbrella. Some societies, such as the ACS, stand ready to provide employment seminars by their staff at the site where their members have been terminated. Such cooperation between societies and employers could serve to reduce suspicion and acrimony between them for the benefit of all, especially the professionals who are threatened with job loss. We turn next to an examination of what the employers themselves can do to alleviate unemployment stress among professionals.

ROLE OF THE EMPLOYER

Employers play a pivotal role when it comes to the problem of unemployment since it is they who make the decisions on terminations and hiring. A variety of strategies are available to employers when they are faced with making difficult decisions on retrenching professional personnel. Not only are there alternatives to terminations, but even when such retrenchment becomes inevitable, the employer can contribute greatly to help facilitate reemployment and adjustment.

Alternatives to Terminations

Employers have developed a wide range of responses to deal with cutting professional personnel costs that do not necessarily entail terminations. A variety of alternatives to reductions in force were developed as part of the federal government's policy to deal with cutbacks in the Department of Defense that began in

1969 (Valdes, 1971). Similar policies were also developed in private industry. In a survey of 105 large industrial companies, all of whom had significant cutbacks in their work force during the severe recession of 1974–1975, it was revealed that most turned to less extreme approaches than outright dismissals to trimming personnel expenditures (Hershfield, 1975). The most widespread practice among the companies was to not fill vacancies caused by normal attrition. For higher-level personnel, reduction through attrition was practically universal. This approach certainly appears to be a most painless way of reducing personnel costs. Nevertheless, since a major adjustment may be required in the work role of those high-level personnel who do not choose to leave, problems of stress can ensue when a hiring freeze is in effect.

Voluntary separation was further stimulated by encouraging early retirement, and this was practiced by about one-third of the companies undergoing retrenchment of high-level personnel. The companies emphasized that they were encouraging, but not requiring, early retirement since such a requirement would violate age discrimination laws. Generally, those choosing to retire early were offered generous pension arrangements and other benefits. Such early retirement programs are apparently quite popular. For example, IBM, which has a traditional policy of not terminating workers for economic reasons, offered early retirement during periods of retrenchment to employees with 25 or more years of service in the company; of those eligible one-third accepted such an option in 1971 and almost one-fourth in 1975 (*The New York Times*, 1975a). These early retirees received two years' salary in addition to their pensions. No indication was given as to what percentage of eligible professionals chose to retire early. Although early retirement is more widely available for higher level personnel than for blue-collar workers (Hershfield, 1975), there is considerable evidence indicating that most professionals prefer working to retirement (Kaufman, 1974c; Sheppard, 1977). Given this strong attachment to their work, it is unlikely that many professionals will choose to retire early, even with generous inducements from employers. Therefore, as a policy designed to stimulate attrition among professionals, early retirement has severe limitations.

Given the unpredictable nature of natural attrition and early retirement, other approaches to personnel cost reductions, short of terminations, have been used (Hershfield, 1975). Only about one in 20 companies cutting costs among high-level personnel resorted to actual reductions in pay and benefits, but many postponed increases in pay and benefits. The latter practice seems to be directed more at the highest-paid employees, since almost half of the companies apply it to their managerial employees but only about one in 10 treat their blue-collar workers this way, regardless of whether or not they are unionized. In fact, there have been instances when professional unions have taken the intiative to head off impending dismissals by foregoing a salary increase for its members (Buder, 1976a,b).

Another way of responding to the need for cutting personnel costs is to reduce the time professionals spend at work. This can be accomplished painlessly by encouraging employees to take their paid vacations during slow business periods. Although over one-third of the companies undergoing retrenchment used such paid vacations (Hershfield, 1975), the approach is useless once vacation periods have been exhausted. A more useful alternative to dismissals which some companies have introduced is shorter workweeks, with corresponding reductions in pay. However, this practice is applied to higher-level personnel less often than to others (Hershfield, 1975). For example, only one-fifth of the companies retrenching used short work schedules with managerial employees—less than half the rate for blue-collar workers. There is an apparent reluctance to put decision-making personnel on a shorter work schedule. Nevertheless, professionals have successfully adapted to various work-sharing modes (Lazer, 1975; Meier, 1979) and they would certainly accept such schedules if the only alternative is job loss. There have been proposals for work sharing which is supplemented by unemployment insurance benefits (Fleischman, 1976; Kihss, 1975; Levitan and Belous, 1977; Lynton, 1975). This would necessitate legislation encouraging reduced work time to fight unemployment. Another variation on the theme of work sharing is scheduling employees for alternating periods of work, which only about one-fifth of the companies used for high-level personnel (Hershfield, 1975). This approach has a disadvantage in that states typically require a minimum number of consecutive days of unemployment before paying unemployment insurance benefits. This disadvantage may be overcome through layoff rotation, with each employee not working the minimum period required for unemployment compensation and then returning to work in accordance with a schedule worked out between management and employees (Homjak, 1978).

It should be obvious that personnel cuts can, and often are, carried out without resorting to dismissals. Some have suggested that it is the white collar employees, whose jobs are not protected by unions, who should be the focus of experimentation with alternatives to terminaton (Lynton, 1975). Unfortunately, in most of the practices just discussed, either company control over personnel cutbacks is inadequate (as in natural attrition or early retirement) and hence fails to ensure that terminations can be avoided, or the individual may suffer in terms of salary or utilization (as in work sharing). Although the latter type of losses are usually preferable to losing one's job completely, the resulting underemployment can be stressful to many professionals. However, for some, such as women with home responsibilities, alternatives such as work sharing may be an ideal compromise to accommodate career and family needs (Griffel and Kaufman, 1977). Indeed, research indicates that sharing of professional positions works quite well (Meier, 1979).

There are, of course, other innovative alternatives to terminations. One example is that of one company lending employees to another as has been done in Japan to maintain job security (*The Economist*, 1978). Another approach is that of transferring ownership of a financially troubled company to its employees, a practice that is beginning to take root in the United States (McManus, 1974; Stern and Hammer, 1978). These examples should suffice to indicate that both employers and employees can go to great lengths to find alternatives to terminations.

Retraining, Skills Conversion, and Transfer

Employers can turn to yet other methods of personnel retrenchment in which individual losses are not only minimized but may also be turned into gains. These methods include transfers, skills conversions, and retraining that can lead to totally new careers. Although internal transfers can be used in times of retrenchment, they may be limited if, for instance, there are too many specialists in a particular field. Transfers for such individuals would have to be into a totally new area of specialization and hence, may require some type of skills conversion or retraining.

The government as an employer frequently seeks alternatives to terminations, and political considerations are likely to play a major role in attempts at minimizing job loss. A case in point was the closing of the NASA Electronics Research Center (ERC) in Cambridge, Massachusetts, and its conversion into the Transportation Systems Center (TSC) for the U.S. Department of Transportation (Rollins, 1970; Shapely, 1971). Although almost half of the ERC professionals were offered positions in the new TSC, skills conversion was most effective for the applications-oriented engineers; scientists involved with research were terminated. However, even those who underwent conversion found that the transfer from one federal agency (NASA) to another (DOT) not only changed the type of work they were doing, but required a major change in their approach to solving problems—where factors such as public policy and cost became at least as important as technology. This type of radical conversion is relatively rare (Teich and Lambright, 1976), but it serves as an example of how political forces can come to the rescue of at least some professionals and redirect their efforts toward socially useful goals. Such redirection has occurred in a more gradual manner in a number of large American laboratories (Teich and Lambright, 1976).

Although there is a lack of statistics on the extent to which conversions or retraining to avoid terminations is used in industry, there are some notable instances of its successful application. Perhaps the most prominent one is that of IBM, which, as we have noted, has a long-standing policy precluding terminations of its personnel which was adhered to even during the depths of the Great Depression. This guarantee of job security comes as close as possible to the model of the Japanese corporation, where employees are hired for life (at least until the recession following the Arab oil embargo of 1973).

IBM avoided terminations during the 1970s not only through early retirement but also by retraining and physically relocating some 5000 employees as part of the most extensive corporate reeducation program in the United States (*Business*

Week, 1975). Although precise statistics were not made available, it was reported that the retraining tended to result in higher-status jobs, including professional staff positions, with a commensurate increase in pay.

Evidence is accumulating that involuntary transfers create great stress among professionals and their families (Burke, 1974; Foster and Liebrenz, 1977). Indeed, it may very well be that retraining for a new career plus the need to pick up roots and physically relocate is no less stressful than losing one's job. Certainly, for those who are reluctant to do either, the change is certain to increase their stress. As we have already seen, those who are willing to be retrained tended to be reluctant to relocate, and vice versa. Therefore, if any change is to be made, the professional should be given the choice of one or the other as an alternative to termination.

However, at IBM (which for many quite literally means "I've Been Moved"), relocation and retraining are part of the organization culture and hence may be more acceptable to its employees. Furthermore, in the IBM approach, which emphasizes personal growth and development of the individual, adjustments to changes in career and home are likely to be rapid. Alan A. Mclean, IBM's industrial psychiatrist, assessed the benefits of the retraining program and concluded: "When the company pays attention to the individual in a highly individualized way it fosters a real, honest increase in self-worth and self-esteem" (*Business Week*, 1975, p. 112).

Aside from the motive of corporate commitment, the no-termination policy at IBM was feasible since some parts of its organization were growing while others were declining. Many companies were not so fortunate and, unlike IBM, could not maintain a full-employment policy. A majority (55 percent) of major American corporations that had to carry out cutbacks in personnel costs among their high-level employees resorted to permanent separations (Hershfield, 1975). Of particular interest is that companies were less likely to carry out such permanent separation among blue-collar workers, but rather turned to temporary layoffs for these employees, even for those who were not union members. The possibility of recall, plus generous supplementary employment benefits provided by some union contracts, give the blue-collar worker much greater protection than the professional. Indeed, the analysis of company practices in cutting personnel costs concluded that it may be the higher level employee "who undergoes the most severe career and lifestyle dislocation during a recession" (Hershfield, 1975, p. 22). This does not differ from the conclusion arrived at in Chapter 2.

Outplacement

Interviews with corporate personnel executives revealed that there was little agreement on what constitutes fair treatment for a terminated employee (Mendleson, 1974). Increasingly, it appears that fair treatment involves the employer providing assistance to cushion the effects of termination. Such assistance can range from merely providing severance pay to a host of elaborate support services. In response to the mass terminations of professionals in the 1970s, some employers established a new personnel function—outplacement—which "can be described as a series of services to terminated employees to minimize any period of unemployment following termination" (Scherba, 1973, p. 41).

We noted in Chapter 6 that relatively few unemployed professionals found their jobs through their employers outplacement service, despite the fact that a majority of organizations claim they provide such assistance (Miner, 1978). Nevertheless, all indications are that a carefully designed outplacement service, either developed as an in-house function or provided by a specialized consultant, does have great potential. Even some types of assistance that are relatively simple to develop can be quite useful. For example, TRW established an outplacement center for its professionals and found that over half of those terminated reported that the most valuable assistance provided was the up-to-date listings of job openings (Lehner, 1971). The counseling provided ranked next in importance, followed by assistance in preparing résumés. Furthermore, three-fourths of those who found new jobs they liked said they would return to their former company if given the opportunity. Apparently, successful outplacement can help assure a positive attitude toward one's former employer despite the termination experience.

Although there has been some criticism of outplacement as "a corporate guilt trip" that handles mostly failures (Welles, 1978), the limited evidence that does exist tends to be positive. For example, it has been reported that "there is statistical evidence that persons who use outplacement training and services find jobs earlier than co-workers who do not participate" (Scherba, 1973, p. 44). More specific data are available from an analysis of outplacement training provided by PPG Industries to facilitate the reemployment of their terminated employees, which reported the following:

> The results of the outplacement training have been shown to be effective. Of the 45 research professionals who were thrown into an unfavorable labor market, 38 participated in the training. There is a significant inverse correlation between the length of unemployment and participation in training among professionals (McIntosh, 1973, p. 13).

Somewhat limited results were reported in Corning Glass's experience with their outplacement program, whose "major objectives are to restore self-confidence and to give 'a nuts and bolts' course in how to organize the campaign to find a new job" (Faber, 1975, p. 4). Although the program was found to have no great impact on the percentage of those who obtained new jobs, it did appear to result in better positions. For example, those who took the course obtained jobs with higher salaries than in their previous jobs, whereas nonparticipants found jobs paying an average of $1000 a year less than they received at Corning.

The objective results reported thus far with outplacement indicates that its potential value is more in helping professionals adjust to job loss and sustaining or restoring their self-confidence than in actually placing them in jobs. As discussed in Chapter 7, appropriate counseling is valuable not only in teaching professionals how to find jobs, but also, and more important, in serving to build their self-confidence so that they are psychologically prepared to deal with the demands and frustrations of a job search. To assist in this process of adjustment, employers can turn to staff psychologists or to one of several private consulting firms that offer extensive outplacement assistance.

A rather elaborate outplacement program which focused on adjustment was developed at Alcan Aluminum Ltd. of Canada by a staff psychologist to help 200 middle-aged professionals and managerial employees embark on a new career outside the organization (Cuddihy, 1974). A special unit was set up to deal constructively with the personnel cutback and included the staff psychologist, two outside consultants, and a line manager from the personnel department. The termination process involved a number of approaches designed to deal with minimizing the stress involved with job loss, as well as assisting in the job search. Since the program involved so many aspects of outplacement, it would be informative to examine some of its more innovative features, which included the following procedures:

1.   Prior to the termination interview by the immediate supervisor, the special unit checked the employee's medical history through the company's physician to determine whether termination was likely to be exceptionally traumatic. If such evidence was found, a meeting was held between the immediate supervisor, a member of the special unit, and the physician to discuss how to handle the termination interview. The supervisor often role-played the interview and, if necessary, a script was written out indicating precisely what should be said. If medical or psychological problems became apparent during the termination interview, the immediate supervisor would arrange for an appointment with the medical center or the special unit as soon as possible after the interview.

2.   Immediately after the termination interview, the employee met with the personnel manager, who provided information on company assistance that included support for travel to search for a new job and a financial settlement to cushion the termination. The personnel manager also provided basic packaged information on job hunting, financial management, and so forth. Although these are elementary types of information, the personnel manager is considered to have a crucial role because, according to the staff psychologist,

he is the employee's first point of contact after the termination interview; the success of a program like this depends heavily on his skills. He is a key man because he has credibility. . . not only has he worked as a manager, but his age, years of service, and level in the organization are about the same as those of the people that he will deal with in this kind of termination process (Cuddihy, 1974, p. 63).

It should be noted that the way in which the termination decision is communicated can have detrimental effects on attitudes toward the employer as well as the individual's psychological well-being (Briar, 1976). Unfortunately, many first learn of their termination in a written communication or, even worse, find out second-hand after others have been informed of the decision (Briar, 1976; Miner, 1978). It has been suggested that "sensitivity to the upset and fear of the dislocated worker is blocked when the employer can hide behind a memo or letter" (Briar, 1976, p. 45).

Communication of the termination decision by the right person is also critical, as was indicated some time ago by Erving Goffman (1952) in his analysis of "cooling the mark out." In this case, the terminated professional would be the mark "who would have to be cooled." According to Goffman (1952), "cooling represents a process of adjustment to an impossible situation. . . . A process of redefining the self along defensible lines must be instigated and carried along. . . . One general way of handling the problem of cooling the mark out is to give the task to someone whose status relative to the mark will serve to ease the situation in some way" (pp. 456–457). The case of Alcan exemplifies how careful consideration can be given to the individual's well-being in communicating the termination decision by an appropriate and well-trained person.

3.   Immediately after the interview with the personnel manager, the employees being terminated were provided with a new office, which included secretarial support, stationery, telephones, and duplicating facilities. The reason for this change was explained by the staff psychologist:

> This abrupt move from his old office and friends might at first upset the employee but it has definite positive aspects. First, the employees in this temporary office space soon meet and begin to help each other by exchanging information about jobs, contacts, newspaper ads, and so forth. Second, there is a clear psychological advantage for the employee in being able to look for work from a secure job base while not having to cope with his old job's responsibilities or with the embarrassment of his friends. The space is available to the employee until he finds a job, regardless of how long that takes. Third, the move emphasizes that a 180-degree turn has been taken: in this new setting the employee is forced to think positively about the challenge ahead of him instead of focusing bitterly on the past (Cuddihy, 1974, p. 66).

4.   To assist the terminated employees to become more active and assertive on their own behalf, they were introduced to one of the two outside consultants as soon as possible after the interview with the personnel manager. Each consultant specialized in a different professional area, with one responsible for technical personnel, such as engineers, physicists, and chemists; the other dealt with managers, economists, lawyers, accountants, and those technical people who had been away from their field for some years because they moved up the administrative ladder. During appointments made at the employee's convenience, the

consultants spent 8 to 10 hours with each individual, providing guidance through a series of exercises and trial interviews to determine job preferences and to strengthen interview skills. The consultants also provided guidance in the preparation of résumés as well as encouragement to use various methods of job hunting. According to the staff psychologist: "This process has an added advantage, in that it involves a fair amount of activity very soon after the employee's termination, so that he is kept occupied. This is good therapy for that early traumatic period" (Cuddihy, 1974, p. 66). This initial phase has been referred to as the "ventilation" period, since it is the time when terminated employees typically vent anger and resentment against their former employer (Welles, 1978).

5.   Within a day after the employee's first visit to the outside consultant, an interview was held with the staff psychologist, who noted that he "tries to help the employee understand both the experience he has just been through and the problems that he will have to face during one of the most difficult periods of his life. . . . I try to explain to the employee that anxiety and tension are normal and entirely understandable during the job hunting period" (Cuddihy, 1974, p. 67). This begins the second phase of outplacement: rebuilding the terminated individual's ego (Welles, 1978).

All employees were offered a rather complete confidential psychological assessment designed to help them become aware of their strengths and weaknesses and to enable them to market their abilities more realistically. The assessment was spread over a two-day period and involved an interview followed by tests and measurements of intelligence, aptitude, interest, and personality.

The individual received feedback on the assessment in about 10 to 14 days. During this period, employees worked with the consultants and actively began their job search, including interviews for new positions. The planning and carrying out of the actual job search is typically the final phase of outplacement (Welles, 1978). It was observed that during this period most Alcan employees began to lose confidence and self-esteem; and this loss was reinforced when there were not replies from initial job contacts, which is not at all unusual in the early search stage. A typical comment was: "I'm not mad at Alcan anymore, but I guess I'm no good. I was just kidding myself all these years. I must really be incompetent" (Cuddihy, 1974, p. 67). A shifting of blame to oneself apparently occurs as the resentment dissipates.

When the employees returned to the psychologist for feedback on the assessment, their confidence had fallen to such a degree that they no longer believed in their own abilities. The staff psychologist observed that: "In 99 percent of the cases, the employee will underestimate his intelligence by a fairly substantial margin. When told just where he stands on a national average, he either cannot or will not accept this information" (Cuddihy, 1974, p. 67).

It is possible that the outplacement process compressed the stages of unemployment by not only forcing the individual to get involved in the job search almost immediately but by requiring the type of career reevaluation that typically does not occur until stage III. Indeed, if outplacement does not result in rapid reemployment, a ''sixth-week-slump'' reportedly occurs (Welles, 1978) that appears comparable to the discouragement experienced in stage IV of unemployment.

Given the loss of confidence and self-esteem, the assessment feedback session at Alcan was of crucial importance. During this session, which lasted three to five hours, the test results were explained in detail and the employee was encouraged to engage in a dialogue with the psychologist and even question or challenge the results. At the end of the feedback process the psychologist provided a verbal summary of the results and his recommendations. The interest of employees in this part of the process was indicated by the fact that some even brought a tape recorder to the session for later reference. The assessment process apparently played a major role in helping the psychological adjustment of the individual. Its value was noted by the staff psychologist:

> We have found that the most important thing to come out of the assessment process is the restoration of self-esteem and confidence. The employee knows that the psychologist is being as straightforward and objective as possible, and (perhaps for the first time in his working life) he is hearing—and facing—the good and the bad about himself, told honestly. He finds out that he is not as bad as he had begun to think he was; that he is a relatively stable, intelligent, worthwhile human being who has some very valuable, marketable skills to offer, even at age 50 or 55.

> The employee is now in a state of mind to turn his back on the company and move forward in a new direction. He can tell himself that they were wrong, that they missed their chance to use his valuable executive know-how, and that now he will show them by using his new-found enthusiasm to find a job elsewhere (Cuddihy, 1974, p. 68).

Such an enthusiastic evaluation is probably warranted given the positive changes in confidence and self-esteem among the unemployed that has been found to result from job counseling. It would appear that assessment and counseling by the employer are crucial in preparing professionals for the frustrations they are likely to encounter in their job search. At Alcan, despite the fact that the professionals terminated were all older—ranging in age from 40 to 62—over nine-tenths of those who used the outplacement services found new jobs in less than four months. Most were reemployed at salaries equal to or better than those of their previous position. No indication was given, however, of the reemployment success among those who did not choose to use the services provided. If the results of other studies on the effects of job counseling can serve as a guide, it is likely that those who did not receive outplacement assistance were not as successful in reemployment.

As noted earlier, job loss is often highly traumatic to professionals, but it can also serve to launch them on new and even more rewarding careers. In discussing the new jobs obtained by the professionals terminated by Alcan, the staff psychologist also found this to be true:

> It is too early to assess whether all these people will be better off in their new jobs, but early feedback is very encouraging. Many of them have told us that they are pleased with the change, some even admitting that it was the best thing that ever happened to them. Some have expressed great new confidence in themselves, because they feel that, on their own, they found more challenging jobs under adverse conditions (Cuddihy, 1974, p. 69).

As with so many other employers, the outplacement process at Alcan was a new experience, and although it contained many innovations, certain improvements are possible. One would be to supplement the individual assessment with an ongoing group counseling approach. The effectiveness of sharing experiences and receiving peer support has been noted in Chapter 7. Such a group approach, the "Stress Management Workshop," was developed at the Equitable Life Assurance Society of the U.S. primarily to deal with the psychological problems of employees whose jobs were abolished (Manuso, 1977). Projective tests (e.g., the TAT) administered before and after participation in the workshop indicated a significant increase in feelings about career capabilities and hopefulness. It was concluded that the workshop served "to detect and prevent stress-related disorders, including depression, not to treat these disorders; and, to bolster employees' psychological resources at a time when these resources were needed most" (Manuso, 1977, p. 601). Clearly, a group approach can go far to reduce the stress of job loss and should be included as part of outplacement activities.

Another change in the termination process would provide cutback victims with the longest possible advance notice. At Alcan the employees were generally notified only several days prior to their termination date, although they usually had been identified as "redundant" three to six months before. This short notice of termination may have been detrimental to the adjustment of the individual. One clinical psychologist involved with counseling professionals who are victims of terminations, strongly advocates giving advance notice, as his following exhortation indicates:

> Provide cutback victims with the longest possible advance notice. This is of utmost importance. The longer the time, the easier it is to adjust—emotionally and operationally—to the departure. A man finds it easier to look for a new job while still on the payroll. His panic feelings are attenuated and he will present himself more favorably in critical interviews. The objection to longer advance notice—namely, that "the man will lie down on his job once he knows he's leaving"—has simply not been observed by many managers I've talked to (Lehner, 1971, p. 45).

There is, in fact, some evidence that having advance notice of termination has little effect on performance. For example, a study of blue-collar workers in four companies revealed no significant changes in absenteeism, lateness, or production among employees who received a one-month advance notice of impending layoff (Hershey, 1972). It was concluded that the study did "raise questions concerning management's traditional practice of announcing layoffs as close as possible to the last day worked, [and]. . . it would appear that it is mutually advantageous to give employees as much notice as possible" (Hershey, 1972, p. 275). Other research has indicated that a longer period of advance notice about termination facilitates reemployment (McKenna, 1973). Thus, the limited evidence that does exist comes out clearly in favor of providing advance notice of termination, preferably as soon as such decisions are made.

Unfortunately, investigations have revealed that about eight-tenths of all employers give their employees less than four weeks' advance notice of termination, despite the fact that most reported that they provided some type of outplacement assistance (Miner, 1978; Heylin, 1976). In one study of unemployed professionals, 43 percent received only a few hours' notice of termination (Leventman, 1974). Thus, it would appear that employers could improve the effectiveness of outplacement merely by providing longer advance notice of termination. This approach may even increase cost-effectiveness if outplacement is successful in helping employees find new jobs well before their termination date.

The federal government has recognized the problem of inadequate lead time in mass terminations, and has attempted to rectify the situation by increasing the separation notice period in order to facilitate the placement of employees affected by reductions in force (Valdes, 1971). If termination decisions are made well enough in advance, the employability of those affected can be enhanced through continuing education. Employer support for continuing education during periods of slow economic growth has even been suggested as "a novel way of reducing the work force without management having to take the initiative—attrition though overeducation" (Siegal, 1976, p. 45). In fact, there is some indication that when employer-supported continuing education does not lead to career advancement in the organization, voluntary termination is likely (Kaufman, 1977). Thus, encouragement of continuing education when combined with outplacement efforts would appear to hold much promise of enhancing the reemployment prospects of professionals slated for termination.

Not only can advance notice affect individual adjustment to job loss, but perhaps even more important is the process by which the termination decision is arrived at, as well as communicated. The use of participative decision making is suggested in the complaint of a Civil Service employee terminated from an urban drug rehabilitation center:

> We were treated with callousness and disdain. It never occurred to those making the decisions to disrupt our lives that we employees might have some input and viable

ideas regarding the situation. Many workers were willing to volunteer to be laid off and many others were capable of offering interesting and practical alternatives. No effort was made to communicate frankly with the employees nor were any efforts made to assuage the panic and anxiousness of the civil service staff. In all the situation was as ugly and anxiety provoking as possible (Greenhalgh and Jick, 1978, p. 7).

When it comes to cutting personnel costs, participative decision making is not likely to be attractive to employers. Yet such an approach, by building trust and involvement, may turn out to be the best method of dealing with terminations for the benefit of employers as well as employees. Outplacement that evolves out of participative decision making would be expected to be more responsive to employee needs and, thus, to enhance their reemployment prospects. Such employer support can be more critical than that of the family (Schlossberg and Leibowitz, 1980).

As employers gain more experience with outplacement, improvements in techniques are inevitable. However, one ingredient to the success of outplacement is essential—top management commitment to the program. As Alcan's staff psychologist explained: "One of the most important factors in making this whole scheme work is the total commitment, both moral and financial of the companies senior management. Without this the program will fail" (Cuddihy, 1974, p. 64). Companies that have received such top level commitment to assisting terminated employees have frequently carried this responsibility well beyond outplacement and, as we shall see shortly, have instituted ongoing career planning programs.

Reentry Counseling

Reentry counseling has generally been associated with the support given to women who are reentering the work force after a long hiatus in their careers. As in the case of reentry for women, the loss of self-confidence and competence, as well as the development of an inhibition toward work among the long-term unemployed, are very real problems for them as well as for their new employers. This was recognized as far back as the Great Depression, when the following was noted:

The social and emotional maladjustment of previously acceptable workers has progressed to the point where many are unemployable. The loss of opportunity to use their skill possessed in earlier years had led to a loss of the skill itself and has forced many to forget their former occupations. "Inertia" habits growing out of extended absence from work have reduced the occupational fitness of some.

Today, employers reemploying or contemplating the addition of personnel must consider and are considering the predicament which industry faces. The recruiting, training and assimilation of these workers are presenting, and may be expected to present, even more than they do now, some real problems (Lange, 1935, p. 50).

Even when one enters a new job after voluntarily leaving a former position there occurs a type of culture shock which can last from only a few hours to several months (Gray, 1975). For the professionals who had been through an extended period of joblessness this shock is likely to be of long duration. If the organizational environment is not supportive or does not ease the professionals back into challenging and productive work then it is doubtful whether their self-esteem and feelings of competence can be restored. Furthermore, if one is not socialized into the new job, disillusionment and detachment from work are likely to follow (Gray, 1975). As we have already noted, reemployment even in one's field does not necessarily serve to restore professionals to the psychological state that existed prior to job loss.

Employers are beginning to recognize the need for special treatment when hiring unemployed professionals, as the observations of one insurance executive indicates:

"In considering the unemployed professional for a position, it is wise to remember that this individual may very well be lacking in self-esteem and confidence. . . . Also, from the unemployed person's point of view, so much is at stake in one interview as to make the individual overly nervous. In the case of a depressed and nervous applicant, an outside professional, such as a consulting psychologist, could probably do a better job of assessing that person's true potential" (Wendt, 1978, p. 42).

From the perspective of employers, it would be in their own best interest when hiring a professional who has just come through the experience of unemployment, not only to do a better job of assessment but also to provide some formal reentry counseling. This is not as far-fetched as it sounds, since research has demonstrated that only a formal type of orientation to a new job is related significantly to subsequent employee effectiveness (Gannon and Paine, 1972). Since employers are likely to encounter an ever increasing number of professionals who are hired after experiencing job loss or underemployment, it would be in the interest of all concerned to provide formal reentry counseling.

Career Planning and Development

As a result of personnel cutbacks and limited growth, some organizations have put increased emphasis on career planning and development of their remaining high-level personnel (Decker, 1978; Van Atta, Decker, and Wilson, 1975). Only through such planning and development can employers assure continuing vitality of their most valuable workers and ultimately their own future viability. Effective career planning can also help reduce the likelihood of future cutbacks among professionals, by assuring a high degree of knowledge and skill utilization. Underutilized professionals are prime candidates for termination when personnel costs have to be reduced. Even if personnel cutbacks do come, those who have thought seriously about their career options and recognized both their strengths and weaknesses are likely to cope more effectively with involuntary termination. With employment problems, as well as second or even third careers, likely to become the norm for professionals, the value of career planning and development becomes even more crucial.

Employers can and do provide career planning and development programs beginning with entry into the organization and ending with retirement (Knowdell, 1978; Walker and Gutteridge, 1979). Outplacement and reentry counseling activities could be integrated, when necessary, into ongoing career programs. As we have already noted, some career programs have even grown out of outplacement efforts. Thus, the capabilities developed to provide assistance for one type of career problem are readily transferable to others. Many employers have recognized that they share a responsibility for the careers of their professionals. Although it is obvious that employers can do much to assist in career planning and development, it is ultimately the responsibility of the individual professional to deal with his or her self-development, even when it is precipitated by job loss.

Another aspect of career development involves organizational change to increase employee participation in decision making. We have already suggested participatory decision making in dealing with terminations, but this leadership style may be particularly important when dealing with the problems that follow employee cutbacks, as one management consultant explained:

> When a company is struggling to survive, whatever structure it started out with hardens. If the organization was authoritarian to begin with, chances are it will become tyrannical. If there was participatory leadership in there before the crisis, people will probably come together to work things out.

> There should be no illusion that the exercising of authority alone carries the key to good performance. I have seen some departments using participative management which are working very well within a classic organizational structure. This isn't always spotted, because it isn't expected. Upper executives assume that everybody is managing the way they are. So pockets of participation exist, flourish, and are rewarded. And nobody knows quite how they are doing it.

> The chief advantage of instituting participatory leadership during a time of crisis is that it is capable of providing more alternatives than can be imposed from above. This type of management is in a better position to get the best ideas from the largest number of people. There is the additional advantage of having more acceptable decisions, since everyone has had a hand in their formation.

> Management that has not consulted its employees, on the other hand, is apt to be judged as wrong no matter what it does. This is independent of the value of the decision. Again, management does not go about willfully cutting throats—they simply do the best they can within the confines of the system they have inherited. It's just that some of these systems are not very good.

> So they ought to be changed. As soon as the cutback has been effected (Langley, 1971. p. 37).

Equitable Life Assurance Society of the U.S. may be an example of a system that was in need of participitory leadership in dealing with the effects of mass terminations of high-level personnel, many with long-term service in the company (Meyer, 1978). Not withstanding the "Stress Management Workshops" provided by Equitable to employees whose jobs were abolished (Manuso, 1977), the personnel director, in a memo to top managers, recognized that employees "identify closely with those terminated" and "that managers must learn to operate effectively in an environment of heightened employee anxiety and reduced employee confidence and trust in management" (Meyer, 1978, p. 30). While an employee-relations consulting firm was called in by Equitable to deal with those who had turned against the company, there was no indication that organizational changes directed toward participatory management were even considered.

Carrying out appropriate changes in the organizational system could go far to enhance the credibility of an employer's concern about the careers of its professionals. Participatory interventions can be advantageous to employers, as well as employees, since they are likely to minimize the anxiety, resentment, resistance to change or loss of work motivation and productivity that have been found to occur among termination survivors (Blonder, 1976; Greenhalgh, 1978). As employers become more open to interventions involving organizational change, there is likely to be an increasing acceptance of career planning and development.

The experience employers are acquiring in the planning and development of careers can be put to use in collaborative efforts with institutions of higher education. Such collaboration has been growing for some time in a number of areas, including cooperative work–study programs for students, college placement for graduates, and continuing education for the employer's professional personnel. Employers can also provide academic institutions with unique capabilities for career planning and development, especially in dealing with hard-to-employ graduates. For example, AT&T donated an assessment center for use in the Careers in Business program at New York University—a collaborative educational effort to redirect humanities Ph. D.s into management positions. An AT&T vice-president summarized the experience:

> The assessment center module used in the NYU Careers in Business project was designed to evaluate skills and abilities important to management success. The module was patterned after similar Bell System programs and focused on communications, interpersonal and administrative skill areas. The profile developed by the assessment staff was fed back to the participants for personal career planning and self-development. Participants stated that they found the assessment experience challenging and enlightening in terms of management responsibilities (Harrison and May, 1978, p. 6).

Although collaboration of this type between industry and academic institutions to deal with the employment problems of university graduates is still a rare exception, such activities are likely to increase. Some of these areas of collaboration are referred to in our discussion of academic institutions, which we turn to next.

ROLE OF ACADEMIC INSTITUTIONS

Colleges and universities, as the institutions most responsible for the education of professionals, have a central role to play in helping to ameliorate the problem of unemployment and underemployment among their graduates. These institutions can do this not only through their traditional function as the primary source of professional workers but also in ways that are directed toward facilitating the employability of those graduates experiencing difficulty in finding work appropriate to their background and abilities.

Entry Restrictions

Although some professionals feel that there should be stricter licensing laws to exclude those who do not meet standards of competence, they are generally reluctant to have institutions of higher education decrease their number of students or increase the length of professional training to discourage students from seeking entry, even in the face of widespread unemployment (Estes, 1973). There is some evidence that students choose their major field in response to changes in the job market (Freeman, 1976), but colleges cannot depend entirely on such individual decisions in determining the numbers of students entering a particular area of study. It seems clear that, at least from the perspective of the graduate, educational institutions would be acting irresponsibly if they did not put some limitation on entry to training for certain professions, such as teaching, which have become saturated.

In some countries where the federal government exerts greater control over policy on higher education, reductions in selected fields have been carried out on a national level because of high unemployment rates among college graduates. For example, Britain cut teacher training by more than half (Scott, 1977), and in Denmark the government restricted entry of students into various fields, including medicine, with the biggest reductions—24 percent—in psychology and teacher training (Duckenfield, 1977).

In the United States some public educational institutions have initiated cutbacks in their programs to reflect more limited employment opportunities in certain fields. For instance, the City University of New York planned a 50 percent reduction in the training of new elementary and secondary school teachers by the 1980s (Buder, 1976c). Cutbacks at similar levels were also planned in the number of students admitted to nursing programs. Largely in response to the ''Ph.D. glut,'' many states began conducting reviews of existing doctoral programs, closely scrutinizing their quality as well as demonstrated need (Griffiths, 1978). In New York State, 21 percent of the doctoral programs reviewed were closed, generally on the initiative of the universities themselves and prior to receiving a final rating from the Commissioner of Education. It is noteworthy that although "the review process has enabled universities to close programs known to be deficient when the internal politics of the institution otherwise would not have allowed proper action to be taken. . . ., professors in programs that have been surrendered are usually not terminated" (Griffiths, 1978, pp. 5–6).

Some state universities have attempted to limit enrollments in response to a tight job market in some fields (*The Chronicle of Higher Education*, 1977b; Smith, 1977), but such responses are more likely the exception than the rule. Financially pressed private colleges, in particular, were certainly not thinking of restricting entry at a time of declining enrollments. In fact, some private institutions were turning to sophisticated marketing techniques to attract more students (Fiske, 1978; Maeroff, 1979). It would therefore appear that restricting entry is not a very acceptable approach to dealing with a surplus of professionals, for either the institutions of higher education or their graduates.

Curricula Adaptation

Since cutting back on student admissions is anathema to colleges and universities that are financially hard pressed and need to maintain or increase enrollments in order to survive, certain compromise approaches would appear to be necessary. One possible compromise is to adapt the curricula in which reductions are required to meet changing job market needs. This approach would be especially attractive to universities hard hit by declining enrollments. Schools of education, in particular, have been in the forefront of designing curricula that are intended to lead to alternative careers (Coughlin, 1977). These alternatives to teacher training appear to fall into two broad categories—those that emphasize social service and those with a concentration on public policy and education.

It is too early to tell whether the graduates of alternative career programs are any more successful in finding jobs than are those completing the more traditional education. The emphasis of many alternative career programs on training for the public sector may be creating a new category of unemployed professionals, especially if educational institutions are merely attempting to shore up shrinking enrollments with little consideration for the future job market.

Increased Career Orientation

As college graduates have encountered increasing difficulties in finding suitable employment, the debate within institutions of higher education on their role in preparing their graduates for work has intensified (Jacobson, 1977b). Many colleges and universities began to acknowledge that the future of their institutions is dependent to a great degree on how effectively they can prepare their students to succeed in the job market. Surveys reveal that most employers do not feel that colleges are providing the type of preparation needed for the working world (Jacobson, 1977a). College graduates tend to agree. In fact, a nationwide follow-up of college graduates who had already established themselves in careers found that only 38 percent rated their college education as very useful in providing the knowledge and skills for the jobs they held (Bisconti and Solmon, 1976). The area of study most frequently recommended as needed for their jobs was business administration, which was chosen by 45 percent of college graduates and ranked high in almost all professions. This strong need for more practical knowledge and skills may explain why graduate schools of business and management grew phenomenally during the 1970s, going against the downward trend in the growth of enrollments in most graduate fields.

There appears to be a general agreement that higher education must somehow accommodate the problems relating to the world of work without losing its academic integrity (Jacobson, 1977b). However, the conflict between academicians and employers over the need for vocational or career-oriented education may have been exaggerated. Colleges and universities appear to have recognized that some kind of occupational orientation must begin to shape curricular plans (Fields, 1978; Jacobson, 1977b). For their part, employers do not go as far as requiring a vocational-oriented education for college students but, rather, favor greater exposure to practical on-the-job realities by means of such methods as cooperative-education programs or internships as complementary to academic classroom activities (Jacobson, 1977a). Private companies are willing to support students in such experiential programs, since it is in their own interest. For example, one company found that coop students not only come back to work for them after graduating but also emerge as better performers (Phillips, 1977). The need for experiential work applies even more to the hard-to-place liberal arts graduate (Cooper, 1976). Thus, it would appear that there is no lack of innovative approaches that could take into account the career development needs of students while maintaining educational integrity.

Continuing Education and Retraining

Aside from restricting entry into programs for which job opportunities are limited, adapting the curricula of such programs, or providing more career-oriented experiences, institutions of higher education can play a more direct role in dealing with the problems of unemployment and underemployment among college graduates. We have already seen in Chapter 7 how some academic institutions had become directly involved in retraining professionals for new careers. However, it was the federal government that provided the funds and, together with interested professional groups, even the initiative for these retraining programs. Such initiative has also been taken by hard-pressed municipalities that have had mass terminations of professionals, especially elementary and high school teachers. For example, the New York City Board of Education had urged local colleges to offer night and weekend courses so that terminated teachers could be certified in other fields in which there were 1200 job openings (*The New York Times*, 1976). Under the law these certified professionals would be given preference in hiring.

Professionals seem to favor government assistance for continuing education and retraining in dealing with unemployment. Indeed, unemployed professionals are even willing to accept welfare aid when it is contingent on retraining for available jobs (Briar, 1976). Most respondents in our study felt that government aid to enable them to remain up to date with developments in their field would be useful while they were out of work (Table 8.1). However, support for such a proposal appears to increase with reemployment success, which may imply that those least successful in their job search are more concerned about finding work than about staying up to date in their field. This speculation tends to be reinforced by the fact that professionals who remained without a job were most in favor of temporary work in government projects, but least supportive of government educational aid as useful methods for coping with unemployment. For those continuously employed, the exact reverse was true. So although education and training may help improve the employability of jobless professionals, there are no substitutes for the creation of appropriate jobs for those in need of work. Indeed, some have observed that continuing education and retraining is most effective when it is designed for professionals who become reemployed, to supplement what they learn on their new jobs (Katz, 1971). Such programs would be not only job relevant, but also supported financially by employers.

The importance of continuing education for maintaining the mental health of the unemployed was recognized as far back as the Great Depression (Pratt, 1933). For example, a so-called "Leisure Time University" was organized in Worcester, Massachusetts, providing the unemployed with course curricula in such diverse fields as business, sales, law, economics, psychology, and mental hygiene. As suggested in Chapter 7, unemployed professionals may enroll for courses in their field in an attempt to maintain their self-esteem. We found that among the unemployed who maintained high self-esteem, support for government assistance for staying up to date in their field was most prevalent among younger professionals ($r = -0.36$, $p < 0.05$) and those with a strong need for self-fullfilment ($r = 0.41$, $p < 0.05$). However, for the unemployed who had low self-esteem, such an approach was more acceptable to those who felt most burdened ($r = 0.42$, $p < 0.05$) and were weak in personal control ($r = 0.40$, $p < 0.05$). It appears that if updating with the help of the government is to be carried out for the purpose of growth, self-esteem must be maintained; but such growth may be more attractive to the younger professionals (Kaufman, 1974c).

For individuals with low self-esteem educational assistance is more welcome by those with greater difficulties and who believe they are not in control of their lives. It may very well be that the latter group feels so desperately in need of a job that they would be willing to accept any strategies to improve their employability. In general, those in stage II of unemployment were most in favor of updating assistance with seven out of ten supporting it. It is those professionals who are at the peak of their job search who apparently feel that participating in an updating program would be most useful in helping them return to work.

Although colleges and universities are placing much greater emphasis on continuing education programs and part-time curricula to meet the demands of a changing student market as well as professional relicensing (Vidal, 1976a,b; Watkins, 1975), few have taken the initiative to respond to the updating or retraining needs of unemployed and underemployed professionals. The major exceptions are the community colleges whose career-oriented programs are being directed toward dealing with the problems of unemployment (Jacobson, 1977c). A growing number of college graduates are turning to the community colleges for retraining in more marketable skills. Such retraining has undoubtedly expanded under the impact of CETA funding, which is received by most community colleges (Tirrell, 1977). In addition to offering career-oriented educational programs that are attractive to out-of-work and underemployed professionals, community colleges have also been in the forefront in their response to providing assistance to those seeking work. For example, a consortium of community colleges in southeastern Michigan designed a course to develop job-seeking skills, titled the Employment Search Planning Program (Cooke and Moch, 1976). This course included educational components such as planning the job search, contacting organizations, preparing a résumé, and going through a job interview. The building of self-confidence was expected to accompany the development of job-seeking skills. Such courses could be required as part of continuing education and retraining programs in order to help facilitate successful employment.

Although the career-oriented curricula of community colleges have been most responsive to the problem of joblessness, four-year colleges and universities also possess the capabilities to provide appropriate continuing education and retraining programs for unemployed professionals. However, university programs designed to correct a supply-and-demand imbalance within a profession may have their limitations. A case in point involves retraining or respecialization programs in psychology, which were surveyed by the American Psychological Association (Albin, 1978). At least 54 psychology departments reported retraining Ph.D.s, more than half of them in clinical psychology. Although most participants in such programs already had a doctorate in some other specialty in psychology (typically one not in demand), second Ph.D.s were also granted to those in fields as diverse as philosophy, physics, engineering, chemistry, and geology. However, the total number retrained has been limited by a lack of funds. Despite the American Psychological Association's policy strongly supporting retraining, funding for such programs has not been forthcoming from the National Institute for Mental Health (NIMH). As the head of the Psychology Education Branch at NIMH notes: "Every new program we fund is paid at the expense of an old one. Retraining is an extreme luxury and not a high priority for us" (Albin, 1978, p. 2). Although some universities have provided teaching fellowships to Ph.D.s accepted for retraining in psychology, funding remains the major obstacle to the growth of such programs.

Tuition payments are clearly an obstacle for unemployed professionals who are financially hard-pressed, but institutions have attempted to deal with this problem in various ways. For example, a deferred tuition program initiated by PMC Colleges in Chester, Pennsylvania, allowed unemployed professionals to return to school for undergraduate and graduate "refresher" courses (Caruth and Vogelsang, 1972). Tuition costs were deferred until six months after the participants were working in full-time professional jobs. No interest was charged on the deferred tuition and students were allowed up to two and a half years from the date of registration to begin payments. Another approach is exemplified by the special program for the unemployed at the weekend college of Wayne State University arranged between the college and the Michigan Employment Security Commission (*The New York Times*, 1975b). Under this program the unemployed enrolled in classes for one day a week, while remaining available for work.

Although the schemes described above may reduce the financial burden of updating or retraining to some degree, they do not go far enough. One problem is that those who return to school to enhance their employability can have their unemployment benefits terminated since they may not be available for full-time work (Briar, 1976). It would make a great deal more sense to permit unemployment insurance recipients to improve their employability any way they can while searching for a job. Indeed, some policy analysts have advocated that unemployment insurance be replaced with a "fund whose basic premise would be that an individual is entitled to the means for retraining or taking further training in order to achieve his highest level of personal and national usefulness" (Striner, 1972, p. 64). Such a fund could come about as a result of a total change in national policy requiring us to "rethink our basic philosophy of education and develop a *reentry system* for the education and training of all citizens *throughout life*" (Striner, 1972, p. 58). Such a change has, in fact, been advocated by the National Commission for Manpower Policy, which has called attention "to the importance of developing flexible structures that would enable people to have careers with periods of work interspersed with periods of recurrent education or manpower training, possibly tied into the retirement and Social Security system" (National Commission for Manpower Policy, 1976, p. 58). These policy changes would certainly be supportive of those who advocate expansion of our colleges and universities to serve all, including the unemployed, who could fill idle time by learning new knowledge and skills (Bowen, 1977).

Unfortunately, such changes will not come rapidly enough to deal with the more immediate education and retraining needs likely to be required by jobless and underemployed professionals. Hence, for the near future, cooperation among colleges and universities, government, employers, and other institutions are required to support continuing education and retraining programs for professionals in need of meaningful work. Government assistance is likely to be most useful in the form of direct tuition assistance to the unemployed or underemployed, without necessarily jeopardizing jobless benefits. The resources of employers can also be brought to bear on the problem through their support of fellowships, cooperative education programs, and internships (Cooper, 1976). Of course, the new knowledge and skills acquired should be relevant to jobs that are available. As we already noted, retraining is most effective when tied to specific job openings.

Perhaps a harbinger of the type of cooperative effort being advocated is a demonstration project at New York University directed toward retraining humanities Ph.D.s for careers in business (Harrison and May, 1978). Although sponsored by the University of the State of New York Board of Regents, the project was funded by contributions from corporations and private foundations, with a matching grant from the National Endowment for the Humanities. Fifty Ph.D.s were selected from 500 applicants for intensive seven-week cram courses in subjects related to business and management. The program was tuition-free and each participant received a $750 stipend to pay for food and dormitory accommodations at New York University. For those participants who desired to continue studying for a Master's of Business Administration degree, N.Y.U. offered one semester credit for the seven week program that could be applied toward the four semesters required to complete the M.B.A. The N.Y.U. faculty taught the academic courses, and 35 corporations provided executives who gave informal talks to the students about the "nuts" and "bolts" of business life to help in their reorientation and socialization into the private sector. Shortly after the first program ended, about 40 percent of the participants had already found positions in business, and half returned to work in academia or continued graduate study (Scully, 1978). Cooperative efforts such as the Careers in Business program clearly demonstrate that institutions of higher education have a key role to play in imparting new knowledge and skills to professionals who are seeking to enhance their employability or change their career.

Facilitation of Midcareer Change

The return to college by both the employed and the unemployed, particularly for purposes of career change and job-related studies, is likely to increase in the future, with or without employer or government assistance. Those at midcareer or beyond will account for much of this expansion. In fact, adults aged 35 or older who were enrolled in undergraduate or graduate degree programs increased from 800,000 in 1972 to 1.2 million in 1976 (Young, 1973, 1977). This dramatic increase occurred at a time when overall college enrollments were leveling off. Over three-fourths of the older students were in the labor force and more than eight out of ten were studying part-time.

Educational institutions may have to respond to the needs of the growing adult student population in more ways than just providing job-related courses. The need to change careers is common to both these older working students and the educated unemployed who returned to school, although for those without jobs this change may be involuntary. The need for a new approach to continuing education for these unemployed professionals was recognized by the University of California at Berkeley when they participated in the Aerospace Employment Project (AEP) described earlier. The experience of Berkeley is most informative:

> For several decades Berkeley University Extension has taken the traditional steps of providing the resources of the University of California for innovative as well as orthodox forms of continuing education. This new form of continuing education, requiring a different style of instruction for educated unemployed "students" at mid-career—students with entirely different motivations, objectives, psychological characteristics, and perceptions of self—now appears as a challenge for the extended university.
>
> Accordingly, the styles of instruction and curriculum suitable for younger students at the first step in the learning process, or even for graduate students, do not seem appropriate for programs concerned with mid-career transfer. While the format at Berkeley comprised lectures, group discussions, "rap" sessions, field trips, and readings, we also experimented with role playing and simulation games (e.g., The Community Land Use Game, The Policy Negotiation Game, etc.). We now believe the orientation program should have included more advice on how to go about getting a job, workshops on promoting career development, recognizing and revising one's assumptive biases, therapeutic dialogue (analyzing mutual anxieties associated with unemployment and an uncertain future) and understanding and managing counterculture forces. Further workshops might deal with maximizing one's human effectiveness potential and overcoming the usual unwillingness of adults to consider a change in goals and objectives. (Such unwillingness tends to render necessary learning experiences irrelevant.) (Jones and Fox, 1973, pp. 111–112).

Educational institutions are in a position to provide assistance to ease the stress of career change, particularly among those whose change was involuntary because of job loss. One example of how a university can provide such assistance to professionals undergoing job change is a course offered at Catholic University, titled the Strategy of Career Transition (Hyman, 1975). In some respects this course covers the same type of job search skills provided by the counseling approaches discussed in Chapter 7. However, the initial emphasis of the course is on the psychological adjustment of the individual. According to the developer of the course, it "deals with the emotional aspects of midcareer transition, thus freeing the job seeker to search effectively. It seeks to counter panic behavior, which may cause frantic job hopping and deep distress to the unemployed and their families'' (Hyman, 1975, p. 23). The techniques used ranged from psychological testing to determine what the participants needed from their job to role playing designed to establish a realistic strategy for finding and keeping new jobs. Among the more than 2000 participants who had completed the course, it was found that one out of three ''were in the wrong fields to begin with and were interested in and qualified for at least two other fields which would give them greater job satisfaction'' (Hyman, 1975, p. 26).

For professionals who were in the wrong field, the loss of a job provides an opportunity to carry out a long-needed career change. Many professionals end up in the wrong careers because of faulty or insufficient counseling received in college or even earlier. This inadequacy was noted in a report by the Carnegie Commission on Higher Education (1973), which called for the strengthening of both college placement services and counseling programs. College placement officers can provide the counseling and contacts to help unemployed professionals find appropriate jobs. However, many with work experience may not use the college placement office since its services tend to focus on entry-level jobs for recent graduates. Nevertheless, it could well be that in response to job market changes, academic counselors are changing their own orientation. A case in point is that of the counselors who volunteered from local colleges and universities in the Boston area to advise unemployed professionals about further academic training and its relationship to jobs (LaMark, 1972). A further broadening of the focus in counseling as well as in placement will undoubtedly accompany the increase in the number of graduates who are returning to school to initiate new careers.

Cooperative Job Development and Placement Services

Institutions of higher education will be under strong pressure from their more mature clientele to adapt their placement services to include job development activities for all age groups. Attempts to improve college placement have included the establishment of cooperative arrangements with the Employment Service, which can cater to experienced professionals as well as recent graduates. Although such cooperation had been attempted on about 40 campuses in the mid-1960s, it came under severe criticism because it was perceived as not only being ineffective, but also as representing another step toward government control over professional placement (Brown, 1965b). Perhaps a more acceptable approach is for a college or university to join with other institutions of higher learning in their local area to form a consortium to pool their job development and placement resources. Cooperative ventures among academic insitutions are fairly common and are increasing (Magarrell, 1979; Watkins, 1978).

Regardless of the framework selected for job development and placement services, there is a need to focus on particular types of professionals who encounter difficulties in the job market. The University of California has established two geographically separated Educational Career Services offices that specialize in the placement of teachers throughout the country (Smith, 1977). Such placement efforts become even more crucial as Proposition 13-types of taxpayer revolts slash teachers and other professionals from civil service payrolls. Among others encountering great difficulty in placement are those whose graduate education prepared them for academic jobs. In response to their need, the University of Michigan, under a grant from the Alfred P. Sloan Foundation, established an office to provide such individuals with career counseling and placement in nonacademic positions (Coughlin, 1978). For such services to be effective, job development must complement career counseling. Indeed, the Careers in Business program described earlier was designed to overcome resistance by employers to hire Ph.D.s in the humanities for entry-level management positions. As the program's developers explained:

> We hope to make Ph.D.'s more visible—and therefore more acceptable—in the business community. At the same time we hope to insure the continuity of graduate programs in the humanities by showing business leaders that people with advanced training in literature, history and philosophy can bring needed insight, perspective and skills to the nonacademic world (Lovenheim, 1977, p. 9).

Indeed, even critics of such retraining programs suggest that their real value is in "overcoming the predjudices of potential employers" (Shapero, 1972, p. 46). The success of the Careers in Business project is due in no small measure to the jobs that developed out of a close corporate involvement with the program. However, college placement offices are not likely to have experience in job development, but they can learn much from the professional self-help groups. Perhaps the most important lesson to be learned is that out-of-work professionals are not only willing to carry out job development activities for themselves and their peers but are highly effective in doing so. As an additional incentive, educational institutions can offer tuition assistance in return for job development services provided by unemployed professionals who return to school. Such job development could be coordinated through professional self-help groups. This would certainly be an economical way for colleges and universities to improve the employability of their students who have returned to school with the expressed purpose of attaining such improvement.

It is clear that institutions of higher education can play a multifaceted role in dealing with the problems of jobless and underemployed professionals. By providing relevant, comprehensive, and integrated programs involving continuing education and retraining, career counseling for students of all ages, and job development and placement, the colleges and universities can play a major role in the adjustment of their graduates to the uncertainties of an ever-changing job market while simultaneously helping to assure their own survival. The resources for the development of such programs and services can come not only in the form of government assistance of various types, but also from business and industry (Cooper, 1976; Meyer, 1975). Such a pooling of resources in a cooperative effort may in the final analysis be the key to promoting the health and well-being of not only the professionals who are seeking work but also the institutions that educate and employ them.

SUMMARY AND CONCLUSIONS

Although the experience of job loss appears to result in self-blame, most professionals attribute the problem of unemployment to government policies, societal priorities, or the "system." This resentment can be manifested in a variety of ways. Although we found that most of those experiencing joblessness supported changing priorities in the society and political lobbying by professional societies as well as unionizing in order to deal with the problem of unemployment, relatively fewer endorsed a more activist or radical approach to change. In general, it was the long-term unemployed who supported a more activist political approach.

Apparently, those professionals who had not been able to maintain their self-esteem in the face of joblessness were most willing to attack the system when subjected to high unemployment stress. However, professionals who were in stage II of unemployment—the period of concerted effort—tended to be most in favor of government assistance in the form of temporary work and educational support as well as political lobbying by their professional societies to attain such help. Since these professionals were still highly motivated to return to work, the less radical solutions to unemployment, such as temporary jobs, were more congruent with their needs. The implications are clear—providing for the needs of unemployed professionals to return to work may be effective only if it occurs before they have become work-inhibited and prone to accepting more radical solutions.

Propensity toward political activism was more prevalent among the underemployed than among those without work. The underemployed are no longer struggling with the everyday needs of economic survival. But with the fulfillment of their higher order needs blocked they may direct the anger resulting from their career frustrations against society. It would appear that when work no longer provides professionals with esteem or fulfillment, they must look elsewhere to satisfy these needs. A thwarted desire for job involvement could be redirected toward political involvement. We should, therefore, expect an increase in support for political activism and societal change concommitant with the increase in the number of underemployed professionals.

In dealing with the plight of unemployed as well as underemployed professionals, a concerted societal response is called for which demands the active involvement of the government, professional societies, employees and academic institutions. A summary of the potential roles of these institutions are as follows:

1. *Government* has long attempted to play a role in ameliorating the problem of unemployment. There is no doubt that such government involvement can be considerably improved, especially in providing assistance to professionals who are in search of work.

Although professionals who have been out of work appear somewhat wary of certain government controls to deal with unemployment, they nevertheless support intervention in the form of public job creation. This is particularly true of those in stage II of joblessness. Hence, intervention with a federal job program would be most effective well before work inhibition sets in. Programs established under the Emergency Employment Act or the Comprehensive Employment and Training Act have apparently helped considerable numbers of jobless professionals to return to work, but to what degree that work resulted in underemployment is unknown. What is clear is that federal job creation programs in both the public and private sectors are applicable to professionals and are most effective when there is a coordination of efforts involving retraining, job development, and placement assistance. It would appear that creating jobs to utilize the talents of unemployed and underemployed professionals in work dealing with societal problems is the most direct way in which the government can contribute to the overall adjustment of the individuals involved while helping to cure the ills of the nation.

It has been suggested that a centralized office should be established within the federal government to deal more effectively with policy and programs relevant to the special problems of unemployed and underemployed professionals on a nationwide basis. Furthermore, changes in the existing unemployment insurance system and the Employment Service appear necessary. Although unemployment insurance can cushion the financial blow of job loss and permit the professional to engage in a more intensive job search, it may also contribute to the work inhibition of the long-term unemployed. Therefore, any overhaul of the unemployment insurance system should involve its redirection toward encouraging continuous employment and/or retraining. Changes could include the determination of employer contribution rates to unemployment insurance on the basis of whether or not alternatives to termination were used. In addition, work-sharing approaches such as a shortened workweek or retraining could be subsidized by unemployment compensation. All indications are that Professional Placement Offices of the Employment Service can be considerably improved by including needed services, such as career counseling, guidance in job search, and intensive efforts at job development and referral. It was suggested that volunteer self-help groups of unemployed professionals could assist not only in providing such services but also in helping to change the image of the Employment Service as the option of last resort.

2. *Professional Societies* represent of their constituencies, and have important roles to play in dealing with the employment problems of their members. Placement services are typically provided by professional societies for their members but are often not very effective. Cooperative placement efforts with the Employment Service have, however, turned out to be successful. Such cooperation has involved Employment Service assistance in placement at annual meetings and organizing volunteers, usually unemployed professionals, to carry out job development and matching activities at employment offices for themselves and their colleagues. Although such cooperative efforts could go far not only in improving the services provided by professional societies but also in enhancing the image of the Employment Service, they are still more the exception than the rule. Professional societies have also provided their expertise in government-supported projects involving skills conversion and retraining of unemployed professionals. Furthermore, the societies can assist in carrying out and disseminating job market forecasts in their field.

Restrictions on the numbers of those practicing in an overcrowded field can be attained by means of professional licensing and renewal of licenses based on continued competence. Although not yet widespread, such licensing practices are likely to grow as professionals as well as the public increase their demands that their interests be protected. Professionals generally support more activism by their societies, such as political lobbying, to protect their interests. There even appears to be increasing militancy, as indicated in the growth of professional unions. Support for more actions such as unionization and strikes, is prevalent not only among those most affected by joblessness but also among young graduates and the underemployed. Pressure is likely to increase from these groups for more militant tactics to deal with their career interests. An indication of such trends is the establishment by professional societies of guidelines on employer responsibility in dealing with terminations of their members. A possible harbinger of the future is the investigation and identification of employers regarding their compliance with termination guidelines. Professional societies can also cooperate with employers in assisting the placement of professionals slated to be terminated. Such cooperation could serve to reduce suspicion and acrimony for the benefit of all concerned.

3. *Employers* make the decisions on terminations and hiring. Thus employers are in a key position to apply a variety of strategies to avoid terminations. Even when terminations are inevitable, employers can facilitate the adjustment and reemployment of those experiencing the trauma of job loss.

Many employers have turned to less extreme approaches than outright dismissals for trimming personnel costs. The difficulty with some popular alternatives to terminations, such as natural attrition or voluntary early retirement, is that employer control over personnel cutbacks is limited and involuntary separations may have to be used as well. This is especially true for early retirement, since professionals typically are so involved with their work that few will voluntarily leave their jobs even when the employer offers generous inducements for early retirement. Employers do have control over salary and working hours and thus limitations on either or both can serve as effective alternatives to terminations if a reduction in personnel costs is required. In particular, various approaches to work sharing appear as attractive ways to reduce personnel costs without resorting to terminations. Work sharing is likely to result in some underutilization and stress, but it would appear to be preferable to job loss, especially since it tends to minimize disruption of the professional career and promises the opportunity to return to full utilization when conditions improve. Other alternatives to termination involve a reshuffling of personnel using internal transfers or retraining programs for new career positions. Since either career change or transfers involving geographic relocation are likely to result in high stress, professionals should be given the choice of one or the other as an alternative to job loss.

When terminations become unavoidable because of retrenchment, many employers have provided a variety of outplacement services directed primarily to minimizing the period of unemployment after termination. These services can include the provision of information on job openings, job and career counseling, psychological assistance, preparation of résumés, improving interviewing skills, and various support services needed to carry out an effective job search campaign. Indications are that the potential value of outplacement is more in helping professionals adjust to job loss and sustain or restore their confidence and self-esteem than in actually placing them in jobs. A key factor in the success of an outplacement program is top management's commitment and support. It is in management's own interest to develop effective outplacement programs since they can serve to maintain a positive image of the organization through a sincere effort to provide useful assistance to those terminated.

For professionals who have experienced an extended period of joblessness, returning to work can be a shock and create problems for them as well as their employers. Therefore, it would be in the interest of all concerned if employers provide reentry counseling to help restore the professionals' self-esteem and feelings of competence and ease them back to challenging and productive work. Finally, by providing effective career planning and development from entry to retirement, employers can help minimize not only the number of terminations but also the stress of job loss when personnel cutbacks become unavoidable.

4. *Colleges and universities,* as the institutions responsible for educating professionals, can play a central role in helping to ameliorate unemployment and underemployment problems among their graduates. One option open to institutions of higher education, albeit not a very attractive one, is to restrict entry of students into fields that have an oversupply of graduates. Deliberate cutbacks in student enrollments have been carried out in some public colleges and universities, but financially hard pressed private academic institutions are understandably reluctant to further diminish declining enrollments. One possible compromise is

adapting curricula in which reductions are necessary to meet changing job market needs. Schools of education have been in the forefront of adapting curricula that are intended to lead to alternative careers. Even academic curricula that do not have specific occupational goals, such as liberal arts programs, can increase their career orientation and thereby prepare their graduates for the job market while maintaining educational integrity. One way of accomplishing this is to complement the academic curriculum with exposure to the practical realities of work by means of cooperative education programs, internships, or similar experimental approaches that are attractive to both students and employers.

Academic institutions can also help facilitate the employability of those graduates who are experiencing difficulties in finding appropriate work, by providing them with continuing education and retraining programs. Institutions of higher education are in a position to provide not only the formal course work to facilitate midcareer change but also the counseling, job development, and placement services so crucial to the reemployment success of professionals who are jobless or underemployed. As the number of older students increases, colleges and universities will be under strong pressure to provide for the needs of this more mature clientele and provide the types of services required for easing midcareer change. The success of continuing education and retraining programs to deal with the problems of jobless and underemployed professionals may very well depend on academic institutions taking the initiative in the development of such programs while obtaining the cooperation and support of employers and the government. This type of cooperation may be the key to the future growth and development of both professionals who are seeking work and the institutions that educate and employ them.

It is clear that the roles of various societal institutions overlap in dealing with the employment problems of professionals. Such overlap can easily result in duplication of effort and inefficiency. Attempts at reducing such inefficiency by the integration of efforts to place professionals in appropriate jobs are dealt with in the final chapter, to which we now turn.

CHAPTER NINE

Directions for Future Policy and Programs

Since many of the issues discussed in this book are interrelated, it is appropriate to end with an integration of conclusions reached in previous chapters. A systems model approach will be used to summarize broadly the process of adjustment to unemployment stress as well as to arrive at some possible directions for future policy and programs in dealing with the problems of the professional job market. The global criterion of potential policy and program effectiveness will be the health and well-being of the individual, which, as we have noted, can ultimately affect societal health. Moreover, we explore changes that may be required to enable psychologists and mental health specialists to apply their knowledge and skills more effectively to the problem of unemployment stress. Since the problem is one in which not only the government, but also employers, educational institutions, and professional societies play a role in policy and programs, our analysis and recommendations will integrate how the contributions of each may best facilitate adjustment of the individual professional who is in search of work.

ADJUSTMENT TO UNEMPLOYMENT: A SYSTEMS MODEL

Although some efforts have been made to develop a systems model of unemployment stress (e.g., Estes, 1973; Ferman, 1979; Gore, 1975), they do not appear to be comprehensive enough to explain adequately the complex process of coping and adjustment relevant to joblessness. In an attempt to remedy this deficiency, a parsimonious systems model is proposed that takes into account the current state of knowledge about the process of adjustment to unemployment stress. This tentative model is depicted in Figure 9.1 and, although developed primarily for unemployed professionals, it may be applicable to many other workers as well.

Central to the model is the unemployment stress typically experienced as a result of involuntary job loss. Unemployment stress may have several dimensions,

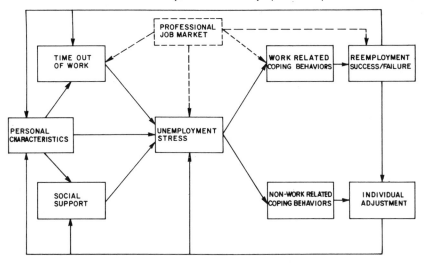

Figure 9.1. Model of individual adjustment to unemployment stress.

but it generally involves individual psychological and physiological reactions to the disruption created by joblessness. The severity of unemployment stress is affected by many factors, which are often interrelated. The most important of these factors appear to be the personal characteristics of the unemployed, the social support they receive, and the period of time they spend out of work. A pervasive environmental factor affecting unemployment stress is the nature of the professional job market. However, our description of the model will focus on the individual since job market factors are generally beyond personal control.

Personal Characteristics

As a result of involuntary unemployment, some professionals experience severe stress, whereas others are minimally affected. Individual differences in personal characteristics have been identified that are likely to increase the severity of stress that accompanies joblessness. Those professionals who are most prone to unemployment stress are likely to possess one or more characteristics of which the following are typical:

1. Male.
2. Female head of household.
3. Between 30 and 40 years old.
4. More than one dependent.
5. Limited financial resources.

6. Disadvantaged background (e.g., minority-group member).

7. Highly educated (especially if a Ph.D.).

8. Technical professional (especially if in R&D).

9. Dissatisfied with career choice, but no alternative career.

10. Nonreligious.

11. Previous adjustment problems (e.g., psychiatric history).

12. Previous unemployment experience.

Professionals possessing even only a few of these personal characteristics would be highly prone to stress in their reactions to job loss. For example, male professionals in their 30s with dependents and limited financial resources should experience extremely high levels of unemployment stress. An awareness of the personal characteristics associated with high unemployment stress can be useful not only to those providing counseling assistance but to employers in developing more effective outplacement and reentry programs.

Social Support

The amount of social support received by the jobless professional can play an important role in moderating the severity of unemployment stress. Social support can be obtained from a variety of sources, including the following:

1. Spouse.

2. Family.

3. Friends.

4. Professional colleagues.

5. Community groups.

6. Former employer.

Of course, the nature of one's social support system would depend on various personal characteristics, such as marital status or profession. Different types of social support are provided, depending on the source. Certain people, such as one's spouse, family, and friends, can provide great emotional support. Furthermore, having ties with community groups such as those of a religious nature may also provide strong emotional support. However, support that is more instrumental in nature, such as assistance in finding a job, would be more likely to come from one's professional colleagues or a former employer's outplacement efforts. It is apparent that having a social support network that provides both emotional and instrumental help serves to keep unemployment stress levels down. Therefore, it would be important for counselors and others providing assistance to the jobless to encourage maintenance and development of an adequate social support network that provides both emotional and instrumental assistance.

Time Out of Work

The period of time spent out of work is affected by personal characteristics such as age, financial resources, and family responsibilities, as well as job market factors. Unemployment stress appears to be affected by the duration of joblessness in a curvilinear fashion that is similar to that predicted by various theories of stress. As time out of work increases, four rather distinct periods or stages of unemployment through which many professionals pass have been identified:

1. Shock, relief, and relaxation.

2. Concerted effort.

3. Vacillation, self-doubt, and anger.

4. Resignation and withdrawal.

Although there is generally an increase in stress when job loss is anticipated, the reaction when the actual termination occurs is an immediate shock followed by a period of reduced stress accompanied by relief and relaxation. This first stage can last about one or two months. As stress starts to increase, stage II begins and a concerted effort is made to find a job. Only after several months of intensive but fruitless job hunting does one enter stage III of unemployment, wherein high stress accompanies the vacillation, self-doubt, and anger resulting from a lack of success in finding work. Stress remains at a high level during stage III for about one to two months. If no job is found at the end of this period, stress begins to drop considerably as the fourth stage, resignation and withdrawal, is entered. This final stage of relatively lower stress is characterized by acceptance of one's jobless state. It is clear that the detrimental effects of unemployment stress can be kept at a minimum if specific interventions or coping behaviors occur at an appropriate stage. This is addressed further in the sections that follow.

COPING WITH UNEMPLOYMENT STRESS

Various types of coping behaviors have been identified that attempt to deal with the reduction of unemployment stress. These coping behaviors can be broadly classified on the basis of whether or not they are work related. The focus will be on adaptive, as opposed to maladaptive, coping responses.

Work-Related Coping Behaviors

There are several types of coping behaviors that are directed solely toward reemployment. These work-related coping behaviors include the following:

1. Job search.
2. Retraining/continuing education.
3. Relocation.
4. Job counseling.

Of all the work-related coping behaviors, the job search is most directly instrumental in finding a position. As we have noted, the job search is most intensive during the second stage of unemployment and may be accompanied by high stress. The other work-related coping behaviors are intended to improve a professional's employability and each strategy may be more appropriate at a particular stage of unemployment and for individuals with certain characteristics. For example, job retraining may be more acceptable to those who are in the third stage of unemployment and who because of family roots cannot relocate to find work. For professionals with limited work experience or those who are dissatisfied with their career choice, job counseling would be appropriate as early as possible. Since relocation is in itself a stressful experience, it may be most appropriate as an intervention early in stage II when motivation to find work is greatest. The choice and effectiveness of work-related coping behaviors may be strongly influenced by the professional job market. For example, the type and intensity of the job search, as well as attempts at relocation or retraining, will be affected by how difficult a job market is encountered by the professional.

Non-Work-Related Coping Behaviors

There are various types of non-work-related coping behaviors that are used to help reduce the stress resulting from the unemployment experience. These can include the following:

1. Life-style change.
2. Financial assistance.
3. Political or union involvement.
4. Mental health assistance.

One major response to dealing with the economic problems created by the loss of income is to reduce spending and carry out a drastic change in life-style, which for married men often involves role reversals. In addition, seeking financial assistance may also be necessary. Some may deal with their frustration and anger by becoming politically involved or by joining in collective action through union activities. Others who experience extreme psychological stress may turn toward some type of mental health assistance. With the exception of the latter, these coping behaviors may or may not be maladaptive. However, there are a host of responses to unemployment stress that are clearly maladaptive, such as attempts at escaping through alcoholism or outward aggression involving criminal acts or child abuse. Regardless of whether or not non-work-coping behaviors are adaptive, they are unlikely to be elicited if reemployment occurs shortly after job loss.

REEMPLOYMENT SUCCESS AND FAILURE

Work-related coping behaviors are directed toward attaining reemployment success within the constraints imposed by the professional job market. Such success does not only mean finding a job but also to what degree the job meets the individual's goals in terms of utilization of knowledge and skills, growth potential, salary, security, and so on. Conversely, reemployment failure occurs not only when a job cannot be found but also when the new job is not very congruent with one's career goals. Taking a job out of desperation that merely provides an income but leaves an individual highly underemployed is a good case in point. The evidence indicates that, at least for professional workers, underemployment can be a highly stressful experience comparable to that created by unemployment. Therefore, stress is likely to continue if a professional becomes underemployed following job loss. This stress may lead to a non-work-coping behavior such as political or union activism. However, continued failure to find a job is likely to affect unemployment stress in accord with the stages of unemployment, with stress increasing up to stage III and diminishing in stage IV. The type of coping behaviors elicited change accordingly.

ADJUSTMENT TO JOBLESSNESS

There are many changes that the unemployed undergo as they adjust to joblessness. This adjustment typically involves psychological changes directed toward reducing unemployment stress. By the time stage IV of unemployment is reached, these changes involve an overall psychological deterioration that typically includes at least some of the following symptoms:

1. Loss of self-esteem.
2. Loss of personal control and feelings of helplessness and hopelessness.

3. Work "inhibition," occupational rigidity, and feelings of professional obsolescence.

4. Social isolation.

5. Psychosomatic disorders.

For those who reach stage IV, the withdrawal and resignation to a state of joblessness is an adjustment process whereby unemployment stress is greatly reduced. Similarly, the adjustment attained by means of some non-work-related coping behaviors may serve to reduce stress, but possibly at the price of deterioration in the individual's well-being. For example, adjustment in stage IV may involve social support from one's spouse, which may not only reduce stress but also reinforce work-inhibition. The more rapid and successful the reemployment, the less likely that psychological deterioration will occur. Although successful reemployment should serve to eliminate much of the stress created by unemployment, a full restoration of the psychological state extant prior to job loss may be difficult to attain.

Many personal characteristics, such as sex or minority status, are stable and do not change following job loss, but others, including financial resources and career choice, could be greatly affected by the process of coping and adjustment. For professional workers, becoming underemployed may serve not only to further their psychological deterioration, but also to create a new source of stress stemming from dissatisfaction with their work role. Thus, professionals who cope with joblessness by accepting positions that leave them underemployed may be worse off in terms of adjustment than they were when out of work.

In sum, it would appear that unemployment stress can be reduced by successful reemployment as rapidly as possible following job loss. Typically, this stress reduction is accompanied by an improvement in one's psychological well-being. However, unemployment stress may also be diminished by a failure to find work, which can result in one's adjustment through withdrawal and resignation to being in a jobless state. Although this can be viewed as an adjustment to unemployment stress, it would probably be extremely maladaptive, since for most professionals it is dysfunctional to both a return to work and a restoration of individual well-being.

ROLE OF THE MENTAL HEALTH PROFESSION

It should be clear by now that the mental health profession can contribute its knowledge and skills to dealing with problems created by job loss. However, such contributions have been relatively limited. In this section we examine briefly the role of the mental health profession in dealing with job loss as a community as well as an organizational problem and as an area of future research.

Unemployment as a Community Mental Health Problem

A study of community mental health workers—psychologists, psychiatrists, social workers, and paraprofessionals—found that they do regard economic factors such as unemployment as pertinent to their clients problems (Dooley and Catalano, 1977). However, many community mental health workers lack adequate information on the impact of economic change, as the following results indicate:

> Despite the apparent importance of economic conditions for their work, 43 percent of the staff members reported receiving no information or guidance regarding the impact of economic change during the last year. Another 19 percent reported, at most, some related reading in lay periodicals or newspapers. Just 36 percent reported either in-service training or reading in professional journals pertaining to economics and mental health (Dooley and Catalano, 1977, p. 222).

The potential problems resulting from such a lack of information or guidance was noted in another study with respect to social workers but is also applicable to other mental health professionals:

> It is possible that social workers, lacking information about joblessness and the social-psychological importance of work, may treat unemployment as a symptom. . . .

> Obviously, a lack of jobs will hinder job seeking success. Yet if the client is told that job attainment is contingent on success in treatment with a counselor rather than on the availability of jobs the client may be programmed to fail. This is not because the therapist's strategies are ineffective but because the ability to get a job may be related to the availability of work and to the abundance of jobs in one's line of work, *not* treatment success (Briar, 1976, pp. 101–102).

One question that arises concerns whether or not the mental health professional should deal with job counseling. The adequacy of such counseling provided by the Employment Service has been noted, and improvements would certainly be in order. However, some resistance to doing this counseling may come from professionals themselves, despite their potential contributions, as is indicated in observations of social workers:

> Social workers have avoided working in employment agencies; employment counseling may appear superficial to treatment-oriented social work practitioners. Yet they could enhance the current quality of counseling services and generate an awareness of the catastrophic effect of unemployment on some persons and families. Moreover, the despondent, suicidal person might receive more relevant services than are currently available in public employment offices (Briar, 1976, pp. 102–103).

What may be required is an unfreezing of attitudes on all sides regarding the role of the mental health professional in dealing with the problems of joblessness. Perhaps an appropriate place to begin would be with the education and training of mental health professionals. It was surprising to find that psychologists, psychiatrists, social workers, and paraprofessionals did not differ in their attitudes or knowledge regarding economic factors and mental health (Dooley and Catalano, 1977). It was suggested that this lack of difference, regardless of education or professional role, "may be partially due to the relative absence of attention to economic factors in the curricula of the mental health disciplines" (Dooley and Catalano, 1977). In addition to curricula changes designed to provide mental health workers with the knowledge to deal with the problems of job seekers, employment counseling skills can be developed through appropriate work placements. For example, one social work teacher found that "it is possible to weave the skills of a caseworker into the tasks of an employment counselor. This has been done . . . in at least one agency on an experimental basis with students with effective results" (Briar, 1976, p. 106).

Even if mental health professionals acquire knowledge and skills relevant to employment counseling, they may not want to attend to the job-finding problems of clients but, rather, prefer helping those who need intensive psychological services. It was suggested that if this is the case, "there is no reason why the paraprofessionals could not attend to the job seeking problems and actually assume full responsibility for managing caseloads where the primary task is finding jobs for clients" (Briar, 1976, p. 102). It is clear that barriers such as a lack of background or a reluctance to provide help on the part of mental health professionals vis-à-vis job-finding problems of clients, combined with the Employment Service's continuing neglect of job seekers' psychological needs, call for alternative approaches to deal more effectively with the unemployed.

A highly promising alternative is the self-help group that incorporates assistance from mental health professionals or paraprofessionals, with an appropriate division of labor. Self-help groups of unemployed professionals have typically worked closely with the Employment Service and with community-oriented programs such as Start-Up. Some common problems encountered by self-help groups of unemployed professionals include a loss of continuity in leadership and experience when volunteers are successfully reemployed as well as a cessation of support services because of an improving job market. There is clearly an ongoing need for such groups and their support services. The demise of community support such as that provided by Start-Up was lamented by counselors, as the reactions of one of them indicates:

> I am keenly sorry to see Start-Up close, because I think the services here could be utilized for a long time and in lieu of this agency closing, I would like to see a similar agency that would be centrally located with job and resource information. It is amaz-

ing how many people do not know what is available to them. . . . People need support, but often are afraid to ask (United Way of King County, 1974, p. 21).

Despite the withdrawal of formal support, some self-help groups of unemployed professionals formed in the recession of the early 1970s have continued to function in areas that were hard-hit, such as Seattle and Boston. Perhaps even more significant is the fact that mental health professionals have volunteered their services to such groups. They thereby provide not only professional psychological assistance but also much needed continuity of experience in dealing with unemployed professionals. It would thus appear that self-help groups are serving a very real need among professionals in search of work, regardless of changes in job market conditions.

It has been suggested to psychologists that by establishing consultative relationships with or by helping form self-help groups for specific problems or populations, they can contribute to preventive community mental health (Hirsch, 1977). Interventions involving self-help groups to deal with problems of the unemployed are highly promising, judging by the success of pilot projects such as the job club. Thus, the problem of unemployment stress is certainly one in which the community psychologist and other mental health workers can make a major contribution.

Unemployment as an Organizational Mental Health Problem

While the approach to dealing with unemployment as a community mental health problem holds much promise, interventions prior to job loss would appear to be even more effective. Therefore, the burden for initiating such mental health interventions falls largely on the shoulder of employers who are forced to reduce personnel costs. We have already noted how organizations can effectively utilize the services of psychologists in their efforts at outplacement of terminated professionals. However, even organizational psychologists may have only a limited knowledge of the impact of job loss as well as how to deal with it. Here, too, the integration of such knowledge into the curricula of organizational psychology would be appropriate. As we have amply demonstrated, such knowledge does exist. Indeed, some tentative guidelines to the organizational psychologist can even be derived based on what we know of adjustment to unemployment stress:

1. When reducing personnel costs, emphasis should be on alternatives to termination, such as natural attrition, early retirement, eliminating salary increases, reducing pay and benefits, shorter work schedules, internal transfers, and retraining.

2. If termination decisions have to be made, individual differences in personal characteristics should be considered in order to minimize unemployment stress.

3. Notification of termination should be made as soon as possible after the actual decision by an appropriate individual.

4. Outplacement activities should begin simultaneous with notification of termination, to help absorb the initial shock of job loss.

5. Outplacement should provide emotional, as well as instrumental, support not only to hold down unemployment stress but to minimize the resentment and hostility toward the employer generated by termination.

Mental health considerations should also be incorporated into the personnel practices of organizations hiring high-level personnel who have just been through a period of joblessness. Examples of such considerations include the following:

1. Attention should be paid to potential reentry problem cases, particularly among the long-term unemployed, to help ease them back into a productive work role.

2. Appropriate placement, focusing especially on avoiding the creation of situations that result in underemployment, should enhance adjustment and help minimize stress.

3. Assignment to positions involving relocation should be made with care, since geographic change can create additional stress and exacerbate problems of adjustment.

4. Retraining programs and career change may be most appropriate for those who have gone through a long job search but have not yet reached the final stage of withdrawal and resignation.

It would thus appear that employers could contribute positively to individual, as well as organizational, mental health not only by having their psychologists, counselors, and human resource specialists provide effective outplacement services to those terminated but also by paying closer attention to reentry problems when hiring those who have just gone through a period of joblessness. The reentry problem, in particular, has not received as much attention as it deserves.

Of course, many employers, particularly small firms, would not be in a position to provide much in-house assistance and in such situations the support provided by self-help and community groups would be invaluable. Indeed, since job loss is both a community and an organizational problem, a scenario for the future could very well involve cooperative efforts between those involved in community mental health and employers who are forced to carry out terminations. Such cooperation could go far in enhancing efforts to improve the quality of work life, as well as mental health.

Research Needs

Although a body of knowledge has begun to emerge concerning the psychological impact of unemployment and underemployment, the limited amount of research carried out thus far raised more questions than it has answered. Psychologists and other social scientists still have many questions pertaining to the problems of joblessness and how to deal with them. There is an obvious need for more and better research to provide answers to these questions. A few behavioral scientists have attempted to identify general research needs and these include the following:

1. *Multiple levels of analysis* are needed, ranging from macro approaches using national and local data in epidemiological research to the micro or individual level of analysis (Brenner, 1976). However, it is the research focusing on the individual level that is most useful to psychologists. Even Brenner, who is responsible for much of the epidemiological research on unemployment, has recognized that "with research on a 'microscopic' level, a clearer picture can be obtained of the causal mechanisms by which economic changes are associated with societal pathologies" (Brenner, 1976, p. 103).

2. *Replication of research* has been called for to assure generalizability of results (Dooley and Catalano, 1979). Such replication should also extend to cross-cultural studies. Brenner (1976) has carried out some limited cross-cultural replications of his research and believes that: "Extension of this comparative research to other countries will bring us closer to understanding the sources of pathological response to changes in the condition of the economy" (p. 101).

3. *Longitudinal studies* are necessary to follow up individuals who experience joblessness (Brenner, 1976; Dooley and Catalano, 1977; 1979).

As Brenner explains:

> In this type of research, for example, population cohorts would be followed and intensively examined over periods of several years, in order to ascertain the effects of the economic changes specific to their lives, as these changes tend to be associated with specified pathological conditions. Such microscopic studies of the lives of individuals should help to identify how strongly each of the several sources of economic trauma affect the tendency toward serious physical and mental health pathologies and aggression in the population (Brenner, 1976, p. 103).

Other researchers concur with Brenner, and call for the monitoring of stress reactions via longitudinal studies:

> "Unlike retrospective studies based on archival data, future studies should observe the processes which lead to successful as well as unsuccessful adaptation to economically precipitated stress. Such monitoring would help determine which of the sev-

eral explanations offered for complex findings such as Brenner's are correct'' (Dooley and Catalano, 1977, p. 224). Although some longitudinal research has been carried out with terminated blue-collar workers, such studies with professionals are notably lacking.

4. *Evaluation of coping responses* to unemployment stress is needed to determine what strategies are most effective (Dooley and Catalano, 1977; Liem and Liem, 1979). Of particular interest to some researchers are the formal and informal ways families seek counseling to obtain relief (Dooley and Catalano, 1977). With the possible exception of studies on social support, an area where more research is also required (Hirsch, 1977; Liem and Liem, 1979), evaluation of individual and family coping with unemployment stress has not received the attention it deserves. Here is where longitudinal studies involving monitoring of coping strategies would be useful, as the following explanation indicates:

> Prospective monitoring of family coping strategies would also determine whose behavior is disordered by the experience of economic change—those experiencing the direct or the indirect impact of job changes. . . .

> Prospective monitoring would not only help clarify the relationship between economic change and catastrophic measures such as suicide and institutionalization; it should also help identify successful and unsuccessful coping strategies. Such information would be invaluable to mental health workers who deal with families seeking help and to agencies attempting primary prevention in school, work, and home environments (Dooley and Catalano, 1977, p. 224).

5. *Evaluation of institutional responses* to deal with unemployment stress is needed to ascertain which approaches should be emphasized in policies and programs (Brenner, 1976; Dooley and Catalano, 1977). As Brenner has pointed out:

> It would be important to evaluate the effects of non-economic ameliorative programs. . . in light of national, regional, and local economic trends. It may be that, in many instances, the ameliorative programs are completely overwhelmed by the effects of the economy. In other cases, it may be that such programs act as important buffers to the effects of economic trauma and have prevented much greater pathology (Brenner, 1976, p. 102).

6. *Identification of high-risk groups* with respect to unemployment stress requires further research (Brenner, 1976; Dooley and Catalano, 1977). Although work has already been done in this regard, as is indicated by our review in Chapter 3, some researchers have called for the use of subsamples to obtain ''a profile of response to economic change by socioeconomic class, sex, and age cohorts. . .enabling investigators to identify high and low risk groups'' (Dooley and Catalano, 1977). Brenner strongly supports such an approach, noting that:

It is vital that efforts be taken to study populations that tend to undergo substantial economic difficulty which is heightened by national economic adversity. . . .In addition, age, racial, occupational, and industrial groups that are particularly vulnerable to the instabilities in the national economy represent a priority for substantial study, since one would want to target specific ameliorative economic policy where it would presumably provide the greatest benefit (Brenner, 1976, p. 102).

On the basis of the limited evidence we have, it is the professional workers who are most affected by unemployment stress. However, with the exception of a few small-scale studies, professionals have been generally neglected in research on unemployment and mental health.

7. *Increased support for research* relevant to unemployment stress is called for, especially given the potentially destructive effects of joblessness and underemployment on the individual and society. Although government agencies such as the National Institute for Mental Health (NIMH) have sponsored studies and conferences focusing on the psychological effects of unemployment (Herbert, 1978), these efforts still appear rather limited relative to the gravity of the problem.

To be useful, psychological research on unemployment must be linked with action-oriented policy and programs. Behavioral science knowledge and techniques played a crucial role in an action-research and policy development program established by New York State solely to tackle the problems of public sector job displacement (Jick, 1978). Other public policy areas, such as the development of a national health program, could benefit from research on the effects of unemployment stress.

Eventually, public policy research efforts must begin to focus on broad societal changes that can eliminate the causes of joblessness and underemployment. One such fundamental change requiring policy research could involve the education, work, and leisure cycle, as indicated in the following proposal on work-sharing by government analysts:

The shortage of jobs, especially preferred jobs, could easily persist for the rest of this century. Traditional remedies of macroeconomic expansion and public jobs might not be enough. . . .

Work sharing in the form of more cyclic life patterns is an alternative for coping with the job shortage problem. . . . One advantage of this approach is that it can deal with a number of social problems simultaneously, particularly the inadequate access to leisure and education throughout life, and the rigid ''lockstep'' progression from school to work to retirement. The goal of making work, education, and leisure more accessible merits high priority on the Nation's policy research agenda (Best and Stern, 1977, p. 9).

Although the government has provided the major source of support for research on unemployment, it is clear that employers, professional societies, and academic institutions all can make contributions relevant to their own interests. Given their limited resources, however, cooperative research efforts would make a great deal of sense, particularly when the development of policy and programs are pertinent to more than one type of societal institution. To demonstrate how such cooperative ventures could be capitalized on in a programmatic way, we now turn to the development of a hypothetical professional employment system.

AN INTEGRATED PROFESSIONAL EMPLOYMENT SYSTEM

Government policy and programs dealing with unemployment have, quite rightly, focused on helping those who, because of their limited skills and external barriers such as discrimination, experience the greatest job market difficulties. However, concentration of policy and programs on the employment problems of those possessing the most limited skills has resulted in the relative neglect of those at the other end of the spectrum—the growing number of educated workers who cannot find professional-level jobs. Some may argue that because of their education and other advantages they are perfectly capable of helping themselves and do not need assistance, but the evidence we have reviewed indicates that this is not necessarily the case.

Although those in search of professional jobs probably invest considerable time, effort, and resources in finding meaningful work, all indications are that the positions they are seeking are becoming ever more elusive and difficult to locate. Of course, there are external barriers, such as a lack of professional-level jobs in some fields. But even when such jobs do exist, the often inadequate dissemination of information about their existence, combined with the limited knowledge among many educated workers regarding how to find appropriate work, can serve to create unemployment and underemployment where there need not be any. Furthermore, those educated jobseekers who are not successful in finding professional-level work can eventually become work-inhibited and no longer make an effort to find employment. Therefore, improvements in the situation must come not only by changes in the employment system for professional-level jobs but also by those changes being directed at enhancing the employability of individuals seeking such jobs.

Such changes do not necessarily require a radical overhaul in policy or programs dealing with professional employment, which is not likely in the near future. The most realistic strategy is to first focus on the improvement and development of that which already exists in order to evolve a more effective and integrated professional employment system. Since various societal institutions can and do play important roles in dealing with the problem of unemployment and underemployment among professionals, it would be appropriate to integrate these roles and reduce duplication in order to improve the effectiveness and efficiency of the overall system. Such an integration is suggested in the systems model depicted in Figure 9.2. In this model an attempt has been made to show in broad terms how the various roles of the government, professional societies, academic institutions, and employers can be closely interconnected to effectuate an improved professional employment system whose primary goal is to facilitate rapid adjustment to joblessness through meaningful work.

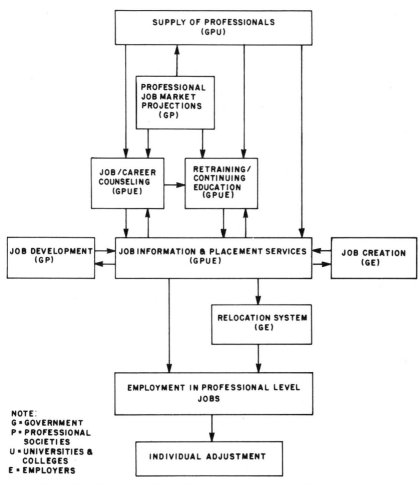

Figure 9.2.   Integrated professional employment system for individual adjustment.

Since the government is already involved in many of the roles depicted in the model, one possible strategy would be to develop policies directed toward the improvement of existing public services and their integration with the interventions that can be provided by other institutions. This becomes more concrete if we examine each part of the model in a logical sequence.

1. *Job market projections*. To the extent that job market projections are accurate, they can be quite useful in helping shape policy that can affect the supply of professionals. Perhaps the clearest examples of this was the projected low demand for teachers that could have been translated into policy decisions affecting the supply of teachers. More accurate job market projections also serve to improve the effectiveness of counseling, retraining, and continuing education programs. The federal government has traditionally provided job market projections through the Bureau of Labor Statistics. One way in which the quality of these projections could be improved is by obtaining the involvement of the professional societies, whose expertise can make important contributions regarding future supply and demand as well as skills conversion in their respective fields. However, the involvement of industry executives or academic administrators in the leadership of some professional societies may result in some bias in their orientation vis-à-vis supply and demand, and this should be taken into account whenever participation is solicited.

2. *Supply of professionals*. Based on job market projections, the supply of professionals can be controlled to some degree. For example, the projections of a low demand for teachers have resulted in cutbacks in Ph.D. and teacher-training programs. In addition to controls on curricula, the government can also limit or expand the supply by means of the support it provides via fellowship and other student assistance programs in specific fields. Indeed, this had been practiced to some degree in response to changing national priorities.

Not only do universities and government have a responsible role to play in applying controls to supply, but the professional societies do as well. By means of licensing and recertification, the number of professionals in some fields can be controlled to some degree while quality is maintained. Also, by providing accurate information about the job opportunities in particular fields, the professional societies, in conjunction with government efforts, can help to either encourage or discourage new entrants. Furthermore, in those fields where there is a professional or state accreditation of curricula, the growth in the number of accredited programs in each field can be limited by requiring new as well as existing programs to meet rigorous standards of need as well as quality.

3. *Job and career counseling*. Using better information about the current and future professional job market, counselors can provide more accurate guidance concerning job and career opportunities. This can result in a more effective and realistic matching of the special needs of professionals with their choice of jobs.

Such counseling can be carried out in several different settings, depending on who is seeking the help and for what purpose. Because of the extensiveness of its operations and access to job information, the professional placement offices of the Employment Service appear to have the greatest potential for providing widespread counseling assistance as well as referrals to community programs for psychological and other help. Job and career counseling in specific fields can be provided by the respective professional societies, whose expertise can be integrated with that of the Employment Service. Academic institutions can also cooperate with the Employment Service, primarily through their college placement offices, to provide more effective job and career counseling to students as well as to graduates of all ages. Even employers have begun to offer job and career counseling, sometimes as an outplacement activity, but increasingly as part of ongoing in-house career development programs. Regardless of setting, a prerequisite to effective counseling is accurate collection and dissemination of information about job and career opportunities.

4. *Retraining and continuing education.* For those desiring a career change or updating to improve their employability, some type of retraining or continuing education may be appropriate. For many, such decisions can best be made after some career counseling. As in the case of career counseling, the effectiveness of retraining and continuing education programs depends on an accurate needs assessment based on high-quality information about supply and demand in the professional job market. Academic institutions, because of their potential capabilities, could play a major role in professional retraining and continuing education. In addition, continuing education programs for updating or upgrading could be offered by some professional societies, whereas job-oriented professional retraining could probably best be provided by employers. Regardless of where the retraining or continuing education programs take place, the government can play a supportive role not only by providing assistance for the unemployed and underemployed to encourage their enrollment, but also by sponsoring assessment and skill conversion studies to help assure that the programs are linked to real job opportunities.

5. *Job information and placement services.* Central to the integrated professional employment system are job information and placement services. Effective provision of such services requires a coordinated effort among all relevant institutions, but as in almost all aspects of the employment system, the government can play a central role. Although the Employment Service and its professional placement office may have many limitations when it comes to providing information and placement assistance to professionals, it does possess a great potential. This is indicated by the successful results attained when efforts have been directed toward the special placement needs of professionals. One innovative approach that has already proved to be effective is to have professional societies integrate their capabilities with those of the Employment Service. Similarly, close relationships

can be fostered between each professional placement office and local college placement offices as well as employers of professionals. By concentrating an integrated professional job information and placement system in one center that also provides assistance involving counseling, retraining, continuing education, and relocation, the Employment Service could radically change its image as the option of last resort.

6. *Job development.* Any professional job placement system is worthless if it has few job openings. Therefore, job development becomes crucial to the success of the system. Although job development activities would appropriately be centered at the professional placement offices of the Employment Service, these activities could best be carried out with the direct involvement of the professional societies, possibly by their members who are seeking work. Participation by unemployed professionals in job development has been highly successful. Although these professionals worked as volunteers, it would appear that they could also be hired on a temporary basis, until they "self-destruct" their jobs by finding appropriate work through their job development activities. A reward system for effective job development activities could also be instituted.

7. *Job creation.* Although the issue of job creation by the government is controversial, it would appear to be necessary in a situation where job development is ineffectual because of a widespread lack of jobs. Perhaps most controversial is the temporary work provided under various public job programs. It should be noted that many unemployed professionals would be quite willing to accept temporary jobs created by the government. However, these jobs would have to be meaningful and not just "make work" positions which would result in underemployment. Efforts at job creation must also involve the private sector, with the government providing incentives to employers to hire professionals in need of meaningful work. Moreover, federal stimulation of demand for permanent professional level positions could be accommodated through such means as R&D funding to solve important national problems. Employers would be responsible for retraining and placement of the educated unemployed and underemployed in permanent professional-level positions. Such openings as well as those resulting from job creation would be listed by the professional job information and placement system.

8. *Relocation system.* When professional-level jobs are scarce in a particular geographic area, frequently the only way to find such positions involves relocation. However, many would choose to change their careers or even take a job that leaves them underemployed rather than relocate. Nevertheless, even for those who are willing and able to relocate, certain types of assistance and incentives can be provided to support their move. Perhaps the most important part of an effective relocation system is accurate, up-to-date information on job openings. Such information can be provided by means of computerized job-matching systems that would store data on job openings as well as on individuals seeking work.

By means of real-time computer-assisted job-matching systems that could transmit data anywhere in the country, lists of professional-level job openings could instantaneously be made available to those who desire to relocate. Furthermore, job openings could be matched immediately with individual qualifications. Incentives, in the form of relocation grants to pay for the costs of moving and resettling, could be a joint responsibility of the employer and the government. As an incentive for employer participation, such relocation grants could be made available only to those who list positions in the job-matching system. To facilitate adjustment, employers would also be expected to provide counseling to help alleviate the stress created by relocation and reemployment.

From this brief description, it should be clear that the suggested systems model is not a radical departure from that which already exists. Nevertheless, the model does imply two major changes in the existing system. The first change involves a considerable increase in the types and quality of assistance provided by the professional placement office's of the Employment Service so that they are transformed from options of last resort to vital centers attractive to those seeking help in finding professional-level jobs. The second change, closely related to the first, calls for the integration of relevant information or services provided by professional societies, academic institutions, and employers with those of the professional placement office. All indications are that with the type of integration being proposed here, public placement efforts can be made attractive to employers of professionals as well as to those seeking professional-level jobs.

Whereas overall policy and programs could best be determined on a national level, implementation would be the responsibility of local professional placement offices. However, participation by representatives of professional societies, academic institutions, and employers should be on both the national policymaking level as well as on the local level to help assure a meaningful coherence between policy and implementation. By centralizing policy and decentralizing implementation of an integrated professional job information and placement system, problems of unemployment and underemployment can be reduced considerably among those seeking professional-level jobs. Insofar as it provides rapid and meaningful employment, such a system would go far to help restore the psychological well-being of the increasing number of professionals who will be suffering from job loss or underemployment.

ALTERNATIVES TO TERMINATIONS

It can be argued that job loss is just one of those life events that is difficult to avoid, especially given the fluctuating job market conditions over the span of a professional's career. However, unlike most stress-creating life events, job loss because of economic decline is not necessarily inevitable. This has long been demonstrated by Japanese industry, although some terminations did occur as a result of the recession following the Arab oil embargo of 1973–1974. In the United States, IBM is perhaps the best example of major employers that have a no-termination policy. Other employers have rescued both their company and their jobs by passing ownership to the employees. It is clear that when there is a commitment by the employer to social responsibility that extends to the health and well-being of its employees, alternatives to terminations can be developed.

Unfortunately, judging by past history, social responsibility on the part of employers comes slowly unless encouraged by legislation. It would appear that attempts at achievement of full employment in the United States through legislation could require employers to utilize some types of alternatives to terminations. Some western European countries have already established such policies (Reubens, 1970). Many employers in the United States do use a host of alternatives to mass terminations. These include internal transfers, retraining, natural attrition, early retirement, postponing salary increase, reduction of salary or benefits, and various types of work sharing.

Several types of government-controlled incentives could be applied to encourage the use of alternatives to terminations. One such incentive involves the use of unemployment insurance (Henle, 1976; Lynton, 1975). An overhaul of the unemployment insurance system is long overdue, and one objective could be to have it redirected to encourage continuous employment. Since employers typically contribute to unemployment insurance according to the volume and frequency of their layoffs, their contribution rates could be adjusted in response to whether or not they used alternatives to terminations. A reduction of the contribution rate would follow adoption of alternatives, whereas rate increases would occur if terminations were carried out. Unemployment insurance could also be used to subsidize work-sharing approaches, such as a shortened workweek. Under this scheme employees can be assigned to a part-time schedule and still be eligible for unemployment compensation for the days they do not work. Although this may entail a certain degree of underemployment, the continuity of their jobs and a high income would surely result in less stress for professionals than would a complete loss of job and income. There is, of course, the expectation of a return to full-time work when conditions improve. Although work-sharing approaches are applicable to all workers, they would appear to be most easily implemented among higher-level employees, who typically are not unionized, thus precluding lengthy union–management negotiations (Lynton, 1975).

It should be clear that whatever approach is used as an alternative to termination, some stress is created among those affected, but it is likely to be considerably less than that precipitated by job loss. It would be appropriate to investigate the various alternatives to terminations for professionals, as well as other workers, using stress-related criteria in addition to those involving cost. The objective, of course, would be to minimize both. Thus, by providing appropriate alternatives to terminations, the cost in both human and economic terms can be substantially reduced for the benefit of all.

A GLOBAL PERSPECTIVE

The problem of the educated unemployed and underemployed has become worldwide, reaching epidemic proportions in many developed as well as developing countries. It is a problem that is likely to continue well into the future, threatening the health and stability of individuals as well as societies. Unfortunately, concerted measures carried out on a global scale are not likely, although groups such as the International Labour Organization and the Organization for Economic Cooperation and Development have expressed concern.

Until such time as a global effort can be mounted to deal with the problem of professionals in search of work, responsibility remains primarily with each individual country. No society can afford to squander those human resources that can contribute most to improving its quality of life. Indeed, it is the rapidly increasing numbers of educated workers who are likely to have the greatest influence on the shaping of future societies. Thus, if for no other reason than self-interest, national efforts must be devoted to helping assure proper utilization of professionals. Not to do so will lead to mass frustration of expectations and psychological deterioration among educated workers, which could, as past evidence indicates, contribute to political turmoil and conflict on a global scale.

References

Abramson, L. Y., Seligman, M. E. P., and Teasdale, J. D.Learned helplessness in humans: Critique and reformulation. *Journal of Abnormal Psychology,* 1978, **87**, 165–179.

Adams, L. P. *The Public Employment Service in Transition, 1933–1968.* Ithaca, N.Y.: New York State School of Industrial and Labor Relations, Cornell University, 1969.

Adams, W. *The Brain Drain.* New York: MacMillan, 1968.

American Institute of Aeronautics and Astronautics. *AIAA Employment Workshops: V.II. Analytic Report.* New York: AIAA, 1972.

Aiken, M., Ferman, L. A., and Sheppard, H. L. *Economic Failure, Alienation, and Extremism,* Ann Arbor, Mich.: University of Michigan Press, 1968.

Albin, R. S. Retraining: The second time around. *APA Monitor,* December 1978, 5, 21.

Alden, J. Job hunting after the next layoff: It'll be tougher. Here's why. *New Engineer,* June–July 1973, 11–12.

Allen, T. L. Aerospace cutbacks: Impact on the companies and engineering employment in southern California. Doctoral dissertation, Massachusetts Institute of Technology, 1972.

American Chemical Society, *Professional Employment Guidelines.* Washington, D.C., 1975.

Anderson, C. R. Coping behaviors as intervening mechanisms in the inverted U stress–performance relationship. *Journal of Applied Psychology,* 1976, **61**, 30–34.

Anderson, C. R. Locus of control, coping behaviors, and performance in a stress setting: A longitudinal study. *Journal of Applied Psychology,* 1977, **62**, 446–451.

Andrisani, P. J., and Abeles, R. P. Attitude development and work experience during the middle years. Paper presented at the meeting of the American Psychological Association, Washington, D.C., 1976. (a)

Andrisani, P. J., and Abeles, R. P. Locus of control and work experience: Cohort and race differences. Paper presented at the meeting of the American Psychological Association, Washington, D.C., 1976. (b)

Andrisani, P. J., and Nestel, G. Internal-external control as contributor to and outcome of work experience. *Journal of Applied Psychology,* 1976, **61**, 156–165.

Arnstein, G. E. Match: Square pegs for square holes. *Phi Delta Kappan,* November 1965, 122–125.

Asher, S. M. Unemployment among engineers: An Indian experience. Doctoral dissertation, Syracuse University, 1972.

Aun, E. M. New horizons for aerospace professionals, *Manpower,* January 1973, 3–8.

Ausmus, N. F. Occupational information systems and the Department of Labor. *Journal of Employment Counseling,* June 1977, **14**, 54–58.

Austin, A. Soviet outcasts meet Western scientists. *The New York Times,* April 15, 1980, Cl, C3. (a)

Austin, A. In Soviet science training, strengths are marred by flaws. *The New York Times,* September 2, 1980, C4. (b)

Austin, A. Moscow police bar scientists meeting. *The New York Times,* December 1, 1980, All. (c)

Azevedo, R. E. Scientists, engineers, and the job search process. *California Management Review,* 1974, **17**(2), 40–49.

Azrin, N. H., Flores, T., and Kaplan, S. J. Job-finding club: A group-assisted program for obtaining employment. *Behavior Research and Therapy,* 1975, **13**, 17–27.

Babec, J. A., and Lee, J. W. The cooperative placement center: Corporate action to assist terminated employees. *Personnel Journal,* 1970, **49**, 819–823.

Bailyn, L. Career and family orientations of husbands and wifes in relation to marital happiness. *Human Relations,* 1970, **23**, 87–113.

Bain, T. *Labor Market Experience for Engineers During Periods of Changing Demand.* Manpower Research Monograph No. 35. U.S. Department of Labor. Washington, D.C.: U.S. Government Printing Office, 1974.

Bakke, E. W.*The Unemployed Worker.* New Haven, Conn.: Yale University Press, 1940.

Bakke, E. W. *Citizens without Work.* New Haven, Conn.: Yale University Press, 1947.

Bamundo, P. J. The relationship between job satisfaction and life satisfaction: An empirical test of three models on a national sample. Doctoral dissertation, The City University of New York, 1977.

Barmash, I. New jobs for old hands. *The New York Times,* May 29, 1977, Sec. 3, 1.

Barnes, D. Job matching via satellite.*Worklife,* December 1977, 12–15.

Barnes, P. Fringe benefits of a depression: Bringing back the WPA. *The New Republic,* March 15, 1975, 19–21.

Barraclough, B. M., Nelson, B., and Sainsbury, P. The diagnostic classification and psychiatric treatment of 25 suicides. In N. L. Barberow (Ed.), *Proceedings: Fourth International Conference for Suicide Prevention,* Los Angeles, Calif., October 18–21, 1967, 61–65.

Bar-Yosef, R. *Vocational Retraining in Israel.* Jerusalem: Department for the Retraining of University Graduates, Ministry of Absorption, 1977.

Bar-Yosef, R., Shield, G., and Varsher, Y. *Job-Seeking Professionals* (in Hebrew). Jerusalem: Work and Welfare Research Institute, Hebrew University, 1975.

Bar-Yosef, R., and Varsher, Y. *Occupational Absorption of Immigrant Engineers* (in Hebrew). Jerusalem: Work and Welfare Research Institute, Hebrew University, 1977.

Bar-Yosef, R., and Weinberger, R. *Retraining for Immigrant Professionals* (in Hebrew). Jerusalem: Work and Welfare Research Institute, Hebrew University, 1975.

Battelle Memorial Institute. *A Survey of Aerospace Employees Affected by Reductions in NASA contracts.* Columbus, Ohio: Battelle Columbus Laboratories, May 20, 1971.

Beller, I. Latin America's uenmployment problem. *Monthly Labor Review,* 1970, **93** (11), 3–16.

Berg, L. *Education and Jobs: The Great Training Robbery.* New York: Praeger, 1970.

Best, F., and Stern, B. Education, work, and leisure: Must they come in that order? *Monthly Labor Review,* 1977, **100**(7), 3–10.

Bezdek, R. H. Alternate manpower forecasts for the coming decade: Second guessing the U.S. Department of Labor. *Socio-economic Planning Sciences,* 1973, **7**, 511–521.

Bisconti, A. S., and Astin, H. S. *Undergraduate and Graduate Study in Scientific Fields.* ACE Research Reports **8**(3). Washington, D.C.: American Council on Education, 1973.

Bisconti, A. S., and Solmon, L. C. *College Education on the Job—The Graduates' Viewpoint.* Bethlehem, Pa.: The CPC Foundation, 1976.

Blonder, M. D. Organizational repercussions of personnel cutbacks. Doctoral dissertation, City University of New York, 1976.

Bowen, H. R. *Investment in Learning: The Individual and Social Value of American Higher Education.* San Francisco, Calif.: Jossey-Bass, 1977.

Bozza, L. Is college preparation enough? *The Social and Rehabilitation Record,* February–March 1975, 25–28.

Bradshaw, T. F. Jobseeking methods used by unemployed workers. *Monthly Labor Review,* 1973, **96**(2), 35–40.

Brandwein, R. Mass layoff of defense scientists and engineers: A case study. *Proceedings of the National Symposium on Stabilization of Engineering and Scientific Employment in Industry,* San Jose State College, San Jose, Calif., November 1966, 38–48.

Brayfield, A. H., Wells, R. V., and Strate, M. W. Interrelationships among measures of job satisfaction and general satisfaction. *Journal of Applied Psychology,* 1957, **41**, 201–205.

Breed, W. Suicide, migration and race: A study of cases in New Orleans. *Journal of Social Issues,* 1966, **22**, 30–43.

Breed, W. Male suicide—Los Angeles and New Orleans compared. *Bulletin of Suicidology,* December 1967, 11–14.

Breed, W. Five components of a basic suicide syndrome. *Life Threatening Behavior,* 1972, **2**(1), 3–18.

Brenner, M. H. Economic changes and mental hospitalization. *Social Psychiatry,* 1967, **2**, 180–188.

Brenner, M. H. Economic changes and heart disease mortality. *American Journal of Public Health,* 1971, **61**, 606–611.

Brenner, M. H. Fetal, infant, and maternal mortality during periods of economic instability. *International Journal of Health Services,* 1973, **3**, 145–159. (a)

Brenner, M. H. *Mental Illness and the Economy.* Cambridge, Mass.: Harvard University Press, 1973. (b)

Brenner, M. H. Trends in alcohol consumption and associated illnesses. *American Journal of Public Health,* 1975, **65**, 1279–1292.

Brenner, M. H. *Estimating the Social Costs of National Economic Policy: Implications for Mental and Physical Health, and Criminal Aggression.* Library of Congress, Congressional Research Service. Washington, D.C.: U.S. Government Printing Office, 1976.

Brenner, M. H. Personal stability and economic security. *Social Policy,* 1977, **8**(1), 2–4.

Briar, K. H. The effect of long-term unemployment on workers and their families. Doctoral dissertation, University of California, Berkeley, 1976.

Brown, D. G. *Academic Labor Markets.* A report submitted to the Office of Manpower, Automation and Training, U.S. Department of Labor, September 1965. (a)

Brown, D. G. The pros and cons of government-financed placement of college teachers. *Phi Delta Kappan,* November 1965, 125–129. (b)

Brown, T. D. An *Analysis of Reemployment and Unemployment of Engineers Laid Off from NASA Aerospace Contracts Between June of 1968 and October of 1970.* Cambridge, Mass.: Harvard University, October 1972. NTIS No. PB213761.

Bucher, G. C., and Reece, J. E. What motivates researchers in times of economic uncertainty? *Research Management,* 1972, **15**(1), 19–32.

Buder, L. Licensing of teachers is urged. *The New York Times,* July 7, 1976, 38. (a)

Buder, L. Layoff of 308 school supervisors averted by foregoing salary rise. *The New York Times,* September 9, 1976, 34C. (b)

Buder, L. City University is planning 50% cutback in teacher-training programs. *The New York Times,* September 23, 1976, 46. (c)

Bulman, R. J., and Wortman, C. B. Attributions of blame and coping in the "real world." *Journal of Personality and Social Psychology*, 1977, **35**, 351–363.

Bureau of National Affairs. Recruiting practices. *Personnel Policies Forum*, Survey No. 86, March 1969.

Burke, R. J. Personnel job transfers: Some data and recommendations. *Studies in Personnel Psychology*, Spring 1974, **6**, 35–46.

Burks, E. C. Loss of jobs in New York City is sharply reduced. *The New York Times*, September 2, 1976, 34.

Business Week, How IBM avoids layoffs through retraining. November 10, 1975, 111–112.

Camil Associates. *Recruitment, Job Search and the United States Employment Service*. U. S. Department of Labor, Employment and Training Administration, R&D Monograph 43. Washington, D.C.: U.S. Government Printing Office, 1976.

Caplan, R. D., Cobb, S., French, J. R. P., Harrison, R. V., and Pinneau, S. R. *Job Demands and Worker Health*. HEW Publication No. (National Institute for Occupational Safety and Health) 75-160, 1975.

Caplow, T., and McGee, R. J. *The Academic Marketplace*. New York: Basic Books, 1958.

Carey, M. L. Revised occupational projections to 1985. *Monthly Labor Review*, 1976, **99**(11), 10–22.

Carnegie Commission on Higher Education. *College Graduates and Jobs: Adjusting to a New Labor Market Situation*. New York: McGraw-Hill, 1973.

Cartter, A. M. The academic labor market. In M. S. Gordon (Ed.), *Higher Education and the Labor Market*. New York: McGraw-Hill, 1974, 281–307.

Cartter, A. M. *Ph.D.s and the Academic Labor Market*. New York: McGraw-Hill, 1976.

Caruth, D. L., and Vogelsang, R. L. Programs to assist unemployed engineers, scientists and technicians. *Marquette Business Review*, 1972, **16**, 128–136.

Catalano, R., and Dooley, D. Economic predictors of depressed mood and stressful life events in a metropolitan community. *Journal of Health and Social Behavior*, 1977, **18**, 292–307.

Catalano, R., and Dooley, D. Does economic change provoke or uncover behavioral disorder? A preliminary test. In L. Ferman and J. Gordus (Eds.), *Mental Health and the Economy*. Kalamazoo, Mich.: W. E. Upjohn Institute for Employment Research, 1979, 321–326.

Cavan, R. S. Unemployment—Crisis of the common man. *Marriage and Family Living*, 1959, **21**, 139–146.

Cavan, R. S., and Ranck, K. H. *The Family and the Depression*. Chicago: University of Chicago Press, 1938.

Cerra, F. Job agents are assailed on basis of survey of ads. *The New York Times*, August 7, 1977, 25.

Chambers, W. N., and Reiser, M. F. Emotional stress in the precipitation of congestive heart failure. *Psychosomatic Medicine*, 1953, **15**, 38–60.

The Chronicle of Higher Education. Student protests hit West Germany. June 20, 1977, 2. (a)

The Chronicle of Higher Education. 10-per-cent cut sought in N.C. teacher education. November 7, 1977, 2. (b)

Clarity, J. F. Bethlehem steel eliminating 2500 from office staff. *The New York Times*, October 1, 1977, Sec. 3, 25, 31.

Clopton, J. C., Jr. An exploratory study of career change in middle life. Doctoral dissertation, University of Cincinnati, 1972.

Clymer, A. "Conservatives" share "liberal" view. *The New York Times*, January 22, 1978, 1, 30.

Cobb, S., and Kasl, S. V. *Some Medical Aspects of Unemployment*. Ann Arbor, Mich.: Survey Research Center, Institute of Social Research, University of Michigan, May 1971.

Cobb, S., and Kasl, S. V. *Termination: The Consequences of Job Loss*. National Institute for Occupational Safety and Health Research Report No. 76-1261, June 1977.

Cofer, C. N., and Appley, M. H. *Motivation: Theory and Research*. New York: Wiley, 1964.

Cohn, R. M. The consequences of unemployment on evaluations of self. Doctoral disssertation, University of Michigan, 1977.

Comptroller General of the United States. Reemployment assistance for engineers, scientists and technicians unemployed because of aerospace and defense cutbacks. Report to the Congress, B-133182, 1973.

Conner, T. Aerospace professionals: An analysis of their unemployment problems and employment opportunities. Doctoral dissertation, Claremont Graduate School, 1973.

Constance, J. A. The strike at Stevens Tech. *New Engineer,* June 1977, 25–27.

Cooke, R. A., and Moch, M. K. Facilitating the job-seeking process. In O. Moles (Chair), *Ameliorating the Impact of Unemployment: Established Programs Versus Individual Needs*. Symposium presented at the meeting of the American Psychological Association, Washington, D.C., September 1976.

Cooper, A. C. Putting the liberal arts graduate to work, *Personnel,* 1976, **53**(2), 61–65.

Coopersmith, S. *The Antecedents of Self-Esteem*. San Francisco: W. H. Freeman, 1967.

Corson, W., Nicholson, W., and Skidmore, F. *Experiences of Unemployment Insurance Recipients during the First Year after Exhausting Benefits*. Final report, U.S. Department of Labor, Manpower Administration, No. DMLA-11-34-74.01-4, 1976.

Coughlin, E. K. Making education degrees marketable. *The Chronicle of Higher Education,* May 9, 1977, 7.

Coughlin, E. K. Can new Ph.D.'s find employment and satisfaction outside academe? *The Chronicle of Higher Education,* March 27, 1978, 10.

Coyne, J. C., and Lazarus, R. The ipsative–normative framework for the longitudinal study of stress. Paper presented at the meeting of the American Psychological Association, New York, September 1979.

Crittenden, A. Women work and men change. *The New York Times,* January 9, 1977, Sec. 3, 22.

Crowley, M. F. Professional manpower: The job market turnaround. *Monthly Labor Review,* 1972, **95**(10), 9–15.

Cuddihy, B. R. How to give phased-out managers a new start. *Harvard Business Review.* July–August 1974, **52,** 61–69.

Culhane, C. Unemployment among professionals lifts taboo concept of manpower planning. *National Journal,* 1971, **3,** 1661–1666.

Cummings, J. More are seeking second degrees in colleges. *The New York Times,* January 7, 1976, 29.

Danielson, L. E. *Characteristics of Engineers and Scientists*. Ann Arbor, Mich.: University of Michigan Press, 1960.

Davis, D. D., Johnson, C. D., and Overton, S. R. Job placement for handicappers: Developing a natural helping system. Paper presented at the meeting of the American Psychological Association, New York, September 1979.

Dear, E. P. Computer job matching now and tomorrow. *Personnel,* 1970, **47**(3), 57–63.

Decker, W. D. Forces that influenced the career management programs of today. *Proceedings, 86th Annual Conference of the American Society for Engineering Education.* Washington, D.C.: ASEE, 1978, 1–9.

Dennis, T. L., and Gustafson, D. P. College campuses vs. employment agencies as sources of manpower. *Personnel Journal,* 1973, **52,** 720–724.

Dewhirst, H. D., and Holland, W. E. Effect of organizational change on career goals of scientists and engineers. *IEEE Transactions on Engineering Management,* 1975, **EM-22,** 114–119.

Diamond, D. Plight of the fired executive. *The New York Times,* October 20, 1974, Sec. 3, 5.

Diggory, J. C. *Self-Evaluation: Concepts and Studies.* New York: Wiley, 1966.

DiNunzio, M. *Aerospace Employment Project: Finding New Careers in Local Government for Unemployed Engineers and Scientists.* National League of Cities and U.S. Conference of Mayors, NTIS No. PB213670, August 1972.

Dipboye, R. L. A critical review of Korman's self-consistency theory of work motivation and occupational choice. *Organizational Behavior and Human Performance,* 1977, **18,** 108–126.

Dipboye, R. L., Fromkin, H. L., and Wiback, K. Relative importance of applicant sex, attractiveness and scholastic standing in evaluation of job applicant resumes. *Journal of Applied Psychology,* 1975, **60,** 39–43.

Dohrenwend, B. P. The social psychological nature of stress: A framework for causal inquiry. *Journal of Abnormal Social Psychology,* 1961, **62,** 294–302.

Donig, C. Personal communication, *Berliner Psychologische Beratungstelle,* May 25, 1978.

Dooley, D., and Catalano, R. Money and mental disorder: Toward behavioral cost accounting for primary prevention. *American Journal of Community Psychology,* 1977, **5,** 217–227.

Dooley, D., and Catalano, R. Economic, life, and disorder changes: Time-series analyses. *American Journal of Community Psychology,* 1979, **7,** 381–396.

Dorfman, D. Male potency and the Dow Jones Industrial Average. *New York Magazine,* October 20, 1975, 10–12.

Drucker, J. H. To be 60 and jobless. *The New York Times,* July 9, 1975, 36.

Drucker, P. F. Planning for "redundant" workers. *Personnel Administrator,* January 1980, **25,** 32–34.

Dublin, L. I. *Suicide—A Sociological and Statistical Study.* New York: Ronald Press, 1963.

Duckenfield, M. Denmark to call a halt to college growth. *The Chronicle of Higher Education,* January 24, 1977, 6.

Durkheim, E. *Le Suicide.* Paris: Alcan, 1897.

Dyer, L. D. Managerial jobseeking: Methods and techniques. *Monthly Labor Review,* 1972, **95**(12), 29–30.

Dyer, L. D. Job search success of middle-aged managers and engineers. *Industrial and Labor Relations Review,* 1973, **27,** 969–979.

Early, J. F. Effect of the energy crisis on employment. *Monthly Labor Review,* 1974, **97**(8), 8–16.

Eaton, B. C. Defense engineers: Do they have special reemployment problems. *Monthly Labor Review,* 1971 **94**(7), 51–54.

Eckland, B. K., and Wisenbaker, J. M. *National Longitudinal Study: A Capsule Description of Young Adults Four and One-half Years after High School.* Report No. RTI/884/51-01 S. Raleigh, N.C.: Center for Educational Research and Evaluation, Research Triangle Institute, February 1979.

The Economist. Rent-a-worker. May 27, 1978, 86–88.

Eisenberg, P., and Lazarsfeld, P. F. The psychological effects of unemployment. *Psychological Bulletin*, 1938, **35,** 358–390.

Elder, G. H. *Children of the Great Depression: Social Change in Life Experience.* Chicago: University of Chicago Press, 1974.

El-Khawas, E. H., and Bisconti, A. S. *Five and Ten Years after College Entry.* American Council on Education Research Report, **9**(1), 1974.

Engel, G. L. Sudden and rapid death during psychological stress—Folklore or folk wisdom? *Annals of Internal Medicine*, 1971, **74,** 771–782.

Engineering Manpower Commission. *Assuring the availability of engineers necessary to attain national goals.* New York: Engineers Joint Council, April 1975.

Estes, R. J. Emotional consequences of job loss. Doctoral dissertation, University of Pennsylvania, School of Social Work, 1973.

Estes, R. J., and Wilensky, H. L. Life cycle squeeze and the morale curve. *Social Problems*, 1978, **25**(3), 277–292.

ETA Interchange. Job search, relocation plan takes shape. March–April 1977, **3**(3), 6–7.

Faber, H. Corning, N.Y.: Hometown absorbs the shock. *The New York Times,* September 14, 1975, 4.

Falcocchio, J., Kaufman, H. G., and Kramer, P. Travel patterns and mobility needs of the physically handicapped. *Transportation Research Record*, 1976, **618,** 13–15.

Faver, C. A. Women's life satisfaction as a function of values and roles. Paper presented at the meeting of the American Psychological Association, Montreal, September 1980.

Feerst, I. Are aliens in engineering a threat to your job? *New Engineer*, July–August 1977, 29–34.

Fenichel, O. *The Psychoanalytic Theory of Neurosis.* New York: Norton, 1945.

Ferman, L. A. Economic deprivation, social mobility and mental health. Paper presented at the meeting of the American Psychological Association, New York, September 1979.

Ferretti, F. Financial crisis crippling New York's public schools. *The New York Times,* December 12, 1976, 1, 8.

Fidell, L. S. Empirical verification of sex discrimination in hiring practices in psychology. *American Psychologist*, 1970, **25,** 1094–1098.

Fidell, L. S. Employment status, role dissatisfaction and the housewife syndrome. A paper funded by the National Institute on Drug Abuse, California State University, Northridge, Calif., undated.

Fields, G. Major effort: Colleges help students who can't choose a field by providing flexible curricula, special courses. *The Wall Street Journal,* October 12, 1978, 48.

Fineman, S. A Psychosocial model of stress and its application to managerial unemployment. *Human Relations*, 1979, **32,** 323–345.

Finison, L. J. Unemployment, politics, and the history of organized psychology. *American Psychologist*, 1976, **31,** 747–755.

Finison, L. J. Unemployment, politics, and the history of organized psychology, II: The Psychologists League, the WPA and the National Health Program. *American Psychologist*, 1978, **33,** 471–477.

Fishman, L. Results of the Martin layoff study with special reference to engineers and scientists. *Proceedings of the National Symposium on Stabilization of Engineering and Scientific Employment in Industry,* San Jose State College, San Jose, Calif., November 1966, 62–73.

Fiske, E. B. Job outlook good, students jam accounting course: Colleges, overwhelmed, strive to curtail enrollment. *The New York Times,* August 9, 1977, 25.

Fiske, E. B. Hard-hit schools turn to marketers. *The New York Times,* January 22, 1978, Sec. 3, 1.

Flaim, P. O. Employment and unemployment during the first half of 1974. *Monthly Labor Review,* 1974, **97**(8), 3–7.

Fleischman, H. Joblessness: Share-the-work remedy. *The New York Times,* December 19, 1976, Sec. 4, 16.

Folger, J. K. The job market for college graduates. *Journal of Higher Education,* March 1972, **43,** 203–222.

Foltman, F. F. *White- and Blue-Collar in a Mill Shutdown: A Case Study in Relative Redundancy.* Ithaca, N.Y.: New York State School of Industrial and Labor Relations, Cornell University, 1968.

Foster, L. W., and Liebrenz, M. L. Corporate moves—Who pays the psychic costs? *Personnel,* November–December 1977, 67–75.

Fox, W. S., and Wince, M. H. The structure and determinants of occupational militancy among public school teachers. *Industrial and Labor Relations Review,* 1976, **30,** 47–58.

Frankel, M. M. (Ed.). *Projections of Education Statistics to 1986–87.* U.S. Department of Health, Education and Welfare. Washington, D.C.: U.S. Government Printing Office, 1978.

Freeman, E. S., and Fields, C. L. *A Study of Black Male Professionals in Industry.* New York: Recruiting Managerial Consultants, 1973.

Freeman, R. B. *The Over-educated American.* New York: Academic Press, 1976.

Freeman, R. B. *Black Elite: The New Market for Highly Educated Black Americans.* New York: McGraw-Hill, 1977. (a)

Freeman, R. B. The new job market for black academicians. *Industrial and Labor Relations Review,* 1977, **30**(2), 161–174. (b)

Freiman, G. A. Soviet teacher's "J'accuse." *The New York Times Magazine,* November 25, 1979, 122–127.

Friedlander, F. Importance of work versus non-work among socially and occupationally stratified groups. *Journal of Applied Psychology,* 1966, **50,** 437–441.

Galbraith, J. K. *The Great Crash, 1929.* Boston: Houghton Mifflin, 1961.

Gallup Opinion Index. Sixteen million Americans would move to another country. May 1971, Report No. 71, 24.

Gallup Opinion Index. Economic predictions. 1977, Vol. II, Survey No. 964-K, 934.

Gannon, M. J. Sources of referral and employee turnover. *Journal of Applied Psychology,* 1971, **55,** 226–228.

Gannon, M. J., Foreman, C., and Pugh, K. The influence of a reduction in force on the attitudes of engineers. *Academy of Management Journal,* 1973, **16,** 330–334.

Gannon, M. J., and Paine, F. T. Sources of referral, job orientation and employee effectiveness. *Proceedings of the Academy of Management,* Minneapolis, Minn., August, 1972, pp. 36–38.

Gaynor, A. F. Unpublished data from the San Fernando Valley Section IEEE, personal communication, December 7, 1971.

German, P. S., and Collins, J. W. *Disability and Work Adjustment.* U.S. Social Security Administration Report No. 24 GPO, 1974.

Gerston, G. J. City job agency has few openings. *The New York Times,* February 14, 1974, 16.

Ghiselli, E. *Explorations in Managerial Talent.* Pacific Palisades, Calif.: Goodyear, 1971.

Ginsburg, S. W. What unemployment does to people. *American Journal of Psychiatry,* 1942, **99,** 439–446.

Ginther, S. Law school graduates. *Occupational Outlook Quarterly,* Fall 1975, **19,** 2–3.

Ginzberg, E. *The Unemployed.* New York: Harper, 1943.

Ginzberg, E. The outlook for educated manpower. *The Public Interest,* No. 26, Winter 1972, 100–111.

Globerson, A., and Baram, B. *Retraining for Professionals* (in Hebrew). Tel Aviv: Tel Aviv University, 1971.

Goble, F. G. *Toward 100% Employment: An AMA Survey Report.* New York: AMACOM, 1973.

Goffman, E. On cooling the mark out. *Psychiatry,* 1952, **15,** 451–463.

Goldman, A. L. 66% of teachers who were laid off reject return offer. *The New York Times,* October 10, 1977, 1.

Goldman, A. L. New professional-licensing plan backed in Albany. *The New York Times,* April 8, 1979, 22.

Goldstein, T. Job prospects for young lawyers dim as field grows overcrowded. *The New York Times,* May 17, 1977, Cl, C55.

Goldstein, T. A.B.A. president-elect warns on unemployment of young lawyers. *The New York Times,* August 6, 1978, 30.

Goldstein, T. California takes lead in lawyers amid continued shortage of jobs. *The New York Times,* September 18, 1979, A21.

Golladay, M. A. *The Condition of Education.* Washington, D.C.: U.S. Government Printing Office, 1976.

Goodchilds, J. D., and Smith, E. E. The effects of unemployment as mediated by social status. *Sociometry,* 1963, **26,** 287–293.

Goodwin, L. *Do the Poor Want to Work? A Social–Psychological Study of Work Orientations.* Washington, D.C.: The Brookings Institution, 1972.

Goodwin, M. Problems of the unemployed executive. *The New York Times,* September 28, 1975, Sec. 3, 2.

Gore, S. The influence of social support and related variables in ameliorating the consequences of job loss. Doctoral dissertation, University of Pennsylvania, 1973.

Gore, S. A conceptual approach for the study of unemployment as a stressful life event. In H. Proshansky (Chair), *Unemployment—America's Major Mental Health Problem.* Symposium presented at the meeting of the American Psychological Association, Chicago, 1975.

Gore, S. The effect of social support in moderating the health consequences of unemployment. *Journal of Health and Social Behavior,* 1978, **19,** 157–165.

Gould, J. M. *The Technical Elite.* New York: Augustus M. Kelley, 1966.

Granovetter, M. S. *Getting a Job: A Study of Contacts and Careers.* Cambridge, Mass.: Harvard University Press, 1974.

Grasso, J. T., and Myers, S. C. The labor market effects of investment in human capital. In A. I. Kohen et al. (Eds.), *Career Thresholds,* Vol. 6, 53–92 U.S. Department of Labor, Employment and Training Administration, R&D Monograph 16. Washington, D.C.: U.S. Government Printing Office, 1977.

Gray, H. L. On starting a new job. *Journal of Occupational Psychology,* 1975, **48,** 33–37.

Greenhalgh, L. A. *Cost-Benefit Balance Sheet for Evaluating Layoffs as a Policy Strategy.* Ithaca, N.Y.: The CSEA–New York State Continuity of Employment Committee, New York State School of Industrial and Labor Relations, Cornell University, 1978.

Greenhalgh, L. A. and Jick, T. *The Closing of Urban State Agencies: Impact on Employee Attitudes, Perceptions, Careers, and Economic Security.* Ithaca, New York: The CSEA–New York State Continuity of Employment Committee, New York State School of Industrial and Labor Relations, Cornell University, 1978.

Greenhalgh, L. A., and Jick, T. The relationship between job insecurity and turnover, and its differential effects on employee quality level. Paper presented at the 39th Annual Academy of Management Meeting, Atlanta, Ga., August 8–11, 1979.

Greenhaus, J. H., and Badin, I. J. Self-esteem, performance and satisfaction: Some tests of a theory. *Journal of Applied Psychology,* 1974, **59,** 722–726.

Greenwald, H. P. Scientists and the need to manage. *Industrial Relations,* 1978, **17,** 156–167.

Griffel, A., and Kaufman, H. G. *Part-time Work and Women.* Jerusalem: Work and Welfare Research Institute, Hebrew University, 1977.

Griffiths, D. E. Doctoral programs must pass a new test. *New York University Education Quarterly,* 1978, **10**(1), 2–8.

Gupta, D. K. The socio-economic impact of unemployment and income inequality: A cross-national study (1958–67). Doctoral dissertation, University of Pittsburgh. 1977.

Gurin, G., Veroff, J., and Feld, S. *Americans View Their Mental Health.* New York: Basic Books, 1960.

Gurin, P., Gurin, G., Rao, R. C., and Beattie, M. Internal–external control in the motivational dynamics of Negro youth. *Journal of Social Issues,* 1969, **25,** 29–53.

Gutteridge, T. G. The economic consequences of unemployment and the search for work among displaced technical professionals. Unpublished paper, 1975.

Gutteridge, T. G. Labor market adaptations of displaced technical professionals. *Industrial and Labor Relations Review,* 1978, **31,** 460–473.

Guyot, J. F. *The Costs of Savings in New York City's Fiscal Crisis Report B. A Year of Layoffs for Civil Servants.* New York: State Legislative Institute, Baruch College of the City University of New York, 1976.

Haefner, J. E. Race, age, sex and competence as factors in employer selection of the disadvantaged. *Journal of Applied Psychology,* 1977, **62,** 199–202.

Hall, D. T., and Gordon, F. B. Career choices of married women: Effects on conflict, role behavior, and satisfaction. *Journal of Applied Psychology,* 1973, **58,** 42–48.

√ Hall, D. T., and Mansfield, R. Organizational and individual response to external stress. *Administrative Science Quarterly,* 1971 **16,** 533–547.

Hall, O. M. Attitudes and unemployment. *Archives of Psychology,* 1934, No. 165.

Hammer, E. G. Conservation of technological human resources in the U.S. *Public Personnel Management,* 1974, **3,** 403–408.

Harmon, D. K., Masuda, M., and Holmes, T. H. The social readjustment rating scale: A cross-cultural study of western Europeans and Americans. *Journal of Psychosomatic Research,* 1970, **14,** 391–400.

Harrison, D. G., and May, E. R. *Careers in Business, Campus to Corporation.* New York: The University of the State of New York, September 1, 1978.

√ Hartley, J. F. The impact of unemployment upon the self-esteem of managers. *Journal of Occupational Psychology,* 1980, **53,** 147–155.

Hawks, I. The Russian immigrant's vocational crisis. In S. A. Grossman (Chair), *Stress Reactions to Work Crises.* Symposium presented at the meeting of American Psychological Association, Montreal, September 1980.

Hecker, D. E. The jam at the bottom of the funnel: The job outlook for college graduates. *Occupational Outlook Quarterly,* 1978, **22**(1), 37–39.

Helmer, J. *Bringing the War Home: The American Soldier in Vietnam and After.* New York: Free Press, 1974.

Henle, P. *Work-Sharing as an Alternative to Layoffs.* Congressional Research Service, July 19, 1976, HD5106 Gen. 76-134E.

Henle, P. Trade adjustment assistance: Should it be modified? *Monthly Labor Review,* 1977, **100**(3), 40–45.

Henry, A. F., and Short, J. F., Jr. *Suicide and Homicide.* Glencoe, Ill.: Free Press, 1954.

Hepworth, S. J. Moderating factors of the psychological impact of unemployment. *Journal of Occupational Psychology,* 1980, **53,** 139–145.

Herbert, W. Mental health parley focuses on economy. *APA Monitor,* July 1978, **9**(7), 1, 8, 9, 29.

Hershey, R. Effects of anticipated job loss on employee behavior. *Journal of Applied Psychology,* 1972, **56,** 273–275.

Hershfield, D. C. Reducing personnel costs during recession: Are there alternatives to the layoff? *The Conference Board RECORD,* 1975, **12**(6), 20–22.

Herzberg, F., Mausner, B., and Snyderman, B. *The Motivation to Work.* New York: Wiley, 1959.

Heylin, M. Layoff investigations: A progress report. *Chemical and Engineering News,* October 25, 1976, 57–59.

Hinrichs, J. R. Unpublished data, personal communication, Management Decision Systems, Inc., Darien, Conn., January 1976.

Hinrichs, J. R. Getting fired: Organizational problem solving from the employee's perspective. In L. L. Cummings (Chair), *Dealing with Poor Performance: Supervision, Training and Terminations.* Symposium presented at the meeting of the American Psychological Association, New York, September 1979.

Hinrichs, J. R., and Ferrario, A. A cross-national study of manager's job attitudes. Paper presented at the 18th International Congress of Applied Psychology, Montreal, 1974.

Hirsch, B. J. The social network as a natural support system. Paper presented at the meeting of the American Psychological Association, San Francisco, 1977.

Holen, A. S. Effects of professional licensing on interstate mobility and resource allocation. *The Journal of Political Economy,* 1965, **73,** 492–498.

Holmes, T. H., and Rahe, R. M. The social readjustment rating scale. *Journal of Psychosomatic Research,* 1967, **11,** 213–218.

Homjak, W. W. Layoff rotation. *The Personnel Administrator,* September 1978, 46–53.

Horowitz, M. A. *Increasing the Employability of Applicants in Professional Occupations.* Professional Placement Office, Division of Employment Security, Commonwealth of Massachusetts. NTIS No. PB199179, September 1968.

House, J. S. The relationship of intrinsic and extrinsic work motivations to occupational stress and coronary heart disease risk. Doctoral dissertation, University of Michigan, 1972.

Hoyt, J. W. Periodical readership of scientists and engineers in research and development laboratories. *IRE Transactions on Engineering Management,* June 1962, 71–75.

Human Behavior. The Lockheed engineer syndrome. January–February 1972, 54.

Hunt, P., Schupp, D., and Cobb, S. *An Automated Self Report Technique.* Mental Health in Industry Document 1966-1, Institute for Social Research, University of Michigan, January 1966.

Hyman, S. D. Changing careers in midstream. *Manpower,* June 1975, 22–26.

IEEE. *Petition for Amendments to the IEEE Constitution.* New York, Undated.

Industrial Research. Opinion poll results: Retraining not adequate. August 1971, 55.

Institute of International Education. *Open Doors: 1978–79 Report on International Educational Exchange,* 1980.

Jackson, E. F. Status consistency and symptoms of stress. *American Sociological Review,* 1962, **27,** 469–481.

Jacobson, D. Time and work: Unemployment among middle-class professionals. Unpublished manuscript, Department of Anthropology, Brandeis University, undated.

Jacobson, R. L. Colleges are still weak in vocational training employers complain. *The Chronicle of Higher Education,* January 24, 1977, 4. (a)

Jacobson, R. L. Higher education and the job crises: Public disillusionment provokes a debate. *The Chronicle of Higher Education,* March 28, 1977, 3. (b)

Jacobson, R. L. Two-year colleges prepare to fight for new clientele. *The Chronicle of Higher Education,* April 25, 1977, 6. (c)

Jacques, E. Death and the mid-life crisis. *International Journal of Psychoanalysis,* 1965, **56,** 502–514.

Jahoda, M., Lazarsfeld, P. F., and Zeisel, H. *Marienthal: The Sociography of an Unemployed Community.* New York: Aldine-Atherton, 1971 (1933).

Jick, T. Coping with job loss: An integration of research, application, and policy development. *Industrial Relations Research Association 30th Annual Proceedings,* 1978, 266–273.

Jick, T., and Greenhalgh, L. *The Relocation of a Rural Hospital Unit: The Impact of Rumors and Ambiguity on Employees.* The CSEA–New York State Continuity of Employment Committee, 1978.

Johnson, M. *Counterpoint: The Changing Employment Service.* Salt Lake City, Utah: Olympus, 1973.

Johnston, J., and Bachman, J. G. *Youth in Transition,* Vol. 5. Ann Arbor, Mich.: Institute for Social Research, University of Michigan, 1972.

Joint Economic Committee. *Trends in the Fiscal Condition of Cities: 1978–1980.* Washington, D.C.: U.S. Government Printing Office, 1980.

Jones, R. J., and Azrin, N. H. An experimental application of a social reinforcement approach to the problem of job-finding. *Journal of Applied Behavioral Analysis,* 1973, **6,** 345–353.

Jones, W. W., and Fox, W. H. The educated unemployed. *Public Personnel Management,* 1973, **2**(2), 108–112.

Justice, B., and Justice, R. *The Abusing Family.* New York: Human Sciences Press, 1976.

Kahn, R. L., Wolfe, D. M., Quinn, R. P., Snock, J. C., and Rosenthal, R. A. *Organizational Stress: Studies in Role Conflict and Ambiguity.* New York: Wiley, 1964.

Kantor, M. B. Some consequences of residential and social mobility for the adjustment of children. In M. B. Kantor (Ed.), *Mobility and Mental Health.* Springfield, Ill.: Thomas, 1965, 86–122.

Kardiner, A. The role of economic security in the adaptation of the individual. *The Family,* 1936, **17**(6), 187–197.

Kasl, S. V. The optimal measures of the impact of manpower programs on health. Paper presented at a Conference on the Evaluation of the Impact of Manpower Programs. The Center for Tomorrow, Ohio State University, Columbus, Ohio, June 15–17, 1971.

Kasl, S. V., and Cobb, S. Blood pressure changes in men undergoing job loss: A preliminary report. *Psychosomatic Medicine,* 1970, **32**(1), 19–37.

Kasl, S. V., Cobb, S., and Brooks, G. W. Changes in serum uric acid and cholesterol level in men undergoing job loss. *Journal of the American Medical Association,* 1968, 2–6, 1500–1507.

Kasl, S. V., Gore, S., and Cobb, S. The experience of losing a job: Reported changes in health, symptoms, and illness behavior. *Psychosomatic Medicine,* 1975, **37,** 106–122.

Kass, O., and Lipset, S. M. America's new wave of Jewish immigrants. *The New York Times Magazine,* October 7, 1980, 44, 100, 102, 110, 112, 114, 116–118.

Katona, G., and Strumpel, B. *A New Economic Era.* New York: Elsevier, 1978.

Katz, D., Gutek, B. A., Kahn, R. L., and Barton, E. *Bureaucratic Encounters: A Pilot Study in the Evaluation of Government Services.* Ann Arbor, Mich.: Institute for Social Research, University of Michigan, 1975.

Katz, I. Evolving public and industrial policies based on recent experiences in the retraining of engineers released by advanced technology companies. Paper presented at the 92nd Winter Annual Meeting of American Society of Mechanical Engineers, Washington, D.C., November 28–December 2, 1971.

Kaufman, H. G. Relations between unemployment–reemployment experience and self-esteem among professionals. *Proceedings, 81st Annual Convention, American Psychological Association,* 1973, 601–602.

Kaufman, H. G. Career interruption, obsolescence and professional career reentry among women engineering graduates. Paper presented at the Engineering Foundation Conference on Women in Engineering. Updating of Skills: Retraining and Reentry, Henniker, N.H., August 1974. (a).

Kaufman, H. G. The graduate management degree: Is it really the road to success? *New Engineer,* February 1974, 31–34, 42–48. (b)

Kaufman, H. G. *Obsolescence and Professional Career Development.* New York: AMACOM, 1974. (c)

Kaufman, H. G. *Career Management: A Guide to Combating Obsolescence.* New York: IEEE Press/Wiley-Interscience, 1975.

Kaufman, H. G. Factors affecting the relationship between continuing education and performance: A state-of-the-art review. In National Science Foundation, *Continuing Education in Science and Engineering.* Washington, D.C.: U.S. Government Printing Office, 1977, 235–243.

Kaufman, H. G. Technical obsolescence: An empirical analysis of its causes and how engineers cope with it. *Proceedings, 86th Annual Conference of the American Society for Engineering Education.* Washington, D.C.: ASEE, 1978 194–207. (An abridged version was also published in *Engineering Education,* 1979 68(8), 826–830.)

Kaufman, H. G. *Factors Related to the Utilization and Career Development of Scientists and Engineers: A longitudinal study of involuntary termination.* A final report submitted to the National Science Foundation, Grant No. SRS 77-20737, 1980. NTIS No. PB81180226.

Kerlinger, F. N., and Pedhazur, E. J. *Multiple Regression in Behavioral Research.* New York: Holt, Rinehart and Winston, 1973.

Kihss, P. A day of jobless pay proposed in states work-sharing plan. *The New York Times,* September 5, 1975, 18.

King, C. T. The unemployment impact of the Vietnam war. Doctoral dissertation, Michigan State University, 1976.

Kleiner, M. M. Interstate occupational migration: An analysis of data from 1965–70. *Monthly Labor Review,* 1977, **100**(4), 64–67.

Kleinfield, N. R. Zenith to lay off fourth of workers to trim its costs. *The New York Times,* September 28, 1977, D1, D7.

Knack, P. The personal cost of cheating on unemployment insurance. *The New York Times,* February 19, 1978, Sec. 4, 17.

Knowdell, R. L. The implementation of a career/life planning program in an industrial setting. *Proceedings, 86th Annual Conference of the American Society for Engineering Education.* Washington, D.C. ASEE, 1978, 17–23.

Kohen, A. I., and Shields, P. M. Determinants and consequences of service in the armed forces during the Vietnam era. In A. I. Kohen et al. (Eds.), *Career Thresholds*. Vol. 6 155–189. U.S. Department of Labor, Employment and Training Administration, R&D Monograph 16. Washington, D.C.: U.S. Government Printing Office, 1977.

Komaroff, A. L., Masuda, M., and Holmes, T. H. The social readjustment rating scale: A comparative study of Negro, Mexican and white Americans. *Journal of Psychosomatic Research*, 1968, **12**, 121–128.

Komarovsky, M. *The Unemployed Man and His Family*. New York: Arno Press, 1971 (reprint of 1940 edition).

Kopelman, R. E. A causal-correlational test of the Porter and Lawler framework. *Human Relations*, 1979, **32**, 545–556.

Korman, A. K. Self-esteem variable in vocational choice. *Journal of Applied Psychology*, 1966, **50**, 479–486.

Korman, A. K. Self-esteem as a moderator of the relationship between self-perceived abilities and vocational choice. *Journal of Applied Psychology*, 1967, **51**, 65–67. (a)

Korman, A. K. Relevance of personal need satisfaction for overall satisfaction as a function of self-esteem. *Journal of Applied Psychology*, 1967, **51**, 533–538. (b)

Korman, A. K. Toward an hypothesis of work behavior. *Journal of Applied Psychology*, 1970, **53**, 31–41.

Korman, A. K. *The Psychology of Motivation*. Englewood Cliffs, N.J.: Prentice-Hall, 1974.

Korman, A. K., Greenhaus, J. H., and Badin, I. J. Personnel attitudes and motivation. *Annual Review of Psychology*, 1977, **28**, 175–196.

Kornhauser, A. *Mental Health of the Industrial Worker: A Detroit Study*. New York: Wiley, 1965.

Kotschnig, W. M. *Unemployment in the Learned Professions*. London: Humphrey Melford/Oxford University Press, 1937.

Kryger, B. R., and Shikiar, R. Sexual discrimination in the use of letters of recommendation: A case of reverse discrimination. *Journal of Applied Psychology*, 1978, **63**, 309–314.

Kubler-Ross, E. *On Death and Dying*. New York: Macmillan, 1969.

Kweller, I., Zalkind, S. S., and Dispenzieri, A. *A Longitudinal and Comparative Analysis of the Stress Effects on Civilian Personnel of an Announcement to Close Some Naval Shipyards*. Baruch College of the City University of New York, 1972.

Ladd, Jr., E. C., and Lipset, S. M. Faculty support for unionization: Leveling off at about 75 percent. *The Chronicle of Higher Education*, February 13, 1978, 8.

Laderriére, P. Recent trends in conditions for teacher recruitment and their implications in member countries. In *Teacher Policies*. Paris: OECD, 33–61 1976.

Ladinsky, J. Occupational determinants of geographic mobility among professional workers. *American Sociological Review*, 1967, **32**, 253–264.

LaMark, H. V. C.E.S. for unemployed engineers. In D. D. French (Ed.), *Continuing Engineering Studies Series*, No. 6. Washington, D.C.: American Society for Engineering Education, 1972, 43–46.

Lange, W. H. Regaining lost skill. *Personnel Journal*, 1935, **14**, 55–59.

Langley, G. How to manage the survivors of a cutback. *Innovation*, February 1971, **18**, 32–39.

Langner, T. S., and Michael, S. T. *Life Stress and Mental Health*. New York: Collier-Macmillan, 1963.

Langway, W. E. The results of the Long Island Defense Layoff Study with specific reference to engineers and scientists. *Proceedings of the National Symposium on Stabilization of Engineering and*

Scientific Employment in Industry, San Jose State College, San Jose, Calif., November 1966, 49–61.

Lawler, E. E. *Motivation in Work Organizations.* Monterey, Calif.: Brooks/Cole, 1973.

Lawlis, G. F. Motivational factors reflecting employment instability. *Journal of Social Psychology,* 1971, **84,** 215–223.

Lazarsfeld, P. An unemployed village. *Character and Personality,* 1932–33, **1,** 147–151.

Lazarus, R. S. The concepts of stress and disease. In L. Levi (Ed.), *Society, Stress and Disease,* **1** 53–58. London: Oxford University Press, 1971.

Lazarus, R. S., and Launier, R. Stress-related transactions between person and environment. In L. A. Pervin and M. Lewis (Eds.), *Perspectives in Interactional Psychology.* New York: Plenum, 1978, 287–327.

Lazer, R. I. Job sharing as a pattern for permanent part-time work. *The Conference Board RECORD,* 1975, **12**(10), 57–61.

Lefkowitz, J. Self-esteem of industrial workers. *Journal of Applied Psychology,* 1967, **51**(6), 521–528.

Lehner, G. How to manage the victims of a cutback. *Innovation,* May 1971, **21,** 42–47.

Leventman, P. G. The technical professional: A study in career and disillusionment. Doctoral dissertation, Bryn Mawr College, 1974.

Leventman, P. G. Nonrational foundations of professional rationality: Employment instability among scientists and technologists. *Sociological Symposium,* 1976, **16,** 83–112.

Levinson, D. J. *The Seasons of a Man's Life.* New York: Knopf, 1978.

Levinson, H. *Executive Stress.* New York: Harper & Row, 1970.

Levitan, S. A., and Belous, R. S. Reduced worktime: An alternative to high unemployment. In R. Taggart (Ed.), *Job Creation: What works?* Salt Lake City, Utah: Olympus, 1977.

Levitan, S. A. and Taggart, R. Employment problems of disabled persons. *Monthly Labor Review,* March 1977, **100**(3), 3–13.

Levy, F. Extraversion and reactions to stress. Unpublished paper, 1977.

Levy, L. C. Jobless becoming entrepreneurs. *The New York Times,* February 23, 1975, Sec. 3, 1, 15.

Lewis-Beck, M. S. Determining the importance of an independent variable: A path analytic solution. *Social Science Research,* 1974, **3,** 95–107.

Liem, G. R., and Liem, J. H. Social support and stress: Some general issues and their application to the problem of unemployment. In L. Ferman and J. Gordus (Eds.), *Mental Health and the Economy.* Kalamazoo, Mich.: W.E. Upjohn Institute for Employment Research, 1979, 347–379.

Lindsey, R. Some who believe in a no-work ethic. *The New York Times,* June 1, 1975, 45.

Lipset, S. M., and Schwartz, M. The politics of professionals. In H. Vollmer and D. Milk (Eds.), *Professionalization.* Englewood Cliffs, N.J.: Prentice-Hall, 1966, 299–310.

Little, C. B. Stress responses among unemployed technical–professionals. Doctoral dissertation, University of New Hampshire, 1973.

Little, C. B. Technical–professional unemployment: Middle-class adaptability to personal crisis. *The Sociological Quarterly,* 1976, **17,** 262–274.

Lodahl, T. M., and Kejner, M. The definition and measurement of job involvement. *Journal of Applied Psychology,* 1965, **49,** 24–33.

London, M., Crandal, R., and Seals, G. W. The contribution of job and leisure satisfaction to quality of life. *Journal of Applied Psychology,* 1977, **62,** 328–334.

Loomba, R. P. *A Study of the Reemployment and Unemployment Experience of Scientists and Engineers Laid Off from 62 Aerospace and Electronic Firms in the San Francisco Bay Area During*

1963–1965, San Jose, Calif.: Manpower Research Group, Center for Interdisciplinary Studies, San Jose State College, NTIS No. PB177350, February 15, 1967.

Loomba, R. P. *An Examination of the Engineering Profession*. San Jose, Calif.: Manpower Research Group, Center for Interdisciplinary Studies, San Jose State College, 1968.

Lovenheim, B., Ph.D.'s Look beyond the ivory tower. *The New York Times*, May 1, 1977, Sec. 12, 9.

Lynch, J. J. *The Broken Heart: The Medical Consequences of Loneliness*. New York: Basic Books, 1977.

Lynn, F. Poll finds economy and taxes are the voters main worries. *The New York Times*, October 28, 1974, 1, 26.

Lynton, E. F. *Alternatives to Layoffs*. A conference held by the New York City Commission on Human Rights, April 3–4, 1975.

Maeroff, G. I. Students flock to job-related courses. *The New York Times*, November 3, 1975, 1. (a)

Maeroff, G. I. College enrollments rise 8.8%, greatest surge since the sixties. *The New York Times*, December 10, 1975, 43. (b)

Maeroff, G. I. Colleges, facing decline, advised to lure students. *The New York Times*, January 1, 1979, 6.

Magarrell, J. Black graduates found gaining biggest payoffs from degrees. *The Chronicle of Higher Education*, May 16, 1977, **14**(12), 1, 10.

Magarrell, J. One-fourth of U.S. colleges join cooperative ventures. *The Chronicle of Higher Education*, September 10, 1979, 7.

Malm, F. T. Recruiting patterns and the functioning of labor markets. *Industrial and Labor Relations Review*, 1954, **7**, 507–525.

Manpower Report of the President. Washington, D.C.: U.S. Government Printing Office, 1975.

Manuso, J. S. J. Coping with job abolishment. *Journal of Occupational Medicine*, 1977, **19**, 598–602.

Marcus, R. L. Has advertising produced results in faculty hiring? *Educational Record*, 1977, **57**, 247–250.

Marsh, L. C. *Health and Unemployment: Some Studies of Their Relationship*. Toronto: Oxford University Press, 1938.

Marshall, H. D. *The Mobility of College Teachers*. New York: Pageant Press, 1964.

Martinez, T. *The Human Marketplace: An Examination of Private Employment Agencies*. New Brunswick, N.J.: Transaction Books, 1976.

Maslow, A. M. A theory of human motivation. *Psychological Review*, 1943, **50**, 370–396.

Masuda, M., and Holmes, T. H. The social readjustment rating scale. *Journal of Psychosomatic Research*, 1967, **11**, 219–225.

Maxwell, K. G. Job hunting problems of married professional women. Unpublished paper, May 1977.

McIntosh, S. S. Outplacement—The new responsibility in termination. *The Personnel Administrator*, March–April 1973, 10–13.

McKenna, J. B. *Labor Market Experience of Persons Who Received Advance Notice of Employment Termination*. Report No. 4, Research Branch, Ontario Ministry of Labour, August 1973.

McManus, G. J. I'm giving the workers my company. *Iron Age*, July 8, 1974, **214**, 49–50.

Mechanic, D., and Volkart, E. H. Stress, illness behavior, and the sick role. *American Sociological Review*, 1961, **26**, 51–58.

Meichenbaum, D. A Self-instructional approach to stress management: A proposal for stress innoculation training. In C. Spielberger and I. Sarason (Eds.), *Stress and Anxiety,* Vol. 1. 237–263 New York: Wiley, 1975.

Meier, G. S. *Job Sharing: A New Pattern for Quality of Work and Life.* Kalamazoo, Mich.: W.E. Upjohn Institute for Employment Research, 1979.

Mendleson, J. L. What's ''fair'' treatment for terminated employees? *Supervisory Management,* November 1974, **19**(11), 25–34.

Merrett, S. The education–occupation matrix: An Indian case study. *International Labour Review,* 1971, **103,** 499–510.

Mesa-Lago, C. Unemployment in socialist countries: Soviet Union, East Europe, China and Cuba. Doctoral dissertation, Cornell University, 1968.

Mesa-Lago, C. Unemployment in a socialist economy: Yugoslavia. *Industrial Relations,* February 1971, **10,** 49–69.

Meyer, M. C. Combining resources for survival: A look at two institutions, *Personnel Journal,* 1975, **54,** 628–630.

Meyer, P. S. Traditionally paternal, Equitable Life rattles staff by mass firing. *The Wall Street Journal,* December 11, 1978, 1, 30.

Miao, G. Marital instability and unemployment among whites and non-whites. *Journal of Marriage and the Family,* 1974, **36,** 77–86.

Michelotti, K. Educational attainment of workers. *Monthly Labor Review,* 1977, **100**(12), 53–58.

Miner, M. G. *Separation Procedures and Severance Benefits.* Washington, D.C.: The Bureau of National Affairs, Inc., Personal Policies Forum Survey No. 121, April 1978.

Mockbee, J. Personal communication, NASA Goddard Space Flight Center, Greenbelt, Md., January 1978.

Mooney, J. D. An analysis of unemployment among professional engineers and scientists. *Industrial and Labor Relations Review,* 1966, **19,** 517–528.

Moore, Jr., W., and Wagstaff, L. H. *Black Educators in White Colleges.* San Francisco: Jossey-Bass, 1974.

Mottur, E. R. *Conversion of Scientific and Technical Resources: Economic Challenge—Social Opportunity.* Monograph No. 8. Washington, D.C.: Program of Policy Studies in Science and Technology, The George Washington University, March 1971.

Murphy, H. B. M. Migration and the major mental disorders: A reappraisal. In M. B. Kantor (Ed.), *Mobility and Mental Health.* Springfield, Ill.: Thomas, 1965, 5–29.

National Center for Educational Statistics. *The Condition of Education.* Washington, D.C.: U.S. Government Printing Office, 1978.

National Commission for Manpower Policy. *Proceedings of a Conference on the Role of the Business Sector in Manpower Policy.* Special Report No. 41, November 1975.

National Commission for Manpower Policy. *The Quest for a National Manpower Policy Framework: Facilitating Recurrent Education and the Flexibility of Working Life.* Special Report No. 8, April 1976, 58.

National Manpower Advisory Committee. *Federal Manpower Policy in Transition.* U.S. Department of Labor, 1974.

National Research Council. *Science, Engineering and Humanities Doctorates in the United States: 1977 Profile.* Washington, D. C.: National Academy of Sciences, 1978.

328 References

National Science Foundation. Unemployment rate for engineers, June/July 1971. *Science Resources Studies Highlights,* September 1971, NSF 71-33.

National Science Foundation. *Immigrant Scientists and Engineers in the United States.* NSF 73-302. Washington, D.C., 1973.

National Science Foundation. *The 1972 Scientist and Engineer Population Redefined,* Vol. 2: *Labor Force and Employment Characteristics.* NSF 75-327. Washington, D.C., 1975. (a)

National Science Foundation. *Projections of Science and Engineering Doctorate Supply and Utilization 1980 and 1985.* NSF 75-301. Washington, D.C., 1975. (b)

National Science Foundation. Private industry employment of scientists and engineers in 1975 shows a 5-year decline. *Sciences Resources Studies Highlights,* May 1977, NSF 77-312.

National Science Foundation. Scientific and technical personnel in private industry, 1960–70 and 1975. *Reviews of Data on Science Resources,* No. 30, March 1978, NSF 78-302.

National Science Foundation. Employment of scientists and engineers increased between 1976 and 1978 but declined in some science fields. *Science Resources Studies Highlights,* March 1980, NSF 80-305.

National Society of Professional Engineers. *Executive Summary of the Technology Utilization Project.* Washington, D.C., 1973.

Neuringer, C. Attitudes toward self in suicidal individuals. *Life Threatening Behavior,* 1974, **4,** 96–106.

The New York Times. Ceylon: "If we don't die here. . . ." April 11, 1971, Sec. 4, 1.

The New York Times. Engineering group modifying charter. November 10, 1972, 19.

The New York Times. Loss of skilled worrying India. March 4, 1974, 5.

The New York Times. 1,900 accept plan offered by IBM on early retiring. April 12, 1975, 33. (a)

The New York Times. Detroit jobless return to school. October 26, 1975, 59. (b)

The New York Times. Psychologist sets up a job club and helps members find work. November 29, 1975, 33. (c)

The New York Times. Retraining of ex-teachers is urged. November 7, 1976, 63.

The New York Times. Frustrations of jobless university graduates are erupting in Italy. March 7, 1977, 6. (a)

The New York Times. Caracas sends 6,500 to study abroad. March 13, 1977, 14. (b)

Niland, J. R. *The Asian Engineering Brain Drain.* Lexington, Mass.: Heath, 1970.

North, D. S., and Houstoun, M. F.*The Characteristics and Role of Illegal Aliens in the U.S. Labor Market: An Exploratory Study.* Linton & Co., Inc. Washington, D.C., March 1976, NTIS No. PB252616.

Novaco, R. W. Stress inoculation: A cognitive therapy for anger and its application to a case of depression. *Journal of Consulting and Clinical Psychology, 1977,* **45,** 600–608.

O'Brien, J. E. Violence in divorce prone families. *Journal of Marriage and the Family,* 1971, **33,** 692–697.

Office of Technology Assessment. *Forecasts of Physician Supply and Requirements.* Washington, D.C.: U.S. Government Printing Office, 1980.

Opinion Research Corporation. Rising unemployment, not inflation or energy, still is the top problem facing the nation. *ORC Public Opinion Index Report to Management,* July 1975.

Oppenheimer, E. A. The relationship between certain self constructs and occupational preferences. *Journal of Counseling Psychology,* 1966, **13,** 191–197.

Oppenheimer, M. The unionization of the professional. *Social Policy,* 1975, **5,** 34–40.

Ornstein, A. C. Quality, not quotas. *Society,* 1976, **13**(2), 10, 14–17.

Orpen, C. Work and nonwork satisfaction: A causal–correlational analysis. *Journal of Applied Psychology,* 1978, **63**, 530–532.

Orzack, L. H. Work as a central life interest of professionals. *Social Problems,* 1959, **7**, 125–132.

Oser, A. S. Recession is drawing many into sales. *The New York Times,* October 31, 1975, 31.

O'Toole, J. The reserve army of the underemployed. *Change,* May 1975, 26–63.

Palen, J. J. Belief in government control and the displaced worker. *Administrative Science Quarterly,* 1969, **14**, 584–593.

Palen, J. J., and Fahey, F. J. Unemployment and reemployment success: An analysis of the Studebaker shutdown. *Industrial and Labor Relations Review,* 1968, **21**, 234–250.

Palmore, E. Physical, mental, and social factors in predicting longevity. *Gerontologist,* 1969, **9**, 103–108.

Parade Magazine. The price of unemployment. October 5, 1975, 6.

Parnes, H. S., and King, R. Middle-aged job losers. *Industrial Gerontology,* 1977, **4**(2), 77–95.

Parrish, J. B. Women in professional training. *Monthly Labor Review,* 1974, **97**(5), 41–43.

Paykel, E. S., Scaling of life events. *Archives of General Psychiatry,* 1971, **25**, 340–347.

Perez de Tagle, O. G. The stage theory of balanced educational–economic development and its application to developing countries with educated unemployment. Doctoral dissertation, University of Wisconsin, 1973.

Perline, M. M., and Presley R. W. Labor mobility and the "net advantage" theory. *Personnel Journal,* 1973, **52**, 1040–1045.

Perrella, V. C. Employment of recent college graduates. *Monthly Labor Review,* 1973, **96**(2), 41–50.

Phillips, J. J. Is cooperative education worth it? One company's answer. *Personnel Journal,* 1977, **56**, 505–507.

Phillips, L. E. Mandatory continuing education for licensed professionals is here to stay. *Association Management,* April 1978, 79–86.

Pierce, A. The economic cycle and the social suicide rate. *American Sociological Review,* 1968, **32**, 457–462.

Powell, D. H. The effects of job strategy seminars upon unemployed engineers and scientists. *The Journal of Social Psychology,* 1973, **91**, 165–166.

Powell, D. H., and Driscoll, P. F. Middle-class professionals face unemployment. *Society,* 1973, **10**(2), 18–26.

Powell, E. H. Occupation, status and suicide: Toward a redefinition of anomie. *American Sociological Review,* 1958, **23**, 131–139.

Pratt, G. K. *Morale: The Mental Hygiene of Unemployment.* National Committee for Mental Hygiene, 1933.

Quindlen, A. New York is facing vast job turnover. *The New York Times,* January 22, 1979, A1, B3.

Quinn, R. P., and Staines, G. L. *The 1977 Quality of Employment Survey.* Ann Arbor, Mich.: Survey Research Center, Institute for Social Research, University of Michigan, 1978.

Rabinowitz, S., and Hall, D. T. Organizational research and job involvement. *Psychological Bulletin,* 1977, **84**, 265–288.

Rahe, R. H., McKean, J. D., and Arthur, R. J. A longitudinal study of life-change and illness patterns. *Journal of Psychosomatic Research,* 1967, **10**, 437–452.

Rangan, K. Leadership in Sri Lanka shaken by outbreak of student protests. *The New York Times,* December 15, 1976, A14.

Rees, A. Information networks in labor markets. *Proceedings of the 78th Annual Meeting of the American Economic Association*, New York, 1966, 559–566.

Reid, G. L. Job search and the effectiveness of job-finding methods. *Industrial and Labor Relations Review*, 1972, **25**, 479–495.

Reubens, B. G. *Hard to Employ: European Programs*. New York: Columbia University Press, 1970.

Rickard, T. E., Triandis, H. C., and Patterson, C. H. Indices of employer prejudice toward disabled applicants. *Journal of Applied Psychology*, 1963, **47**, 52–55.

Rickard, T. E., Triandis, H. E., and Patterson, C. H. Indices of employer prejudice toward disabled applicants. *Journal of Applied Psychology*, 1963, **47**, 52–55.

Ritchey, P. N. Explanations of migration. *Annual Review of Sociology*, 1976, **2**, 363–404.

Rittenhouse, C. H. *The Transferability and Retraining of Defense Engineers*. Washington, D.C.: The U.S. Arms Control and Disarmament Agency, November 1967.

Ritti, R. R. Underemployment of engineers. *Industrial Relations*, 1970, **9**, 437–452.

Ritti, R. R. *The Engineer in the Industrial Corporation*. New York: Columbia University Press, 1971.

Roberts, S. Inflation, recession—and families. *Social Casework*, March 1975, 182–185.

Roberts, S. V. White males fight back on minority job programs. *The New York Times*, November 24, 1977, A1, B17.

Roderick, R. D. An organizational analysis of the hiring of engineers. Doctoral dissertation, University of Illinois at Champaign–Urbana, 1970.

Rollins, R. H. Closing of the NASA Electronics Research Center: A study of the reallocation of space program talent. Master's thesis, Massachusetts Institute of Technology, 1970.

Rosen, B. C. The achievement syndrome: A psychocultural dimension of social stratification. *American Sociological Review*, 1956, **21**, 203–211.

Rosenfeld, C. The extent of job search by employed workers. *Monthly Labor Review*, 1977, **100**(3), 58–65.

Ross, S. S. Guidelines of professional engineers: Does anyone really care. *New Engineer*, November 1973, 18–21.

Rotter, J. B. Generalized expectancies for internal versus external control of reinforcement. *Psychological Monographs*, 1966, **80** (1, Whole No. 609).

Ruffner, R. N., and Sale, R. T. *The Impact of Unemployment on Handicapped People*. President's Committee on Employment of the Handicapped, March 1975.

Runciman, W. G. *Relative Deprivation and Social Justice*. Berkeley, Calif.: University of California Press, 1966.

Rushing, W. Income, unemployment and suicide: An occupational study. *Sociological Quarterly*, 1968, **9**, 493–503.

Santhanam, M. L. Levels of anxiety among unemployed and underemployed. In T. E. Shanmugam (Ed.), *Researches in Personality and Social Problems*. Madras, India: University of Madras, 1973, 257–272.

Sanua, V. D. Immigration, migration and mental illness: A review of the literature with special emphasis on schizophrenia. In E. B. Brody (Ed.), *Behavior in New Environments*. Beverly Hills, Calif.: Sage, 1970, 291–352.

Sarason, S. B. *Work, Aging, and Social Change: Professionals and the One-Life–One-Career Imperative*. New York: Free Press, 1977.

Schaar, K. Behaviorist to help labor reduce dole roles. *APA Monitor*, June 1976, **7**(6), 6.

Scherba, J. Outplacement as a personnel responsibility. *Personnel*, 1973, **50**(3), 40–44.

Schlossberg, N. K. and Leibowitz, Z. Organizational support systems as buffers to job loss. *Journal of Vocational Behavior*, 1980, **17**, 204–217.

Scott, P. A new dilemma for British universities: How to cope with a falling birthrate. *The Chronicle of Higher Education*, May 2, 1977, 7.

Scully, M. G. Worldwide job crisis faces university graduates. *The Chronicle of Higher Education*. September 27, 1976, 4.

Scully, M. G. Some humanists "make it" in the corporate world. *The Chronicle of Higher Education*, October 16, 1978, 10.

Searls, D. J., Braucht, G. N., and Miskimins, R. W. Work values of the chronically unemployed. *Journal of Applied Psychology*, 1974, **59**, 93–95.

Sears, R. R. Sources of life satisfactions of the Terman gifted men. *American Psychologist*, 1977, **32**, 119–128.

Segrè, J. Self-concept and depression: Mothers returning to work or remaining at home. Paper presented at the meeting of the Eastern Psychological Association, Washington, D.C. March 1978.

Seligman, M. E. P. *Helplessness: On Depression, Development, and Death*. San Francisco: W. H. Freeman, 1975.

Selye, H. *The Stress of Life*. New York: McGraw-Hill, 1956.

Semas, P. W. Faculty unions focusing on job security. *The Chronicle of Higher Education*, November 1, 1976, 3.

Seybolt, J. W. Work satisfaction as a function of the person–environment interaction. *Organizational Behavior and Human Performance*, 1976, **17**, 66–75.

Shabecoff, P. Ford staff finds job front is difficult despite help. *The New York Times*, December 7, 1976, 61.

Shaffer, R. A. More Americans take jobs for which they are overqualified. *The Wall Street Journal*, January 16, 1976, 1, 16.

Shama, A. Psychological effects of stagflation on the middle class: Findings from a longitudinal study. Paper presented at the meeting of the American Psychological Association, New York, September 1979.

Shamot, D. Professional employees turn to unions. *Harvard Business Review*, May–June 1976, 199–227.

Shanker, A. Where we stand: How come an "easy" job attracts so few? Why laid-off teachers refused to return. *The New York Times*, October 16, 1977, 7.

Shanthamani, V. S. Unemployment and neuroticism. *Indian Journal of Social Work*, 1973, **34**, 43–45.

Shapely, D. R&D conversion: Former NASA lab now working on transportation. *Science*, 1971, **171**, 268–269.

Shapero, A. Effects of government R and D contracting on mobility and regional resources. In W. H. Gruber and D. G. Marquis (Eds.), *Factors in the Transfer of Technology*. Cambridge, Mass.: MIT Press, 1969, 179–218.

Shapero, A. Making the technical unemployed productive again. *Innovation*, May 1972, **31**, 38–49.

Shapero, A. The displaced, uncomfortable entrepreneur. *Psychology Today*, November 1975, **9**, 83–86, 88, 133.

Sheppard, H. L. Worker reaction to job displacement. *Monthly Labor Review*, 1965, **88**(2), 170–172.

Sheppard, H. L. Factors associated with early withdrawal from the labor force. In S. L. Wolfbein (Ed.), *Men in the Pre-retirement Years*. Philadelphia: Temple University School of Business Administration, 1977, 163–215.

Sheppard, H. L., and Belitsky, A. H. *The Job Hunt: Job-Seeking Behavior of Unemployed Workers in a Local Economy*. Baltimore: Johns Hopkins Press, 1966.

Sheppard, N., Jr., Chicago job training partnership offers a model for U.S. proposal. *The New York Times*, April 10, 1978, D1.

Shipler, D. K. Making it—Russian style. *The New York Times Magazine*, February 11, 1979, Sec. 6, 38–46.

Shuster, A. Many European teachers jobless as economies lag, birthrates dip. *The New York Times*, December 29, 1976, 3.

Siegal, S. R. The night-school MBA: Long investment, low return. *MBA*, May 1976, 44–45.

Silk, L. Top business group's plan on attacking unemployment. *The New York Times*, January 12, 1978, D1, D10.

Silverman, C. *The Epidemiology of Depression*. Baltimore: Johns Hopkins Press, 1968.

Silverman, D. Employment service: "There must be a better way." *The New York Times*, August 19, 1977, A20.

Singular, S. The business schools: A bull market in applicants. *MBA*, May 1975, 34–36.

Slote, A. *Termination: The Closing at Baker Plant*. Indianapolis, Ind.: Bobbs-Merrill, 1969.

Smith, L. H. Employment prospects brighten a bit for some teachers in California, *Monthly Labor Review*, 1977, **100**(11), 49–52.

Social Science Data Center. Personal communication, University of Connecticut, Storrs, Conn., March 1978.

Solmon, L. C. Attracting women to psychology: Effects of university behavior and the labor market. *American Psychologist*, 1978, **33**, 990–999.

Solmon, L. C., and Hurwicz, M. L. The labor market for Ph.D.'s in science and engineering: Career outcomes. Paper presented at the Eastern Economics Association, Washington, D.C., April 28, 1978.

Srole, L., Langner, T. S., Michael, S. T., Opler, M. K., and Rennie, T. A. C. *Mental Health in the Metropolis*. New York: McGraw-Hill, 1962.

Staines, G. L., and O'Connor, P. The relationship between work and leisure. Unpublished paper, University of Michigan Survey Research Center, 1979.

Stang, D. Who succeeds in the academic job market? *APA Monitor*, September/October 1976, 31.

Stang, D. J., McKenna, W., Kessler, S. J., Russell, V., Sweet, S., Rosenfeld, P., Peleg, M., and Kafton, A. Predicting success in the academic psychology job market. Working paper, American Psychological Association, Washington, D.C., 1976.

Stanic, V., and Pym, D. *Brains Down the Drain: The Misuse of Highly-Qualified Manpower*. Anbar Monograph No. 12. London: Anbar Publications, 1968.

Stanley, D. T. *Running Short, Cutting Down: Five Cities in Financial Distress*. Washington, D.C.: The Brookings Institution, March 1976.

Steinmetz, S. K. *The Cycle of Violence: Assertive, Aggressive, and Abusive Family Interaction*. New York: Praeger, 1977.

Stern, R. N., and Hammer, T. H. Buying your job: Factors affecting the success or failure of employee acquisition attempts. *Human Relations*, 1978, **31**, 1101–1117.

Stevens, D. W. Job search techniques: A new index of effectiveness. *The Quarterly Review of Economics and Business*, 1972, **12**(2), 99–103.

Stevens, G., and Marquette, P. Black MBAs: Room at the top? *MBA*, August–September 1978, 39–42.

Stevens, N. D. The effect of job-seeking behavior on obtaining a job. *Journal of College Placement,* April–May 1972, 46–50.

Stevens, N. D. Job seeking behavior: A segment of vocational development. *Journal of Vocational Behavior,* 1973, **3**, 209–219.

Stevenson, G. Computers launch faster better job matching. *Worklife,* July 1976, 3–8.

Stotland, E. *The Psychology of Hope.* San Francisco: Jossey-Bass, 1969.

Striner, H. E. *Continuing Education as a National Capital Investment.* Kalamazoo, Mich.: W. E. Upjohn Institute for Employment Research, 1972.

Strumpel, B. Economic life-styles, values, and subjective welfare. In B. Strumpel (Ed.), *Economic Means for Human Needs: Social Indicators of Well-being and Discontent.* Ann Arbor, Mich.: Institute for Social Research, University of Michigan, 1976, 19–65.

Stuart, R. G.M. sets dismissal of 18,000: White-collar cut is made amid slumping sales. *The New York Times,* April 26, 1980, 33–34.

Super, D. E. Self concepts in vocational development. In D. E. Super, R. Starighevsky, N. Matlis, and J. P. Jordann (Eds.), *Career Development: Self-Concept Theory.* New York: College Entrance Examination Board, 1963, 1–16.

Super, D. E. Career development. In J. Davitz and S. Ball (Eds.), *Psychology in the Educational Process.* New York: McGraw-Hill, 1970, 428–475.

Taeuber, K. E., and Sweet, J. A. Family and work: The social life cycle of women. In J. M. Kreps (Ed.), *Women and the American Economy: A Look to the 1980's.* Englewood Cliffs, N.J.: Prentice-Hall, 1976, 31–60.

Tagliabue, J. Executives wanted, German ads say. *The New York Times,* May 13, 1980, D7.

Teich, A. H., and Lambright, W. H. The redirection of a large national laboratory. *Minerva,* 1976, **15**, 447–474.

Thompson, P. H. The effects of unemployment on engineering careers. U.S. Department of Labor Contract No. 81-25-72-10, November 1972.

Thompson, P. H. Who gets laid off. *IEEE Spectrum,* December 1973, 68–75.

Tiffany, D. W., Cowan, J. R., and Tiffany, P. *The Unemployed: A Social Psychological Portrait.* Englewood Cliffs, N.J.: Prentice-Hall, 1970.

Tirrell, J. E. *Community and Junior Colleges and the Comprehensive Employment and Training Act.* Washington, D.C.: American Association of Community and Junior Colleges, 1977.

Triandis, H. C. Factors affecting employee selection in two cultures. *Journal of Applied Psychology,* 1963, **47**, 89–96.

Trumbull, R. Upsurge of racism in Toronto afflicts South Asian immigrants.*The New York Times,* February 27, 1977, 1, 13.

Ullman, J. C., and Gutteridge, T. G. *The Effectiveness of Mailed Applicant-Opening Matches as a Placement Device and as Labor Marketing Information: A Study of the National Registry for Engineers.* Springfield, Va.: National Technical Information Service, Operations Division, 1973.

Ullman, J. C., and Huber, G. P. *The Local Job Bank Program.* Lexington, Mass.: Heath, 1973.

U.S. Department of Commerce, Bureau of the Census. *1967 Census of Business.* Washington, D.C.: U.S. Government Printing Office, 1970.

U.S. Department of Labor. *Job Seeking Methods Used by American Workers.* Bulletin 1886, Washington, D.C.: U.S. Government Printing Office, 1975. (a)

U.S. Department of Labor. *Ph.D. Manpower: Employment Demand, and Supply 1972–85.* Washington, D.C.: U.S. Government Printing Office, 1975. (b)

U.S. Department of Labor. *Educational Attainment of Workers, March 1975*. Special Labor Force Report 186. Washington, D.C.: Bureau of Labor Statistics, 1976.

U.S. Department of Labor. *Occupational Outlook for College Graduates, 1978–79*. Bulletin 1956. Washington, D.C.: Bureau of Labor Statistics, 1978.

U.S. Office of Education. *Placement Services for Personnel in Higher Education*. Washington, D.C.: U.S. Department of Health Education and Welfare, 1961.

U.S. Senate Committee on Labor and Public Welfare. *National Science Foundation Conversion Programs, 1971*. Hearings before the Special Subcommittee of National Science Foundation. Washington, D.C., U.S. Government Printing Office, 1972.

United Way of King County. *Start Up*. Seattle, Wash.: 1974.

Valdes, W. C. Perspectives on reduction-in-force. *Defense Management Journal*, 1971, **7**(1), 3–8.

Van Atta, C. M., Decker, W. D., and Wilson, T. Professional personnel policies and practices of R&D organizations. In H. G. Kaufman (Ed.), *Career Management: A Guide to Combatting Obsolescence*. IEEE Press/Wiley-Interscience, 1975. 122–192

Vanderslice, T. A. The vital need for technology and jobs. An executive speech reprint. General Electric Company, Schenectady, N.Y., 1976.

Ventre, F. T., and Sullivan, L. N. *Review and Assessment of Post Orientation Careers of ADAPT (Aerospace and Defense Adaptation to Public Technology) Participants*. Cambridge, Mass.: Massachusetts Institute of Technology, 1972, NTIS No. PB232204.

Vetter, B. M. *Supply and Demand for Scientists and Engineers: A Review of Selected Studies*. Washington, D.C.: Scientific Manpower Commission, 1977.

Vetter, B. M., Babco, E. L., and McIntire, J. E. *Professional Women and Minorities: A Manpower Data Resource Service*. Washington, D.C.: Scientific Manpower Commission, 1978.

Vidal, D. Continuing-education schools thrive. *The New York Times*, September 1, 1976, 2. (a)

Vidal, D. More and more adults seek more—and different—education. *The New York Times*, October 24, 1976, Sec. 3, 12. (b)

Vinokur A., and Selzer, M. L. Desirable versus undesirable life events: Their relationship to stress and mental distress. *Journal of Personality and Social Psychology*, 1975, **32**, 329–337.

Vroom, V. H. *Work and motivation*. New York: Wiley, 1964.

Walker, J. W., and Gutteridge, T. G. *Career Planning Practices: An AMA Survey Report*. New York: AMACOM, 1979.

Walsh, J., Johnson, M., and Sugarman, M. *Help Wanted: Case Studies of Classified Ads*. Salt Lake City, Utah: Olympus, 1975.

Ware, F. A. An analysis of the validity of commercial industry employment barriers facing unemployed aerospace engineers and aerospace scientists. Doctoral dissertation, Georgia State University, 1974.

Watkins, B. T. Continuing education eyes advanced training. *The Chronicle of Higher Education*. November 17, 1975, 11.

Watkins, B. T. States sending professionals back to the classroom. *The New York Times*, September 11, 1977, Sec. 12, 3.

Watkins, B. T. Modest growth projected for cooperative ventures. *The Chronicle of Higher Education*, November 27, 1978, 13.

Watson, G. Morale during unemployment. In G. Watson (Ed.), *Civilian Morale*. New York: Houghton Mifflin, 1942, 273–348.

Weintraub, A. R., and Thornton, R. J. Teachers strike: The economic and legal determinants. *Journal of Collective Negotiations in the Public Sector*, 1976, **5**(3), 193–206.

Weisman, A. D., and Hackett, T. P. Denial as a social act. In S. Levin and R. J. Kahana (Eds.), *Psychodynamic Studies on Aging*. New York: International Underwriters Press, 1967, 79–110.

Welles, C. Is outplacement a corporate guilt trip? *Esquire*, August 29, 1978, 56–59.

Wendt, G. R. Hiring unemployed professionals. *Personnel Journal*, 1978, **57**, 40–42, 44.

Wheaton, W. L. C., Jones, W. W., and Fox, W. H. *Adapting Professional Manpower from Aerospace to Urban Government: Final Report, Aerospace Orientation Program*. Berkeley, Calif.: University of California at Berkeley, NTIS No. PB221622, 1972.

White, B. J. The criteria for job satisfaction: Is interesting work most important? *Monthly Labor Review*, 1977, **100**(5), 30–35.

Wiener, Y. Task ego-involvement and self-esteem as moderators of situational devalued self-esteem. *Journal of Applied Psychology*. 1973, **58**, 225–232.

Wilcock, R. C., and Frank, W. H. *Unwanted Workers: Permanent Layoffs and Long-Term Unemployment*, New York: Free Press of Glencoe, 1963.

Wilkes, P. Jobless, in the suburbs. *The New York Times Magazine*, June 8, 1975, **13**, 79–86.

Williams, F. E. *Russia, Youth and the Present-Day World*. New York: Farrar & Rinehart, 1934.

Williams, J. M. *Human Aspects of Unemployment and Relief*. Chapel Hill, N.C.: University of North Carolina Press, 1933.

Williams, L. K. Some correlates of risk taking. *Personnel Psychology*, 1965, **18**, 297–310.

Wilson, J. A. Motivation underlying the brain drain. In K. Baier and N. Rescher (Eds.), *Values and the Future*. New York: Free Press of Glencoe, 1969, 431–452.

Wiseman, M. Public employment as fiscal policy. *Brooking Papers on Economic Activity*, 1976, **1**, 67–114.

Wortman, C. B. Causal attributions and personal control. In J. H. Harvey, W. J. Ickes, and R. F. Kidd (Eds.), *New Directions in Attribution Research*, Vol. 1, New York: Halstead Press, 1976, 23–52.

Wortman, C. B., and Brehm, J. W. Responses to uncontrollable outcomes: An integration of reactance theory and the learned helplessness model. In L. Berkowitz (Ed.), *Advances in Experimental Social Psychology*, Vol. 8. New York: Academic Press, 1975, 278–332.

Yancey, W. L., Rigsby, L., and McCarthy, J. D. Social position and self-evaluation: The relative importance of race. *American Journal of Sociology*, 1972, **78**, 338–359.

Yanov, A. Economic colonialism in the Soviet. *The New York Times*, August 11, 1977, A17.

Young, A. M. Going back to school at 35. *Monthly Labor Review*, 1973, **96**(10), 39–42.

Young, A. M. Going back to school at 35 and over. *Monthly Labor Review*, 1977, **100**(7), 43–45.

Name Index

Subject Index